The Therapeutic Experience and Its Setting

The Therapeutic Experience and Its Setting

A Clinical Dialogue

Robert Langs, M.D.
and
Leo Stone, M.D.

NEW YORK • JASON ARONSON • LONDON

CONTENTS

CLASSICAL PSYCHOANALYSIS AND ITS APPLICATIONS

A Series of Books
Edited by Robert Langs, M.D.

PREFACE
by Robert Langs

This book was born out of controversy. It is an attempt through dialogue to identify some of the major issues in clinical psychoanalysis and psychotherapy today, many of them quite neglected. I am deeply grateful for having had the opportunity to exchange ideas with Leo Stone, a gifted and dedicated psychoanalyst. However, the experience was not without its difficulties. I was very much aware that at moments of dispute I was in disagreement with an analyst of many excellent years of experience, someone who had written boldly and creatively regarding important clinical issues. I knew too that at times my arguments became repetitious and perhaps tedious, though I tried always to link them to some piece of clinical material and to add fresh perspectives with each review. I knew as well that I was exposing myself to criticism and possibly even to misunderstanding, and that I could not predict how I would be experienced by the reader of these dialogues. And yet despite all of these concerns, I felt that my commitment to the field of the dynamic psychotherapies must take precedence, and that the issues must be joined so that not only might I grow in some small way, but that many others might also take up the challenge and profit thereby.

These dialogues took place during 1976 and 1977. In reviewing them I was pleased to see that the basic structure of my adaptational-interactional viewpoint was well established. I would have wished to have been able to more clearly utilize the concept of the adaptive context than I had, and to differentiate more specifically between Type One derivatives (evident inferences drawn from the material from the patient and understood in relative isolation) and Type Two derivatives (derivatives consistently, dynamically, and unconsciously organized around the prevailing adaptive context within the therapeutic interaction at the moment). I wish too that my conceptualization of the validating process had been sharper, and that I had more clearly discussed the nature and functions of the ground rules or framework in terms of the critical functional and unconscious communicative importance of the analyst's establishment and maintenance of these tenets. It is through the latter that the distinctly human and therapeutic qualities of this dimension of psychoanalysis and psychotherapy truly come to light. While these would have provided me with better tools for discourse, I have realized in retrospect that it was this very dialogue with Leo Stone that motivated me to more sharply conceptualize many dawning areas in my thinking.

Nonetheless, the basic line of thought I present in this book stands as an adequate representation of my present viewpoint. If anything, I have subsequently more firmly established its clinical basis and its theoretical elaboration. My present thinking calls for no fundamental revision of the ideas presented here.

I must state again how deeply appreciative I am to Leo Stone for having agreed to participate in this exchange. I am indebted as well to Jason Aronson for his support of this project, to Sheila Gardner for invaluable secretarial assistance, and to Jan Blakesley for constructive editorial advice.

Finally, it is my personal hope that the development of psychoanalysis and psychoanalytic psychotherapy will find positive stimulus through these dialogues. I know that I personally gained important perspectives and grew through these exchanges. It is my hope that the reader will be afforded a similar experience.

PREFACE
by Leo Stone

This dialogue (or series of dialogues) grew out of what I had initially thought would be quite casual informal conversations undertaken at Dr. Langs's suggestion. Somehow, this implicit mood persisted throughout our meetings, even after I became aware that our conversations would probably be offered to a wider audience than I had at first expected. A silent recording apparatus is a very unobtrusive reminder of the outer world. And the atmosphere of an after-hours, friendly, freewheeling chat does not make for guardedness. Further, there is certainly a seductive appeal in just "speaking one's mind," at times even "sounding off."

The discussions came at a time when I was intensely preoccupied in my active hours with other matters—clinical, administrative, and related concerns. I was, in the schoolroom sense, "unprepared"— either with any detailed review of my own writings of many years ago, or with any detailed familiarity with certain more esoteric contributors on the current psychoanalytic scene. If I was tempted at moments to correct these deficiencies—to "cram"—I stoutly resisted this ignoble, ad hoc urge. Dr. Langs more than compensated for my lacks. He was primed for debate.

While these interviews have been edited, I do not believe that the spontaneous off-the-cuff quality has been changed. Except for the removal of occasional, thoroughly egregious remarks more appropriate to an ephemeral bull session, there was a special effort to avoid interfering with the original mood.

One thing is certain: the dialogues do represent the actual points of view of the two participants, however much the proportions and emphases may be influenced by the nature of spontaneous give-and-take exchanges. Unless edited to the point of utter artificiality, one's views can hardly be expected to emerge in this context in the systematic and considered manner characteristic of scientific papers. For this perspective on my own thinking, I refer the reader to my previously published work. On the other hand, the immediate emergence of responses under dialectical—intellectually adversary—pressure probably does have a subtly, uniquely informative quality in its own right. I earnestly hope that the reader will find this to be true.

This hope is only the stronger because at moments I felt like Ferdinand the Bull in a flowered pasture, suddenly beset by a determined picador who had only lately invited him to graze in blissful peace. Dr. Langs was gracious enough to mention his awareness (with implicit apology) of the peculiar inequalities of our respective roles. I must therefore—and I do—accept full responsibility for my acquiescence in this transaction. Because of my profound convictions regarding my intellectual positions, I trust that I held my own. If it is unlikely that my technical procedures, with either a psychoanalytic or a psychotherapeutic case, would be the same as they were a few decades ago, this does not affect the basic differences in our views, as these arose in relation to the special issues raised by Dr. Langs. Also, while no one is likely to maintain an absolute and permanent unalterability in his attitudes in the face of intelligent dialectical exchange, I do believe that Dr. Langs and I, while mutually respectful and attentive to one another, did end in an essential intellectual standoff. Since the material speaks for itself, there is no need (or justification) for a detailed summary of the many-faceted elements in this (not unproductive) disagreement.

Naturally, there were some important areas of agreement between us, largely with regard to the critical significance of certain problems, respect for the germane responsibilities, and the need for an open-minded, persistent approach to both. On the whole I found these discussions most rewarding. They were refreshing, even when somewhat disconcerting, and invariably stimulated further thought and investigation. Despite the head-on quality of certain intellectual confrontations, a friendly relationship of gradually increasing importance was maintained at all times. I hope that this in itself—in some unspecifiable way—speaks for a significantly affirmative quality in the entire process.

Chapter 1
TWO BASIC POSITIONS

Langs: Let me begin by trying to orient you. Here's what happened. I started to write a book that would be a systematic clinical study of the psychoanalytic situation, in terms of the interaction between patient and analyst. I roughed out an approach, and then I started to delve into the literature. I had previously written two books on the techniques of psychoanalytically oriented psychotherapy (Langs, 1973, 1974), in which I had tried to rethink our basic methodology, but in writing them I had not really extensively examined the literature. (There was, of course, a bibliography of the basic sources.) I had decided—and at least as far as I'm concerned this is very much in the spirit of what you said in your 1974 paper—that it was important really to flesh out the literature, see what I could find if I really dug hard. During the same time I was starting to make clinical observations of a rather different quality from my earlier ones, particularly in terms of interaction. And what I discovered was an entire literature that was wholly new to me, and I think that I am fairly well read—as indeed your works reveal you to be.

Stone: I would certainly not call myself erudite.

Langs: I was going to ask you something about your picture of yourself and some of your writings, and where, for the moment, you feel they fall in the history of psychoanalysis. To continue with my introduction: I started to look at the literature and I was really amazed at the number of papers and writings that were unfamiliar to me, that I had never been exposed to, or, less often, that I had read, and you know how you can repress those papers.

Stone: I'm sure that's true of all analysts.

Langs: Yes. Well, I began to make abstracts for myself; my publisher, Jason Aronson, saw them, and he said, "Why don't you do this more systematically?" Initially, it was more a burden for me than not, for it was not clinical and I wanted to do something clinical. But it soon became a very interesting project because it brought me, for example, into the Kleinian literature—and I noticed that you are one of the few classical analysts who is aware of some of the papers written by the Kleinians; you acknowledge some possibility of their being useful. It brought me to writings on interaction, which they are concerned with in a limited, I think, way, and it brought me to a language related to interactional processes—one that I was struggling to develop based on my widening clinical observations.

Stone: This was the study of the psychoanalytic situation?

Langs: Right. The name of the book that I eventually developed was *The Therapeutic Interaction* (Langs, 1976b) and I ended up focusing on the relationship, the interaction, and the framework; the last is the area I would like to concentrate on with you today—the framework of the psychoanalytic situation.

Actually, when I finished writing the abstracts—and there are over five hundred—I decided that it was like Mount Everest: it was there and I had now to climb and explore it. I think, as you know—you must have had this experience with *The Psychoanalytic Situation* (Stone, 1961)—that if analysis, as Freud (1937) said, is one of the impossible professions, then the analytic relationship is something that is virtually impossible to master—in one's writings and in one's clinical work. We try to achieve relative mastery, but there are always flaws; there are always possible criticisms.

Currently, that's what I'm working on. I've done a very long critique of the literature, and a synthesis. I'm in the middle now of the final revisions.

Stone: You're going to see other analysts as part of that project?

Langs: Yes, that's what I'm planning—a series of dialogues. And I'd like to tell you exactly what happened, because I think it reflects one of the fundamental difficulties of our profession. Occasionally I will be at a dinner party with colleagues and we'll get to talking shop. My ideas are somewhat radical in the eyes of many. They have to do in part with the psychoanalytic situation and with the ground rules—an area of interest to you, of course. And at one such party one of your students took exception to some of my ideas in this area— indeed, he started to get very frustrated, actually even angry. In fact, I've learned not to discuss these matters at social gatherings; they're too loaded for that kind of setting. In any case, he said, "Look, why don't you go and talk to Dr. Stone; he's a friendly fellow, and very open. See if his position is clearly represented in *The Psychoanalytic Situation* (Stone, 1961), if it has changed, and so forth." And as I considered the suggestion it occurred to me that not only could it lead to seeing you, but that there was a broader issue involved: namely, that one of the characteristics of the psychoanalytic literature is determined by the fact that we're all so relatively isolated. Even critiques tend to be offered in isolation; there's not much give and take, and very little opportunity to exchange ideas. So I thought, maybe that's what I should be doing: since I have the literature in some sort of perspective, whatever its merits, I should go to the people who have made that literature, like you, and open a discussion. I feel somewhat presumptuous in taking on something like this, but I believe somebody should do it.

Stone: Certainly somebody should. And you've been dreaming and writing and editing, and thinking about it, so why not you?

Langs: Well, that's how I came to call you. I'm really glad to be here. I think, as you said in 1975, that a lot of problems and issues in psychoanalysis are not being debated. And many of these issues come up in your writings. In reviewing the literature, I found that *The*

Psychoanalytic Situation (Stone, 1961) was one of the most often mentioned, most often referred to pieces of work in the analytic literature. People turn to your work there again and again, and, of course, to the "Widening Scope" paper (Stone, 1954), which was a landmark at the time it was presented. Other papers that you have written are referred to and they're important, but as I see it, one of the essential things in your contribution has been the development of new ideas about the indications for analysis, the nature of the relationship, but especially about the conditions or framework of the analytic situation. I think that you've made important contributions to the concept of transference, and I hope we can discuss this later. But your turning to a study of the psychoanalytic situation itself was, in my opinion, a piece of genius. And I think that this area is still a critical one, and that there are still many unresolved issues. I think that, for example, my two books on technique (Langs, 1973, 1974) were based in part on your thinking. And it seems to me that before we even get to issues involving the analytic relationship and transference, the conditions under which an analysis takes place constitute a very crucial factor.

Stone: There is still a lot of disagreement about that, even in our own group.

Langs: Well, let's start there. What's the disagreement?

Stone: Well, just take a microscopic example. A distinguished colleague believes that the transference is something that occurs universally. No disagreement about that; clearly it is a universal component of all human relationships. But he feels that the only thing that's different in the analytic situation is the way the transference is handled. I, from my side, would agree that it is certainly handled in distinctively different ways but this isn't the only difference. I am convinced that the analytic situation, with its rule of abstinence and its central communicative field consisting of free association, has a dynamic effect, that it promotes, you see, a particular regressive trend of transference that ultimately gives rise to a transference neurosis. And this trend of transference is quite unique; something like it occurs elsewhere only in obviously pathological circumstances. Transferences to a teacher or a family physician or a priest or any of the innumerable similar phenomena we know are different from the analytic transference. (These are just examples of frequent spontaneous transferences.) I think that while little elements of agreement appeared here and there, the essentially opposing, if not antithetical, views persisted in our discussions. Now, as to how this would affect practice, I think both of us agreed that the differences might be very slight, but that they might appear now and then, and in a crucial way.

Langs: I think they might be very crucial, given a certain interlude in the analytic situation where there arose an issue related to the—well, for the moment, we have to call it the ground rules. I hope eventually to show you why I would prefer to call this dimension the frame or the framework, or even the container. In such an instance, someone with your viewpoint would be more inclined to understand it dynamically and to interpret in that area first, than to turn immediately to interpretations of other contents. Whereas those who take the other position might tend to put aside the issue related to the framework more readily, thinking that it was peripheral, rather than central. I must say that you immediately touch upon an issue that I think is absolutely crucial, one of the basic technical precepts—the need to analyze an issue related to the frame as a first-order technical task—that comes to the fore when you begin to appreciate the importance of the framework.

Stone: Yes. Here was just an example, you see, of the type of disagreement. How that represents or doesn't represent things that go on in our society at large, what the distribution of opinion would be, I don't know. But there are differences in that respect, I am sure. There are many others who would share our disagreement.

Langs: Because you have written on these problems, you've undoubtedly been exposed to the debates that are involved, and I would like to hear them. I become involved in them in much more limited ways. Basically, I teach only residents at this point. And I do know the issues that this work raises for them. But let me ask you one other question that's related, though somewhat tangentially. Are you saying that because of the special conditions of the analytic situation, the ground rules—the rule of abstinence and the rest—the transference experience in the analytic situation comes up in a form that is, as I term it, analyzable, whereas in the outside world where you will see transference manifestations, they are not expressed in an analyzable form? Does that help distinguish between the expressions of transference within the analytic situation and outside it, or would you put it differently?

Stone: That's a sort of secondary, pragmatic view of it. I meant something very much more fundamental first, and from that I would proceed to possible technical considerations. Because what you said, in a sense, represents what my "opponent" believed—or approaches it: that the essential distinction is that the analytic transference is analyzed instead of just accepted. Although your emphasis was on the "analyzable form." This is true, but it is not the primary distinction. What I mean is that there is something about the analytic situation that has a specific, dynamic effect of its own that gives a special quality and quantitative depth (let us say) to the transference. Now, it does produce or contribute strongly to the transference neurosis, which is, of course, the phenomenon par excellence that we hope to analyze with greatest effect. That's true. But by the same token, you see, lack of awareness of the dynamic power of the situation, however silent and unexpressed that power may be, could lead also (and paradoxically) to an unanalyzable situation. You know, by an exaggerated interpretation of the concept of abstinence with a person whose ego is not as strong as that of some others (I use "strong" in its usual connotation among analysts) one could produce a regressive transference neurosis of such tenacity and severity that it could be analyzed only with the greatest difficulty, if at all. Whereas some sense of the power of the process and situation in itself might avert this.

Langs: Now, I didn't say "analyzed"; I said "analyzable," and that refers to qualities determined by both the patient and the analyst— which is the point that you are making. You are also saying that transferences arise in dynamic interaction with how the analyst creates and manages the therapeutic environment.

Stone: Yes. The dynamic origin of the transference is the special and neglected issue here.

Langs: You and I both have a very strong appreciation for the frame; I think we can explore and clarify it through this dialogue. as I have said, to an exaggerated degree. That is, to be "tough" with a rules that may produce in the transference a quality that interferes with its analyzability. I think we can exchange a lot of interesting ideas in that respect. I would also say that my focus has been exactly in the opposite direction.

Stone: Well, let me note that my focus has been in that direction because I thought that was the neglected direction. I am also interested in the other direction. I approve no more of people who adopt actively parental or coddling, not to speak of more obviously harmful positions in relation to patients, than I do of those who sit like graven images with their patients. It's just that I feel that those errors have been understood from early on; in fact sometimes understood, framework of the psychoanalytic situation (Langs, 1975b) I as I have said, to an exaggerated degree. That is, to be "tough" with a patient is regarded as all right. To be a little gentle with a patient is always suspect. To raise a fee is natural, good analytic work. To lower a fee is, a priori, dubious indulgence. To withhold information is, a priori, good. To give a little information because you think it, as a matter of judgment, desirable at the time is, a priori, bad. It was such trends that turned my interest in this direction.

Langs: I did want to inquire about the historical perspective involved in your writing *The Psychoanalytic Situation* in 1961—the climate of psychoanalysis at that time. In a paper I wrote on the framework of the psychoanalytic situation (Langs, 1975b) I suggested that you, in 1961, were looking at certain very evident problems in the application of that framework. I, on the other hand, writing fourteen years later, was looking at a very different set of problems.

Stone: That may very well be.

Langs: What do you recall of the climate of that time, fifteen years ago?

Stone: Well, it's basically in the book, you see. It was not only the intangible climate, but my experience in supervising candidates, and also analyzing them and sensing their comprehension of technical precepts. I don't want to give the impression that they were all being taught things that I thought were of this nature, because I know that there were colleagues who were very important and influential in the technical indoctrination of students who had attitudes very close to my own, Rudy Loewenstein, for example; these colleagues always took the adult realities of life very seriously in analytic work and I think, if anything, would be somewhat on the gentler side of things. So, it's more the case that the precepts as stated, as carried down from the original Freudian precepts, have acquired a certain rigid literal-ness, and have been invested with a certain aura, as if they were canonical law, rather than being treated as the best possible precepts Freud could distill at the time, in brief statement form, to be applied according to judgment, with due regard for the infinite variety of individual responses. They're all read, and perhaps by some people are taught, in a very literal way. Further, since analytic students, with rare exceptions that are based on the particular analysts and super-visors, are involved in a situation of awe, of tremendous respect for authority, maybe even a search for it, they too will then bring some of this to the teachings. "See," they might say, "this is the way it is!" They don't have, or most of them don't have, religion any more. That is also something where there is a way of doing things. "Don't think too much; thinking up to a certain point is all right. Beyond that, it gets bad, it's dangerous, see!"

In short, I had the impression that there was an overrigid principle of practice that candidates were living by. Somehow or other, special challenges would arise in an analytic situation, which is, however much it may be specified or defined, a living situation in which two human beings are involved. However, a rule was always there to decide important issues summarily and thus avoid the travail of analytic thought and decision. Furthermore, sometimes even the original thinking by our greatest forerunners, as in every other science, I began to recognize, had neglected certain important ele-ments, not only in the pragmatic-empirical sphere, but in relation to classical metapsychological theory, for example in the dynamics and "economics" of transference. Several writers made contributions to the theory of transference following Freud; and some of these were of crucial importance—for example, Ida Macalpine's paper (1950). The climate, I felt, had become overrigid and narrow, although sometimes in a paradoxical sense. On the one hand, older people of good judgment, first by virtue of their sense of security (nobody was looking over their shoulders), second, by virtue of sheer experience, and third, by free intelligence and maturing judgment, would sometimes—not "take liberties"—but would make essential variations because they were desirable, and would still feel that they were following sound principles. On the other hand, younger people could not do so, whether through awe, fear, incapacity to think, or comfort in having a set system of doctrines to go by. That was the climate. From reflecting on these observations, I came to the further conviction that certain principles could be misleading, and in some instances were actually not comprehensively correct. I don't want to get too autobiographical here.

Langs: Please go ahead.

Stone: I had rather a mixed background, you see. My first analytic experience was with a person who was very much on the extreme "left" of analytic thinking—to use an inadequate political analogy—much influenced by Ferenczi on the one hand, but also by the thinking of socially oriented analysts. This relationship was dissolved when the analyst became one of the schismatists, one of those who broke off into a new group. I stayed with the classical group at the New York Institute and have regarded that as my essential analytic commitment throughout. But I had a taste of the other! So, if anything, perhaps for a while I was what you might call overclassical, overrigid. In fact, I mentioned the fact in one of my papers, I think "The Widening Scope" (Stone, 1954), where I felt I might have done a better job with the schizophrenic girl patient if I had been a little less rigid, you see. I was more correct than the correct young analysts I later supervised.

Langs: I would like to clarify this—you had a taste of what sort of analytic experience?

Stone: Of the very "unorthodox"—for example, where you occasionally have social contacts with the analyst, not avoided by the analyst and in fact at times even arranged by him. Maybe even contacts among the analysands in which the analyst participated, and so on. This analyst was a bright and able person. I don't want to do an injustice inadvertently. But I think the methodology was wrong; also, ultimately, the basic conceptions of psychopathology. The therapist, however, was following certain precepts with genuine conviction. I should add, albeit in a tiny terse statement, that my personal analytic experience thereafter was of a decidedly classical, even "orthodox" nature, as represented by the "best" of that persuasion.

Langs: That's quite interesting. There are so many influences of our personal analytic experiences on our subsequent thinking, and they are so seldom discussed.

Stone: Well, anyway, I had a personal taste of "unorthodoxy" in skilled hands. I reacted strongly in the other direction, and then only gradually, mostly through my experience with borderlines, began to reexamine the psychoanalytic situation and process, and the techniques employed. My first paper in this direction (Stone, 1954) now has a somewhat equivocal position in the analytic literature, as you know.

Langs: No, I don't have that picture of it.

Stone: Well, it's very much valued by some people; some others, you know, regard it, especially in the sense of the title, as a false lead. They believe we should go in for the "narrowing scope of indications." I have tried to deal with these criticisms in a recent paper (Stone, 1975). The title, as separated from the content, may be misleading, if one is prone to be misled, or has a strong partisan bias. We do not usually react to papers by title.

Langs: I haven't had much opportunity to review that debate, so I'm not familiar with it.

Stone: It does tend to ignore the content of the paper, you see. There is much in the paper beyond what is stipulated by the title. I admit to having had some personal feeling about this in the past. I think Bak (1970) was a little unfair, because the title wasn't even picked by me! It was the title of the symposium and I was asked to give the initial paper. He made something of a putative slogan-building quality of the title. As a matter of fact, he didn't have too much to disagree with in the content of the paper. However, *de mortuis nil nisi bonum.* Dr. Bak was a very able man. But the point is, that with the observations of certain of these sicker people and how they responded to analytic situations, I initiated and developed a personal trend of interest that has continued to this time, with some fluctuations. But to return to the analytic groups, and the climate I observed in the sphere in which I was involved originally, as student and teacher. You see, there were several years in which, because of severe chronic illness in my family, through which I was almost housebound, I was relatively inactive in the organizational sphere. I did some writing, studying, and my practice, but was not so much actively involved in our institute. I never lost touch entirely, however. I always had some occasional teaching function, perhaps not nearly as much as I would have had otherwise, but very little contact with the administrative situation, although that returned again later (I should say recently), with a bang.

Langs: The return of the repressed.

Stone: You see, the New York [Psychoanalytic] Institute was always my group, even though there was a brief period when I analyzed a couple of people from Columbia [Psychoanalytic Institute] and then, some five or six years ago, I was a Visiting Professor at Columbia for a year. Recently, I have again become involved in candidate analysis at Columbia. The general relationship with Columbia has been cordial. Now, what I meant to say, before I got off on that other tack, was that I was very much aware of these other institutes, like the William Alanson White, and the [Karen] Horney institute, and the Flower Fifth Avenue group. In all of them were people, in varying number, whom I had known years before, in the New York Analytic Society, which is where we all started. The Downstate [Psychoanalytic] Institute was a peaceful budding off, so to speak, rather than an ideological split. There was no fight or intense intellectual debate. The William Alanson White and the Horney situations, and to some degree the Columbia development, were the results of, or were accompanied by, rather intense feelings.

In any case, except in a rare reference, I couldn't accept the stated "deviant" principles of any of these groups as I knew them at the time, so I felt that I had to deal with the essential substratum or foundation of what's called classical psychoanalysis and look for developments there, or the possibility of contributing to such developments.

Langs: Within that basic framework, yes. So these are some of the factors that brought you to define the analytic situation: you were reacting to overrigid students and classical analysts, and to so-called deviant analysts who were tending to define analysis differently, to become much looser in the way they conceived its structure.

Stone: Yes, and that I could not accept. On the other hand, I was somewhat troubled at times by what I felt was too narrow, too doctrinaire a view of the situation and process among ultraclassical analysts. Either a fundamental fallacy in thinking, or something in the mood of interpretation of precepts, or both.

Langs: Yes, it's quite interesting. Was it that when these groups deviated, you're saying it broadly, they tended to take a much more open and loose, but actually ill-defined position regarding the psychoanalytic situation?

Stone: Well, that may not be fair, with regard to Columbia. There were some scientific differences, but as far as the essential definitions, and so on were concerned, they would be essentially the same. Except perhaps in Rado's early minimizing of the importance of transference. However, there were a few other senior analysts there at the same time who did not follow him. The intellectual climate has changed tremendously since Rado stepped down.

Langs: Yes, and it's to your credit that you then decided to reexamine the nature of the psychoanalytic situation in that context, and you came up with what I think is a fundamental set of well-defined precepts, within which the rigidity of certain classical analysts also came under scrutiny. This strictness may have been one of the things that disturbed some of these deviant analysts, if we may call them that—they consistently have objected to the rigidity of the classical analyst.

Stone: It disturbed them, you mean, that a so-called classical analyst was questioning it himself?

Langs: Not so much that—I think that what they felt they were reacting against was similar to the areas of concern to you: that within some quarters of the classical movement there was an over-literal translation of Freud's writings on the ground rules that tended to ignore, of course, his own applications of these rules and their possible—and, I would add, actual—therapeutic potential—an issue that I hope to get into later.

Stone: Well, there were really a great variety of differences. For example, some were largely intellectual. I think Rado placed a tremendous emphasis on adaptational psychodynamics, the preponderant importance of certain ego phenomena. In the early days, the practices of Columbia were a little bit different; I think they would be more inclined to see people three times a week, more than the people at the New York Institute would find acceptable. I think that tendency, and others, have largely disappeared.

Langs: Yes, I think there's been a change.

Stone: On the other hand, I don't know too much about Flower Fifth Avenue. Silverberg was one of the founders there and he came from the New York Society originally, part of the original great schism in which Horney and Thompson and several of their younger followers, and Silverberg, and Sullivan, all went at once, joined by Erich Fromm. Then they split again, ultimately into three present groups.

Langs: Was there a central issue that created that split?

Stone: The issue arose, actually, about the rescinding of the teaching privileges of Karen Horney, in the New York Institute. It was on that basis that the first big split occurred. Then when they all went off, they split again. Horney formed a separate institute; William Alanson White (Thompson, Sullivan, et al.) became independent, and Silverberg went off with others to found a group at Fifth Avenue. But the point is that in some of them there was not only the question of "rigidity." Horney, for instance, had different ideas about the relative importance of certain areas of resistance, or the preponderant importance of the current interpersonal field as against the genetic background; she was much more prone to regard the genetic historical part, insofar as the patient was strongly occupied with it, as a resistance. And the William Alanson White people at that time were tremendously interested in social and sociological elements reflected in analysis—say, in the position of women throughout their development and in their actual everyday cross-sectional or "horizontal" experience and their experience of occupational impediments, as opposed to what they regarded as the exaggerated importance of penis envy, and matters of that sort; the interpersonal psychiatry of Harry Stack Sullivan was very influential in that group. So it was more than a reaction against rigidity; it was often a different view of personality development and analytic process.

Langs: And of the basic conception of neurosis.

Stone: That's right. That went with it.

Langs: You said something else. Let me take you back to it, and pick up one thread which I think is very important. First of all, in developing your study of the psychoanalytic situation, you spoke of that work in part as coming out of your own analytic experience.

Stone: You mean, as analyst?

Langs: No, as a candidate. That's really where you started, you see.

Stone: Oh, as candidate. Let me clarify that, it's a very good question. What I meant was, that I was not prone to look for answers in another theoretical view of things, because I had had a taste of a concept of the analytic situation that ignored what we would regard as fundamental concepts of abstinence, concepts to which I would still adhere with the utmost strictness; and since this was then reflected in an actual split, I was not inclined to look to people and writings that reflected matters which I had already experienced. I was, therefore, more interested in taking what I regarded as essentially sound principles, including the indispensable principle of abstinence, trying to study them and see if, in my humble view, some improved ideas could be developed from that. So, yes, my experience did enter to the extent that whereas somebody else who thought things were too rigid might say, "Well, I'll try out the Horney Institute," or "I'll try William Alanson White." I had already had a little foretaste of that.

It's an odd thing, because Ferenczi, of course, was one of the original contributors to Freud's own thinking on the principle of abstinence. But he went on to experiments with extreme indulgence, and still later tried alternating abstinence and indulgence, and so forth. That pattern was perhaps reflected in the personality and practice of the individual who was important to me in my earliest analytic years. In emphasizing this phase of my training, I may slight the great importance of the second (or "orthodox") phase of my analytic experience. Not only was this, in general, more satisfactory, but it opened my eyes to the fact that scholarship, skill, and classical conviction could be accompanied by manifest human warmth and interest. Indeed, in a sort of "pseudo-paradox" (not pseudo-parameter!) the experiencing of the difference between the practice of a classical analyst of the greatest experience and skill, and the sometimes mindless rigidity of the younger people, was another powerful stream which contributed to my developing interest in technique and process.

Langs: I think what you are touching upon, of course, is that we always have to separate the transference issues in our own work from the intellectual issues. Ultimately, all analytic concepts have to be validated intellectually, but there is a source, and an important source of creativity, in the transference sphere. Winnicott (1949), for example—and this is one of my favorite quotations—felt that all analytic research is an effort to complete the unfinished business of one's personal analysis. The gift is to do it in a creative way.

Stone: There is a lot of wisdom in that. I think that maybe I've overemphasized it to you; but sometimes by inadvertence, of course, one tells something that is important. Because the sequel to my early experience was, I think, that I was overrigid, although not temperamentally—you see, I'm a kind of easy person by temperament, by and large—but because my concept of what was right tended to be narrow, I think I was in my early years of analytic practice, if anything, in the mold of the somewhat overrigid, overorthodox young analysts. However, by the nature of referrals made to me, or the general state of analytic practices at the time, I soon had a considerable accumulation of more severely ill patients. And it's with them that I began to see the impact of this kind of practice. In the "Widening Scope" paper (1954) I mentioned that certain "free" elements in my early training had occasioned a reaction in the opposite direction.

Langs: It is a personal response, but it's also a valid contribution. In fact, in your paper on the training and assessment of a candidate (Stone, 1974) and the paper on problems and potentialities of psychoanalysis (Stone, 1975) you are still occupied with these very issues. In general, there is an interplay between the way we, as candidates, are analyzed, and some of our own views on the psychoanalytic situation. I think that this is a very important issue in its broadest sense, and that it is a determinant of the future of analysis. It's an issue that I would like to explore further, eventually. I think that your comment is appropriate to this discussion; in effect, you sensed something that has to do with the conditions under which we, as candidates, have been analyzed: they promote idealization, doctrinaire thinking, and the search for authority because certain aspects do not, as you say very frankly, get to be analyzed. The conditions of training analysis (they are now changing, I believe) give the analyst power over the candidate and his future, and also include modifications in confidentiality. As a result, the specific conditions of that particular psychoanalytic situation are going to influence the communication and the analyzability of those very dimensions.

Stone: To me that is a disastrous fact of our training.

Langs: I think that you and I, having developed an interest in the psychoanalytic situation, know so well that once you modify the situation the effects are extremely powerful.

Stone: Yes, you see, this matter of the training analyst's "reporting" and his "power" over the candidate's career constitute a gigantic modification, an example of what I mean about a certain type of thinking, since you mention it. You see, here is a gross modification of the analytic situation. Gross! Not a little variation, such as somebody saying, "Hi," instead of "How do you do?" I mean it is like a house with something inexplicable and huge sticking out of the side of it that has no business there. And this was accepted, you see, because in the nature of things, first of all, people like the authoritarian approach; we can't get away from that—otherwise a lot of political trouble would be avoided. Secondly, because it had an honorable ancestory; and thirdly, because it served what was thought to be a very important practical purpose, from the point of view of the institute and the faculty. I don't deny it all meaning. Of course, I think that it's value has been overestimated, greatly overestimated, but it has persisted. And nobody gave a damn. Whereas if somebody said to a patient, who was, let us say, going to have an X-ray for a possible cancer the next day, "Well, I hope it will turn out all right," his technique was suspected. Do you see what I mean?

Langs: A remarkable phenomenom when you consider it especially for analysts: the division in their thinking, the splitting.

Stone: But here you see a massive distortion of the very nature of the analytic situation and its impingement on the transference tolerated, taken for granted. Furthermore, this is how people learn about analysis, by experiencing it! That's part of the "normal" lunacy of some of our work. I don't mean to oversimplify it. Obviously, there are reasons and arguments behind it. But I stand firm on my final judgment of it.

Langs: To anticipate a little bit, I shall provide you eventually with clinical data, not from candidates but related to the functions of the frame, that I think support this aspect of your position in many detailed ways. I think it's a very important issue: it's one of the things that has made analysis unnecessarily difficult. It's one of the segments of analytic history I want to review with you: why has so little research been devoted to the management and functions of the analytic frame? This is why I consider your monograph so crucial. You announce at the beginning: I want to study the nature and function of the analytic situation, of the framework. The fact that as analysts we have all experienced a disfigured and distorted framework is a factor in our not examining that very area. And it is interesting—I might as well mention it here—that it was in the nature of Freud's genius—even though he wrote so few papers on technique—to divide them almost equally between transference and the ground rules (Freud, 1912a,b, 1913, 1914, 1915). It's impressive that he spent so much time on issues related to the basic ground rules. You know that Freud was not a man who wrote lightly; if he spent time writing on the frame, it meant that he knew that it was a very crucial issue. And yes, I think that there is a kind of splitting off, a remarkable level of denial, in the way analysts ignore the specific consequences of the conditions of the so-called training analysis. The other point—and it relates to this subject—is one that you yourself commented on in your 1975 paper and took issue with Szasz about. I have picked it up in terms of the concept of transference, and Szasz's (1963) discussion of Freud's discovery of transference and the defensive elements that were involved. This is not a matter that you took issue with—that transference can be utilized in a defensive way as a concept by the analyst.

Stone: I assume you refer to the tendency to regard all of the patient's reactions as transference. This, of course, was a matter which I criticized in 1954. Regarding the defensive use by the analyst, I would agree with Szasz. I took issue with him in his tendency to reduce this invaluable and central concept much too far. My mention of it was a footnote in my 1967 "Postscript."

Langs: Yes, but to be forthright, as I said before, is so crucial. You were commenting in your paper (Stone, 1975) upon the defensiveness of many analysts, their refractoriness to new ideas, their need for the status quo, and the guarded way they approach these issues. I think that's related to their attitude toward the psychoanalytic situation itself; just as there is a segment of the analytic population that needs a certain kind of inappropriate rigidity for their defensiveness, these analysts also seek rigid rules or ideas. I think there's an interplay there. I must say that my own impressions from a distance tend to run parallel to your ideas—from what I could discern of the literature and prevailing folklore (see Langs, 1976b), I felt that in 1961 the overliteral application of the ground rules constituted a preponderant issue, and this went hand in hand with another attitude—to repeat, avoidance of an examination of the psychoanalytic situation.

The fact of the matter is that there was no really extensive consideration of the analytic situation and of the ground rules from the time Freud wrote his basic papers until your monograph appeared, perhaps with the exception of several papers by Greenacre (1954, 1959), in which she reviewed this aspect as part of her study of transference. She took, I think, a somewhat different position from yours—we'll get to that in a while—but she did not offer a careful or extensive examination of the ground rules or frame—which is a very interesting piece of psychoanalytic history to think about. It appears to be a collective blind spot. Perhaps you have more of a perspective than I do on why this area was avoided.

Stone: Since you bring it up, again, this shows the value of an exchange rather than just a monologue. Because, you see, it returns to my mind that apart from the outright deviations like those of Horney and the William Alanson White school, there were other things, not only the earlier work of Ferenczi, but Alexander and that big group he fathered, which for a while exerted considerable influence and power, but which is now going down the drain even in Chicago. I say that, not to express my opinion of the work, but because in some respects I think it's too bad, what happens to things that fail or are largely wrong. We sometimes lose the opportunity to examine them critically again, and see if there was something good in them. The only heritage from the Alexander experience is the expression "corrective emotional experience," which curiously enough you *occasionally* hear mentioned by very "classical" analysts, as a phenomenon that they recognize, but in a different general context.

Langs: And used in a different sense. Let me make one quick comment about neglecting the potential of failed ideas. One of the findings I have been able to document clinically is that contained within the most destructive intervention is a kernel of positive therapeutic intention. This is what you are referring to on another level, in saying that when things go by the wayside, we should at least extract from them the positive therapeutic intention—actually, not the "therapeutic intention" alone, but the possible germ of scientific truth—sometimes to be gained even in a paradoxical way.

Stone: Which is true in a great deal of Ferenczi's work; some things which Ferenczi suggested are left in our work in an attenuated form. Their marks and influence are felt in classical analysis. There was something about Alexander, apparently, maybe his personality, the publicist in him, or the quick formation of a large group, the exaggerated claims that awakened the antagonism of the classical analyst. In fact, I once wrote a review of Alexander's book (Stone, 1957) in which I covered the general subject, a review for the *Psychoanalytic Quarterly,* with a critique of some of his essential ideas. But I think that there is another reason for the tightening up thereafter. It's like revolution and counterrevolution, in miniature. If somebody is storming the breastworks and saying, "We've got to knock this whole thing over; we're going to see a patient now five, six times a week, and then the same patient maybe twice a week or once a week, or give him a recess of three months, and then take him back," or "We're going to be a tough parent with him, a tough father because his father was too easy with him," or "we're going to be a gentle, kind father because he had a tyrannical father," there is an immediate reaction of emotional resistance. I don't know whether you remember it, but at one point (I think I mention it briefly in that 1975 paper, in relation to the "forty-five-minute hour") there was a period when the "four or five times a week" rule was a cause célèbre in the "American" [Psychoanalytic Association]. It was finally passed as a rule that training analysis wasn't acceptable unless it was at least four times a week, because analysts were seeing candidates three times a week in some institutes. And of course there was the Chicago business of varying frequency according to the state of the transference, and so on. In any case, what I'm trying to say is that the strong trend to revisionism was perhaps also a factor behind the "tightening up" of the classical analysts. This is an understandable phenomenon.

Langs: Greenacre was definitely reacting to that trend; I think in her 1959 paper she specifically addressed herself to that issue, and spoke out against manipulations that actually disturb the analysis of transference-based material. And that issue did persist in the literature for some years.

Stone: Oh yes. There are very few adherents left, I think—or very few institutes that are thus committed.

Langs: I think some are in Los Angeles now.

Stone: Maybe in Los Angeles, in an entirely different sphere of revision, in some references, far more radical. Chicago, at the Institute, has very few people, if any, who are intellectually, technically loyal to the latter-day Alexander view (at least, that is my impression).

Langs: You know, I think that the questionnaire on psychoanalytic practice sent out by the American Psychoanalytic Association may hold a lot of surprises for us. There is—and this I think is very important for the nature of the psychoanalytic situation—a need for us to discuss not only the influence of the frame on the patient, but also on the analyst. This is a neglected issue—perhaps we could begin to approach it. I don't know if you are familiar with a paper written after *The Psychoanalytic Situation* (Stone, 1961): Tarachow's paper on "Reality and the Psychoanalytic Situation" (1962).

Stone: I've read Tarachow's paper, I think, but I don't remember that I was very much influenced by it.

Langs: I haven't reviewed the paper recently, but his viewpoint was similar to yours, prompted in part, I believe, by your concept of primordial transference, which he called an inherent—and interfering—wish for fusion that exists within both patient and analyst. I think that this relates to the way in which the framework is viewed and managed, and also ignored by analysts. As you have said a number of times in *The Psychoanalytic Situation* and elsewhere, the analytic situation, which is very demanding on the patient, is also extraordinarily demanding on the analyst. And the need for pathological defenses, the need for inappropriate gratification—the difficulties in maintaining a relative state of nongratification and particularly the need to renounce inappropriate gratification—is always creating inner pressures for the analyst. I think that the history of psychoanalysis is in part based on responses to these pressures.

You know, you can look at the deviational movements, as you have, from so many different viewpoints. Some have said that each deviant school has given up a particular aspect of the concept of unconscious processes, instinctual drives, and the like. But we can view deviant schools—and, quite often, specific deviations as well—in terms of their prevailing attitude toward the nature of optimal frustration and what has to be renounced by both patient and analyst. I think that this is another dimension that analysts have struggled with again and again. So, what we're dealing with in our discussion is really something that is constantly generating within the analyst potentially disruptive pressures upon his attitude toward, and his dealing with, both the patient and the analytic situation; the outcome reflects his capacity to manage and resolve his inner state and conflicts.

Stone: While the situation involves a sort of epitome of all human mental functions and passions and everything else, it is in a curious way one of the most artificial of human situations. With that specification in mind, I think the analyst is certainly exposed to it and involved with it, just as much as the patient. But, as I have remarked in the past, we hope that he is better able to handle it!

Langs: Very true. Racker (1968), whom you quote, and for whom I have a great deal of respect—I thought he was a very original writer—points out that the difference in the analytic dyad isn't that there is one healthy person and one sick person, but that one is relatively more able to cope and to manage because he has been to some extent analyzed. It's that differential that is crucial—and certainly what Loewald (1960) was referring to in terms of the object relationship that fosters insight and growth in analysis. But I think it's important to recognize the presence of that constant pressure—that constant search for nontherapeutic gratification and the constant need for renunciation by the analyst in his attitudes toward these issues. There can be avoidance as well as positive ways in which these problems are handled.

This preamble leads me to the other point I was going to develop: relationship far too much. But attention to that other sphere of the if you read the literature, what is interesting is that there is an extraordinary trend toward favoring various modifications in technique, and very few analysts who question that trend—I can name offhand just a handful of people who have. For example, I think of the literature developed by Zetzel (1956, 1958) and Greenson (1965, 1967) in terms of the therapeutic and working alliances, which stressed aspects of the analytic relationship that have to do with a dimension other than transference—not the framework, but what I call the nontransference aspects of the patient's relationship to the analyst. But alliance is not the opposite of transference, nor do I like the term "real relationship" because I think it, too, dichotomizes the relationship far too much. But attention to that other sphere of the patient's relatedness to the analyst has spawned a whole literature that is filled with modifications in technique that have not been examined. In addition, if you look at the literature on the ground rules—it's a very sporadic literature—you will find only a few papers on each of the ground rules, and these are relatively poor methodologically. For example, on fees, there is the recent paper by Eissler (1974), and there are several others.

Stone: On fees? During the last two years I would not have seen it unless it spoke of something I was particularly inquiring into. Most of my time was taken up with administrative tasks. It is not likely that I would have been moved to read it.

Langs: It is a very lengthy, very down-to-earth, very solid paper on virtually every aspect of fees.

Stone: Is there a particular issue there that you have in mind? I wouldn't ordinarily read a long paper on fees!

Langs: Not for the moment. I simply meant to suggest that there are isolated papers on each of the ground rules.

Stone: When you say "ground rules," do you mean precepts for behavior and management in certain fundamental spheres?

Langs: Yes, as related to the analytic relationship. The basic agreement—the analytic pact, as Freud initially described it in 1940. And what is remarkable and unfortunate about our literature is that methodologically it is really a poor group of writings. Now, you wrote an essay (Stone, 1961) in which you didn't bring in clinical material, and that's a perfectly legitimate undertaking. Eventually, though, there should be efforts at clinical validation. Other writers have presented a particular modification in a ground rule, or have at times presented clinical material, but nonetheless did not examine directly their own clinical material in order to clarify the issue at hand. I think that's a very crucial flaw.

I learned my psychoanalytic methodology from Jack Arlow, who is a marvelous teacher, and I think I've extended his ideas into what I call the "validating process" (Langs, 1976b). In essence, this requires that after every intervention, even the creation of the analytic pact, or any manipulation of the frame, the analyst must listen to the subsequent material from the patient with that intervention as the organizing factor. He must reexamine associations and behaviors for confirmation. We attend to what these responses tell us about the patient's fantasies about the intervention, and his perceptions of it. I'm a stickler about such efforts. And what I've seen in the literature is a strong tendency to advocate—but not document—modifications in technique. The main critics have been Brenner and Arlow (1966), Rangell (1968) somewhat, and Kanzer (1975). And of course Kanzer, in his review of *The Psychoanalytic Situation*, which you must know.

Stone: It distressed me very much at the time. I thought it was quite unfair, that it contained what I considered strongly tendentious views of what was said.

Langs: Authors are, of course, at the mercy of their reviewers, always. But you did attempt to address yourself a little bit to his critique in the postscript to your book (Stone, 1967).

Stone: Oh yes, without mentioning the review.

Langs: But it was apparent to anybody who had read the review.

Stone: I might have said some sharp things. But time takes the edge off such feelings—perhaps legitimately.

Langs: It's a basic issue because, as I understand it, you're saying that in your opinion what you advocate really fosters the analysis of the transference constellation transference neurosis or whatever— and does not interfere with it? I have in mind two aspects: the kind of flexibility in applying the ground rules that you believe is appropriate to the analytic situation, and the kind of selective adherence to those rules that you also describe. I must mention that I have found examples in the literature in which your work is used to advocate a far greater loosening of the ground rules than I'm sure you intended, you see; that's another hazard of writing.

Stone: That's true.

Langs: Just to take one example: one of the issues that you did not specifically discuss is that of gifts. I know of one or two published clinical vignettes in which an analyst accepted a gift from a patient in an effort to appear "human" (see Silber, 1969 and Gudeman, 1974). The whole problem of how an analyst does best appear "human" comes up in this respect.

Stone: That's the issue I had in mind when I asked about ground rules before when you mentioned fees, and I know there's a tremendous hullabaloo about fees. If you have a seminar with students it's one of the things they invariably ask about. I thought that fees are things that are settled by the ground rules, by rules of intelligent practicality and human decency, but I didn't know that this was a big issue that one writes papers about. And in a way that's true of gifts. If one follows the very literal rule of abstinence, a very strict concept, then you might say that the patient must abstain from giving a gift and that you must abstain from accepting them. I think in general this is true; it's a good rule. The patient pays you a rather fixed and, one would assume, a rationally established fee that's mutually satisfactory. Then the introduction of a gift is a potential distortion, whatever its specific meaning.

Now, what I mean about this thing being settled by common sense within the framework of the ground rules, is that there are situations where, for example, the gift may be unimportant relative to the mood of the patient at the time. I've sometimes given an example like this. A shy, schizoid girl with tremendous social anxiety who comes from a background where Christmas gifts are a sine qua non of relationships with anybody who is important to the individual suddenly comes in at Christmas time with a box of cookies that she made herself, or a handkerchief that she embroidered herself, or something like that. The question is, you see, whether it is important to put this down, and say "No, I don't accept gifts in the analytic situation. The real job is for you to talk to me about it in free association and to come to understand why you feel impelled to give me a gift." First of all, you know darn well why she feels impelled to give me a gift. It's because she gives one to anybody whom she likes or who is important to her. So what if she's not going to get one from you, that's okay. Secondly, the question is whether you estimate that she can accept your rejection of the gift, however gentle, without being hurt, or maybe so hurt and taken aback that she won't be able to tell you much about it. First, she'll think that you're strange and she'll think the whole damn rule is strange. So what, so she gives you a box of cookies! Now, it may be that you can accept this gift and very gently and gradually impart to her the idea that modest as this gift is, and grateful as you are for her kindness and regard and the very fact that she has this warm inclination, the work usually proceeds better if one abstains even from a very benign impulse of this kind and tries to talk about it. That would be the best procedure in the future. Perhaps something can even come up about this gift now?

I just take this as a very simple paradigm. Obviously, there are much more complicated situations. Now, the truth is, to put it boldly, you may learn more even about her impulse to give you the gift, if you accept it gratefully and gracefully, and then ask to know a little more about it, in a very tactful way, than if you refuse it. This may be so at times, because the refusal may be, in a small way, traumatic. What is traumatic, what injures another person's feelings, is always relevant. It is, of course, dependent on the state of that person's pathology, the state of the transference, the background in which this person grew up, how routine this procedure may have been in the life of this individual in the past, or how exceptional and hazardous the undertaking may have been for the patient. Now, that's quite different from a patient walking in, with some big expensive item from Jensen's, saying "Doctor, I thought your wife would like this." The thing may cost $150, and is completely inappropriate in all respects. That is as different a situation as two things can be. So I believe that in the matter of gifts, the rule is in general sound and essentially correct, but the way it is administered and the occasional variations to which it is subject are almost as important as the rule itself. If the writers you mention said that egregious, significantly expensive, inappropriate gifts, gifts that go beyond the token category, should be categorically ruled out at the start, and with other things, one should use all the nuances of judgment, then I'd say, "Fine." I don't know whether that offends your sensibilities.

Langs: You can tell that it does, I suspect.

Stone: People have not paid attention to the basic rationale of my views in *The Psychoanalytic Situation,* as I gather from their responses. For example, in Kanzer's (1963) review, there isn't even a mention of that rationale. All he talks about is, in effect, my "corruption" of the transference neurosis, which I'm most interested in facilitating. If you get a little acid note in my reaction to that review, it's because at that time, it upset me very much. It's many years ago now, and all is "forgiven and forgotten." In any case, what I meant to say was that I started with examining the clinical aspects of the psychoanalytic situation. On the basis of empirical observations, I came to certain "conclusions," tentative, so-called scientific conclusions. From that I went into a deeper consideration of the nature of the situation and there I had certain precursors, Spitz (1965), Phyllis Greenacre (1954, 1959), perhaps others, in examining the situation's infantile underpinnings. I think I developed a fairly consistent theory of the dynamics of the psychoanalytic situation, and the fundamental role of speech as a mode of relatedness between two people in that situation.

That's putting it briefly. I don't think anyone's interested in that; they're interested in the clinical modifications which it implies or which they think it implies, like the people you mentioned who think that everything should be changed, and who quote me as authority for it. I thought I was very careful to specify certain things that cannot and should not be changed. Well, there's an occasional reference to my views on the role of speech, or to the oral elements in speech. You see, under the influence of Hartmann's (1939) admirable work, which has made the ego something separate and in itself, or fated to be separate from the beginning, and of the fixed view of speech as one of the autonomous ego functions, I think people are a little annoyed, intellectually annoyed, that somebody still thinks, as I do, that the mouth has an important role. And maybe that's the reason that these caveats are overlooked; I don't know. Or it may be that it's my style, my written style—I hope I don't talk like that.

Langs: You don't at all.

Stone: My style is so involved and so difficult to read that people get fed up with it, and in that case I can only apologize, you see.

Langs: I must offer a personal note about your style of writing. Some of your reviewers, of course, brought that up. I found, rereading you this time, and I can't tell you how many times I've read *The Psychoanalytic Situation* (Stone, 1961) that . . .

Stone: You probably put it better than I do.

Langs: But I found it very easy to read you this time, once I started to follow the development of your thinking and read your writings sequentially; what you have to say and the way you put it together became for me a very satisfying kind of experience. But I think it also poses a problem for the average reader because you're touching upon areas about which he would tend to be somewhat defensive, and then he uses these reactions to avoid the basic issues. But, let's take that as our point of departure; I find it rather interesting how this is unfolding. Let me tell you something about the recent literature, because I don't think you're particularly familiar with it.

Stone: No, no, I'm not too familiar with the literature in the last couple of years.

Langs: Well now, this goes back some years, and you refer to a bit of it yourself (Stone, 1961). There's a literature that has developed a concept of the psychoanalytic situation and frame in terms of its basic functions, one that stems largely from Winnicott's writings (1958, 1965): it is a trend that is somewhat different from your approach and it raises one theoretical issue, before we get to the clinical aspect. I should say that my own approach came from none of this, but from a third avenue. I would like to get to that later because of what you were saying about your attempt to offer a basic conception of what we might call the metapsychology of the psychoanalytic situation itself.

Stone: A clinical metapsychology, you see.

Langs: Let me approach the historical aspect this way—I think that there are two basic trends to the conception of the psychoanalytic situation in terms of its structure: the creation of a specific set of ground rules and boundaries, and the rules of behavior and of communication. One avenue of approach begins with Freud's basic clinical papers, his papers on technique, in which, as I said before, he devoted about half, perhaps even more, of his space to these ground rules in an attempt to elucidate them pragmatically in terms of his own clinical experience. And he did a remarkable job. Later, he elaborated only a bit—I think, mostly in his 1937 paper, "Analysis Terminable and Interminable." And I think Freud's key concept was the safeguarding of the transference: we need these ground rules because there is a danger that transference gratification might prematurely satisfy the patient's neurotic needs, which he therefore would not analyze.

I would characterize it a bit more adaptively: the analyst would reinforce the patient's pathological adaptation—actually, his maladaptation—and this would preclude the search for more effective solutions. But I think that the safeguarding of the transference was and is a very crucial concept. Ferenczi (1919, 1921, 1925) reworked it— he's another analyst whose work is not studied very much today. I came to Ferenczi through Balint (1968); I don't know how you feel about his book, *The Basic Fault.*

Stone: Some of Balint's ideas have interested me, and I believe I have referred to them. But I have had a great interest in Ferenczi from early on. Balint would seem to have adhered to most of Ferenczi in technical articles.

Langs: Balint, as I understand it, was an analysand of Ferenczi; through his book I came to know something about Ferenczi and his relationship and debates with Freud. And then as I started to review the literature on technique I found that the first papers written by someone other than Freud on transference (after Freud discussed Dora in 1905) were written by Ferenczi. In 1909 he wrote the first of these, "Introjection and Transference" I believe you referred to it. Ferenczi in those early years presented some very important additional ideas.

Next came a mystery that perhaps you can explain—I've asked others, too. In 1934, Strachey made a very significant contribution. I know you refer to him in some detail in the "Postscript" (Stone, 1967).

Stone: Yes. Strachey's paper was delivered at the Marienbad symposium.

Langs: My question is: What happened to Strachey? This paper, whatever you think of it, seems to me a landmark paper, a remarkable paper, and yet he never wrote anything subsequently. I've always wondered why.

Stone: I know. I think he is a very important contributor. I really don't know about his further activities. I always had a lot of respect for that paper. Even though I have some fundamental disagreements with it, I think that as is true of many things which one can't fully accept there is something in it.

Langs: What is the nature of your basic disagreement with it?

Stone: Well, my basic disagreement with it is that it seems to operate within too narrow a sphere. As I remember it, it's almost entirely a superego theory of therapeutic effect. Also it rests too much—perhaps under the influence of Klein—on the archaic oral process. While I, for example, am very much interested in the continuum between incorporation and verbal discourse, I feel that there is nonetheless a profound difference between a communication on the verbal level and an incorporative process. This applies especially to the representational—or essentially cognitive—significance of speech, at the opposite end of the continuum with incorporation. As I remember it, it was the incorporation of parts of the good object, according to Strachey, which gradually replaced the harsh, archaic superego, on the basis of certain well-framed and well-timed interpretations in immediate relation, I think, largely to the hostile transference.

Langs: Yes, he used that as an example. But in terms of "the transference," he termed them "mutative" interpretations.

Stone: I think that is an excessively archaic reduction of the process, and too narrow a conception. Just as, in the clinical sphere, the idea that only a transference interpretation can be "mutative," while it testifies to the genuine centrality of that process, neglects certain practically important ancillary processes and even the basic relationship of transference to extratransference interpretations. I have tried to explicate this relationship to some degree (1967).

Langs: In 1972 *The International Journal of Psycho-Analysis* reprinted the Strachey paper with an appreciation by Rosenfeld, in which he acknowledged that Strachey was referring only to the superego. Rosenfeld broadened these ideas by applying them to the ego and to the self. So that limitation certainly has been modified. I myself use introjection in a particular way that I think is somewhat idiosyncratic. But I feel, just as you do, that you can take the basic mechanism of introjective processes and see its function on different levels of psychic organization, that it doesn't have to be confined to a primitive mechanism.

Stone: In my paper on "Resistance" (Stone, 1973) I explained that one of my conceptions of the process in terms of the fundamental, the real metapsychological—or rather, a part of the actual *psychological* process in analysis—is the gradually accepted, voluntary substitution of verbal discourse and true cognitive understanding for the urge to overcome separation in a literal, corporeal sense. I mean by this insight in its ultimate sense, rather than communication as conceived of in its most primitive expression, that is, of fusion, in which oral incorporation is the most clearly distinguished and clearly defined process of a series. In other words, what Strachey describes in his paper must gradually give way to another remotely derived process. This change is integral with the gradual renunciation of the primordial transference urge. This is a miniature, individual replica of one large component of the original development of speech and language.

Langs: In this context, let me raise another issue that emerged, for me, when I read the British, the Kleinian literature. I found it an interesting experience and I'd like to share some of it with you very candidly. The Kleinians are of course much more interested in interactional processes. And we, as classical Freudians, are much more interested in cognitive processes and verbal exchanges. Now actually, in the analytic situation, obviously, both are going on, and we have tended to focus on the intrapsychic more than on the interactional. What the Kleinians do, unfortunately, is think so exclusively in terms of primitive, interactional mechanisms that they leave out reality.

Stone: Only the transference is emphasized.

Langs: Right. The reality influences, which are enormous, are somehow neglected.

Stone: I would agree. You see, I'm not steeped in the Kleinian literature, but I've read some of their major contributions, and I get the same impression, that they see it only as a transference process; that is, the reality to them is also "transference." It is so interpreted, and largely in its archaic representations.

Langs: Yes, very primitive.

Stone: How they get their therapeutic effects, I don't know, but there is no doubt that they are sometimes effective. It would be an interesting subject for speculation in a different frame of reference.

Langs: Balint (1968) said the reason that they see so much projection and projective identification is that these patients are under the pressure of the attacking, primitive analyst, and that this is the characteristic mode in which this is experienced and defended against. But how they get their therapeutic effects may involve a concept I have something to say about. I call it "misalliance cures" (Langs, 1975a, 1976a); in other words, symptom resolution without insight. Yet, I do not entirely write off their work; their interpretive efforts are often confirmed by the patient—it's worthy of careful study. Again, we'll get back to some of this later.

So, returning now to the history we began to trace out, this kind of practical approach to the analytic situation and the definition of its rules and limits was initiated by Freud.

The next major contribution—and there were many in between: Fenichel had something to say in '41; Menaker (1942) too, as you know; Stern in '48 brought up the analysis of borderline patients and was one of the first to write about modifications in technique; Berman, whom you took issue with, I think very validly, wrote in '49;

and so forth—was really not until 1953, when Eissler's landmark paper on parameters brought up again the construction and nature of the analytic situation from a particular vantage point, that of deviations and modifications in technique. Parameters themselves constitute a specific issue. Many analysts don't appreciate that a parameter is but one type of modification in technique, one that is related to the patient's ego dysfunctions, and that there could be other indications for a modification in the frame. Eissler's concern was very specific: he was writing about schizophrenics, and the deviations were necessitated by ego dysfunctions, and, as you know, Eissler said they had to be minimal, and they had to be self-eliminating—a comment that you took issue with (Stone, 1961). But he pointed out certain dangers, which came up again in the '58 symposium.

Stone: Eissler's paper, which I admired for the clarity of its thinking, even if sometimes it's overclear—you know what I mean, that it doesn't take into account certain things which don't fit into the conceptual schema but are nonetheless powerful human dynamisms—that paper has certain postulates, especially that interpretation is the only valid, true psychoanalytic activity on the analyst's side. In other words, everything else is a "parameter." That's his assumption too. We don't usually say that that is the only effective process which occurs. For example, just the fact that a person comes to see somebody every day is a dynamic part of a process. Clarifications are certainly an essential part of the process—I mean those which can't be regarded as interpretations of the unconscious, and so on. The analyst's patient listening is a dynamically effective "activity," if you wish. But if you accept Eissler's postulate that only interpretation is an incontrovertibly valid activity for the analyst, and that the hypothetically normal ego should respond to it without other adjunctive interventions or attitudes, all right; then from that point on the whole thing follows very excellently. However, see Freud's remarks on the prior necessity of a positive bond (1913, pp. 139-140). It is not that I question the uniqueness of interpretation as a psychoanalytic modality, nor that it is often the decisively effective maneuver. But I have reason to doubt that it is therapeutically effective without other modalities, even with the fictive "normal ego"; further, that in occasional cases its effectiveness, compared with other interventions and attitudes, may, on an empirical basis, be open to some doubt. It would take too long to elaborate this further at this point.

Langs: I'm sure he was under pressure to change his position, though, oddly enough, I agree with it in substance. By 1958 he had come up with the concept of pseudo-parameters and had modified his views a bit.

Stone: I do recall that he spoke of pseudo-parameters. I remember now that even a question—that's right, a question—was considered a parameter, or perhaps a pseudo-parameter. This is rationality—or, at best, logic—that borders on the reductio ad absurdum.

Langs: Would you accept the idea of a base line defined in terms of neutral interventions, which, of course, will ultimately have to be geared toward interpretation?

Stone: Yes, I would accept that, as a sort of standard generalization, but it would then be subject to certain questions. For example, How neutral is properly neutral? What is the desirable criterion of neutrality? Is it the "benevolent neutrality" of Loewenstein (1951), or the sterile computerlike "neutrality" that is still being practiced in certain psychoanalytic quarters (more Freudian than Freud)?

Langs: I'd like to get to these matters of definition a little bit later. Right now, may we continue with the history? After Eissler's paper, as you know, there was the Anna Freud discussion in Philadelphia (1954a), in which she tried to develop further some criteria for flexibility—a position I won't discuss here. By the way her criterion for modification in technique was that there was an upsurge from the unconscious, or a resistance, that overthrows the basic conditions for analytic therapy. At another point, she mentioned the development of an aspect that had a greater malignancy than the analyst could cope with—all of which raises a lot of issues. Then, still in 1954, there were your "Widening Scope" paper, and the others by Jacobson and Anna Freud (1954b).

Stone: Anna Freud (1954b) discussed my paper at considerable length at the Arden House symposium, sponsored by the New York

Psychoanalytic Society. Then, a couple of weeks later, she went to Philadelphia, where she made her own presentation, published in the *Philadelphia Bulletin* (A. Freud, 1954b).

Langs: That's right, this occurred all at the same time. Glover's (1955) comments were interesting, because they are so typical of attitudes toward the basic framework. He has an entire chapter on Ferenczi, which ends, I think, with Freud's (1926) famous phrase— *non liquet.* Glover never could decide: he said, you know that if you deviate you may be gratifying the transference and it may be inappropriate; but on the other hand, if you don't deviate there may be major resistances. And this uncertainty prevails to this day in many quarters.

Stone: I'm sorry I never met Glover personally. I had one patient at least who went to him for quite some length of time in England and I had some brief correspondence with him. Also, once I corresponded with him briefly on a scientific matter. While he impresses one, from his writings, as a very systematic, perhaps dry-minded man, he had a most penetrating insight into certain things that may have been, I think, difficult for him to accept, as they are for most analysts. I quoted him in one of my own papers—a remark he made at the Marienbad Symposium (Glover, 1937). I may be inaccurate as to the verbatim quotation, but the idea is there. He said that in the last analysis, the patient is searching for and reacts to the kind of person that the analyst really is in the depths of his personality. Now, that would be hard for a systematic thinker like Glover to accept, yet it indicates how deeply and honestly he might see certain things. Because this is the kind of understanding that is evaded in the conceptions of analytic technique I have criticized, I tried, in my "Postscript" (1967), to include that aspect. It's a very hard idea, I think, to incorporate in a systematic view of process, because, theoretically (in the classical—especially neoclassical—view), any competent analyst, if he sits and makes the right interpretations, is just the same as another competent analyst.

Langs: Theoretically, perhaps so.

Stone: You know it isn't so, and we know that the patient, especially a sicker patient, who is digging into the nitty-gritty of human emotions and passions, is somewhere going to react to the fact that his analyst may be a person who just doesn't like certain kinds of people, no matter what "neutrality" he presents, and even if he doesn't know it himself, or has no sympathy with this or that kind of feeling, or has a genuine interest in this person as a suffering human being. Now obviously, these are not simple matters. The cornerstone of our work is transference. All of the patient's "perceptions" are not correct. They may, indeed, be miles away from the fact. But to discriminate between the two takes not only the usual cultivated technical perceptiveness and evaluation of response to interpretations, but a willingness and openness to searching self-analysis. The resistances engendered by bedrock in the analyst's personality are much more liable to be "silent"—obstinate passive refusals to get involved or to respond affirmatively to the analyst's efforts. The more usual "transference" responses, even when strongly negative, are more blatant, whether in manifest affect or clearly translatable dream (or equivalent) material. These are the materials on which we base much of our work.

Langs: That's a good point. In the course of my own work—and I am trying to explain to you just how I got there—I have been extraordinarily impressed with the patient's unconscious perceptiveness. This was one of the areas in which I took issue with you, but I think I understand it more clearly now. You have a footnote in *The Psychoanalytic Situation* (Stone, 1961) that may help us to develop some of the contrasts in our positions and some of the ways in which we agree. The footnote was important to me because I became very involved with unconscious perception as a process in the therapeutic interaction. Let me just set the textual context for the footnote for you, on pages 35 and 36. You were discussing neutrality and objectivity, and the analyst's symbolic anonymity. You talked about the patient's accepting the physical arrangements, the routinization, but not the possibility that the analyst is actually not interested in him. So you suggested that at times it may be important specifically to express that interest, but that whether one does or does not verbalize his concern as an analyst, it has to be there.

Stone: It has to be there, right.

Langs: Your emphasis on physicianly commitment is I think, crucial. And then you wrote about the justification for the vacuum that is created in analysis as a means of providing conditions for the expression of transference fantasies, and you went on to say that the same sense of incognito is needed in regard to the question of the analyst's—here, I will quote you: "informing the analysand about one's specifically personal reactions to him, i.e., to him as an individual, other than as a patient, a matter which is often an acutely poignant problem to the analysand."

You took a position here that was a little different, I think, from the one you adopted in dealing with other kinds of questions and information about the analyst—here you accepted limited self-revelations. You went on: "Furthermore, in both these last intimately related instances, there *is* a high degree of feasibility; one *can* control at least the *explicit* and *manifest* communication of the facts of one's opinions and feelings" (Stone, 1961, p. 36). Now comes the footnote: "I omit from extended discussion the nonmanifest (including nonverbal) communications to the patient, especially those of which the analyst may be unaware. These are of very great importance. However, the subject is too large, too complex, too much burdened with problematic nuances, for 'incidental' treatment. I should like to state, however, that I do not subscribe to the mystique which assigns to such attitudes a universally preponderant power, and which tends, correspondingly, to find, in most transference fantasies, perceptions of important truths concerning the analyst's basic attitudes" (Stone, 1961, p. 129). How would you clarify that statement?

Stone: All that I meant was this. I recognize the fact that the patient's perceptions of things that are not consciously communicated by the analyst may be very important. I mean, he may react to the analyst as an individual, sometimes with a high degree of perception about him in general, or sometimes in connection with his specific countertransferences to the patient, or his transferences to the patient—to follow the distinction that Gitelson (1952) made between the analyst's transference and his countertransference. But the point is this: he doesn't always perceive those things correctly. And there is an interplay between his actual perceptions and the power of the transference which can be of quasihallucinatory power in extreme instances. I have sometimes found the most startling examples in which patients, under the sway of the transference, genetically determined, have been utterly and profoundly mistaken about my attitudes toward them. Sometimes these have been attitudes of long standing, well developed in my mind and feeling.

Of course, there can always be a scientific doubt. You can always say that they read something about me that I didn't know—granted. But there have been several instances where there was very little likelihood that that was so—instances where my conscious knowledge of myself, my feeling toward them, my self-analytic exploration, which goes on almost all the time to some degree, utterly and flatly contradicted and invalidated the patient's perceptions. After all, we have little else to depend on in these matters. Ergo, while the patient's conscious and unconscious perceptions are important and we have to be deeply and unflinchingly watchful about them (just as we have always to be watchful about countertransferences). I must conclude that the "mystique," the idea that the patient is always "reading you" correctly and that what he does and says and feels is always in response to what you feel, has had a period of flowering, a kind of fashion, which I thought had become exaggerated, at times to an absurd degree. You hear young doctors talk about how the patient thought this or that, said this or that, "and of course he was responding to how I felt." Sometimes, yes; sometimes no; and one would not want this to become an established principle. It would be like turning things upside down—like Poe's story about the lunatic asylum ("The Strange Case of Dr. Tarr and Professor Fether"). In one section of my "Postscript" I believe that I attempted some dialectical application of both sides of this problem. Obviously, many factors will enter into the balancing and ultimate preponderance of the important elements in this interaction.

Langs: It's interesting, because it seems that the thinking on these concepts tends to fluctuate. For example, I would take a position that is a little different in two ways. One is that when I wrote of unconscious perception, I did so in terms of primarily indirect communications of unconscious perceptions not the manifest things the patient says about the analyst so much as the indirect, derivative communications: perceptions, and yet conveyed through derivatives.

Stone: In the course of the analysis?

Langs: Yes, in any session, if you just monitor the material from the patient for unconscious perceptions of yourself. Most often the patient will be talking about himself or somebody else, but you keep asking, Is there something related to myself—the analyst?

Stone: Oh, I think there's something related to the analyst, in every hour (see Freud's original comment [1926]). The only thing I would emphasize is that the preponderant dynamic element is most often the transference, and that we must rely on the analyst's trained perceptiveness and honest self-analysis of the countertransference and general humility as to his actual traits to make the principle useful. If this fails, then, of course, everything is haywire.

Langs: What I think you're saying—and there was also a period where this was said too about countertransference—is that when the analyst experiences something, it must be something the patient wants to create. Now, there is both truth and falsity about that.

Stone: You're right; that sometimes happens. The patient may actually bring about or elicit a given response. And sometimes it's a valuable key to a useful interpretation. But it isn't always so. Some things may arise spontaneously in the analyst, in relation to a given personality, a manifestation of his own ongoing inner processes— his "transference."

Langs: Right. Sandler (1976)—by the way, again in the *International Review of Psycho-Analysis*—wrote an interesting paper on this very subject: he talked about the patient's attempts to evoke reactions in the analyst, and he very much saw the outcome as a combination of the patient's needs and efforts, and the analyst's own propensities. Obviously it is.

Stone: Propensities or vulnerabilities, whatever. Or some inevitability in the personal interaction, if not headed off by interpretive insight, or at least utilized productively in its occurrence.

Langs: Now, when I began to study this literature and this subject, the thing that struck me was that while you were concerned with and responding to a particular trend, which still exists in some quarters, toward viewing everything—to state it in the extreme—as valid and perceptive, I was reacting to the exact opposite: my colleagues were seeing everything—or nearly everything—as distorted. They were saying that every response of the patient is transference, that the patient very seldom perceives accurately and that it's mostly a matter of distortion. They even called the patient's relationship to the analyst the "transference." And my findings, which I'll detail later, were that very often that isn't the case either, that it depends on the individual situation. The patient's valid perceptions and functioning were often being ignored. Much of it was expressed unconsciously, through derivatives. One has to be prepared for either possibility, without the bias which usually tends to favor the view that it is the patient who is distorting things.

Stone: With that I fully agree. And probably one's emphasis and accent will depend on what one is confronted with. For example, I have mentioned to you already that I was always very impressed with that problem. That is where my interest got under way, in the 1954 paper, and I came back to it in a different perspective in the paper that followed *The Psychoanalytic Situation*—the "Postscript," written in 1967. That remark of Glover's (1937), in the Marienbad symposium in the thirties, impressed me deeply—the fact that the patient somewhere, somehow, always has some reaction, at the very bottom, to what kind of person the analyst really is ("at the very bottom" is my own spontaneous paraphrase, of course). Well, this can be regarded as ambiguous, and yet it is in one sense definite, for it states a fact. It doesn't say how the patient reacts, but that the patient does react. But it implies that there is a high degree of perceptiveness and that if there are powerful distortions or trends of any kind, whether they might in other walks of life be regarded as good or bad, somewhere these will enter into the course of the analysis, if utilized by the evolution of the patient's transference and his capacity to resolve that transference. I'm talking about the patient's perception somewhere that this person (the analyst) dislikes a certain kind of other person, among whom the patient may classify himself. Even if there is not the slightest demonstration of it, or anything the least bit wrong in the analyst's behavior in any sense, I do believe it has an influence. To that extent, I believe that the perception is always there, although the perception may be tremendously distorted by the anticipations of the patient's pathological transference. That there are variations in depth and acuteness of perceptiveness, whether due to neurotic inhibitions or "autonomous" deficits, is no doubt an additional factor in these transactions.

Langs: The one person who has accentuated this the most is Harold Searles (e.g., Searles, 1965, 1972, 1975). He has written very extensively about this topic, almost entirely about schizophrenics.

Stone: Mostly psychotics.

Langs: Even though he said that his work applies to neurotics, his papers have tended to be ignored by most subsequent writers who explore the analytic interaction. And yet, he's a very sensitive writer. In the '70s (Searles, 1972), he wrote a paper about a delusional woman patient who was able to perceive and incorporate aspects of his own unconscious functioning and fantasies of which he wasn't aware until he detected them in the patient and finally got in touch with them. My own course of thinking led me, first, to believe that the patient makes certain unconscious perceptions. Later I took another step: the patient actually introjects certain contents and fantasies from the analyst and then he works them over, depending on his own valid needs and neurotic distortions. More rarely, the patient may unconsciously distort at the very beginning. Obviously, we come back to how crucial it is for the analyst to know himself.

Stone: To know oneself, of course. I am certain it is the only way one can try to work one's way through that maze. In the last analysis (no pun intended!) one can't rely on the patient to analyze the analyst, so he can then analyze him. I don't mean to be a "wise guy!" If the analyst has humility, such incidents can sometimes be crucially helpful. I just feel that the ultimate critiques and perceptions are the analyst's responsibility. If he can't hack it—too bad for the analysis. Paradoxes have their place. I have always been fascinated by Tertullian's *Credo.* But I would not like to see it securely installed in scientific methodology.

Langs: Self-knowledge is the basis for the analyst's reality testing and his assessment of the patient—and so much more. It is absolutely crucial. I found a tremendous resistance to these ideas in some quarters. I think this is related to your present-day problem paper (Stone, 1975). I read that paper with tremendous sympathy because in some small way I have been trying out new ideas and I find the most enormous resistance among my colleagues. I find them very frightened of new ideas; I find them responding not on the basis of data or observations, but entirely on prejudice. And if you happen to be directing your thinking toward processes within them, and to ways in which the patient is perceptive of them, for example, they are very threatened and protest very loudly.

Stone: I have made it clear that I think this is one of the formidable problems of psychoanalytic progress.

Langs: I thought your paper was remarkably outspoken. Few people have been willing to point to these kinds of difficulties with analysis.

Stone: Yes, that's a glaring thing. One can observe it in any friendly, informal discussion or in formal debates.

Langs: That's how I came here, as I mentioned earlier—through a dinner-party discussion with one of your students who became furious with me, didn't want to listen or discuss. And that's what prompted me to say, Okay, let's talk it out.

Stone: You mean he thought you had me wrong, or he didn't agree with what you were saying?

Langs: He didn't agree, one; and two, he felt that I was misrepresenting you. In fact, this encounter spawned my whole idea of going to people who have stated a position and talking it out with them. I think it can be very productive.

Well, let me continue with this brief overview of the history and then we'll get to the clinical data. I had mentioned Clover (1955)—and even before Glover, there is someone who, I think, deserves brief mention; she's had great influence on me, at least. That is Marion Milner.

Stone: I've read some of her things but I can't say she's greatly influenced me. I probably should know more about her.

Langs: Well, that's one of the reasons I started on my book, *The Therapeutic Interaction:* there's a whole literature that I know you would get tremendous pleasure out of. If one gets over or beyond some of the prevailing prejudices among classicists toward Kleinian thinking—because we certainly can't accept some of the Kleinian concepts—there are embedded in them some very brilliant ideas. Now in 1952, even before your "Widening Scope" paper (Stone, 1954), Milner made a passing reference to the framework, to the ground rules; I found it by reading a paper by Masud Khan (1960). In it, Milner, who was an artist, apparently said, Let's think of the analytic situation—the conditions of an analysis—as one would the frame of a painting.

Stone: Milner wrote one paper devoted to somebody's drawings.

Langs: Yes, it's actually a fascinating book (Milner, 1969). She said, in her 1952 paper, Think of the frame of a painting as setting off the reality inside from the reality outside. So the frame does two things: it demands a sphere of influence—in other words, it creates a boundary. And it also indicates that within the frame, the laws of interaction and communication can be different from those that prevail outside—if you create it that way. So, she was thinking of the laws related to art, and implying that more primary-process kinds of things can dominate within the frame; the transference illusion can develop. This has been said, of course, in other ways: the transference illusion can be created because there is a secure frame around the analytic situation. This comment does in a way restate what Freud had said and what you yourself also examined—I can't say often enough how relevant I believe to be your stress on the importance of examining the nature and the functions of that frame, the psycho-biological matrix, as you call it. You know, the frame is taken for granted by so many analysts who don't realize how crucial and functional the matrix and the framework are.

Stone: They have taken this "frame" for granted. Yes, that's a widespread though hardly universal view of it. This is the setting in which you perceive things and interpret them according to certain rules, with little thought as to how or why they are meaningful, or how the fundamental process is facilitated by this context. There is interest in providing a steady background for the cognitive processes of the analysis, and the rule of abstinence is thought both to protect the transference from contamination and to provide incentives for deeper-going analytic work. This view derives largely from Freud. That the situation itself is a powerful dynamic phenomenon is epigenetic, so to speak—a latter-day view, or, as I see it, discovery. Incidentally, "frame" and "psychoanalytic situation" are not really congruent concepts. Not quite, but something like the difference between a human being and the skin that bounds him.

Langs: Milner's thinking was fascinating in that it constituted the first three-dimensional metaphor, so to speak, of the ground rules. It gave one a little more of a feeling of depth. I tried to extend this imagery into a terrarium tank or a water tank with fish and animals, indicating that you need a boundary, and that you have certain conditions that prevail within there so that these animals can survive, and so forth. But the analytic frame includes the analyst—it is partly human—and ultimately it defies metaphor. It is not only a matter of the frame itself; how the analyst manages it is filled with unconscious communications. However, Viderman, in 1974, called the realm within the frame the "analytic space." I called it, following the Barangers (1966), the "bipersonal field." You will perhaps recall that Nacht and Viderman (Nacht, 1957, 1963; Nacht and Viderman, 1960) advocated many "selective" modifications in basic technique. But Viderman attempted in the 1974 paper to define the analytic space (I'll mention some of what he said later).

So, Milner didn't write a basic paper on the frame, but made some very important remarks. But I think that before you published *The Psychoanalytic Situation* (Stone, 1961) there were two major contributions to the study of the framework. The first, by Greenacre (1954), was a very practical extension of Freud's work. There she said that her clinical experience led her to take the ground rules seriously, that she tended to advise adherence to them, and that she maintained her position with few exceptions. In fact, as one of the first analysts specifically to refer to what I later called "therapeutic misalliances," she said that modifying the frame can create a narcissistic alliance with the patient that will undermine the therapeutic alliance by gratifying him, by feeding into his narcissism. She developed her main ideas in several papers on transference, acting out and other topics (Greenacre, 1954, 1959). Some of her work was, by the way, a reaction to Alexander (1954), who recommended a variety of modifications and so-called corrective emotional experiences. Again, it's interesting that her papers partly come out of her reactions to the literature of her time; we all write in such a context. And so she spoke in favor of the basic utilization of the frame.

The other important analyst who wrote before 1961 was Winnicott (1958, 1965), who introduced an idea that I think is truly ingenious. That is, he argued that the framework itself can actually be therapeutic, it offers a hold, a "therapeutic hold." He saw this hold as something like a primary maternal preoccupation, the hold of the mother with the newborn infant. He was not suggesting that the analyst touch the patient, but that if you maintain a secure frame you offer the patient a secure setting which provides him with a basic matrix out of which his ego may develop—an environmental matrix. He said, I think as early as 1956, in his contribution to the symposium on transference, that with certain kinds of patients—and it's interesting how so much of this kind of understanding comes out of working with nonneurotic patients—sometimes just maintaining the therapeutic hold has to do all the therapeutic work for long periods. One does not interpret, one responds to the patients. Well, he doesn't quite identify it as the patient's tests of the frame as Viderman (1974) did later, but this is really what he's implying.

Stone: You are referring to the set, dependable quality of the analytic situation? Greenacre (1954) in one of the earlier papers mentions, although she doesn't use this terminology, unless she refers to it later, that she thought that merely the analyst's quiet, confident, continuing with the work, unalarmed and undisturbed by the patient's carrying on, was in itself an important contribution. And I myself believe that within reason all these things are true. But it is important to remember (if, indeed, it is recognized at all!) that passive adherence to rules can also take on a negative twist with certain patients, at certain junctures. There are destructive parents, you know, who never hit their children—or even speak an angry word. "Above reproach," so to speak.

Langs: There's no question that any position that you take regarding the frame—and I'm going to show you some of this later on—can be abused and used for destructive ends, by taking it to an extreme.

Stone: Not even consciously abused, but owing to a lack of genuine awareness, as I see it, of the dynamics of the analytic situation, certain "correct" attitudes can become destructive. That's where I differ from most of my colleagues.

Langs: Why? What would their position be?

Stone: Well, I mean it is not generally or widely accepted that the "vacuum" itself is dynamic other than as a "hold," or a "holding" for the patient; that it can evoke regression; that it can induce tremendous augmentation of transference demands, and that it can—if the patient's adult ego is not satisfied with the rationality of the analyst's position (in his complete "neutrality" and his inaccessibility)—lead to, I think, antitherapeutic results: severe regressions and, sometimes, unanalyzable transference responses. You have an angry patient who is also regressing in a transference sense and feeling justified. I doubt that this would happen with a person like Winnicott because I would guess that there was probably something communicated from him that was very gentle and considerate and accepting. But I must stress the sphere of reality perception in the sense of adult ego functions. Somehow, at least in the relative sense which is so generally important in analysis, the cognitive and affective deprivations established by the analyst must be perceived as rational and appropriate by the patient.

Langs: One of the answers to the differences in our positions lies here. I have to say at this point—it may be immodest but I don't know how to put it any other way—that I think I can maintain what would be considered as a rather stringent frame in an extremely kind, benign way, and in an extremely rational way as well. Such a position comes not out of any countertransference problem, but out of a real faith in the basic curative potentials of such a frame, and I am convinced that this rationale does get communicated to my patients. It think that you are right in saying that people who strictly apply the ground rules more blindly and without my perspective will often utilize these tenets as a vehicle for expressing their destructive countertransference. I think moreover that what you describe as a transference regression in response to such rigidity has in part—I'm sure you would agree—certain nontransference elements, in that the patient actually perceives on some level the destructiveness in the analyst.

Stone: Sometimes it's just the sheer frustration beyond what a "sick person" (Freud's words) can tolerate, but it's made much worse if the patient perceives that this is either groundless or irrational; that the analyst, for example, nonsensically delays for weeks telling him when he's going on his vacation (and the patient can't make his own plans) because the analyst "doesn't answer questions," even though such a question has to be answered sooner or later. Then, of course, a further dimension is added to the situation, because the patient perceives the analyst as either a fool, or a rigid, thoughtless adherent to a meaningless rule—or, as you say, may perceive and react to some kind of sadistic, frustrating countertransference. Then his regression in the context of a growing transference is more severe than what would occur in an ordinary everyday human situation.

Langs: One of the points I want to develop—again I'm anticipating myself—is that I observed many modifications in the framework, and I observed them in the hands of therapists who were using them consistently to express their countertransferences. Rigid adherence in a senseless way is the other side of the coin. I would agree a delay such as you describe reflects some degree of destructiveness. But what all of this says to me for the moment (I think this is crucial), is that much of the negative reception of your position regarding the understanding of the dynamics of the psychoanalytic situation derived from the fact that analysts often utilize, let's say, the two spheres—overrigid adherence to and excessive modifications of the frame—to express their countertransference needs, and they resist and resent facing that fact.

Stone: Yes, that's often the case. Sometimes it's just due to a lack of intellectual capacity to go beyond the all-too-convenient "rules of good behavior" to try to understand what the rule is based on, what it means, and how it is therefore to be interpreted and utilized with sensitive discrimination.

Langs: Oh, I can see that.

Stone: Sometimes intellectual naiveté and the search for the universally applicable formula are involved. Granted that most colleagues are very bright and well educated.

Langs: You undoubtedly know that both Greenson (1972) and Annie Reich (1960), who wrote on this point, felt that in addition to countertransference factors in technical errors, there could be intellectual problems. I agree that there can be both, but I truly feel that positions and errors of this kind always have some contribution from countertransferences. I feel, for example, that just as when a diamond is struck, it cleaves along certain lines, so the position one takes on technique and the like is bound to be influenced by inner countertransference pressures.

Stone: I believe you're probably right. To some (variable) degree, it is always at least a participant.

Langs: Well, I'm seen as being a little tough when I take a position like that. But I'm talking empirically, from clinical observations.

Stone: As to what degree, what proportions, these take in given instances I wouldn't want to speculate. As a matter of principle (as least in a didactic sense) I prefer to start with the manifest and demonstrable.

Langs: And I prefer a constant focus on the latent, though it too is demonstrable. This relates to something we have talked about: the great influence that derives from the analyst's having been himself analyzed in a modified analytic situation. This affects his perception of the frame, it fosters distortions and misapplications of it, and even a fear of examining it lest he discover the truth about his own analysis. There are a lot of very powerful factors that have led to blind spots in these areas.

Well, these heavy albeit important speculations take us a little beyond our intended clinical and historical focus.

So, I have briefly outlined the contributions of Winnicott and Greenacre, both of whom were pioneers in the consideration of the analytic frame and setting—the ground rules.

Stone: It seems to me as I listen to you that both Winnicott and Greenacre spoke about the "primary" or "holding" transference, which is the strengthening dimension and constitutes the gratifying part of the transference. I myself tended to stress the separation aspects, the frustrating aspects, in terms of the primordial transference. Greenacre offered a different interpretation of the infantile or archaic meaning of the analytic situation. You see, I shouldn't say "they" in referring to Winnicott and Greenacre, though in a sense they share something in common. Spitz (1965) too, I think, followed Greenacre in certain references. I do not believe I omitted the supportive, gratifying aspects of the analytic situation; but you are right that my great emphasis was on the activation of the sense of infantile separation and "deprivation-in-intimacy." I do not believe that infantile symbiotic needs are gratified. The gratifications (not unimportant!) are at an adult (or protoadult) level.

Distinguished as these colleagues are and much as I admire them, I believe that there was a fundamental error in these interpretations of the analytic, or rather the infantile meaning of the analytic situation, its archaic meaning. I view the analytic situation—I'm not speaking about child analysis—as an adult situation. And the fact that it sets up certain reverberations that go down into the deepest archaic strata of feeling and thought, or what becomes thought, is a matter of the awakening of transference, of the drivelike elements in the relationship. And that it isn't really that the situation provides these gratifications. You can't take two people and put them together, one of them talking all the time, and the other never responding (as in ordinary discourse), or giving any of the gratifications that human beings normally get from one another, even in talking, not to speak of seeking advice or instruction, and view this as largely a system of gratification, as far as infantile urges are concerned, except as you regard transference misperceptions, *faute-de-mieux*, as gratifications. You can view it as an important gratification to the extent that the adult looks to the analyst with full confidence, with the expectation of full tolerance and acceptance, and with the knowledge that he can confide in him or her without reservation, and certainly with the hope of being helped by this person. That is an adult experience, although it may have a variety of unconscious meanings to the patient.

Now, what is awakened by the fact of a "separation-in-intimacy" is a series of urges of various levels of development, and of those, the most primitive, I thought, was this primordial urge to overcome the fact of separation. That I called the "primordial transference." And that, I felt, goes all the way from primitive ideas of merger or incorporation or symbiosis, depending on the individual, up to what I explained as a derivative of the same urge, in the invariably occurring incestuous longing which occurs in all human beings, to me an expression of the basic urge, channeled in the particular developmental phase which the individual is able to attain: he wants just this parent, he wants to return to this parent, he is unwilling to turn elsewhere for gratification. If he does, the same powerful urge converts the new object into the original object by an infantile hallucinatory overriding of adult perception, albeit in a state of repression. Thus a major element in neurotic conflict is initiated. But I think that's a little different from the idea that there is some kind of "holding," in an infantile sense, going on. I would say that there is some kind of gratifying cooperation between two adults which helps the adult patient to sustain the privations imposed on his infantile urges, not dissimilar to what occurs in childhood development. This is supplanted by the patient's perception of the reasonableness of the technical method. Inevitably this is "aided and abetted" in an immediate sense by more primitive transference expectation: you know, magical wishes for some kind of omnipotent deliverance or healing by an omnipotent analyst. This is, of course, an equivocal factor, whose ultimate fate in the analysis can be complicating and complicated. Nunberg (1926) has written penetratingly of such matters. But by and large the patient does his part because he thinks this makes sense, because it's been recommended to him, because he thinks this other person is intelligent and interested, and has a method which, he has decided, will be helpful at this stage of his life. There are, I think, certain important differences between these matters and the "hold," although I do not doubt this may appear too, in its infantile sense, as part of the quasi-hallucinatory system of transference gratification mentioned before, and subject to the same storms of disappointment and anger as other related matters of this kind.

Langs: I know you tended to locate adult aspects in the mature transference, and contrasted it with the primordial. This is, for me, one of the more interesting and novel concepts you have helped to develop in my thinking. When we spoke before, I began to see something of each side: that there is something in these steady functions that you allude to in a person who is not responding with counterhostility, counterseductiveness, and all the rest, that could possibly have the positive, infantile, holding qualities that these other writers have alluded to. But you're saying . . .

Stone: That the "resemblance" which I stressed in 1954—you may remember "not to a rocking chair"—gives rise to the infantile hopes and wishes, and then it is transference in the usual sense, the materialization of the fantasy, all the way from being sung to sleep by mother to whatever variant individual form it takes.

Langs: I'm always trying to trace out the unconscious transference fantasies involved, in the genetic sense of discovering their earlier counterparts. There is in actuality a certain unique deprivation in the analytic situation, but there's also a certain unique kind of gratification, which has transference and nontransference elements.

Stone: The gratification is not the ultimate powerful dynamism. It does help, perhaps indispensably, to sustain the situation.

Langs: That's exactly it; and there are two points that follow. The first is related to the nature of the dynamic power for the analytic work: you need the security first, and then the frustration becomes the dynamism. I agree with that: both play a role. And by the way, Calef, in the 1971 panel on transference, in summing up, using different words, said this very thing: that it is the frustration (he spoke of it in a more sophisticated way), the frustration of love wishes and the like that generates the development of the transference neurosis.

I think you're right and I think he would agree that this aspect has its primitive elements related to each stage of development. It is the driving force of the analytic work, although it needs the secure holding. I would think this is the reason you accentuated this dimension in terms of the dynamics of the analytic work. I accentuated the holding aspects for the moment, in terms of the need for a secure frame. Both have their place.

It interests me that your sensitivity to the separational and deprivational aspects of the analytic relationship and setting led you to
argue that one can take frustration too far and be too depriving. And
because of my current focus on the holding and positive aspects—I've
learned something about my own thinking from this—my position
is that such a hold offers enough gratification that I can be necessarily depriving, because I am already giving the patient something
very powerfully helpful. Isn't it clear that the setting, the frame,
creates both for the patient—a unique hold and an equally unique
form of deprivation? Both are essential to the analytic unfolding.

Stone: Well, it is again a question of quantities. I do believe that
the hold, the steadiness of the analyst, the tolerance of the analyst,
and all of these things probably operate more, I would say, in
relation to the "adult"—to the mental and emotional responses of
the adult patient—in the give and take of responses. Mind you, I'm
not dogmatic, nor do I feel absolutely certain of my position. There is
no doubt that it may awaken infantile fantasies that something is
being gratified, just as the interpretation, after a while, may be
experienced as being fed, or, in the negative transference, as, for
example, being scolded. But the genuinely affirmative qualities
operate, I think, in the sphere of feeling of the adult.

Langs: You know that, for me, raises another point. Friedman
(1969), who wrote a paper on the therapeutic alliance, and spoke of
different ways in which the therapeutic alliance was conceived of in
the writings of Freud, Fenichel, and the rest, gets around to the
importance of hope for the analysand. He discusses your work
(Stone, 1961). Now some people who have written about the
therapeutic alliance have immediately stressed nontransference factors, and reality, and mature qualities in the patient that don't have
transference elements to them, while you made it very clear that you
felt there were transference contributions to the therapeutic alliance.
Now when Friedman commented on your work, he saw both the
primordial and mature transferences as contributing to the therapeutic alliance, while as I reviewed your work, I felt that you were really
saying—and are now—that it is the mature transference that is more
relevant to the therapeutic alliance.

Stone: Yes, to the therapeutic alliance. The other furnishes a certain driving power which at times is on your side and at times may be violently disruptive. It is a powerful, archaic force and it may sustain analyses for some time, in the sense that the urge to union is there, to reestablish, or to establish it for the first time in a postnatal sense; but of course, obviously, in its very nature it could also do the opposite, and turn to extreme disruptive anger, in response to frustration. It is not a rational or quasi-rational force. In the past, I believe, I compared it to sailing close-hauled, to windward—a fraction of the adverse wind used to propel one on one's own course. With optimum skill in dealing with a patient who is not "too sick," we hope to harness this powerful "ill wind," and get it to "blow some good." Whereas the so-called mature transference, which is a poor term, I recognize that . . .

Langs: Yes, it is.

Stone: It's never really taken, and yet it is a meaningful term. I mean it comprehends a factor that has not, I believe, been categorized before: that there is a transference which operates in the analysis, which is independent of primitive, strictly primitive, let's say, bodily wishes, and which derives from the phase of childhood where other things are wanted from a parent, and that these are often represented in the analysis—for example, the wish to be listened to. How many people have you known who said they couldn't talk to their mothers? She'd turn away, or do something else, or she'd correct them, or say something irrelevant. To be listened to, to be talked to, even to be taught language originally—which, as you remember, I thought was one prototype of the acceptance of interpretations in analysis. Yes, it is a poor term but it does mean something important!

Langs: I see what you're trying to get at. I would see this as actually a mixture of transference and nontransference. I would definitely want to include primitive versions of it as well. Benedek (1962) said in her review of your book in the *Psychoanalytic Quarterly* that she wasn't sure how well your classification of transference would hold up and what it meant, because it was different from what had been said before. There are remarkably few classifications of transference, you know, very few, beyond Freud's initial efforts at identifying positive and negative, hostile and erotic forms.

Stone: She felt, as I recall the review, that it was part of the system of ego functions expressed in transference? I forget the exact words.

Langs: I think, however, that what you're really saying is that there is a transference sphere that has to do with primitive and more sophisticated forms of separation, frustration.

Stone: It is the effort in both instances to overcome separation; you know, as we talk I get my own thinking together. The "mature transference" is the effort to overcome separation in the secondary sense, and in a mode compatible with healthy development. I mean, the child learns to talk to his mother. He learns to communicate his wishes by speech. He wants his mother to teach him things, and so on. And this is a mode of bridging the gap of separation which can go on through life. That's different from wanting to snuggle permanently against her breast, not to speak of wanting to crawl into her belly! I call it a transference because, in analysis, it often appears as a literal repetition of the past, including its frustrations. Because it coincides with affirmative strivings of the cooperative patient in many important respects, it can easily elude notice. It often supports the therapeutic alliance. But it is not fully congruent with it. It does repeat the past, and it can become a resistance, like any other transference modality. It is not just the expression of a phase of maturation, although the attainment of a certain level of maturation would have been a prerequisite for its appearance.

Langs: One is accepted and the other is wanting not to accept, wanting to gratify, wanting to fuse and merge.

Stone: To obliterate separation summarily, in a primitive sense.

Langs: Right, this is what you were struggling with. One has to do with working out adaptive ways of resolving; the other has to do with neurotically gratifying.

Stone: Yes, so that's why I spoke of speech as constituting a bridge over separation. I mean, in human life in general. It is the chief avenue of adaptation of the infant to the fact that people exist separately. To be sure, there are other modalities, some independent, some ancillary—locomotor development, manual skill, capacity for thought and planning, and others.

Langs: That's one thing Benedek commented on; she felt that you had overvalued the verbal and had not been sensitive to nonverbal spheres. I think again and again as I read the monograph (Stone, 1961) that you do acknowledge this other area—very much so. It becomes a matter of accent—where one decides to do some investigating. Just as you acknowledged unconscious perception, you were acknowledging nonverbal forms of interaction, but showing that the use of speech ultimately should be the goal—well, the means of attainment, a vehicle for resolution.

Stone: I'm sorry, I wandered from something you were saying.

Langs: Oh no, that's all related to it. I think it began to help me put into perspective some of the ways in which we came at the subject of transference and the frame at different points in history and from different vantage points. In my overview (Langs, 1976b), I didn't know quite where to put the issue of primordial versus basic primary transference, but now you've helped clarify it.

In Benedek's review in the *Quarterly* (1962), she alluded to your contribution: she was concerned with clarifying the concept of transference, the basis of your ideas about primordial transference, and she said that she didn't know how to evaluate it, how to assess it; it was an original idea. But I think that we're achieving some kind of assessment now: apparently there are certain inherently, basically primitive gratifying aspects of the analytic relationship as well as certain inherently primitive depriving aspects. You focused on the deprivational aspect because this is what generates the fantasies that become analyzable in terms of the transference constellation.

Stone: Because they to me are the primitive dynamic motor power of the whole process. Of course, there are other motivations, of different quality, at various levels. As for what's gratified, well, that's a very nice question. That is the infantile wish and the fantasy gratification which are integrated in the adult grafiicaton obtained from somebody to whom you are looking for help. These are, of course, anticipated before the fact. They form the infantile nucleus of that antipation, and maybe even contribute certain elements of a priori trust, which might not be so readily established in reality. What I mean is that, otherwise, the skeptical patient has to be convinced that there is some sense in all this, to "come and talk with somebody and out of this you're going to get over your terrible stomach aches." You see, it isn't an a priori appeal to ordinary modes of thought. On the other hand, there is something at the very bottom of one's psychic structure that does respond to that. And that, as I see it, is largely in this primordial thrust to overcome separation, and which gets a positive representation, perhaps borrowing a term and "misusing" it in a different sense, in the "holding" aspect. That's in the sense of holding the person to the situation, the phenomenon that Freud thought of as the positive transference in its affirmative sense; you know, trust, liking for another person, expectation of help, and so forth. But that the real power comes from the deprivational aspect, the real dynamic power that motivates the development of the transference and ultimately the transference neurosis in its everyday details and phase specifications—is my profound conviction. This I have called "deprivation-in-intimacy" and I have elaborated on it in past work. If you're exposed to somebody all the time and your intimate confidences and profound conscious and unconscious expectations receive no ordinary informational or affective responses, a regressive trend of expectation is strongly stimulated. (Incidentally, I want to mention that I regard Ida Macalpine's paper [1950] as of prime pioneer importance.) Then, if you want milk, you have to find it in what he says, and then he tells you it isn't milk, it's just your wish fantasy. If you want sexual gratification, no, it isn't forthcoming from the analyst; you just have to fantasy it, or act it out somewhere else, whereupon he tells you that your "acting out" impedes analytic understanding, the effective utilization of interpretations, and, ultimately, the awareness that you have invested the analyst with images derived from your early life, and thus directed at him the longings aroused by them. Ultimately, in being able to accept verbal understanding as the bridge of contact with the analyst instead of bodily gratifications, one repeats the original separation from the mother of bodily care—to whom speech remains the basic bridge over separation.

Langs: As I said before, Calef, in the 1971 symposium on transference, also emphasized a view of transference manifestations deriving from the frustrational aspects of the analytic situation. Now Winnicott accounts for the therapeutic role of frustration in two ways. I think the first way—the one that Khan and he write about the most—is the analyst's inevitable failures, which the patient then makes use of for analytic work.

Stone: Which the analyst should admit frankly, as I remember it.

Langs: He doesn't admit that as frankly as Margaret Little (1951) does.

Stone: I do think that an actual mistake or lapse should be admitted, for several reasons; preeminently to preserve the integrity of the situation, and to support the patient's reality sense.

Langs: Winnicott and Khan feel that the analyst should recognize his error and view it as an actual mistake which then gives the patient a current opportunity to work over an earlier failure and to be angry about it. In other words, the actuality of the working over based on an immediate traumatic experience is very much emphasized in this way of thinking. I think that deprivation comes up in a second way for them, in that inevitably one wishes for more gratification. Isn't this really what you're saying—and inevitably, one is going to be frustrated?

Stone: Without artifacts there is frustration for the patient in analysis; it's built in. I think of it as a situation of high frustration, whether manifest or not. To be sure, there are certain balancing gratifications at all levels and—certainly—the persevering system of transference wish, expectation, and fantasy.

Langs: You know where this shows up. Clinically, one finds—I'm sure if you went over your own experiences too—that once the analyst does make a modification in technique—in the frame—the patient wishes for more. Do you know that Freud (1912b) described that? It's interesting to find, when you pick up a clinical concept, that there are earlier versions of it already in the literature. Freud says that if the analyst begins to reveal his personal life, the patient will become insatiable for such communications. Greenacre (1954) restated that; she had observed it; I've observed it. I've observed two things: if the therapist or analyst who is prone to modify the frame does this as a kind of consistent pattern, the patient will himself consistently seek these deviations. He seeks more and more of them, eventually to the point where inevitably he will have to be frustrated. This issue comes up in the writings of Kohut (1971, 1977), in his discussion of the establishing of a narcissistic transference by acceding to certain gratifications. I have found, however, that inevitably the patient will want more and more, to the point of frustration and then rage.

Stone: Well, possibly he has the latent frustration and rage then, primarily. But what I was wondering about was what you meant by "revealing his personal life." I have never approved of or suggested revealing one's personal life. What I have felt is that too great a fuss may be made about the withholding of a trivial fact, sometimes actually stimulating resistances, when it lacks a commonsense element of rationality. For example, in a quite usual analytic setup, one may have one's office where one's wife walks (or runs) down the hall chasing one's kid, and then find it a terrible breach of analytic precept if the patient asks, "Are you leaving on your vacation in July or August?" to tell him, or similarly with "Are you going to be in this country or Europe?" Such matters may be very important for some patients to know, where there is a high degree of anxiety. One may frequently, of course, judge it best to withhold such information, or to delay the communication. On the other hand, the ill-timed, arbitrary, unexplained mute response to such queries may have adverse effects on the process, while a simple, well-timed response may not seldom bring forth the fantasies that were sought by not responding. I have never thought that one should ever tell a patient any intimately personal data about oneself, as a general principle.

Langs: Yes, you're very specific about that. What I meant was that this was Freud's example; this happened to be the way in which he illustrated it.

Stone: Yes, that the patient will want more and more. Sure, you start a trend of gratification, the patient will exploit this, and will even establish special means for eliciting this form of gratification. It is, of course, the analyst's job to detect and interpret this tendency, and to avoid gratifying it, when it is a regressive demand. However, I doubt that arbitrary, undiscriminating withholding is adequate prophylaxis for such complications. It may sometimes stimulate them in distorted form (spying, etc.), and it may inhibit the verbal presentation of questions, speculations, and fantasies. A "black-or-white" rule is no substitute for judgment.

Let me just come back to something you said before, where you mentioned Masud Khan and Winnicott, about one's real mistakes and what they may mean in the analysis. I may be somewhat misguided because I don't know intimately enough just what they mean, but I'm old-fashioned enough to believe that pending demonstration to the contrary, a mistake is a mistake. It can't be thought of as intrinsically affirmative if it's really a mistake. To me, the admission may be important; sometimes even of affirmative value.

Now, certain things that we regard as mistakes may prove in retrospect not to have been mistakes, and we may then change our view of them. You know, the sort of things that have happened even in internal medicine. At one time a low-protein diet was ordered in chronic nephritis with albuminurea, and then later a high protein diet because you're losing albumin, and god knows what else. I have had experiences that have given me much thought and that I have never fully solved in a larger sense. I don't know if you include in your interest this kind of mistake I mean. I used to at times cite to students, when I was talking about the analyst's emotional reactions, including evanescent episodes of irritation and so on, an instance involving a very pesky but pathetic and interesting young girl (in the days when I had that kind of patient; now I have mostly people of mature years, with a background of a few analyses. It's a different kind of patient population, almost entirely professional people.)

The patient was a young woman who used to commute in from some remote place in Long Island where she worked. She came from the West, very othodox Protestant background, entirely inimical to even the basic concepts of analysis. But anyway, she was a very courageous, tenacious little woman, who came to see me over a few years and eventually married some guy from the South and went down there with him and bore a lot of children. I used to think she was built like a mosquito, even wondered how she could ever sustain the marital intimacy, not to speak of having the succession of five children of which she informed me. Anyway, she had a "habit" of forcing responses in the analysis, not readily susceptible to interpretation. She came in from this place where she worked—it was at least an hour and a half by railroad—returning the same distance after the hour. She came in once or twice flimsily dressed, in a blinding rainstorm, so that I would have to lend her an umbrella. Once it was a snowstorm, and she had no money to pay for her return trip. I had to get some money to lend her for her ticket. You see, the issues would be forced by the situation (ordinary "human decency," you know!). You could interpret these matters morning, noon, and night. And gradually it did take effect. Because this woman had a rather surprisingly good analytic result in the end. It started with a great fear of men; I mean, virginity was taken for granted, and any kind of contact was feared. These matters underwent gradual change.

But once she put me in a bind that overcame my usually very effective controls. She wanted to change her schedule around, and she seemed really to need the change. It was, from her point of view, a reasonable request, but it was what transpired thereafter that was so odd. (Here I "reconstruct" the dialogue.) I said, "Well, I can rearrange things and I can see you at two o'clock on Wednesday." "No, I can't do that; I can't make that because of an office meeting." I said, "All right, I can see you at the end of my schedule on Thursday." (I'm making up these hours.) "I think it's important that you have your full schedule this week and I can" . . . "No, then it will be [this way or that way], and I have the trains, and there's a special conference with my employer." I said, "Look now, I'm afraid we might simply have to omit the hour; you've got something coming up that's very important, and that happens once in a while." "I feel so depressed this week and I have this special something or other coming up." I said, "All right. One more try. Since you do seem so very distressed, and you have all these problems, I'll—I'll see you in my lunch hour Tuesday, I'll still have a little time left over." "No, I can't do that." At this point, I had a pad in my lap. I threw my pencil down on the pad and I said, "Look this just seems impossible to me. We'll just have to do without the hour. Anything I propose is no good!"

She was silent for a moment, and blanched. It was still relatively early in the hour. "Oh," she said, "I'm frightened! I thought you were really angry with me. That you were going, if not to put me out of the analysis, never to have any use for me anymore. And my heart almost stood still; I was so upset. I was so frightened!'' And then she went on to recount an episode of her early life which she had mentioned in the past, as a part of her history, the way patients often do; it was not new. That she had had some trouble at school, and had gotten very distressed about it, and had swallowed an "overdose." She was a girl of twelve or thirteen; her father, a very religious small-town man, had gotten terribly angry with her. There had been some fuss between them about this school issue, about her studying or taking this course, or whatever it was. And as I said, being a righteous, thoroughly religious man, he had said that her behavior was terrible, terrible what she had done to him, and he would never again pay any attention to her school work, and that was it. And he didn't! She had apparently provoked this situation to provide something that was like the actuality of threat of rejection by me, as her father. She recognized the similarity in the emotion, she recaptured what she had experienced then. It was bad enough to have swallowed the pills; but her father was, in effect, going to disown her.

There is only one point that I'll make: there was tremendous expedition of her analysis thereafter. She moved forward much more rapidly and did a lot of good work. She had an analysis for three and a half or four years, then married some fellow from the South. For a long time I got follow-up cards from her, usually Christmas cards, or the announcement of the birth of a child. But there was always that puzzle in my mind because I had one or two similar less dramatic experiences. Here I had made a mistake, I had lost control of myself, albeit in a limited way. Maybe I shouldn't have been so "giving" in the first place, or certainly if I were, I should have at least contained myself and said, "Well, I guess I'm sorry we can't make it; we'll just have to accept the fact that you'll have one hour less." Instead, I threw my pencil down and showed unmistakable irritation, which she recognized. I think the saving thing (and this is very important) was that she knew I was not really hostile to her. I had been patient with her; and she could accept this outburst. But something happened; this was a catalytic thing in the analysis. Something provided a sense of reality about an experience; that sense of reality apparently had never been recovered. Even though she had told me that experience more than once. It was as if the transference-countertransference dramatization was a sine qua non for genuine insight. Now whether Winnicott and Khan mean mistakes like that or they mean mistakes in interpretation, I don't know.

Langs: I think they mean all kinds. Your vignette touches upon a number of things that are pertinent. Here is a modification in the frame, in terms of your neutrality. And what I have found is that these are powerful stimuli for the patient's reactions. In fact, I did a study of each of Freud's case histories from this viewpoint (Langs, 1976c, 1978a,b).

Stone: Of course, there remains the question of defining "neutrality" in its affirmative sense, in its psychoanalytically appropriate nuances. In the instance given, there was no question of the loss of psychoanalytically neutral "poise," for the moment. But as I mentioned earlier the whole matter is one for extended discussion, rather than simplistic affirmation.

Langs: That's true. In Freud's cases, though, I can show you the reactions of his patients to his alterations in the frame as measured by today's standards. In general, modifications stimulate a great deal of material that has to be understood largely in terms of the patient's perceptions of the implications of that modification of the frame, including the analyst's countertransference-based reactions. Now, that this may generate viable analytic work is very true. One of the observations I've made, and I think this is what you're touching upon, is that any modification of the frame, whether it's valid or not, is a powerful, adaptive stimulus for every patient. It is the most consistent pattern I have discovered—I have three vignettes from your clinical material which involve alterations of the frame, which we'll get to later, and I'll show you in each one of them a strong reaction by the patient. I've never seen an exception to it. In other words, this is a very powerful force and instigator.

Stone: You mean the instance where I told the patient where the toilet was (mentioned, I believe, in *The Psychoanalytic Situation*)?

Langs: No, one had to do with an additional session that you gave (Stone, 1947).

Stone: Oh, the fellow who never would ask for a change of hour? It was the opposite of the instance above; he might have to miss something very important, yet it never occurred to him to ask for a change.

Langs: I'll tell you which clinical vignettes I have in mind; perhaps you'll think about them. Two other instances are in your paper on transference sleep (Stone, 1947). Two segments came from that patient whom you gave an extra session and whom you allowed to owe you money.

Stone: Oh, that's in an old paper, published in 1947. Some of the small details may be unclear in memory; although the paper and his analysis are very clear indeed, in larger outline.

Langs: Yes, it's that early paper on duodenal ulcer and transference sleep (Stone, 1947). On the whole, patients tend not to be as grateful as you might think for these gratifications, these modifications. The unconscious response is quite different from the conscious one. The kind of incident you were describing with your patient is very common. I can show you that kind of reaction with this other patient too.

Stone: Which kind of incident?

Langs: Where the patient does something to frustrate the analyst's special offer, to create—instead of accepting it as a gratification—to create a provocation.

Stone: Please explain, illustrate.

Langs: This also happened with the patient whom you allowed to owe you money—he turned out to be concealing money from you (Stone, 1947).

Stone: Here I think you have two patients criss-crossed. One was a malignant oral character (mentioned in "The Widening Scope") who was that and remained that even though slightly improved, who bought his girlfriend a ring instead of paying me, when he got some money from his mother. The other fellow, the ulcer man, didn't owe me money in the sense of the fee, due each month. He underpaid and then . . .

Langs: You say in the paper that you offered him partial credit. I'm quoting you: "Of special importance was the patient's disclosure, after long concealment, with great guilt, that his earnings had been very large, out of all proportion to the small fee that he was paying on a partial credit basis" (Stone, 1947, p. 29).

Stone: That is right; I now recall the "partial credit basis." Because it may have been that the fee was so small that I couldn't have accepted it at all, if there weren't some credit arrangement.

Langs: What happens, though, is that such offers from the analyst become occasions for sabotage, for provocation by the patient.

Stone: Well, he paid up and he admitted the concealment later, spontaneously, with an acceptance of a reasonable increase in his fee. This was the result of analytic work. I agree that any contingent or flexible "loose-ends" arrangements are susceptible to manipulation. But I cannot agree that there must necessarily be sabotage or provocation or whatever. What is latent in the patient's personality can also manipulate a very clean and neat frame. And I persist in the (quaint?) notion that considerations of equity and humanity must often be given priority over a geometrical neatness of the frame. Genuinely reasonable frame modifications can be analyzed. Latent rage in a masochistically unprotesting individual about a really exorbitant fee can ruin an analysis, often irreparably.

Langs: On the whole, patients tend to react in a very mixed way to these kinds of interventions—an aspect I'd like to get into. I am not advocating the frame for the frame's sake. I am suggesting that adherence to the frame is necessary for the patient's therapeutic needs—a finding that is always validated in the patient's indirect, derivative material. But the point that I'm making for the moment is that they react powerfully, always—even if the modification is justified by an emergency—and Greenacre (1959) said this too. Even a suicidal patient, with whom you make life-saving special interventions, will eventually express hostility toward you for invading his autonomy.

Stone: My own experience is different. I understand such matters "in principle." I regret that I have not found them to be very important in a practical sense. I suppose that the patient dying of pneumonia may resent the doctor's use of antibiotics. But that can be better handled than the opposite!

Langs: Yes, this point is something I'd like to go over with you—in terms of clinical data. Without such material, my point sounds harsh—but it is not.

Stone: Depends on what the nature of the invasion is, it depends on the nature of the situation. I don't believe that this is always so. And this is, of course, with full respect for the profound importance of "autonomy," and the need to maintain it wherever reasonably possible.

Langs: Let me make it clear. I'm not saying that this is necessarily the preponderant or the conscious reaction, nor that he will not appreciate the fact that his life was saved, but I am saying that eventually there will be a kernel of recrimination.

Stone: Of course, it's a complicatedly mixed sphere, but I maintain strongly that empirical and pragmatic realities must be given their preponderant role, where vital issues are at stake. If distortions result from certain necessary interventions they will have to be interpreted and worked through later, no doubt. But the idea, for example, if you permit me to resort to a reductio ad absurdum, that to maintain the integrity of the analytic situation you should let the patient jump out of a window, instead of pulling him back later and risking some recriminations, I don't hold with.

Langs: Under those conditions, of course, the analyst has to be prepared to intervene beyond the frame and accept that part of the patient's reaction as well. I think that is very crucial. But we must remember too that the unconscious ramifications of the analyst's interventions can't always be analyzed away.

Stone: I agree fully that one must be alert to analytic consequences. With this girl mentioned above, all these things came up, in due course. Even the fact that I had to go in and get her an umbrella because she didn't have a coat on, and it was raining torrents. She may in some way have staged the whole situation herself to force an act of "concern," as in other instances. That's all part of analysis. It is true also—and this I have seen in consultations, as well as in my own analytic experience—that sometimes there is a kind of testing of the analyst as a person. But are routines always more important than simple human needs?

Langs: The frame is such a remarkably sensitive aspect of the analytic relationship, both in terms of the deprivation and the hold, that it is absolutely universal, that when there is any kind of modification, for whatever reason, if you look at the subsequent material with that as your adaptive context you will always find particularly powerful unconscious—and sometimes conscious, too —communications and perceptions in response to the modification of the frame. It can be a source of very important analytic work. And the more you consider the implications of the frame, the more effective that work is.

Stone: I don't want to seem to be taking too strongly partisan a view here, because I do recognize the other side. But from the point of view that I'm interested in, it clearly can be forgotten that the patient is also reacting to the frame, and can sometimes develop very powerful reactions to an exaggerated adherence to that frame. The frame can have powerful unconscious meanings that have little to do with technical realities. Now, like all older people, I'm sure that people have had different experiences. I've seen people who have had one, two, three, four, and more past analyses, so that I know that their reaction to rigid adherence of the frame can sometimes be as destructive as a rationally motivated, even sometimes rather striking deviation from the frame; as when an analyst may go to see the patient in the hospital if he's sick for a long time, and sitting at his bedside, conduct an analytic hour, or similar procedures. Some people won't do that, although they might acknowledge that you should go in and say "hello" to the person, if he has been very sick for a long time. I think the situation is analyzable in relation to the rationality and appropriateness of what motivated the deviation. If the analyst deviated from the frame because of his own positive or negative countertransference, then there may be a lot of trouble—much more, of course, if it eludes the analyst's awareness.

Langs: Definitely. We're approaching some of the issues I want to raise later. Your point of view, in terms of the rationality of the situation, brings me back to a comment by Freud that I wanted to quote to you: Freud, in 1912, said in his recommendations to physicians practicing psychoanalysis: "But in psycho-analytic relations things often happen differently from what the psychology of consciousness might lead us to expect" (Freud, 1912b). It seems to me that we have to keep that in mind when considering the unconscious repercussions for the patient, and the way in which the patient unconsciously and validly perceives the modification in technique, however humanely motivated.

Stone: Not only humanely, but also rationally, and with due regard for the importance of the predictable unconscious repercussions. One does assume that a reasonably well-trained analyst knows the difference between offering the patient a drink because it's a cold day and coming to see him because he is desperately depressed in a prolonged surgical hospitalization.

Langs: Let me leave you to think over the vignettes I mentioned, and some others that came up first in your "Psychoanalysis and Brief Psychotherapy" paper (Stone, 1951). What I want to develop next time is some data on a kind of universal way in which patients react to modifications in the frame.

Before we finish today, though, I did want to complete my outline of the relevant history. Let me mention another very important paper, which you may know, by a Kleinian named José Bleger. It appeared in 1967 in the *International Journal of Psycho-Analysis* and is entitled "Psychoanalysis of the Psychoanalytic Frame."

Stone: I don't believe that I know it—or at least I don't recall it.

Langs: Bleger further extends Winnicott's concepts. He sees the frame again as the nonprocess, the constant, which provides the basic environment for the development of the patient. He sees it as creating a basic symbiosis rather than deprivation, the symbiosis out of which ego . . .

Stone: That's where I differed from most of these studies.

Langs: Exactly. In stressing that aspect, again, he was saying something about the basic qualities of the hold. But to get to the immediate point: I was looking over your clinical material, and if we accept basic methodology and an adaptive viewpoint, we should in principle be able to take any intervention—verbal or management—and then look at the subsequent material from the patient for both perception and fantasy, conscious and unconscious responses. With this in mind, there are two vignettes that I'd like to call to your attention: one is from the transference sleep paper (Stone, 1947), on page 26, where you describe a dream. This is the ulcer patient; for the moment, both excerpts are from his analysis.

I will read part of this section: "The following dream occurred in a period of restlessness and depression following a brief spring vacation" (Stone, 1947, p. 20). The patient had taken sedatives; he then had a dream in which "he was looking at the bottle from which he had just taken the sedative. There was one capsule in it which seemed slightly chewed. To his dismay, the chewed appearance was due to two small worms in the bottle, which had heads like little rag dolls. He immediately became concerned lest he had done himself harm by ingesting something contaminated by worms" (Stone, 1947, p. 20).

That was the dream. And basically your interest in this particular dream had nothing to do with the frame at all. You then say, last thing in this paragraph, that this dream was brought to you on an extra Saturday visit, which the analyst had proposed in place of granting the patient's urgent wish for the prescription of a sedative.

Now, just in terms of the manifest content of the dream, in the adaptive context of the alteration of the frame, we can say that the patient had a dream of contaminated medication in response to the offer of an additional session. And this is the theme that I want to develop, this mixture—the spoiled offer of help that the patient validly experiences when the frame is modified.

Stone: He was given an extra hour instead of a sedative. So that the sedative in the dream, the contaminated pills, may have had more to do with certain genetic aspects of the transference, motivated by the current transaction. He was getting some extra time from a parent and that obviously mobilized something in his sibling relationships.

Langs: Yes, there's much more genetic material.

Stone: He had a brother, I know, I believe older than he—and a younger sister? Please remember that it's a long time since I've reviewed the material. It was published thirty years ago and written several years before that.

Langs: He had a brother and sister, if I remember. No, my only point . . .

Stone: That my discussion didn't include the reference to the deviation?

Langs: Well, I know that was not your interest at the time. I just want to show you specific clinical material from your own papers to indicate how consistently this type of reaction to a modified frame appears.

Stone: Let's say that nowadays, where there is something like an extra hour, or an hour on a weekend or the like, it would practically always—not just "practically" but always—appear in my interpretative view of what happened. No doubt about it. There would be recognition of what this means to a patient, even, for example, to be the only patient on a Sunday, or the like, if there is an emergency. No question, no argument about the process importance of the fact. However, that doesn't dispose of the validity of the intervention.

Langs: The other place in this paper (Stone, 1947) where this issue comes up has to do with the money. When I read that the patient had been paying on a credit basis, I said, "All right, let's go back to the last dream and look at it in that context." It's a crude form of analytic methodology, but you weren't giving associations. Most analysts do not attempt to investigate or validate the patient's unconscious responses to an alteration in the frame. The preceding dream is the following: "In a pithy dream expressing the essential non-specificity of his passive wishes"—you were interested in his dynamics—"the patient is receiving a packet of bonds with which to 'make his fortune.' The donor is his mother, then his father, then alternating; then he is uncertain about the identity" (Stone, 1947, p. 28).
Now I think it is fair to postulate that this is related to the fee arrangement, and again, it reflects not only a partial distortion of its

meanings, because, of course, you're not giving him a fortune, but also it contains a kernel of truth: that a patient to whom credit is given is receiving certain special gratifications.

Stone: Well, I don't know what the associations were to that dream. Perhaps you have them at hand? Insofar as you see this in relation to the credit arrangement (and its impact on the transference) this was probably very much closer in time to the patient's decision to "confess" his concealment than to the beginning of the analysis. This, as I said, was an analytic result. The concealment was a function of his character. Also, we may be focusing a bit too narrowly. It isn't as though he were not having special financial relations with his parents, which obviously also enter into the dream. There were financial goings-on with them, which, I believe, were mentioned in the paper. But certainly the transference would be central.

Langs: There the genetic issue comes up—which I'd like to talk about, and which you brought up too in terms of repeating past, pathogenic relationships in the analytic relationship, as compared to frustrating them. The genetic ties: are they being reenacted or not? That's crucial. Now, the final example comes from a brief psychotherapy (Stone, 1951). You describe a young man who reacted well to a short period of treatment for hypochondriacal fears, who came in one session and suggested to the therapist that the therapist see his wife. The way it was handled was that the therapist indicated that he was reservedly willing to see the wife. In other words, he acknowledged to the patient the possibility of a modification and the patient then returned without his wife—didn't accept the offer—but reported the dream. In it, a man called him from the office, addressing him as Bill, and said, "We couldn't help it, standing there, and I just kissed your wife." Then the extract goes on: "The patient started for the place, found himself with a blonde in an apartment, and had a seminal emission" (Stone, 1951, p. 233). Here you report some nice associations: He recalled that he had proposed a foursome date with Bill's and his wife.

Instead of a threesome, you have a foursome. Again the unconscious meanings begin to emerge in regard to the proposal, as well as to the therapist's acceptance of the proposal. That is, this dream is not an entirely distorted view of the therapist's acceptance.

Stone: There's no question about that so far as the unconscious transference response is concerned.

Langs: Now, the argument comes up, in this way . . .

Stone: But you will acknowledge that sometimes you have to see a patient's wife?

Langs: No, I wouldn't acknowledge that.

Stone: Well here we have an important disagreement. This is where the difference between the idea of the unconscious meaning and the overriding clinical necessity or indications is not separated by you. Whereas I separate them. I say, if you see the patient's wife for some good reason—in four-fifths of analyses it never happens, or even nine-tenths, or more—but, let us say, for some good reason like a crisis in the family, which does occur occasionally. A threatened divorce or what not, or insuperable fighting which you can't handle only by analyzing in your patient, may not only justify such intervention but sometimes make it necessary. Then, if the modification brings up unconscious constructions of what it means to the patient for you and his wife to be in contact, they're analyzed. Only in a psychotic might the analysis of such material be impossible. This of course should be anticipated, and would provide a genuine contra-indication.

Langs: There are two things about this, and this is what I would like you to think about; I have more clinical material. My own observations—and I'm not referring for the moment to your thinking—indicate that the juncture at which inexperienced therapists invoke a deviation is virtually always dynamically determined, in part by countertransference and its contributions. That's number one. In terms of actualities, of timing, whatever justification they have, there is always a detectable, additional element that has contributed to the problem that necessitated the deviation, to the stalemate, and to the way of dealing with it beyond the usual therapeutic situation. And the second point is this: the entire implications of the situation become very different if the therapist or analyst frustrates the wish and analyzes it instead of gratifying the wish and then subsequently analyzing it. That actuality is, I think, a very important issue.

Stone: It's very important, of course. I hate to make short shrift of such an important thing, but here again I would invoke the principle that the clinical necessity, given due circumspection regarding possible hazards, including unconscious impacts, is the overriding issue, and we have to assume that the analyst knows his countertransference; that he is not consenting to see the patient's wife because he wants to see her, but because he thinks the marriage may break up (unnecessarily) if he doesn't have the opportunity to talk with her, or preferably with the two of them. I've rarely seen the wife other than with her husband. The analyzability of the situation thereafter will be feasible, of course, in relation to the depth of the psychopathology but also very much in relation to the degree of the demonstrable practical necessity for the intervention.

Langs: Up to a point, I will agree with that principle.

Stone: In the same sense I have stated—I don't know whether I have written it—in informal settings, in conferences, and so on, that the application, in general, of the rigid rule of abstinence is feasible, apart from other factors that determine analyzability, in direct proportion to the capacity of the patient's ego to comprehend as rational the problems posed by the general meaning of the psychoanalytic situation especially as reflected in the rule of abstinence and deprivation. This in turn has two facets: the basic capacities of the patient's ego, and the rationality of the processes with which it is confronted. This ability to understand the rule of abstinence in the first place is one side of the same coin as the ability to understand, perhaps retrospectively, an overriding necessity to deviate at a given time. In retrospect, if this has been a major deviation, which is rare, I think, subsequent analyzability, in the light of renewed abstinence, would be dependent on those factors. I think we can clarify the issue later. Is something always more analyzable if frustrated? Well, it depends on what you frustrate. If you frustrate a patient's curiosity about whether your wife is American or German, this is no "big deal." This would be routine, ordinarily. If you frustrate a patient's need for an urgently needed extra hour or for you to see him with his wife, when a terrible storm is going on, then I would say you are better able to analyze it after the gratification than after the frustration, granted that the latter may also be possible, if the patient's ego is not too severely invaded by his psychopathology.

Langs: That is an issue that I think can only be further resolved through specific clinical material. And I will say this much, because I don't think this is a final answer, that the patient will consistently, unconsciously perceive such deviations in terms of some difficulty within the analyst. Now whether that's a valid perception or not, that we'll debate.

Stone: Yes, we shall. Apart from the fact that I do not believe the patient will always unconsciously perceive this as you say, any more than he *always* perceives the systematic deprivations as certain individuals can, and do. I think he will *sometimes* perceive it that way, and is more likely to do so if it *was* a countertransference expression.

Langs: That brings up another basic issue I wanted to think out: how can we empirically define those analytic deviations based primarily on countertransference, and those invoked primarily in terms of therapeutic need? It is that assessment that determines the extent to which the patient is distorting.

Stone: The question of therapeutic need could, I suppose, if all the facts were available, be evaluated in clinical objectivity. The role of the countertransference can usually only be evaluated in clinical objectivity. The role of the countertransference can usually only be evaluated by the analyst himself—or by his own analyst! But all of that, like most important things, is not as simple as the statement. I think that the distortion of the real relationship—you don't like that term, but you know what I mean—including the clinical relationship can be so serious that it makes the question of what may intrude into the patient's unconscious perceptions and his transference reactions *relatively* less important (in the case of the relatively intact ego). These matters are accessible. And let us not forget that the patient's unconscious also reacts to realities, including injudicious applications of the rule of abstinence. I mean, there is no question that I have seen issues where a disaster would have occurred, let's say, if I didn't see both partners in a marriage during a crisis. And that thereafter if the patient evolves fantasies and dreams of his wife exposing her breasts to me, or similar fantasies extrinsic to the reality, the fantasies can be analyzed and separated from the reality. These fantasies all have a genetic background, they can be analyzed and they can be brought into relationship with what really occurs. If the subject is a neurotic patient within the ordinary scope of the pathology, he will usually see it without too much trouble, and he will be able to separate the fantasy from the fact that the event occurred for a real purpose. I have not had much trouble with that. You see, some colleagues stress that difficulty a great deal. They say if you say "Boo" it's going to come back into the analysis, presumably in some seriously obstructive way. All right then it comes back as "Boo" and you analyze the fact—I'm just making this up for fun— that he was frightened by somebody saying "Boo" once as a child, and you said "Boo," and he has been uneasy with you since then. Now this was, of course, not the same as your saying that you have to go out of town next week. Things occur, regardless of what we may want in the analytic situation. We may have to go out of town, interrupt the analytic situation; that also has a transference impact. The patient reacts to it. You went away, he thinks, because you're being sued for malpractice, or you went away to give a paper, or you went away to receive an honorary LL.D., or whatever. Sometimes the fantasies lend themselves to productive interpretation. These episodes often occur. Now these are "accidents"; we accept them; we have to. Why can't one accept the "accidents" that are produced by special aspects of a person's sickness at times? I mean, like going to see a patient in a hospital if he's laid up for a long time.

Langs: Well, some of my thinking has to do with interactional processes and the way in which the patient introjects the unconscious nature of your intervention. And there are things to be said on both sides. What you're saying is that to fail to intervene in a crisis produces a destructive introject. No question about it.

Stone: Even unconsciously—apart from the fact that it interferes with an adult relationship in a way that may be irreparable.

Langs: The adult aspects of the relationship, and what I will call—because I am discussing this in terms of the bipersonal field concept—the therapeutic qualities of the relationship or of the field, are very much influenced by these interactions. So I think there's still a lot for us to hammer out.

Stone: I think we're just getting into that. Even those excerpts regarding my own patients—I probably haven't looked at that "ulcer" paper in twenty years.

Langs: I know; when people quote some of my own writings, it can be disconcerting. And I know I've put some pressure on you, but I trust you see the value of my ultimate goals—to learn as much as we can about the psychoanalytic frame and process. Perhaps we can stop here—I'm sure we'll both give this first meeting a good deal of thought.

Chapter 2
MODIFICATIONS IN TECHNIQUE

Langs: Last time, as you no doubt remember, we ventured rather briefly into the clinical material related to the ground rules. I want to go back to it, but before we do so, let me explain a little how I got into this area, and how my thinking developed. Perhaps it will help to set the context for our discussion of the clinical material.

I had been working as a supervisor of psychotherapy, with young residents who are error-prone and vulnerable to countertransference problems. I collected a lot of clinical material, and wrote a two-volume clinical text on this basis—*The Technique of Psychoanalytic Psychotherapy*—an empirical book (Langs, 1973, 1974). In it I devoted an enormous amount of space to the ground rules of psychotherapy, although I believe the book is really, in many ways, almost equally applicable to analysis. Maybe we can discuss the differences and the areas of overlap between the two later. I take a position that's rather different from many others, but I believe I am finding more and more evidence for my contention that psychotherapy too needs a defined frame, that it has its own ground rules.

Stone: This I always thought, but I felt it "needed more work." I still think so.

Langs: A lot of analysts go to psychotherapy to let go of their countertransferences; I think this is unfortunate. I think you addressed yourself to the issue in the paper on analysis and brief psychotherapy (Stone, 1951).

Stone: Yes.

Langs: That goes back a way. I found, clinically, that many issues come up in connection with the framework; that management of the framework has a very great influence on the therapeutic situation; and that modifications in the framework have to be dealt with, and can not be brushed aside. The patient would come back to the altered frame in one form or another, over and over again. In fact, I can say that I have extended this repeated observation now to a belief that the one universal in analysis and therapy is that if you modify the frame, however justifiably, you will always get significant responses from the patient, sometimes conscious but especially unconscious. The patient is extremely sensitive to the nature of the framework.

Stone: That, I would agree, is correct. I would not agree that it is always a negative response (i.e., inimical to progress), but the general principle that there is always a response is sound. It may be a useful response. But that the patient also responds to the "frame," even as correctly carried out, and makes all kinds of things of it, that's the other aspect, which is often neglected.

Langs: That's a whole chapter—one that you allude to in your writings: the implications of the different components of the frame. Analysts have just barely begun to investigate this dimension, and I think it's a very important chapter that needs to be written. But I think that one thing that we both very much stand for, one area of definite agreement, is the importance of the frame, of its dynamic meanings, and the patient's great sensitivity to its management. And then, if we can convince people of that at least, let them make the observations. I'm always open to observations. In my own work, then, I had devoted a great deal of attention to the frame and to the importance of it as a "prime therapeutic context," meaning that, in general, you have to analyze that particular area before you get to other problems. You know, there is a tendency among classical analysts to think of therapy and analysis in terms of analyzing the content of derivatives, not to think in terms of the unconscious implications of interaction and actuality, where the frame comes in. I think that today I would argue that there are really two major spheres of analytic activity: one is interactional, the other is verbal; one is interpretive, the other is management. And I think that they're both equally crucial, and crucial to each other. In my analytic training, the stress, of course, was on the interpretive approach—to think in terms of interpreting—and less so on the important aspects of management.

Stone: Do you mean management in its broadest construction? Otherwise, somebody might ask what you mean by management. You're speaking of psychotherapy now?

Langs: I'm speaking of analysis. When I say managment, I don't mean manipulation. I mean the analyst's responsibility to create and manage a frame, to set and maintain the ground rules and boundaries.

Stone: I see; you mean that the analyst creates a "frame."

Langs: I call it a frame and sometimes a container. I'll get to that too. And as Viderman (1974) said, beautifully, every patient in analysis brings his own frame to the situation and will test the analyst's frame again and again. I think this is universal, and the analyst's response is very crucial for what follows. For Viderman, if in response to these tests of the frame the analyst does not secure the frame, he will not get a transference neurosis. And I feel that there is a certain degree of truth in that: without a clear-cut frame, one gets something that is different from an analyzable transference neurosis. Well, I'm a little ahead of myself. Following the completion of my book, I started to make observations related to interaction. The best I can say is this: I took an adaptational approach, not because I had made a conscious decision but because that was the nature of my observations. The clinical data led the way. When I looked at things that were primarily distorted in transference, I noticed that there was always a day residue, always a precipitant. Something happened in the therapy, or in an analysis, that evoked a largely distorted response, but if you took an adaptive context and then listened to the derivatives, you could understand them much more clearly. And if you continued to watch the adaptive stimuli—the things that happened—you could then trace the reactions. Now, Greenson (1967), in his book on technique, really put the day residue to the side. He said there were often reality precipitants, but they were less important, much as Freud (1900) had said about day residues and dreams.

Stone: Yes, I've always had a theoretical reservation about this.

Langs: That's interesting. In what sense?

Stone: Well, in the sense that I feel that the day residue isn't something that more or less accidentally stimulates—or participates in the manifest content. My impression is that the day residue is usually something that achieves its importance, and becomes a "day residue," because it represents either symbolically, or by way of latent associations, a complex that has a real importance in the person's development and neurosis. This is always something that I felt a little bit funny about, so I agree with you on that. I also agree with the fact that what is going on in life, or as you put it more exclusively, in the "frame" . . . You know, there is a funny story connected with that, and I must mention it. A colleague, a contemporary in training although a couple of years older than I, once walked home with me after hearing a very distinguished older analyst, one of our best people, a person who contributed enormously to the literature in a very fine way, in the course of a discussion tell an anecdote from his own practice. At a certain point in the analysis, he said, he crossed his leg, and the patient saw his shoe, and this gave rise to a whole stream of associations and led to a very interesting hour. So my colleague said to me, "You know, I've been thinking, suppose he hadn't crossed his leg! What would have been the course of that analysis?" And we had an interesting discussion reflecting our current level of development, which was that of young to middle-aged analysts in experience. And of course it has always seemed to me that the accidental happenings of life are extremely important for analysis. The old idea that the analysis proceeds in itself, as if it were in a tube, is fallacious; it can't. If it doesn't gain sustenance, some kind of nutrition from the environment, from the analytic situation itself, it's going to be sadly deficient.

Langs: I didn't mean to imply that only reality events within the analysis will prompt transference reactions; external events will do that too. You see, the first truly analytic paper I wrote was on day residues and dreams (Langs, 1971). I made a point that was apparent to you as well, that day residues may be imposed upon us as traumas, but they also can be selected and created unconsciously. Arlow (1969) made that comment earlier, in his paper on unconscious fantasy. There is an interplay between selectively creating day residues and having them imposed on you. Once I took an adaptive approach to what was going on in the therapeutic situation a number of things emerged. One of them, for example, was a concept I called "iatrogenic syndromes." In writing on countertransference from my clinical material, which was largely from the patient—his associations, and the therapist's interventions—I attempted to demonstrate that many regressions and symptomatic relapses in the patient can be prompted by the therapist's or analyst's countertransference responses. I didn't say that this was the only basis for regressions, by any means, but I did say that if you want to find clues to countertransference, there is a whole source, a means of identifying it, in the material from the patient.

And because I was interested in an adaptational approach, I got interested in interaction, and ended up with something—I don't know, apparently I like to call things by names—I called the adaptational-interactional approach, because the adaptational approach is still basically intrapsychically focused. The approach that I'm taking is both intrapsychic and interactional, or interpersonal as Searles (1965) put it; it includes object relatedness in ways similar to the approach of Kernberg (1975) and others, although it differs from theirs in important ways. Now, oddly enough—and this is hard for me to reconstruct because my thinking today is so different from what it was just a couple of years ago—by and large, the classical analyst's main approach to interaction has been through the therapeutic alliance, the sector to which both patient and analyst contribute. When Greenson (1965) wrote of the "working alliance," he pointed out that both the analyst and analysand could contribute to disturbances in this area, and this is where interaction seems to come into play. Transference was see as intrapsychic, as the creation of the patient—it's either Macalpine (1950) or Menaker (1942) who stated this most explicitly; I believe Macalpine said it most clearly.

This was what I was taught. Alliance was seen as mutual—it was interactional—but the classical focus there was on the relatively autonomous functions involved.

Stone: Well, Macalpine was the one who, I found, had contributed more to my thinking in this sphere than almost any other single person except Freud himself. She thought of the transference as a regressive adaptation to the analytic situation. Actually, Esther Menaker too contributed something very important in stressing the "masochistic factor" in the analytic situation.

Langs: Yes, those two papers were quite significant.

Stone: Menaker stressed the importance of the patient's masochism in supporting the psychoanalytic situation, as a response to its frustrations. But, with Macalpine, it was the adaptive reaction to the frustrations of analysis that was so important in stimulating the very occurrence of the transference.

Langs: But that's an interesting comment. It was the Macalpine paper (1950) in which she wrote of transference in terms of it being an adaptation to the analytic situation. Yes, your writings developed some of her early ideas; I can see that connection. But again, because it was an adaptive approach, you looked at the basic framework. Which is interesting, because I got to the frame through an adaptive approach too, and that is something that we share.

So, when I looked at the therapeutic alliance I began to study the pathology of the therapeutic alliance and I coined the term "therapeutic misalliance" or "antitherapeutic alliance" (Langs, 1973, 1974), to indicate that there were situations in which the patient and the analyst could set up an interaction, an alliance, that was not geared toward insight. It could be designed for mutual defense, or neurotic gratification, or something of that kind. So that it was more a misalliance—momentary, one hoped—than an alliance. These occur in every analysis. There are always junctures at which the analyst may unconsciously become involved in a sector of misalliance with the patient, and for a moment, the analytic work becomes derailed. And I began to examine the analytic interaction for indications of misalliance.

Stone: Now, the therapeutic misalliance, you think, would occur because of countertransference, transference-countertransference entanglement?

Langs: In the narrow sense of these terms: that is, it would be a coming together of inappropriate needs within the two participants.

Stone: The "misalliance" operates to intrude or distort the positive or affirmative therapeutic alliance?

Langs: Right. And what I found empirically was that while there could be unilateral disturbances of the alliance sector—where the analyst might do something disruptive of which the patient largely was the victim so to speak, or the patient out of transference-based needs could, as part of his continual efforts to alter the frame, disrupt the alliance, most of the time there was some degree of collusion between the two. It's very important for the analyst to monitor the alliance sector and to try to pick up moments where he goes off in one antitherapeutic direction or another.

Stone: Well, there again it would be a matter of accent. You say you think in most instances it's a matter of collusion. You don't believe that the patient's transference can in itself disrupt the therapeutic alliance?

Langs: Oh, yes, I certainly do.

Stone: I mean—a hostile transference, or transference disappointment in infantile demands, and so on. But that you would regard as in the course of analysis qua analysis—without misalliance. That could occur within the framework of a satisfactory alliance, which can then provide the context for its reduction. What I would deduce is that you believe some transference-countertransference phenomena can distort the therapeutic alliance so that it becomes a misalliance which is then operating against the purposes of the analysis.

Langs: Right.

Stone: Now, when you say there's always collusion, you imply that this distortion of the therapeutic alliance cannot occur temporarily under the stress of the patient's transference—even if we assume the ideal situation, that the analyst is completely on the ball, and not responding pathologically to the transference.

Langs: No. I don't think I said that—not always—but I may have been misunderstood. I didn't say that it doesn't happen; I said that, indeed, as you are saying, it is common for transference needs and distortions to disrupt the therapeutic alliance. What I'm saying is that in my experience—first of all in my experience with residents— most of the time, there is a bilateral contribution to a disturbed alliance. I am also saying that I believe that in the real, actual world of analysis this is far more common than we like to believe.

Stone: With that I would have to agree. Although the "two worlds" are really vastly different.

Langs: It can occur at the behest of the analyst, though ideally that should be less common.

Stone: It's far more frequent than is supposed or accepted. I mean the system of passing the buck always to the patient.

Langs: Exactly. That is a point I speak about again and again.

Stone: Oh yes, in that I would agree with you. But you see, conceptually, it is important to keep in mind that it is part of the work of the analysis that the patient begins to storm with his hostile or unruly erotic transferences, and unless adequately interpreted and properly handled these cause disruptions in the therapeutic alliance. As temporary things they ought to be expected. And if properly handled, they should be short-lived and should have retrospectively a certain unique value if they bring a sense of reality to the patient's transference experience. But I know what you mean: more often than is thought, both people participate.

Langs: And I have the same attitude as you about it. I think they're very important therapeutic experiences. I think they can actualize very important things for both participants, because this is where the analyst can grow a little too, through the proper analysis of such interludes. The only difference, and here's where a very important concept comes to mind and it's an obvious one, is that when the analyst is participating, the first step is not interpretation, it's what I call "rectification." In other words, he has to modify his contribution before he can interpret.

Stone: Yes, if it has been his countertransference or other personal involvement. If we distinguish between countertransference and ordinary conscious responses, getting sore at a patient at certain times, or being unable to stand too much criticism, you know how uncanny patients are in searching out weak spots. How they can attack this guy one way and another guy another way, and sometimes a given analyst can't take it. And that he can rectify, either on a conscious level by self-scrutiny and self-discipline, or if it's true (and warded off) transference to the patient or countertransference of which he becomes aware, he must turn to self-analysis—or, if the situation is too complicated, to the help of another analyst.

Langs: Yes, the unconscious countertransference. The other point I mention again as a tool for identifying and resolving countertransferences—the one that has been most neglected in the literature—is that of the patient: he will undertake unconscious therapeutic work at such times. This is one of my favorite concepts. When I began to study therapeutic misalliances carefully, several things happened. I began to ask: where do they come from; what are their sources? I was seeing many of them in the work of young residents; and I found first that they came out of the therapist's errors. And then we get back to the frame: very often the error was expressed in an unneeded modification of the frame.

Stone: I know, I know. We did discuss some of this before, including the patient's interpretive work. This matter of unneeded "modifications of the frame" is frequently mentioned; and I am sure that it is frequent, just as I am sure that inappropriate pompous rigidity is even more frequent! They sometimes sit pompously and wait for the marvelous analytic revelation to occur. Have you seen the recent paper by Roskin and Rabiner (1976)? Now the modifications of the frame that you think of, that residents are particularly frequently prone to, are what? Being overindulgent?

Langs: The Roskin-Rabiner paper was in the journal that I edit. But you see, mine were not the sit-back type at all. For example, helping a patient to get up after a minor fall, physically touching a patient to help her up (Langs, 1973). Just think of examples that I think I've published. Making physical contact, unnecessarily: the patient is not injured. Even picking up a sweater, unnecessarily (Langs, 1973). Revealing certain facts about themselves under conditions that are different from those you described—that's what interests me and that's one of the vignettes I would like to describe when we get to the clinical material: a case where the therapist on the day of a snowstorm revealed that he lived near the hospital (Langs, 1975b) without getting associations first and without analyzing the entire incident; extensive regression in the patient resulted.

And another important way of modifying the frame is that of giving direct advice, so-called supportive therapy. This is again and again unconsciously experienced by patients as destructive. In one example I published (Langs, 1973), the patient was developing homosexual fantasies and thinking of getting involved homosexually, one factor being that his father had died and that he was sharing a bedroom with his mother. Now the therapist, out of all of the kindness of his heart, but to some degree also out of an inner difficulty, said to him, "You know, you ought to get out of there." This vignette culminated with the patient believing that the therapist wanted to have a homosexual affair with him, and wanted to take him away from his mother for himself. And my point is that these blatant thoughts are not entirely distortions. They contain a degree of unconscious perceptiveness. But these are very active modifications of anonymity, of neutrality, and the like.

Stone: What was the further course of that when he said "I think you ought to get out of there?" What was the patient doing, sleeping with his mother?

Langs: He was sleeping in the same bedroom; I think they were using separate beds.

Stone: But if he had these fantasies about the analyst, was he himself a homosexual, did you say? Or struggling with a powerful unconscious trend of the kind—reactivated as defense by the threatening materialization of his oedipal fantasies?

Langs: He was struggling with conscious homosexual wishes.

Stone: Well, one might assume (unless he were really a manifest homosexual) that he might develop such projections anyway, as part of the transference. Not that I have any doubt that such latent fantasies may have been precipitously mobilized by the intervention. One usually "saves" such interventions until such time as one is convinced that interpretations and clarifications are "of no avail"— that the acting-out resistance has become a "way of life." And then one might offer a considered recommendation, not an "order."

Langs: Let me say something, that brings up some important issues. I don't have the exact vignette with me but I can remember a good bit of it. In fact I refer to it again in a paper on misalliances (Langs, 1976a). There are two factors here: one is a naive resident, the other is a fragile patient who expresses himself very loudly and very clearly. Now with that particular patient, I can go over the sequence because it took a lot of work to restore the frame. But, let's get back to your point because this is a very important problem. It has been said to me many, many times: this would happen anyway, in the course of the unfolding of the transference with a patient with conscious homosexual impulses. I distinguish between saying "in the transference" and saying "in the relationship." That is, I don't call the relationship "transference"; I call the relationship the "analytic" or "therapeutic" relationship, and then talk about primarily transference and nontransference components.

Stone: But transference might sometimes invest that, and he might think of the analyst as seductive, especially in a situation as pathological as the one you describe. I mean, I'm not saying that the fellow should have given that advice. I just don't know enough about the case! But there are times when it might be appropriate for a person to be helped to move out of a home or something like that, by a well-timed and tactful recommendation—as I said before—if the situation supports insuperable resistances, and is obviously intrinsically pathological, and if the patient then distorts this by virtue of his exigent transferences, and he can't understand the interpretation of the transference element, as against the reality of what the analyst intended, then one is probably dealing with a psychotic patient.

Langs: To say that the material would unfold from a homosexual patient in terms of a homosexual transference anyhow is to overlook one important difference: if the analyst has in some way behaved inappropriately, has behaved, let's say, in a seductive way, that then creates a different external and internal situation for the patient. I believe that it actually influences the therapeutic qualities of the field, the bipersonal field (Langs, 1976), and creates a different set of rules—indeed, a damaged frame—and a different unfolding and set of implications from what happens when it comes out of transference frustration.

Stone: Without question. The point is, how necessary was this therapist's intervention? Because there is no question that there are people who get stuck in their parent's home (and "hold") and who at some point, maybe after years of purely interpretative effort, might require some suggestion in the same sense that the phobic patient may have to be told that it's time for him to go out and try to ride on the subway, that one can't go on in the purely verbal sphere without any testing in life. So that the patient comes to know that a part of his therapy includes taking himself out of a situation of impasse, to which he feels tied, and to confront it. Now, I don't know anything about this resident or whether he said this gratuitously, or with proper timing, or whatever, but there are instances where a person can depart, indeed, may have to depart, from the purely interpretative circumscription of his activities, to say something that is of educational import, or that is a statement of a neglected reality, for example, that it is time to try to leave his parent's home. This would usually occur after a few years of most earnest analytic effort, and where you feel that a person is never going to get anything out of purely interpretative work if he doesn't confront this real issue (a built-in acting out, so to speak).

Langs: I would want to add to that that the analyst would have had to spend some time scrutinizing his countertransference to be sure that something isn't being missed, that something wasn't misinterpreted, that he failed to offer the appropriate interpretations that would have enabled the patient to mobilize himself.

Stone: But that's *always* so; that we take for granted. But there are many patients, the fact is, who would just as soon come to analysis for ten, fifteen, or twenty years, and hear interpretations, and stay right where they are. Of course, they're sick people. But by the same token, we are doctors! In such instances I think the analysis itself becomes incorporated in the chronic neurosis, which involves a kind of countertransference participation of the analyst, different from the one that might concern you.

Langs: I would begin to wonder about a misalliance.

Stone: Well, of course. But you see misalliances can take more than one direction. You can have a misalliance of extreme propriety and external continuity of analytic work, sometimes involving a special form of obscure countertransference, supported by the illusion that any ego is the "fictive normal ego" which will surely respond to pure interpretation ultimately, in the light of sufficient time and conscientiousness.

Langs: I would like really to see such clinical material and assess it. You have most clearly delineated certain kinds of modifications in technique. Many of these, of course, fit the definition of a parameter that Eissler (1953) offered, that it is a response to one or more ego dysfunctions. If you read the literature, many therapists and analysts invoke these deviations much earlier in treatment than you suggest, and without this kind of thought or assessment. This particular deviation was made maybe a week or two after the patient mentioned that he was sharing the bedroom with his mother, with just two or three sessions in which the therapist had only begun to explore this with the patient.

Stone: Well, he didn't even know anything about his patient. So almost any activity, even significant interpretation, was out of place.

Langs: In this instance we could agree. But I do believe we have come to a very crucial juncture.

Stone: This is crucial, indeed! Let me say a word about this recent discussion, very briefly (I hope). You see, in psychotherapy we're dealing with something that is, by its nature, different from analysis, although of course intimately related to it, in a derivative sense, and these differences have not been sufficiently well defined. As you said, I tried twenty or twenty-five years ago. That there are many variants and forms of psychotherapy I believe is true, and work must still be done on that, to set up formats like the general format that is relatively well defined in analysis, where we have a fairly formalized situation and methodology, and so on. Not so in psychotherapy. All we know is that we take certain ideas from analysis and extrapolate them into what is often a very different situation. But most of us do recognize that within psychotherapy there is often necessitated a greater focusing, a greater activity by the therapist; although as you suggested earlier, these should be well defined or categorized and governed by rational rules. I mean (to reduce things to an absurdity, for greater clarity) the doctor has no more right to seduce a patient because it's psychotherapy than he has in analysis, or to push him around, or deprive him of his adult rights. But that there is a certain higher degree of activity implicit in the idea of psychotherapy as opposed to analysis is true, insofar as the term (as it usually is) is applied to less intensive work, of lesser duration, with limited and (relatively) planned goals.

Everyone may not subscribe to this: it's poorly defined. But, just for example: the therapist may speak more often, shape the content of the hours, at times not leave the course of communication entirely to free association and an infrequent interpretation. Resistances may often be dealt with holistically, as integrated with impulse, fantasy, or other content. The expression of decorous and appropriate physicianly interest need not be as restrained as in analysis. Even the occasional offering of simple, conservative information or advice, within the physician's sphere of competence, may sometimes be appropriate—not, for example, whom to marry or what the patient's life work should be. And incidentally, I have said in the past, this type of work often calls for greater skill than analysis. It should follow rather than precede analytic training! Of course, there must be a great sensitiveness to transference implications and manifestations. But if activity is kept within the bounds of ethical, dignified, and rational physicianly behavior, the transference manifestations are more likely to be focal breakthroughs rather than massive and general transference neurosis regressions.

What I feel is this. Whether in psychotherapy, or in the analysis of atypical patients, for example, psychotic patients or very severe borderline patients, with severe acting out, or severe regressions, or severe symptomatic exacerbations, whether depression or anxiety, disturbed perceptions or behavioral disturbances . . . Let me break off: a week or so ago, on a week-end, I had a call from the wife of a man who had beaten her. (He was still in a disturbed mood, and she was desperate.) This is no small matter. Say, a psychotic equivalent in a man who is ambulatory and keeps going. To me, there was no choice but to initiate a conversation over the telephone, which did bring matters "under control."

Now this is the important thing: just as I put so much emphasis, in a less behavioral sense, on the ego of the adult patient and its capacity to accept the deprivations, the activities, of analysis as rational and appropriate, I believe, and I'm quite sure I've said so somewhere, maybe in the "Widening Scope" paper (Stone, 1954), that a complementary phenomenon is the rationality and appropriateness of the analyst's behavior—especially when larger deviations are invoked. People have questioned the distortion of an analysis because the analyst had to take extreme steps, let's say with a psychotic patient. You might have had to see that he got home somehow or had to telephone his wife in his presence. These things are infrequent, but they may happen in really extreme situations. The objection has often been made, that the analyst in such instances can't go on and analyze that patient. Well, of course, the analysis may be limited by the severity of the pathology, anyway; that I would acknowledge. But that the analyst can ultimately restore an analytic situation with some of these patients and go on and make considerable headway, I believe is true. To go through a stormy period together may establish a unique bond, difficult to relinquish, difficult to establish with another physician, and of great importance to the more ill type of patient. The criterion that I have usually followed is this: if what the analyst did was rational, and was dictated by the necessities of the situation, the real necessities of the situation, the patient can later come to see such behaviors in that light, and come to accept them in retrospect, and come to accept the fact that such maneuvers are not necessary now, that it is not necessary for the analyst to be in touch with his wife, or to call another doctor, or whatever the hell happened, you see, but that in retrospect such maneuvers were determined by the actualities of the patient's behavior.

All that I have meant with this long-winded discourse is to

introduce the idea that atypical behavior is sometimes necessary or desirable, and that the degree of rationality of that behavior, or let's say, the degree to which it is not determined by the analyst's emotional needs or anxieties, will have much to do with the capacity of the patient to proceed later, and to analyze what happened. And here I should like to mention something that I omitted to say much earlier (or mentioned only partially). It is not superciliousness; as you know, I have great respect for the practice of psychotherapy. However, I think that this practice by residents presents a biased sampling, to be compared only with much circumspection and allowance for many factors of error with the analytic work, or even the psychotherapeutic work, of candidates, not to speak of graduate analysts. Naturally, countertransference acting out is more frequent, and the sheer lack of experience and know-how must contribute heavily to errors of judgment. It's not that any of us are "above it all"—but "percentagewise" (to speak the current lingo) the differences must be very great. Thus your inferences must be influenced by this source, as mine are by many years of supervision of candidates (and graduates) and the analyses and reanalyses of candidates and analysts.

Langs: This criticism comes up from time to time, and I would like to respond. Somewhere, Freud (1918) said we learn little from cases that go well, and much from those that go poorly. Empirically, my work with psychiatric trainees has served me well, and has, I believe, enabled me to generate broad principles, which I have, by the way, consistently validated in my own clinical work and in presentations from more experienced therapists.

Now, it is, of course, quite true that I am observing a rather disturbed bipersonal field and should not conclude that it is representative of a well-run analysis—and I have not drawn such inferences at all. *The Bipersonal Field* (Langs, 1976a) was written to illustrate concepts that I described in a more systematic and balanced way in *The Therapeutic Interaction* (Langs, 1976b). I simply did not want the latter book, based as it is solely on the literature, to appear without some clinical documentation. *The Bipersonal Field* has been misconstrued as a statement of general principles in its totality, and my critics failed to recognize that I fully understood and accounted for the distortions. I then made use of those disturbed therapeutic interactions as a means of highlighting a set of basic and somewhat neglected clinical concepts and techniques that they brought into bold relief. It is erroneously said that I believe that psychotherapy evolves from the therapist's pathology. As a statement of one unfortunate possibility, it is true. As part of a broad principle, however, it would have to be rephrased: psychotherapy is initiated by the patient's pathology and the therapist's ability to help; it unfolds interactionally based on many factors—including the communicated pathology of each participant.

Forgive these extended remarks. I know you've raised a broad question that requires a necessary perspective, but it touched upon a sensitive issue, I guess. So, the form of a given therapeutic interaction will vary with many factors, including those you mention. Nonetheless, the general principles derived, if stated properly and in a balanced way—as I did in *The Therapeutic Interaction* (Langs, 1976b)—can be formulated, I believe, in a manner that is valid for all therapeutic analytic experiences. I am quite mindful of differences, and yet endeavoring to identify universals. Incidentally, these studies actually sensitized me to countertransference expressions, so that I soon was able to identify many subtle forms overlooked by many analysts.

Stone: In any supervisory work, I see candidates with whom isolated countertransferences emerge through occasional lapses in technique. This is rather different from working with someone with poorly controlled countertransferences and considerable confusion regarding the basics of technique—that's a terribly confused situation.

Langs: Yes, but one that provided me with an extensive opportunity to study countertransference effects—and their influence in the therapeutic interaction.

Stone: This also relates to the issue of how slight or benign these effects often may be in their determining the course of an analysis.

Langs: Yes, and it relates to why I tend to emphasize their influence and consequences—an approach that I feel is well taken in the light of evidence that many analysts tend to minimize this aspect of their work with patients. Actually, I believe that the principles I developed in *The Bipersonal Field* (Langs, 1976b) can be discovered and validated by any analyst who listens and formulates along the lines I have been suggesting. Too much so-called analytic work is done at the manifest level; too little attention is paid to derivatives organized around specific adaptive contexts—especially the analyst's interventions and their unconscious implications.

Now, if I may return to the problem of deviations in technique (another area where I feel some analysts have misunderstood my position—I advocate the use of sound and consistent principles, and that is mistaken as rigidity), I would like to say, first of all, and I think we would agree here, that there is always a clinical and subjective judgment involved in assessing the point at which one feels he must invoke a modification in the frame—and this decision is rather clearly open to countertransference-based influence. Secondly, I believe that modifications should be confined, almost entirely, to those that are so to speak forced upon the therapist or therapeutic situation by the patient. And I think this is really what you are saying as well. I will show you, and show you your name quoted (not that this necessarily represents your position) where modifications are invoked for many other more questionable reasons, such as strengthening the therapeutic alliance or being "real" for the patient. There is a paper by Gudeman (1974) in which the patient comes in early in her analysis and offers the analyst flowers and tobacco; he accepted them, saying that he did not want to appear overdepriving, "as Stone had suggested," but these modifications were not forced by the patient and her pathology. This patient regressed severely, and I think this had a great deal to do with the fact that the analyst didn't maintain the boundaries in the first place. What happened then is something that Freud (1912b) predicted, Greenacre (1959) predicted, and I predicted (Langs, 1975a): the patient who obtains a modification in the boundaries will seek further modifications. This patient went from the flowers to the tobacco to asking the analyst to write a letter for her husband's vasectomy. That brings me back to your earlier comment: it would have come up anyhow. My point is that it is different when a fantasy or belief arises when the analyst has behaved in some way that justifies or confirms the fantasy. The hold is different; the valid perception of the analyst is different; the pathogenic past is actually being confirmed; inner, distorted reality is confirmed for the patient. These are important differences. Now, in the situation in Gudeman's paper, there was probably countertransference-based participation on his part, which he himself did not recognize or acknowledge. These are not of the kind of modifications that the pathology and the sickness in the patient dictates in an urgent situation.

Stone: Well, there may, however, be other instances: I don't want to be "too cooperative," so to speak. There may be instances where it is just a matter of the analyst's judgment. But that would usually involve something extraordinary, extraordinary sickness on the part of the patient, or extraordinary vulnerability, or something more subtle, but of equivalent importance; and one would have to know that and know it damn well, to make the judgment that "with this patient I will accept this little token gift." And *most* of the time, especially at the outset, there's no reason why the rules can't be followed, no question about that. However, again, I must add that if Stone's views have been misapplied, so have Freud's (as understood or misunderstood by the epigones). Also—if I may—while I recognize the putative "danger," I do not believe that every concession made to a patient must be followed by increased demands. If that occurs there was something in the patient's character which rendered the concession a mistake in the first place—not necessarily unrectifiable, of course—or, to follow your own special trend of interest, an important countertransference trend has been involved from the beginning. In recent years, I have made home visits to a patient, who made no unusual demands thereafter.

Langs: You have suggested, I believe, two broad indications for modifications: one group is those that you feel are ultimately adventitious and minor: the other are those involving urgent situations. In principle, I would take exception to the ones that are seemingly minor, because I have, empirically at least, found as a rule a countertransference-based contribution at such times. As to the modifications that are required by urgent clinical situations, there I would say something different. Greenacre (1959) said it very nicely: namely, an analyst may often make a modification in an apparent emergency and later find out first, that the patient—and the analyst—have then achieved certain inappropriate gratifications through it, and second, that often the analyst has been involved in a certain degree of complicity.

Stone: There is no "complicity," if one had to do it.

Langs: Well, where the analyst discovers in retrospect that actually there was a blind spot involved; that *unconscious* countertransferences played a role.

Stone: Oh, then that's different. As I said, one has to speak for oneself in such matters—usually. The search for inappropriate gratifications characterizes sick people. If sick enough, they force the issue or—unfortunately—sometimes hallucinate the gratifications. Sometimes an interpretation can be the result of a blind spot. You see, we treat these things almost as if they are reflected only in certain classes of behavior. A person can sit in the analytic chair and never say "Boo" to the patient and hardly ever talk, and only make terse, authoritarian interpretations, but the interpretations can be determined by countertransference or by stupidity, or by lack of empathy. You see, I do object to a certain a priori classification of certain behaviors. And please believe me, I have had patients with multiple past analyses, where some colleagues whose competence, by ordinary criteria, cannot be judged as less than excellent, and who didn't do any of these bad things, such as accepting cookies or similar transgressions, nevertheless succeeded in mixing up some patients so badly that it was almost impossible to extricate them; and they did so just by silently correct attitudes, or quietly disapproving attitudes, or just the slightest note of contempt in their voice at certain times, not to speak of occasions (bursts of irritation) when "authority" was questioned. I get a little emotional when I speak of these matters, because I've had too many such experiences.

Langs: Oh, there are many avenues to misalliance and ruptured alliances that I have specifically studied: number one, let's start there, failures to intervene; the second, of course, is incorrect interventions; and the third is mismanagement of the frame. The reason I'm focusing on that last one is that we've been discussing the frame, but I think it's very important to establish that that's not the only way of disrupting an analysis by any means, nor is misinterpreting; it can be through a failure to intervene at the proper moment. No question about it. The reason I think it's important for us to stress the management of the frame is that analysts have tended to think of mistakes as related to interpretations. One of the things that I said in an earlier paper (Langs, 1975b)—and it was so naive in a sense, and yet so basic—was that sometimes a so-called deviation in technique could actually be a technical error. Now nobody has written about that distinction, or on how to decide, empirically, whether it is so. One of the things that emerged from my observations and surprised me is that even in situations where there has been an emergency, a matter of life and death, and a modification has been invoked, the patient will on some level object to the modification. Now, I'm not saying that it shouldn't be done.

Stone: A patient may resent the fact that he wasn't allowed to commit suicide? This general problem of extraordinary interventions was discussed way back in Philadelphia when Anna Freud gave her paper. I should mention that the patient "objects"—at one level—to being helped to get well! Years ago, an older colleague, long since dead, with a wry sense of humor, mentioned in a clinic conference that a certain patient who had made a rather startling clinical "recovery" had probably done so in gratitude because he had *not* analyzed him!

Langs: Patients feel that their autonomy is disrupted, or they feel inappropriately controlled. It's a very interesting experience, and one has to recognize that there will be this kind of mixed reaction in this particular area, and that it will have to be analyzed. It is not a reason to fail to invoke a life-saving deviation, more a reminder of an important function of a steady frame.

Well, let me quickly fill out my position, then we can do some clinical work. Empirically I found misalliance and countertransference expressions came in the area of management of the ground rules, as well as in the area of intervening. Some of my other finds were that the patient was quite sensitive to the therapist's errors, be it in intervening or management, and would unconsciously perceive them and communicate the results, usually indirectly, in their material. I wrote something on the patient's unconscious perceptions of the therapist's errors (Langs, 1975c).

Initially, the way I defined that concept empirically was that if I, as a supervisor, identified an error and then the patient went on to associate in a confirmatory way, for instance about somebody who was blind, somebody who made a mistake, themes of that kind, I felt this was an unconscious perception of what I had picked up directly. Then through reading the Kleinian literature (see Langs, 1976b) and some of the writings of Searles (1965, 1972, 1975), I got into the more specific interactional mechanisms and realized that not only does the patient perceive the error, he incorporates it. He takes something in from the therapist, the process, the nature of the error, and works over the underlying basis inside himself. At such times, you'll often hear material related to efforts at self-cure. There was a presentation to me last Wednesday night, where the therapist kept making errors—not in regard to the frame, because my residents think long and hard before modifying the frame . . .

Stone: What is the frame they keep, the analytic frame?

Langs: That's another area where there's some difference between our positions.

Stone: Because the frame has to be defined, in any given situation.

Langs: I define the frame of psychotherapy in terms of the face-to-face mode, a lesser frequency of visits, usually twice a week, though it could be once or three times weekly, and I accept all the rest of the analytic frame. Now that's a specific definition.

Stone: Well, that's a very specific and personal definition. You mean that it includes free association?

Langs: Yes, in the operational sense of saying whatever comes to mind.

Stone: But are they supposed to do that, rather than merely having the privilege of saying whatever comes to mind? A difference may lie in their obligatory participation

Langs: I don't present it as obligatory; I say this is the way we will work. Yes, I suppose it has a certain obligatory quality. I would present it in a comparable manner in an analysis. That the way we work is for you to say whatever comes to mind.

Stone: Yes, and the therapist is relatively passive, like the analyst? The therapist makes interpretations along analytic lines, resistance interpretations first, ultimately content interpretations, and transference has a central position?

Langs: Yes.

Stone: Interpretation of the transference has a central position, as it has in analysis?

Langs: Yes, if you include in transference as you just used it both transference and nontransference elements; that is, the way that I would state the relevant principle is that one works where the patient is at for the moment, and that very often, the patient in psychotherapy is in fact dealing with some aspect of the relationship. The rest is appended to the relationship. That is an empirically founded position. When I wrote my technique books (Langs, 1973, 1974), I stated it the other way, the way that I was taught, that in therapy one works with external realities and only more rarely with the transference—so-called. Empirically, I don't feel that this is the case at all.

Stone: Well, if you remember in that paper of mine from which you started to quote a case before, I accented the fact that transference did not assume the same economic role in psychotherapy that it did in analysis, where frequency of contact and the supine position, the lack of visualization, and the analyst's passivity were so important. And that transference could often be indirectly interpreted as integrated into the person's everyday life. Ultimately, certain things which were of an explicitly and narrowly transferential nature, not suited to the still relatively disciplined give-and-take of psychotherapy or the reasonable exchanges of everyday life, would tend to break through, and come into the therapy as interpretable derivatives. Then, of course, it would be extremely important that the therapist be on the alert to interpret them. I think that in the case of the young girl in the "Psychotherapy" paper there was one in which the transference clearly came toward me. But I think that there might be some problem here, because I do not view psychotherapy as something that is "just like analysis," except for the basic concepts of pathology and dynamics, and certain broad principles of technology. I hope this doesn't interfere too much with our communication.

Langs: Oh, I didn't say "identical"; one would, for instance, have to follow through the consequences of the two changes, in frequency and mode. I'm not suggesting that one gets the same intensity of derivatives or depth of work and structural change, but one thing we have to clarify is that when I talk about "transference" in this sense, actually referring to the total relationship, I am talking about both transference and nontransference aspects.

Stone: Yes, right.

Langs: Also, when I talk about "transference" in the narrow and specific sense, I'm really talking about unconscious transference fantasies, not direct references to the therapist or analyst. You know, within our literature, unfortunately, many people equate transference with direct communications about the analyst.

Stone: Of course, transference exists and is operative, whether or not it appears in consciousness. Sometimes, it is "mobilized" with the greatest difficulty—for example, in tenacious acting out. It may appear only in dreams, or in parapraxes, or in the total drift of associations, in a variety of inferential modes.

Langs: You know, Melanie Klein (1952) was the first—not the first to say it, but the first to explicate it. Freud, I know, you quoted as saying that since the patient is conveying this material to the analyst, somehow whatever he's saying has a bearing on that relationship.

Stone: Yes, Freud (1925) did say that everything said in an hour must have some reference to the person to whom it is said, in one of his early papers; that we have to accept the fact that everything the patient is saying has reference to the analyst, in the sense that he's telling it to him, and that one may postulate that the identity of the person he's talking to has something to do with the selection of material.

Langs: Melanie Klein was the one who took that most seriously. Her 1952 paper on transference is a very fine paper. Incidentally, it's not a "Kleinian" paper, in many ways, although she brings in some of her thinking on the earliest phases of mental life. It's a very sensitive paper and I think we, as classical analysts, would accept most of what she says. Klein believed that every communication has some reference to the analyst. Now, I feel that if you include transference and nontransference, and accept it as only one level of what is communicated, that this is true, in analysis and also in psychotherapy—though the form it takes in therapy can be different. We must recognize that there are many variables. For example, with a more primitive patient you may get more primitive derivatives, even in psychotherapy.

Stone: Yes, the forms are different. Sometimes, just because of the infrequency of visiting, there is a breakthrough of intense transference demands. Because there isn't that quieting, partial gratification that goes with frequent visits. That I saw years ago when I had a study group in psychotherapy, which, unfortunately, disbanded after several years; and nobody as yet has gone back and worked over the material.

Langs: I would like to see such work published—but about the breakthrough, the intense breakthrough?

Stone: Yes, I saw one or two instances, where this took intensely pathological form—"too much of a good thing," so to speak. You see, everybody was allowed to practice psychotherapy as he conceived it. I had a kind of zany attitude toward the research aspect. As a matter of fact, that was one of the troubles later, that some of the people wanted to do experimental things, like take two people with similar cases and have them deliberately employ different methods and see how it came out. I couldn't go along with that. I felt it was much better to take a natural historical approach, let the people do what they thought was right and helpful, and then see what happened, simply observing the facts. I remember one instance where it became a problem; the colleague had to consult me, and he was quite panicky about it. He saw a patient once a week, pretty much in an analytic format, lying down and free associating, the therapist quite passive, and this was followed shortly by a very severe transference regression. She gradually came out of it, but with a great deal of sweat and anxiety on the part of the therapist. In that case, there was very little doubt, in my mind, that that particular patient couldn't tolerate this "vacuum" situation, the frustration of the analytic situation, on a once-weekly basis, with the therapist very passive. To be scientific about it, we do not know that this patient might not have had a similar regression in a true analytic situation—say five times a week. But in our work, we do have to make rational inferences; sometimes add the positive and negative inferences together "algebraically," to achieve a dialectical (relative) truth. There are optimum regressions in psychotherapy and psychoanalysis respectively; analysis can utilize a much deeper, more diffuse regression (but not too great!). I believe that the regression in the case mentioned was conditioned not only by severe pathology, but by the undue deprivations of the once-a-week therapeutic situation.

Langs: As my ideas on the importance of the frame—be it in analysis or therapy—evolved, I went back, as I said earlier, to the Freud case histories (Langs, 1976c, 1978a,b). I decided that using as a template today's ground rules, pretty much as you and I define them, I would see how the patient reacted every time Freud stepped out of them, even though they weren't his ground rules. And it's amazing that the same kind of material and the same kind of reactions that are evoked by relatively unneeded deviations in technique today characterized the responses of his patients. In fact, the notes from the Rat Man (Freud, 1909) are an excellent source of this material. As you know, not only did he feed the Rat Man, he did two other things: he sent him a post card and he lent him a book.

Stone: "He was hungry so I fed him," or something like that.

Langs: Do you know that the Rat Man had an absolutely paranoid reaction to that, and that it culminated in a typical dream of the dentist who pulled the wrong tooth, who made a mistake? I think that through the years and this is a piece of history that would be interesting to detail—Freud's ground rules have been somewhat modified; some have been kept quite as he stated them (Freud, 1912b, 1913) and some have been changed. You know, there is the money that he gave the Wolf Man (Freud, 1918; Brunswick, 1928), things of that sort. In that instance, I believe that the deviation was a contribution to the Wolf Man's paranoid episode—it's in all that material. But it's a silently carried out piece of analytic history that through the years we've accepted by and large at least a certain basic framework and I have great faith in that frame as it now stands. I feel that it is a very powerfully effective hold, with therapeutic powers of its own, and it is as effective for the patient in therapy, with certain modifications, as it is for the patient in analysis. But don't misunderstand me, I can be quite active within that frame. And I am. I respond supportively by intervening more empathically, becoming more active at the appropriate moment, and the like, or by reaffirming the frame when the patient impinges on it.

Stone: Well, that probably *is* the most important general consideration. I don't interpret "activity" as giving the patient things, or feeding him. You see, I am very "iconoclastic." I would never even, as some of our European colleagues did at first, and took for granted, eat behind the patient, or take coffee while the patient was there. I'm a "maverick," yet to me this would be unthinkable, unthinkable. So it all depends on where you're sitting when you get very strict about things; you view what somebody else does as unorthodox or unclassical. I think most analysts have stopped that practice now. But years ago it was very common.

Langs: That's very interesting.

Stone: In fact, I once mentioned this to an older person whom I respected in the course of a conversation, and the colleague said, "You mean you wouldn't even take a coffee during an analytic hour?" I couldn't conceive of it, that the patient know that I'm sipping coffee while he's free associating. Imagine what this sets up in him.

Langs: Exactly.

Stone: I say that because you mentioned Freud's feeding of the Rat Man. Of course that's out of the question, except possibly in a war bombardment and where he hadn't eaten for several days! Of course,

we have to remember, and I'm sure you do, that Freud was creating
these things and learning about them as he went along. Genius that
he was, there were some things that he didn't know as well as some of
our early students should, if they're smart, because we can teach them
those things, from the great corpus he initiated. You mean, then, that
you're impressed by the way one can trace the relationship between
such encounters and subsequent untoward effects?

Langs: Right. Also that one's understanding and practices depend
on how one envisions the impact of the modification on the patient.
Do you know that in a paper on erotized transference, Rappaport
(1959) reported that one patient developed an erotized transference in
the presence of his eating his lunch in the sessions—and he never for
a moment thought that that might have had anything to do with it?

Stone: It didn't occur to him that this might have . . . ?

Langs: Absolutely not—that this could have been a factor in the
erotized response of the patient.

Stone: I don't know the particular reason there, but do you know
one reason why a person might overlook that? Simply because it's
validated by authority. You know, if all the big shot older analysts
did it, how can that make any trouble? Like having a dog in the
analytic office! Which was adjacent to my reaction to some of these
explicitly technical things; to the fact that some of the correct
neutralities, some of the lacks of response, could be just as damaging,
in some instances, I thought, more seriously damaging, than lapses
on the gentle or considerate side, assuming that the latter, again,
were not motivated by some chronic countertransference problem.
However, I do also want to fasten down another point, lest we forget
it, in riding our respective hobbies: whatever these "lapses" may be—
yours, mine, Freud's or Rappaport's—the response must involve the
patient's pathology, be it an accusation of blindness, or seduction, or
pulling the wrong tooth. Dreams are dynamic, not just descriptive. If
the pathology is not too severe, and the lapse or mistake not intrinsically damaging or due to a chronic unconscious countertransference distortion, analytic work may rectify the situation, in
occasional instances, with affirmative outcome.

Langs: This is a fascinating area because it touches upon such basic problems, not least the resistances one must overcome in effecting change or presenting new ideas within classical psychoanalysis. It brings me back to my own efforts and the problems I've faced because I attempted to understand and conceptualize interactional mechanisms, introjective mechanisms, and projective identification—I defined them in my own way and I had, I think, a valid and empirical way of defining them (Langs, 1976a,b), not unlike Melanie Klein's (1946), though a bit different. She and her followers tended to think of these mechanisms in very primitive terms. They acknowledge, but underplay, outside influences. But I think that these mechanisms can be used at every level of development, and in increasingly mature forms, and that one can demonstrate that they are influenced by realities too. Anyway, I began to realize that I was dealing with something more than a *perception* of the therapist's errors; there was also an introjection of them and a reading of some of the unconscious meanings. There is then an interplay of sound perceptiveness and response, and distorted and pathological reactions. The former have in general been overlooked.

Stone: You mean that the patient introjects some of the errors of the analyst?

Langs: Yes. In these terms, every technical error, since it's an incorrect intervention for the patient, constitutes a projective identification of the analyst or therapist, a placing into the patient some aspect of his pathology.

Stone: Then this can in effect be a projective identification by the analyst? This phenomenon requires further discussion.

Langs: Exactly. As you know, the Kleinians virtually never write about the analyst's projective identifications, only about the patient's, which is again so defensive (see Langs, 1977b).

Stone: It's very odd, just like their dealing with transference. I agree with the fact that everything that is said in the analytic hour has some element of transference. But not to distinguish between the transference as transference and the numerous realities that may be mentioned constitutes, I think, an important error. You know, if the patient comes in and says, "God, it's an awfully cold day," you don't immediately have to assume that he feels he's being shut out although this may in some instances be the case! (Just as it may be true that his father caught a bad winter cold and died of pneumonia.) I'm just stating the absurdities to make the point. I'm inclined to think that the Kleinians tended in that direction. But I would not say that the Kleinians altogether omit the analyst's projective and introjective identifications. That is, if Money-Kyrle (1956) was a true Kleinian, and if I remember his excellent paper accurately—the one about what happens when the analyst gets "stuck," as to his understanding.

Langs: They do, I believe. This has been part of my criticism of their literature (Langs, 1976b). They tend to think that way and they exclude realities over and over again. You would want to say, "Look, it could be either reality or fantasy or both"; they would say, "It's primitive and intrapsychic." They quickly shift to a very primitive level. This is unfortunate, because these attitudes have turned off so many classical analysts to the important contributions that they made to both theory and technique.

Stone: Turned them away and made them immune to what the Kleinians may have to offer. I can remember Waelder years ago discussing that (as I remember his droll example): A man comes in and says to the analyst, "God, I missed my lunch today and I'm hungry." The analyst says, "You want to take out my bowels and eat them." That, to him, (in jest, I suspect) was a typical Kleinian interpretation.

Langs: Often, they do not work downward from the surface, but they do something else which we should have learned about a long time ago. The see defenses in terms of the contributions of unconscious fantasy. We think of defense much too mechanistically. But Hanna Segal (1967), in a very good paper that represents the Kleinian position, spells it out very clearly.

Stone: She is the colleague who wrote that excellent little book (Segal, 1967) on Melanie Klein. Was that paper based on the same material? I enjoyed the book.

Langs: Yes, they are related. But she too, in the first hour, and I think it was even with a candidate—the candidate said something about being hungry or thinking about milk and she was immediately talking about his wanting to devour her breast. Now, in the first session, without work with defenses, without any preparatory work, it's hard to grasp. I think it was Balint (1968) who said that if you get enough of these interpretations you soon develop a very paranoid position. You're being attacked in a very primitive way and you utilize projective mechanisms to defend yourself. He felt that this is why the Kleinians see so much of it. Yet, despite those limitations, for whatever reason, I didn't let it deter me from studying their work, and I learned a tremendous amount about interaction. And in fact—I don't know if he's going to appreciate it or not—I made a great fuss about a paper by Martin Wangh (1962) that I have not seen referred to in the literature on technique: his paper on the evocation of a proxy.

Stone: That's a familiar title, but it's not clear in my mind.

Langs: It's really a description of the positive aspects of projective identification, the interactional effort to evoke a proxy, to have somebody else experience something for you, to help you to function in a way that you can't mobilize yourself, or experience an instinctual drive expression that you don't want to experience. It fits in very nicely with the Kleinian material.

For me, the Kleinian work that I read coalesced with the observations that I had been making in the interactional sphere. It became clear to me—and this applies also to verbal intervening—that if the therapist makes an intervention that modifies the frame unnecessarily, he then places into the patient some piece of his problems, because it expresses his inappropriate needs, and not those of the patient, and the patient in some way unconsciously perceives, incorporates, contains, works over the relevant contents and inner state, and in general, does two things: accepts it and attempts to cure the introject in an attempt both at self-cure and at cure of the therapist. Searles (1975) has a paper on the subject of the patient as therapist to the analyst; he is one of the rare classically trained analysts to be sensitive to interactional mechanisms.

Stone: The patient tries to cure this bad therapist, this bad parent? This is at least intelligible. That the analyst "places" something "into the patient" is not. Perhaps we will discuss projective identification again.

Langs: Yes. Searles specifically says that he feels that this is a basic human striving, that the infant attempts to give cues to the parent—the mother—that are curative. In fact, he feels that one of the major factors in mental sickness is the extent to which such efforts have been frustrated or misappropriated. (It is a very nice paper, by the way.) I observed this empirically, even in the comments by the patient which, I feel, really constituted unconscious interpretations directed toward the therapist. If they were said directly and consciously, they would have had all the earmarks of an interpretation. And, of course, when I went into the literature, I found that even that idea with which I was so enamored had been presented before, by Margaret Little, in 1951, in her paper on the patient's reaction to the analyst's countertransference. She actually described such interpretive endeavors. It too is a very fine paper.

Well, that's my background: looking at the deviation, taking it as an organizer, as an adaptive context, looking at the material that follows in order to see its unconscious influence on the patient. Time is pushing us, though; it's clear we may have to take more time to go over the clinical material, without rushing it. If you have any clinical material, by the way, that would show the conditions under which you felt that you had invoked a successful modification and had some associations, that would also be very helpful, if it's handy. I have some material, but mine takes a particular direction.

But before we get to it, I wanted, so we don't overlook it, to discuss the other kind of deviation, unrelated to severe pathology, that we mentioned earlier. For example, before vacations, you stated that you felt that it was appropriate, if it was explored and analyzed, to indicate at some point where one is going, or the nature of a hobby or an interest (Stone, 1961). How do you make that decision?

Stone: That's a different issue. That involves a whole theory of a transference, and the question of "resemblances," which I first mentioned around twenty-five years ago. I feel that for the analyst's personality to be kept gratuitously and effortfully hidden, to create the (impossible!) illusion that he is a "blank screen," that he has no real form as a person, is a fallacy. To think that he can literally function as a mirror is to do injustice to Freud's genius. In the first place, it's impossible. Secondly, the artificial effort, instead of enhancing viable transference formation, tends either to stultify it, or to elicit rather "wild" regressive forms. Since I have presented my reasoning in this sphere in the past, I shall not bore you with repeating it here.

In the second place, I had the feeling, a feeling based on what I thought was observation of a clinical sort, not the kind of observation that a laboratory man would accept, but from repeated clinical observations, that this "imitation of a mirror" may facilitate undue regression and may stimulate excessive transference demand, especially if it attains a degree where it is not seen by the patient as rational. For example, to tell a patient—in line with Freud's feeding the fellow, or the analyst eating while the patient is there—to tell a person one's eating habits, not to speak of one's sexual preferences, is of course utterly out of bounds. For the person to have some outline picture of the analyst as a person in relatively neutral reference, especially noninstinctual and nonconflictual references, I thought provided a better basis for the development of the transference than the (presumably) bald, effortfully bald picture. I did not mean that, therefore, one goes about talking a great deal, or conducts the analysis with a great deal of self-revelation. But I did think that certain things fit naturally and simply into place, and are more advantageously told, than withheld. For example, if a patient spoke about sailing and then proceeded to explain in great detail how you did this and how you did that, if you were to say, especially in response to his question, "Yes, I know something about that, it's okay, you can go ahead," I didn't think any harm would ensue. Now, there are people who will say, and maybe you're one of those . . .

Langs: Yes.

Stone: . . . who will say, "Yes, that will come back sometime." The patient will dream of you tying knots on a boat, or something like that, or you going sailing together. Then my response would be, so what. This could in most instances have been a facilitating thing, like a day residue for a dream or the patient responding to his analyst's crossing his legs. It would produce material. Other things (also "nonthings") might produce material, too; but if there were too great an accent on the distance, the inaccessibility, the withholding of innocuous information, it was my observation that this tended to whip up curiosities actively, and make them overintense. Curiosities are normally there, of course. But to give them a spurious over-emphasis was, in short, to intensify transferences to a degree that wasn't always useful. Now, that, I know, is disagreed with by many people. Similarly, as I said, whether one takes vacations in Vermont or Maine would not be, ordinarily, a bit of knowledge liable to occasion severe side-effects, if it seemed natural to answer the question in certain instances. As I've said, the information should not ordinarily be the primary response. But it should remain a matter of the analyst's judgment rather than an arbitrary prohibition. I should say that I have yet to see untoward side-effects from such occasional communications. I have known of a patient who toured around (on the basis of indirect and inadvertent hints) looking for the country home of the analyst who followed the strict prohibition. Incidentally, he found it.

Langs: Yes, I'm going to try to demonstrate this type of deviation.

Stone: Also, I do not think it is especially advantageous for a patient to be spending the whole summer wondering where you are, especially if he has a high level of anxiety. This, I think, is a hell of a waste of neurotic energy.

Langs: Now I know the kind of data to organize for our next meeting. Hypothetically, I would say that the patient would not dream about sailing; he'd dream about somebody exposing himself.

Stone: That, I think, may be related to the inveteracy of your conviction, or to your own experience—with suppressed information? It has not been my experience. The patient may dream of the analyst exposing himself, if that is part of the patient's erotic inclination (in which case, a new tie—or a polysyllabic word—may be the day residue!) or because of the analyst's repressed exhibitionism, in countertransference, if what he says is meant to impress the patient. By the same token, to try the shoe on the other foot, the patient may dream of the analyst's exhibition in response to his "silent" reaction formations. As you know, I believe that much transference "clamor" is due to such exaggerations, whether due to indoctrination or reaction formation. The ironic truth is that—while I have, of course, appeared in erotic dreams, including bilateral disrobing—I do not recall any dreams involving exhibitionism as such.

Langs: Well, I'll try to present clinical data for us to review. But patients will dream. That's what I would expect—that they will see such a comment as a self-revelation.

The issue of separation also concerns me because I feel that it's very important to allow for a maximal analysis of the separation reaction, and anything that's given as a tie, I feel, could have a detrimental effect on that experience.

But I've been meaning to say, throughout our conversation, that I agree with aspects of your position, and I think that you have come to stand for some important ideas. When I talked about the concept of the analyst as a mirror, and my objections to it, everybody said, but Stone has already said that that's an absurd concept and he has made it clear why, and of course I agree. The question comes down to something more than the analyst's humanity. You see, I think that the better metaphor for this aspect of the analyst's functioning comes from Bion (1977), who wrote of the analyst as a container. I think it's a very useful metaphor. It gives depth to his experience and to his interaction with the patient. It has to do with what the analyst has to take in, and it has to do with what he imparts to the patient. It acknowledges the incorporative and metabolic functions of the analyst in terms of his silences, his words, how he communicates, and all the rest. The concept comes up now in this way: if we accept the analyst as a human participant, a container, or however we want to conceptualize it, is it then necessary for him explicitly to reveal information? Will that impair his containing functions or constitute a projective identification on his part?

Stone: See, that's the misunderstanding. I do not feel that the analyst must always be "revealing himself." On the contrary, I think I am generally known as a rather "private" person. Only the analyst ought not to be so fussy about it. One ought not be fussy to a degree where one is an unreal, shadowy figure, because, again, one has to realize that every coin has two sides. As for the analysand dreaming of you exhibiting yourself, I never had that happen in response to my saying "Vermont or Maine"—perhaps I reveal it for reasons other than to tell the patient what nice places to go to! I do not, incidentally, find the "container" view of the analyst very useful.

Langs: That's why I would like to see your material.

Stone: Well, I never saw any ill effects from that sort of thing. My doing that occasionally was the result of seeing the ill effects from the opposite: from seeing patients act as if they were like fish on a hook, or something of the sort, trying to know what kind of a creature this was to whom they were attached, who sat behind them and pontificated every now and then. (As to the "fish on the hook" image—I feel vaguely that I owe someone a credit—perhaps Karl Menninger.)

Langs: One of the convictions I am developing from these conversations is that—well, that we are finding certain areas where we're much more in agreement than our initial positions might have suggested. And it's like you said about Glover (1955), something involved here has to do with very basic analytic attitudes, and a very basic way of conveying an analytic commitment to the patient. What you're saying is that if one has that commitment, then these minor deviations, in terms of your observation, really tend to be rather superfluous. In my observations, the patient is consistently quite sensitive to them, and although the analyst can work through the consequences as long as he is sensitive to them, and can then analyze these minor transgressions, as I would term them, they are realities with some detrimental effects. I have, for example, learned in many ways of the extreme sensitivity of the ground rule of confidentiality. I believe in maintaining it completely, without exception.

Stone: This I believe to be absolutely inviolable, to a degree where I'm regarded as a bit of a freak.

Langs: Well, I too am seen in that way, and I have stated now in writing that I will never publicly refer to a patient of mine, to anybody under any circumstances, and I do adhere to that.

Stone: I won't talk to even another doctor, a doctor of a husband or wife, without it being an emergency that requires it and then with the patient's explicit knowledge and request. So you see, there are some things that I am more strict than the strict about. For example, I don't believe in reporting on candidates for the same reason.

Langs: Right, oh yes.

Stone: I believe that's involved not only with the principle of confidentiality but with the transference, and this is another of the typical, conventionally approved "blind spots" we'll say: that one can insist on the strictness of the analytic situation, but write reports on your patient to somebody. This to me is beyond the beyond.

Langs: That's interesting too, because in many ways you adopt a position very similar to mine, although you are more relaxed and have a less stringent position about exceptions in the extreme than I have.

Stone: Details, small things. I have never answered a question about my personal life or preferences of any intimate kind. People know about my family life only if they heard about it elsewhere, and so on. And in general, I'm a fairly private person. I have a social life, but not such an extensive one that everybody knows about it, and I keep my life quite separate from my practice. What I feel is that whether we call it a mirror or not isn't the important thing, but the straining to preserve an anonymity in an artificial way is important, when the fact is that it's inevitably being invaded and distorted by all kinds of accidents in the natural faultings of life. The doorman might say, "Oh yes, that's Mrs. Stone"; or "How do you do, Mrs. Stone," when the patient is walking in, or whatever. All kinds of similar things. I think I mentioned in passing before that many analysts have their homes and offices together—at one time it was quite prevalent in practice though it is a little bit less so now—but I think that at least half of the colleagues still do, and a kid runs out now and then, or a wife comes out and gets a kid, or a wife leaves the apartment with two children, or a dog, or whatever, so it is nonsense that this "anonymity" is invulnerable, and can be kept pure. The only question is whether there is a difference between gratuitously given information and information of accidental occurrence. Of course, there is a difference, but that doesn't settle all the issues. How important it is, I don't know, and how it will prove itself over time, but the fact is that I have a strong impression that—within the analytic situation—if the analyst is going to strain to be persistently silent about something unimportant, or something which simply is of no more importance than his selection of ties, or that he wears his hair longer than the average or shorter, well, then he might just as well be consistent, and do as indeed an elderly lady analyst did years ago, an American, who was trained abroad—she's been dead now for some time—she sat behind a screen behind the patient. Of course, one should remove all pictures or other ornamentation from the analytic office. I don't know what she could do with her voice. There was no way out of that. Maybe she tried to speak in a monotone, or had it filtered through something. But she did sit behind a screen behind the patient. Told me by two people who had been with her, so I assume it was true. But, you see, I think that is absurd, that's grotesque, and that has a grotesque impact on the patient. As for information—what *could* be more informative?

Langs: I would agree.

Stone: The patient might possibly think he's being treated by a grotesque person who is afraid to be looked at and must conceal her ordinary human form. Well, the question is where do you draw the line? I simply feel that these little bits of information, if in context, if they seem natural, and if they serve to expedite or at least not to impede the flow of associations, not only will do no harm, but might possibly prove, in some instances, to be helpful.

Langs: Another factor in this may be that you think of it in terms of the analyst being uncomfortable with this degree of anonymity; he's straining to maintain it. I think there are analysts—and that's where the middle ground is—who can be very comfortable with such a position.

Stone: There are those who can be very comfortable with it; and there are those who sadistically enjoy it. Certainly, there are also those who are comfortable with it, because they are certain it is the right thing. There are any number of permutations and combinations, positive and negative, which we don't have to describe. For example (in psychological impact): "I don't answer any question.

You want to know when I'm going on vacation? Sweat it out! Maybe when it becomes absolutely necessary I'll tell you. You have to formulate your plans, you're trying to think ahead about it, and so on? I don't answer questions." Sometimes, things of this sort are done, without even a simple explanation of the rationale. Who is a patient, that he has to know why this is done? Does a Yeshiva boy or a parochial school boy have to know why we postulate a God?

Langs: These are, of course, rather extreme examples. I think that part of the issue relates to what reflects the countertransference of the analyst and what does not.

Stone: There I would agree with you. You see, if an analyst has some need to exhibit himself to his patients, that, clearly, will appear in any communication. The truth is that that can even show in the long windedness or flowery language of his interpretations.

Langs: The practice of having the office in the home, with a wife walking around, children walking around, can have an impact. For an example, the patient can unconsciously perceive the analyst as someone who's afraid to be alone with his patients.

Stone: He can interpret it any number of ways, "good, bad, and indifferent." But, of course, it engendered material to be analyzed. As I said, years ago it was the majority practice. I had a setup like that about twenty years ago or thereabouts.

Langs: There could be a valid core to such a perception, it could be unresolvable. These are contaminations that could influence what the patient perceives. You see, one of the areas that I didn't fully develop with you, and that's where the clinical material will come in, is that the patient does make introjective identifications, takes in certain images of the analyst, based on these behaviors and their actual unconscious meanings. Now my experience in general has been that when the analyst modifies the frame, the patient takes in a negative, threatening, seductive, and dangerous . . .

Stone: I know, you seem to see it that way. But with some people it seems to have the opposite effect. In each instance, it would depend on the qualitative and quantitative factors involved.

Langs: I'll show you plenty of clinical material that points this way; if there's anything that you can show me that's the other way, I would like to see it. Beyond this point, which I think is a good point to stop, we have to look at clinical data.

Stone: Oh yes, I agree with you. We should look at clinical data. I would have to think, you know, of long-term analysis, where I have been the second or third or the fourth (or more!) analyst. Now I wouldn't say the contrast has always been with aloofness; in fact, the contrast has sometimes been with rather gross acting out, by analysts in whom you would least expect it. But the other has also occurred; it was one of the things, in conjunction with my own general experience with some borderline patients, the latter having led to the writing up of the "Widening Scope" (Stone, 1954), which gave impetus to my recent interest in the psychoanalytic situation and process. The "borderlines" and later the experience of doing secondary analyses led me to some of my recent ideas. Now if you look for specific instances I would have to think of specific vignettes, which do not risk any exposure of identity. Do you have something from your own analytic practice?

Langs: As I may have mentioned, I do not use material from my own patients in writing books or papers. I do use material presented to me in supervision because it has already been made "public" in a sense, and for necessary reasons. We very much need such material. Analysts in general don't document or analyze the associations and behaviors of the patient that follow a deviation. One of the most interesting examples is in a paper by a fellow named Calogeras (1967), on telling a patient that she could be silent—in other words that she did not have to obey the fundamental rule of free association. The patient felt that she was being controlled and she didn't want to talk, and she was regressing and not doing well, and he wrote a whole paper about the positive effects of this deviation, but she had a dream the night after he made his deviation and he never reported the dream. We are so seldom in a position to look at clinical material in this literature. My own findings are based on extensive studies of clinical data, and they lead me to believe, as a general principle, that when an analyst deviates there will always be some element of countertransference in addition to whatever urgent clinical indicators are present.

Stone: When you say a "deviation," that's the issue. As we agreed before about psychotherapy, which is still, relatively speaking, a no-man's-land despite efforts in the last few decades to try to straighten it out, the deviation is relative to a definition of what is correct. You don't deviate except from what you believe to be right and to be the correct way to do things. So you see, one doesn't deviate if one believes this is a natural and integral part of the process.

Langs: I recall that Anna Freud (1954a) included telling certain homosexuals that they would have to give up the homosexuality as an inherent part of the framework; this is not my position. I believe that there is—in terms of the patient's needs—but one basic set of ground rules for each modality, therapy and analysis. I don't see it as a matter of the analyst's beliefs.

Stone: In a related reference, I can remember hearing one of our older analysts speak—incidentally, a colleague who as far as I know never wrote anything (possibly something very early in her career), but she was regarded as a good teacher and respected as an excellent clinical analyst—she's been dead for some time. She had occasion to discuss something that came up before one of our committees long ago, I don't exactly remember in what context. The important thing was that she made it a condition that the woman give up her lover, if she wished to be analyzed. You see, this I don't understand. I'd feel that if it was a grossly pathological affair one goes on analyzing it to the best of one's ability; then, after a long effort, if you feel that the woman is simply living out a neurosis with this person and won't or can't do anything about it, then you might have to say, "Look, I'm sorry, but the analysis is stymied so long as you live with this man who beats you up every night and who disappears every second week for a week, and so forth, whatever the hell it was" (these last are fictitious, of course).

Langs: I don't believe countertransferences can be ruled out in such situation. You're talking about prolonged intractable analyses—stalemates where you pretty much checked out your countertransference.

Stone: Yes, and where you feel the person's resistances are being served and supported by the continuation of the mode of living or suffering. But this was stated as a condition for getting started. Now that kind of business I don't understand at all. Yet at one time it had a sort of vogue. Incidentally, the constant analysis of one's countertransferences I take for granted as an integral part of adequate analytic technique.

Langs: All I was trying to convey—because I don't make planned deviations except under emergency situations—is that when an inadvertent deviation occurs (and they are inevitable) I would see a certain cluster of effects, and that's what I would like to present next time to you.

Stone: And then you could resume those things that you picked out of my old paper.

Langs: Oh, I have them here; I was planning to get back to them.

Stone: Sorry, I wandered off too far.

Langs: I wanted to allow enough time for us to establish and discuss our respective positions, as a basis for our discussion of the clinical material, and I've been attempting to identify characteristic responses to deviations.

Stone: You mean the negative outcome of "deviations"?

Langs: The negative perceptions and introjections. You remember the vignette about the man who asked for his wife to be seen, and the dream about somebody arranging a foursome? Perhaps the last point that I'll make tonight is that I give a lot of credit to the patient for his capacity to perceive realities in the analyst, but also for his ability to distort! We always have to sort out the two: unconscious perception and unconscious fantasy. When a therapist agrees to see the wife, for whatever reason, under those circumstances he is accepting a ménage à trois in actuality, and may be saying something about, for example, his need for a defense against closeness with the patient. And if the patient has a dream in which he perceives someone arranging a foursome—well, there is a certain degree of truth in that dream, whatever distortions he then makes.

Stone: But again, I think you're blurring the transference with a real situation. It is just this that we hope to cure in the patient! One could say that a woman analyst who accepts a young male patient is thereby fulfilling his oedipal wishes. That, you would agree would be an absurdity. If an analyst agrees to see the wife of a patient for some good clinical reason, he's not arranging a ménage à trois. That the patient may find that in it, I have repeatedly observed—even including a patient who tried to get me to see his wife for no good reason. It was quite obvious. In that instance, to agree would have been gratuitous—and might have lent itself to the interpretation which you generalize too broadly. There have been instances where I have had to see the marital partner, or thought it the constructive, even "saving," thing to do. Your assumption that this must be a countertransference expression which the patient correctly perceives has no general basis.

Langs: Those are the indications we have to go over. I would agree, and so stated in 1974 (Langs, 1973, 1974) that so long as you have the reality you can then analyze the distortion, you can treat the distortion as distortion. What has happened to me over these months is that I have seen fewer and fewer appropriate indications for deviations of that kind. That's where I've become skeptical.

Stone: That is something worth discussing. I'm not so sure about that. You see, for example, as I've gotten older, I sometimes realize that you don't even know the validity of what the patient is telling you with clear certainty, however honest he may be. You see, this is the only human endeavor where your whole stock of information is dependent on the communications of one person. That, while self-evident, is only a recent practical preoccupation. Sometimes it may be important to have at least some other or further information. However, I have not seen people for that reason, although it is sometimes implicit in seeing a family member. I've seen people largely because of severe marital or symptomatic crises, or matters of that sort. So I think that the question of the genuineness of the indication, as I've tried to stress here, in relation to what the patient does with it, is the real issue. Look, the patient can come in, and you can say, "How do you do?" and the patient can then say, "You said that 'do' much more strongly than you usually do, and that means so and so!"

Langs: I have tried to stress the extent to which I use as my criterion the patient's indirect, derivative communications. If you can demonstrate that there was no countertransference contribution to the decision, that the realities truly and entirely call for a deviation, then you are in a position to treat the patient's direct and indirect reactions as distortion. If, on the other hand, there is a kernel of countertransference need as well, then a certain modicum of that reaction has a realistic core. Again, I acknowledge that there are realities that call for such measures; I'm not rigid or blind. I will say this though: empirically, so often, there is an important unconscious countertransference contribution that is overlooked. That is a hard reality that I see again and again.

Stone: The countertransference contribution is no doubt sometimes overlooked, and when it occurs it is no doubt a more subtle error, more difficult to discern than others, but to give the impression and to entertain the idea that all interventions in crises are dependent on countertransference, I think, make us a crazier bunch than we are. We have some crazy people, it's true, but they are not the majority. Besides, we have been worrying about our countertransferences now for more than a few decades. I am sure you would agree that a hidden countertransference can influence a series of the most staid and conservative-sounding interpretations, and thus bollix-up an analysis with remarkable thoroughness.

Langs: You said that in crises many deviational interventions are quite valid. But many, many modifications are made not in crises at all to begin with, and this is where I find so many countertransference difficulties. I find too that short of a suicidal or homicidal threat there are very few crises in which deviations do not have an important countertransference input.

Stone: Again, about minor things and thoroughly optional things, there I would agree that countertransference probably plays a decisive role very often, and that by and large this classic frame, I think, should be maintained. Now that is not to say that I believe the frame is perfect. You see what I mean. I feel that maybe the frame can possibly be improved on; the fact that something is "given" as the frame doesn't prove that it is to go on forever unaltered. But the reasonable maintenance of a frame, until we have a better one, I agree, is an essential constituent of the whole process. All the work operates within that general assumption. Of course, lest I get too "docile," I must remind you that I believe the frame must—or should—be altered ab initio with certain such patients, for as long as may be necessary. Naturally, except for valid reasons, a certain consistency should be maintained.

Langs: One of the observations I've made is the way the frame, and the analyst's management of it, determines the therapeutic qualities of the interaction and of the bipersonal field. When you begin to think of it that way, you begin to realize how important it is. I agree that if I had empirical data that indicated that one or another aspect of the frame impinged in a disruptive way on the patient, I would look to modify it. I have not gathered such data. I would welcome it. I think that would be very interesting to have. Empirical experience should still teach us.

Stone: Oh yes, I think there are still things that we can learn. I remember Anna Freud (1954a) mentioned—I think in that Philadelphia paper, though I can't pin down the reference—that there were some people who even objected to free association; she named a colleague. She also mentioned some people who objected to the regularity of everyday visiting. It's some years since I looked at the paper. Now, you see, I sometimes wonder even about free associations as the unvarying basis of patients' communications, but I have not yet wondered to the degree where I want to abandon the basic rule. I remember that Bob Knight told me about Helmuth Kaiser, whom I quote (or refer to) in that paper on "resistance" (Stone, 1973), who was indeed the ultimate "resistance analyst." Kaiser was at Stockbridge for a while with Bob. This is purely my memory of a personal communication, and it goes back about twenty years (or more), so it's subject to all the hazards of such information. He said that Kaiser had begun to tell his patients, instead of, "Tell me everything that comes into your mind," "Tell me whatever you'd like to tell me." And you know, every once in a while that comes back to me, and I think not that I want to switch to that, but what would that mean in the process? What kind of differences would that introduce? Because free association does have this obligatory aspect.

It does have an abandonment of control involved in it, and it is therefore closer to the hypnotic origins of psychoanalysis than ordinary communication. What would a patient do, how would he feel, how would he react in a situation, if all he knew was that he could say whatever he damn pleased, and what would emerge? That would be an interesting experiment. How would it impinge on the evolution of transference? How would it affect process resistances?

Langs: Calogeras's paper (1967) touches on that issue; that's what he did. I don't know if his data would give you enough of an answer.

Stone: You mean he told the patient what I said above?

Langs: He told her that she did not have to free associate, that she could be silent as much as she wanted.

Stone: Was that an analytic situation?

Langs: Yes, that's what he claims.

Stone: I didn't refer to the right to be silent. That's a different aspect of it. What was suggested is that the "rule" is to say whatever you want, tell him whatever you want to tell him, instead of whatever comes to mind.

Langs: In the Calogeras paper, silence was invoked as a parameter. You know, there were two other points that I wanted to add. Kanzer (1972) wrote a paper on the fundamental rule, and he did point out that there have been changes in the way that it's invoked.

Stone: Yes, the way it's proposed to the patient.

Langs: And the other is that Racker (1968) made a great deal of the fundamental rule because he saw it as essential to what he called the abolition of rejection, which promotes the modification of defenses.

Stone: Well, the affirmative purposes of it we know. Whether there's something else is less clear—but the question gently "haunts" me.

Langs: Let me ask you just to speculate a little, freely, in the terms of your thoughts. What do you feel the difference would be? What is it that you're looking for in this particular alteration?

Stone: That the patient does not sacrifice his autonomy; that he knows he's in a situation where he *can* say whatever he wants. How would the distribution of motivations and energies affect his productions (and his affective responses) under those conditions? That he doesn't *have* to say whatever comes into his mind, but he *can* say whatever comes to his mind, and that he can say particularly what he wants to say. This would be a further step away from hypnosis—relinquishing the last element of authoritarian pressure. Would it come to some earlier focusing of transference elements, bring them closer to consciousness? Would it facilitate, in that sense, the emergence of transference? Or would it, by obviating one of the built-in regressive elements, perhaps inhibit the development of transference neurosis? I don't know. I have a purely experimental view toward it, but a great curiosity. And I have thought that some time with a patient in psychotherapy I would like to try that, see if it makes a difference. I have heard Kaiser criticized as eccentric, but he was a very clever man and I don't remember that Knight ever told me how this turned out with his patients. He just told me this as one of Kaiser's eccentricities.

Langs: It's a good point, not to think of the ground rules as sacred.

Stone: No, nothing in science as such should be sacred. By all means respect a thing for its enormous value and what it has brought to us. But as to whether it is the ultimate answer to everything, one must always say, "I don't know."

Langs: Yes, it's a good note to end on.

Chapter 3
CONFRONTING DIFFERENCES THROUGH A CLINICAL VIGNETTE

Langs: In thinking about our first two meetings, I felt that we had discovered a crucial factor that I, for one, had not previously recognized: we both accept the importance of the frame, of the psychoanalytic setting and situation, but besides that there is the question of whether one is more sensitive to the deprivational or to the gratifying aspects of that frame. This factor colors one's approach to the patient within the same general framework. I must add, recently I found that there are still many analysts, and I think that you had said that you had had similar experiences, who disagree with the emphasis on the frame and its management as vehicles of unconscious communication, and who do not really accept the concept that the frame is important functionally and therapeutically and that it is crucial to what unfolds within the analytic relationship; there's still a considerable amount of resistance. I'm so embedded in this more broad conception of the frame that it's the only way that I can think; and it's confirmed in my clinical observations all the time. But there is still a lot of outside skepticism, criticism, and questioning about even an issue as basic as that.

Stone: There are those who don't regard the frame as having any special, dynamic importance in itself. I think most intelligent analysts whom I know would regard it as important. But the emphasis would be on it being a suitable frame for the cognitive processes and to avoid "contamination" of the affective processes. You know, the nonintervention, the abstinence from any emotional participation and so on, exists solely to permit the optimum emergence of spontaneous material. The recumbent posture and frequent visiting also exist solely to provide a basis for the emergence of "uncontaminated" material. That would be the greatest concession that some would make. I think I agree with you that there are very few who see it as an important participant in itself, a dynamic participant. But I think that most would acknowledge that it has some meaning, at least, when it is not maintained. Maybe that isn't what you were thinking.

Langs: No. I would agree. I would stress too the role of management of the frame in the analytic relationship and interaction. In fact, allow me to expand on this point because I want to ask for your reactions to it, and on that basis we can discuss the clinical material that I have culled out from your writings.

Stone: Okay.

Langs: My own thinking now—perhaps it's a little anthropomorphic—is that the frame and its handling demands respect and consideration whenever it comes up as an issue, as a source of tension. That is, there would be considerable difference in the attitude and technique of such an analyst as you describe, and my own approach, in that I've learned empirically that if an issue comes up in regard to the frame, it must be analyzed and resolved as a first-order problem; if there's been a break in any of its components, any alterations in the frame, this entails another step in basic analytic procedure—rectification. This introduces a concept, which is not especially surprising or novel, though it is rather neglected, and it points up again that there are, as Greenson (1972) put it, many things in analysis beyond interpretation. And the management and rectification of the frame, its correction in reality, are essential before one can effectively return to the analysis of inner contents, of derivatives of unconscious memories and fantasies. I would be very sensitive to any issue that comes up in that area. I would know, based on my experience, that I'm going to have to listen to the material from the patient with the alteration of the frame as my adaptive context. The patient will be reacting to it very powerfully, and his associations will indirectly pertain to it. In other words, there is an order of precedence, of procedure, if you will, not because I say so, but because the patient will continue to work in that area until it gets resolved. Analytic work in connection with frame issues belongs on a par with content interpretations.

Stone: Of course, one would have to have examples of that, insofar as you speak of "continuing to work in that area until it gets resolved." You refer to something that involves a deviation from the usual format or frame?

Langs: Right. Whether it's mutual or the patient imposes it, or even if the analyst or therapist imposes it, it becomes a prime therapeutic and adaptive context; that's one aspect. The second aspect is that these analysts underestimate the important therapeutic qualities of the frame itself. In this regard, Winnicott's (1958, 1965) concept of the analyst's hold is very crucial. Greenacre (1954, 1959) wrote similarly of the basic transference as a kind of maternal hold. This concept also influences one's technique in a second way in that I would be—and am—much more content to be silent and holding, and under less pressure to intervene verbally until the appropriate moment, than would these other analysts, because I feel and have observed that I'm doing something therapeutic by offering a steady frame.

Stone: You mean you're actively aware of that, or have perceived it affirmatively? I think that would be fairly generally accepted, even though all analysts may not think of it in interpretative terms, such as the "holding" and so on. Most analysts would realize, perhaps assert, that something therapeutic is in process just in the maintenance of what you call the "frame" (taking it for granted, of course, from my point of view, that the frame is not set up for a mechanical drawing).

Langs: Oh yes. We have phrases for it, such as the steadiness of the analyst, offering a consistent environment, and all, but recognizing specific therapeutic functions for the frame and hold still make a difference. You see, we develop an image of ourselves as analysts, including some concept of when we are functioning effectively with our patients. It seems to me that the prevailing image of optimal effectiveness involves making a correct interpretation or reconstruction. We set a high value on that.

Stone: You mean it resides in the skill and so on, of interpretation.

Langs: Right. But I would also say that there's a very special skill in knowing how and when to maintain the holding environment.

Stone: By that you mean the passivity, the silence of the analyst?

Langs: The passivity, the silence, the neutrality, the acceptance of the patient's material. It also includes—you know, both Winnicott (1965) and Masud Khan (1969) brought up the concept of not intervening—specifically not intervening at certain times because the hold is more vital to the therapeutic work.

Stone: That I agree with. The only thing that I would feel some caution about would be any implicit exclusion of the fact that an occasional patient, to get the benefits of the "holding" process, would require some greater awareness of the analyst's presence. Even an occasional trivial remark, or as Karl Menninger once said, just an occasional grunt of assent, or a grunt to make it known that you're there and listening, may be important. The very sick patients may at times require that. Otherwise, you see, it will mean that the process will move out into the realm of fantasy, and then possibly a startlingly deep regression. In general, with most neurotic patients, I would agree that the holding process is best implemented by the analyst's tolerant, quiet presence and acceptance of what's going on.

Langs: Nacht (1957, 1963), who is in France, emphasizes quality of *presence* with, let's say, nonneurotic patients. I would simply accept this as an area of debate and in need of empirical study. Winnicott (1958, 1965), in his own clinical explication of the "hold," did exactly what you're saying, in the extreme. The few reports that I have seen of his work show this quite clearly—much like those of Freud. There's a fascinating paper by Guntrip (1975) in the *International Review of Psycho-Analysis*.

Stone: The name is familiar, but I don't think I know the paper.

Langs: Guntrip has stressed object relationships and has studied schizoid phenomena. He was an analyst in England and he was in analysis with Fairbairn at one time, and then with Winnicott. And he wrote a paper, shortly before he died, called, "My Analysis with Fairbairn and Winnicott," in which he described some of his experiences with them—a very fascinating paper. I've developed a great interest in the people who have made our literature.

Stone: Your reading is more extensive than mine, in current or recent literature. I freely acknowledge that.

Langs: I came across it through a discussion in the journal that I edit (the *International Journal of Psychoanalytic Psychotherapy*), in a paper by Glatzer and Evans (1977). Winnicott was very loose with the boundaries, with the ground rules; he would have coffee with patients and he would chat with them. In one of his papers, in which he describes a case, he was working with a schizophrenic woman, and, with his active participation, they just talked about insignificant things for a long period of time, until he felt she was ready for analytic work.

Stone: Yes, schizophrenic in a sense of really psychotic, not as the term is used somewhat loosely now, latent schizophrenic, or potential, or ambulatory schizophrenia. It is an actively psychotic patient who is under discussion.

Langs: Yes, I assume that from the presentation.

Stone: I mention that because, in general, while I am one of those who believes that the "hold," or this salutary effect of the psychoanalytic situation in itself, must in some instances be extended into some activity, I do hold with the principle that the more that that activity can be minimized, the better. It may be just to make a remark now and then, to acknowledge something, to say a word that one might say in a more ordinary situation, to impart a feeling of interest. But as for having coffee with the patient, or going into other activities that bring the relationship closer to the activity patterns of everyday life, I would say that, in my experience, which of course includes some psychotics, but largely "ambulatory" psychotics, it usually isn't necessary, and carries with it hazards that are much greater than occasionally saying, "That's good," or "Yes," or something of that sort, a little remark of approbation or congratulation. But it is likely that others whose experiences have been with much sicker patients than those that I have treated in the last decade have found that such things are necessary.

In fact, I can recall that many years ago at the Menninger Clinic and Sanitarium, I played violin duets with a young man who had a subacute paranoid schizophrenia—sometimes in the hospital, sometimes in my home. It is my (fallible) recollection that he recovered from that attack. Certainly, he improved considerably. It was the one viable initial bridge between us. There is no doubt that with the clinically psychotic person the establishment of contact is the sine qua non of treatment. The persons who have distinguished themselves in this sphere (Simmel, Federn, Sullivan, Fromm-Reichmann and others in earlier days, and possibly Searles, Will, and others more recently) have all had the temperament and the technical elasticity that provided optimal possibilities of such contact. What followed thereafter might vary considerably in character and effectiveness. So, I do not mean to be "critical." I do mean that the principle of "minimization" does remain important. In persons susceptible to extramural office practice, it is my impression that most instances can be contained within the boundaries of professional format (minimizing later disappointment). True, some have treated very sick patients in their offices. Then the format might have to be stretched. I read somewhere in Winnicott of his very tolerant attitude toward a patient who must "widdle on the couch" (if I remember his phrase exactly!). Incidentally, in relation to the question of contact, have you read my review essay in the *Journal of the American Psychoanalytic Association* many years ago (Stone, 1955) of the books by Gertrude Schwing and John Rosen?

With regard to the matter of "presence"—where you mentioned a French analyst, Nacht—"presence" was in my recollection conceived of as an affirmative, rather than a passive, phenomenon. A further extension, in relation to "sick" patients, was the "reparative gift" (Nacht, 1958).

Langs: Yes; it is an important and unresolved issue: the extent to which modifications in the frame are helpful with psychotics and the extent which an unmodified hold proves best. Searles (1965) in his writings states a preference for maintaining the boundaries to whatever extent is feasible. And you and I with your last statement have come much closer to agreeing. The way in which I put it, which is virtually just saying what you have said in another way, is that I believe that the therapist, or analyst, will have to respond to certain impingements on the frame that the patient brings to the therapeutic situation. And at those moments he will, of necessity, respond in a way that stresses maintaining the boundaries and frame, but with sufficient flexibility to react adequately to the patient's imposed needs. In other words, one attempts to maintain the frame and the basic hold, which is what you are saying, within the limits that the patient permits.

Stone: Yes. Or within the limits that will permit the meeting of certain necessities of this particular patient, which may not be met by the more strictly, passively interpreted frame. The patient's masochism does not always know best.

Langs: Right. I don't think I got the point across as clearly as I wanted to. Modifications in the frame become a necessity almost exclusively when they are generated by the patient, for example, in an emergency. He may become suicidal, severely so. One must be careful nonetheless not to modify the frame unnecessarily because of one's own fears or pathological needs. The patient will test the frame, and I think that's very crucial; furthermore it raises another issue that a French colleague, Viderman, has written about (1974).

Stone: Those papers in general I'm familiar with, especially some of the earlier ones.

Langs: His earlier work was with Nacht. In his 1974 paper on the analytic space he developed a very nice metaphor for the analytic situation and a positive concept of the frame. He pointed out that the analyst brings to the treatment situation a particular frame that will foster the development of the transference neurosis or psychosis, and its analysis. The patient brings a different frame, one that is largely designed to maintain his neurosis, and he will test the situation, seek to impose his frame on the analyst, and test the analyst's frame. The analyst, ideally, attempts to meet the test is two ways—by maintaining the frame and by interpreting the unconscious meanings of the patient's efforts to alter it—and thus tries to create the most effective therapeutic frame and hold. With more disturbed patients, though, one may find that there is at times no choice but to respond in a more deviant way. That may also modify the therapeutic outcome, so one tries to limit the deviations—parameters in the narrow sense as defined by Eissler (1951)—to what one decides clinically are the absolute necessities.

Stone: Yes, I agree, but that's a matter of very careful judgment, and those judgments are always influenced in some degree by the analyst's temperament, or maybe certain specific countertransferences, which he is supposed to be analyzing all the time. That judgment may vary to some degree from person to person, we must acknowledge. You know, some people may find themselves more ready to concede things in a given instance. Others may sit tight. In either case, the individual may sometimes "get away with it," sometimes not. I mean this "frame" sometimes has to be stretched. It's only a couple of years ago that I went to see a patient in his home, practically confined to his bed, a man who was so depressed over a period of a few months that the only other alternative would have been to let him go and to let somebody else take care of him permanently (as opposed to a relief doctor during my vacation, both having access to me by telephone). The person is back in analysis, has been for a year or two more, and has made progress. The retrospective analysis of those events comes up now and then, and is necessary. Well, you used to do so and so, and whatever. It has to be explained, and its impingement on his personality processes has to be understood. I mean that now, the essentially classical "frame" has been restored.

Langs: Yes; a situation where the pathology of the patient created an emergency that you had then to respond to.

Stone: Absolutely had to. Or else, let the patient go. And probably that would mean, go to hell (or somewhat more realistically go to a hospital—a matter which was now and then considered).

Langs: I have found that not only will such an experience come up directly in the material from the patient, but I find, and I'm sure that you have too, that if one takes the deviation as the context for listening to the patient's associations, for many months there are indirect, derivative communications of the patient's valid perceptions of the experience, and his distortions of it, and the many, many ramifications of such an event continue to appear in the latent contents for a long time. Of course, this is related to Eissler's (1953) concept that, if the parameter is invoked, one must then attempt to analytically resolve it. As he said, this may not be entirely possible; there may be unmodified residuals, and one has not only to interpret the implications for the patient, one has also to rectify; the frame has to be restored.

Stone: That's one thing to which even early, in that 1954 paper, I tended to demur a bit, to Eissler's very strict criteria. There are some individuals in relation to whom you just cannot accomplish a *restitutio ad integram* of the frame. It can't be. They will require throughout certain "deviations" or "flexibilities" (the last is a term which has nowadays taken on a certain pejorative flavor—as if "rigidity" were a priori a virtue, and "flexibility" a vice!). One has to recognize that. One tries to analyze them the best way one can. There is a question there which borders on semantics. I demur to the the the idea that the continued maintenance of a "parameter" (in its strict sense) means that the process is "not analysis," if the essential goals, dynamic mechanisms, and interpersonal context are maintained, to whatever degree they may be successful. No process, in any case, is expected to be wholly successful, in all instances, certainly not analysis. Some little aspect of the process may have to remain atypical. After all, in surgery or anything else you may have to do some things that are not according to Hoyle, in order to make things come out well. Long ago, I mentioned somewhere that because a sharp scalpel is the surgeon's chief instrument, it does not mean that he must never do blunt dissection with the handle—or even squeeze or press with his fingers. But these matters, I think, are in a way an argument about our own intellectual processes. They have to do more with our own conceptualizations and our semantics, than with the question of the best way to analyze a given patient. I have mentioned elsewhere that Eissler's term, "parameters"—while I have some question about the original premises—has certainly been misused by formulation-hungry colleagues.

Langs: Yes, and you see so little of this discussed clearly in the literature. Seldom does an author present the clinical data and show that he has responded sensitively to the material from the patient in the context of a given modification of the frame. Many analysts will modify the frame and not even attend to the material from the patient in that context.

Stone: It's been done from early on. The frame has been more modified than observed, you see. We have mentioned some examples from the pioneering days. Some have been written into the classical literature, without the slightest self-awareness, as by Brunswick (1928) in her treatment of the paranoid young woman, or by Helene Deutsch (1942) with one of her "as if" patients. Again, I do not say this critically. I believe that there has been an improvement in our awareness of these matters, their meanings, their possible unconscious consequences. But we have also lost something in the path to "rigidification," to the worship of some kind of presumed absolute, whose very underpinnings may still be open to legitimate criticism and study.

Langs: No question about that. Do you have any thoughts that you wanted to mention, about our first two discussions?

Stone: Well, I would have to read them. I found the whole exchange very interesting, myself. Because I found myself sort of free associating at times. Right now I would rather go along with what you have for further discussion.

Langs: I thought that it would be very helpful if we got into clinical material. I think that with clinical data we can really elaborate on some of the important things we want to discuss, and we can get closer to discussing them in terms of clinical evidence. And so I thought I would approach it in this way: I found in your own papers three references to modifications in the frame. And first of all, I want to state that in some ways it's completely unfair of me to do this to you . . .

Stone: Not at all. I can take it.

Langs: . . . because you were not presenting this material in a fashion that was designed to discuss the particular issues that we are developing here.

Stone: No, that's true, but what happened clinically may still be subject to useful discussion at this time, even in long retrospect.

Langs: Well, yes; it helps to bring out some of the points we already spoke of, and I thought it would be helpful to do this from some of your own vignettes even if, as I say, they were not designed to discuss the frame.

Stone: Yet they certainly occurred "in a frame," so it can be so scrutinized. As I said, I can stand it.

Langs: The first example comes from your paper "Transference Sleep In a Neurosis with Duodinal Ulcer," published in 1947, some thirty years ago. It's a marvelous clinical paper. I must say that I really enjoyed reading it as a case presentation—the skill and the detail. It was a unique paper, because analysts seldom offered such specific clinical material. When something did come up related to the frame, you offered some interesting material that we can discuss. But if you look at analytic papers even today, you seldom have the specific clinical material to discuss; you cannot evaluate the presentation. So, in this paper you get to a section on transference sleep, and I will pick up there, and read some of it to you, to orient you—I know how it is with a paper written a long time ago.

Stone: I remember one thing you brought up, about the giving of an extra hour.

Langs: Let me read you the section and then we can discuss it. There is a second modification as well; there are two incidents. Let's start with the first one.
   You say here (p. 26): "A little more than a year after the beginning of the analysis, the patient began to express the conviction that a major purpose of the analysis was that the patient become able to

analyze himself in the future, implying that the need for such treatment would never terminate. With this belief came a later manifestly avowed rivalry with the analyst, the deep sense of failure, the persistent sense of need, and the hostile oral urge for identification, in short, the factors which rendered the patient at times unable to accept the analyst's help at all. Toward the end of the first period of analysis, as the 'sleeping' phenomena became rare, one might think of the patient as in a period of attempted transition from the rejected but persistent passive wishes implicit in it, with preponderant father transference, to an oral clinging to the analyst as a mother, his wife the threatening father, with tentative genital wishes and castration fear. Sibling rivalry, often expressed in earlier dreams (especially the birth or 'entry' of his sister) came conspicuously into the foreground, with material in relation to other patients."

That gives you some background. To continue: "The following dream occurred in a period of restlessness and depression following a brief spring vacation taken after considerable conflict. The patient had also been ruminating with some resentment on pressing and imminent expenses for his daughters."

Stone: Excuse me. He took the spring vacation, or I?

Langs: No, it seems to imply that he did. I was going to comment on that later. At any event, it was an interruption.

Stone: Oh yes. It doesn't make any difference who interrupted, usually.

Langs: Perhaps not on one level, in terms of certain dynamics. But on another level, it was he who modified the frame, and that can make a considerable difference. "To the patient's amazement, he had not had 'stomach trouble' during either the vacation or the transitory depression following it."

Stone: It was obviously his vacation. I have not looked at the material for years.

Langs: Yes, this is interesting in light of what's going on. It shows how the unconscious communication can change; the same association in each different context takes on quite different meanings and dynamics. That's why I prefer having specific clinical material, and I know that you do too.

Stone: I love it. But the damn trouble is that in your later years your patient population is such that it becomes increasingly difficult to give specific material.

Langs: That's why I use supervisory experiences exclusively, to get around that problem, and to get around other issues and complications related to using one's own material and maintaining confidentiality, so I can truly maintain total confidentiality in my own clinical work.

To go on now: "One night when the patient could not sleep, he rose and took one capsule from an old phial of sedatives to which he had not resorted for a long time. On returning to bed, he dreamed that he was looking at the bottle from which he had just taken the sedative. There was one capsule in it, which seemed slightly chewed. To his dismay, the chewed appearance was due to two small worms in the bottle, which had heads like little rag dolls. He immediately became concerned lest he had done himself harm by ingesting something contaminated by worms. The patient, on the basis of past interpretations, but with considerable conviction, related the insomnia, the actual taking of a sedative, and the dream sedative to a breast fantasy. The worms he associated with biting into an apple and the two dolls' heads he associated with the rag dolls his sister kept on her bed as a youngster. The analyst's suggestion that his fear of disastrous consequences from the dream sedatives was connected to his hostility to the prototypes of worms (his sister, his own children) and toward the breast which fed them, he accepted for consideration. This dream was brought on an extra Saturday visit, which the analyst had proposed in place of granting the patient's urgent wish for a prescription for a sedative" (Stone, 1947, p. 26).

Stone: It's interesting to hear a paper some thirty years later. But I must interpolate that supervised material is not the equivalent of one's own analytic work. Not by a long shot!

Langs: The prevailing analytic technique at the time—and perhaps today—is reflected here. I refer to the use of genetic interpretations in isolation, as compared to my own approach: interpreting all aspects of the material in terms of the unconscious implications of the analyst's immediate interventions—spinning out all dynamics and genetics from the here and now. To read on: "The problem of the patient's paradoxical 'sleeping' symptom was further illuminated by a dream in the period of its subsidence. The patient is trying to have intercourse with his daughter Beatrice. His penis is at her vagina, but does not enter; instead it pushes her up bodily toward the ceiling ('Like a little girl on his knee'). He awakens with an erection and a 'slight' ejaculation, which he had been resisting. The patient had been missing his daughter who was away at camp. He remarked on her great charm and attractiveness, his wish to be loved by her as she loved her mother. He recalls jiggling her as a baby on his foot. He remarks on his frequent rigidity and irritability toward this daughter, because she reminds him so much of *himself* when he was young, especially in her charm, attractiveness, and defiant sloppiness.

"In connection with the coital attempt, he mentioned only that he would not wish to *hurt* his daughter. In connection with non-penetration and restraint of ejaculation, he recalled early difficulty in coital penetration and his earlier efforts to diminish the ill effects of his masturbatory addiction."

Stone: Yes, that characterized his early masturbation. I have had a few patients like that. They stopped the ejaculation because "it does less harm." At least that's the frequent rationalization for it. By the way, my own work has for many years centered technically on the transference—this was indeed this paper's central theme. However, I do this without the special emphasis you have repeatedly indicated.

Langs: "He made no spontaneous mention of but accepted with interest the analyst's remark that the same daughter had been equipped with a penis in a previous dream and sexually active in relation to him (as though he were mother, and the daughter was he), that he had been aware of his strong passive rivalry with his own sister for his father's love, and that the difficulty in penetration paralleled closely the position in which he placed the doctor, in connection with his rejection of interpretations by falling asleep. The latter, the patient thought was especially appropriate."

Of late, I have stressed the distinction between direct confirmation and indirect—derivative—validation. I consider only the latter truly psychoanalytic.

"In this manifest dream of incest, obviously multiply determined, the patient turned toward his child as he would have wished his father or mother (with a penis) to turn to him. The frustration is a defense against injury (anatomic or punitive) for both participants, but this seems clearest in this dream on the feminine receptive side. The sexual frustration desired for the parents is also achieved by identification" (Stone, 1947, pp. 26-27).

That gives you a kind of overview of this segment of the material. Now, to select an entirely different focus than the one that you had on your mind when you wrote the paper, let me present what I feel is of interest in light of our discussion. Perhaps we can start there and you can respond.

This sequence begins with the patient invoking a modification in the frame—he had taken a vacation. Now there are, of course, analysts who define the frame differently than I do, largely, I think, because they have failed to put the matter to empirical test. If they had, there would be a far greater consensus. But there are those who maintain that the patient is responsible for all sessions, except when the analyst goes on vacation. And the of course is related, in part, to Greenacre's (1954) concept of the tilted relationship. It's a reminder of the fact that the analyst does indeed establish a frame, that he has an enormous responsibility to do so with discretion, sensibility, and fairness to the patient; and that he has an obligation to maintain the best psychoanalytically validated frame. This is not a matter of "common sense" so-called, but leads into the whole issue of the nature and functions of the frame, and the importance of maintaining it. Eissler, in the paper on fees that I mentioned (1974), stated that if the analyst holds the patient responsible for all sessions, regardless of the reason for an absence, he is operating under what he calls the rule of indenture, which I think is intended as a pejorative term.

Stone: Do you infer that he intended it as pejorative? It is certainly frequent.

Langs: I felt that the word *indenture* implied that it was inappropriate.

Stone: Yes, because an indentured servant was someone who had to serve out his time. Yet what is cited was Freud's rule, established quite early. That doesn't make it sacred or necessarily correct in every instance. It may have been altogether proper and appropriate in those days and under the conditions in which he practiced. Yet Freud (1913) also specified that the patient could relinquish his hours permanently whenever he wished—an important condition.

Langs: I think we would agree, though, that most analysts would not deny the existence of any such ground rule—would simply say that the patient could take a vacation whenever he or she pleased.

Stone: That's at the other extreme; few analysts would go along with that.

Langs: Yes, and I think that the middle of the road is to establish a ground rule related to the patient's responsibility for the session, and then to evaluate a particular request of the patient to go on vacation.

Stone: That I would agree with.

Langs: There are those analysts who would not charge for a vacation where the evaluation had indicated that to the best of their opinion an essential piece of acting out was involved—that there was some realistic need. As you have gathered, I do not find that position validated by derivative clinical material.

Stone: There is an anterior, even more important question: Is the vacation really needed, or very desirable? And how does that balance against its impact on the analysis at this particular juncture? (I omit the question of gross and obvious acting out.) You see, in the patient's mind, it often does revolve largely around the fee. I think that sometimes, and that I believe is one of the problems, too much of the view of analysis revolves around the question of the fee. And there, you know, one might lay oneself open to the charge of being a do-gooder, or "too nice," For example, one hears of analysts, young, middle, or whatever, who, every time the patient gets a ten-dollar increase in salary, feel that there must be a corresponding increase in fee. It's like the income tax. And this is thought to be the only correct view of things, that fees go on a certain slide-rule or ledger basis. This I object to in general principle.

I think that if a person has a substantial increase in income, and has been paying a low fee, of course an increase is indicated. The patient will feel guilty and it's unjust to the analyst if there isn't some rectification. But that everything should revolve around that issue, and it should be watched with a certain hawk-like precision, I feel, introduces something into the analysis that isn't quite right. Equity, of course, should be observed and becomes an integral part of the analysis. Just dealing between the two people is essential, but a numerical literalness, and its intrusive "monitoring," should not be one of the central preoccupations in analysis.

Now, for example, a patient might want to take a vacation. The patient is not a poor person, not a person who is living marginally and just barely being able to be analyzed. One then judges whether this is a bit of acting out, whether he wants to take this vacation essentially to get away from the analysis at an important time, or whether he is a man with a family who has been working very hard; his children can be out of school at this time, his wife very much wants and needs a vacation, and he's very tired and this is a convenient time for them; they may not get another chance for a long time. Why not? You see, there is a reasonable purpose; and there's no particular conflict with the analysis.

How the question of fee would be handled then becomes another matter. To the patient, very often, it is the confronting thing. "Will you charge me?" That, too, I think can be handled with a reasonable degree of flexibility. I believe that a ground rule is important in this practical reality of the relationship. For example, I do believe that it's good for a patient to understand at the very outset, or close to it, whenever it's propitious for the issue to arise, that he is responsible for his hours in the sense that Freud originally discussed it. I forget what the term was. As if he had rented this time, or leased it, and that he would be responsible for it, unless he relinquished his hours.

Now of course there are obviously other things that enter. I don't know how often Freud had consultations. Maybe not too often at the beginning. It would be very serious to him to lose too many hours, which he could not gainfully use because he had committed that time to the patient. But many of us get consultations. Or somebody, for some reason, wants to use the hours. It is always understood, at least by my patients, that any time that I use for professional purposes of course will not be charged to them. But hours that I can't fill, they are responsible for. I think that is fair and reasonable, whether for vacation or other reasons. But even there, I would say there is a little residue of option out on the periphery, where I think one's judgment is important.

For example, I was told once of an analyst who charged his patient for the hours she missed in going to have a baby. Maybe that's all right if you follow a strict, "across-the-board" rule. I would not, temperamentally or otherwise, be able to charge a person for hours lost on that basis. Right or wrong, I would feel it would skew the human relationship adversely; thus, I could not feel comfortable with it. And I think there are other variations. There are some people who are too sick or too infantile in character and personality to be able to accept this ground rule wholeheartedly. Under certain circumstances, such patients say, "Well I was sick; it wasn't my fault." Or "Traffic broke down." In the case of catastrophic weather, I think that with patients like that, in order to preserve the therapeutic relationship, one might vary one's rule. I do think, however, that if the person can accept it, it's better that the general, across-the-board arrangement is maintained, because it is an equitable thing; it is just that the analyst should not have to pay for the patient's trouble in getting to you or for his illness. But as for paying for the hours that you do not otherwise use, that's a matter of honor, you see. Obviously, they don't know whether you use it or not. Perhaps it's too much to remember, but in the appendix of my book on *The Psychoanalytic Situation* this question came up in a discussion by some younger graduates. One man said, he didn't think that it was right to omit the fee when the hour was used because that was letting the patient know something about your practice. That's what I regard as carrying things too far. That's a *reductio ad absurdum*. I think the question of justice and equity is much more important.

Langs: You're stating a position, and a very sensitive position, one that I think is representative of the thinking of many analysts. Let me contrast it a bit with my own conception and practice, because as you know, you kept saying to me, when are we going to get to the issues? Well, we're here, and let me briefly establish them, and then I'll get back to this piece of clinical material to illustrate my points, to try to validate them. The position that you stated is similar to what I was taught, and I accepted it as a student. It's one I experienced personally in my own analysis and on the surface it made a great deal of sense. But there's another principle to consider, one that you would readily include. It happens you didn't mention it, but it was implicit in your discussion, namely, that we are trying to do what is best for the patient and for his analysis, to create the optimal conditions for his analytic experience and work.

Stone: Right. It's more than implicit: the whole discussion has to do with what is best for the analysis, and thus for the patient. It's just that I don't believe that what is inequitable or unkind or insensitive is compatible with good analysis, regardless of considerations of format.

Langs: I think that's first and foremost in deciding how one structures the frame, and it depends on two things that have previously been mentioned: an appreciation of the functions of the frame and a psychoanalytic validating process to confirm the positive value of a given element in that frame. The framework creates what I call a "therapeutic bipersonal field," in which there is open and free communication, where the transference derivatives, the expressions of the patient's pathology, can safely be contained. And the analyst's sound management of the frame generates positive introjects, while mismanagements create negative introjects. But in addition to manifest fairness and sensibility, there is that accent which is very crucial and not generally accepted, that we have mentioned before: there are indirect associations; every association from the patient contains some communication related to the analyst's recent interventions.

Stone: Oh sure, that was Freud's own relatively early observation (1925). Also that one's listening would have to do with a "deviation" I would regard as practically axiomatic. But this only highlights the more general issue. What is far more readily forgotten is that the patient is constantly reacting to the so-called "frame" in its conceptually maintained integrity.

Langs: So, analysts would in general agree, though more in principle than in consistent practice, that we sort out the primarily valid from the primarily distorted material in these observations about the analyst. The accepted approach in the literature was to call the patient's relationship to the analyst "transference," meaning that they thought of it as essentially distorted, until Greenson (1972) got around to saying, "You know, there are things going on that are beyond transference." In addition, the stress has been on manifest rather than latent responses.

Stone: Yes, but I (Stone, 1954) preceded Greenson, in the sense of emphasizing the "real relationship."

Langs: Yes. There were a number of antecedent contributions. I simply meant that he was the one to develop this point in a specific paper.

Stone: True, Greenson then developed the whole sphere into a more elaborate principle.

Langs: I know that in your description of the analytic relationship (1961) you specifically defined three sectors, one of which was veridical. I think also that you there referred to the early work of Menaker (1942) and Macalpine (1950).

Stone: In the old paper (1954, p. 588) I used the term "real relationship"; Greenson referred to it. In 1961, I referred to both, in different references—not explicitly to the veridical sphere which you mention. I don't mean that I'm interested in priorities, only to indicate my early interest in this sphere, and to clarify the facts. Probably Greenson took off from Anna Freud's discussion (1954b) of that aspect of my paper.

Langs: At that time, most analysts would still have called the whole relationship the "transference," though they were aware of certain realities.

Stone: Yes, Anna Freud referred to that in discussing the paper. I mentioned that subject again recently in a long paper, "Problems and Potentialities" (1975). There's a footnote about Anna Freud's discussion: she said that very often analysts overlook the "real relationship" and ascribe everything, especially when the patient is hostile, to transference. But then she said, "I must be careful lest I am uttering subversive thoughts"—or words to that effect. I commented that this attitude toward "heresy" testified to the intellectual climate of the times, that a person of Anna Freud's distinction felt impelled to be "careful," even if possibly in jest. Actually, I didn't define the term, I just used it, as if its existence and meaning were self-evident.

Langs: As I recall, it was inherent to your comments; you didn't isolate it as a factor for study. You used the concept, did you not, as very basic to your thinking about the analytic work with these more disturbed patients?

Stone: Yes, yes. As I recall it now—offhand—the question arose in relation to what older analysts used to think of as cultivating or developing or maintaining a "positive transference"—especially in relation to more severely ill patients. This isn't important in itself. I interrupted you just to straighten out some facts. Recently I noticed that the use of the term "therapeutic alliance," is being repeatedly referred to as if the first time it was ever mentioned was in 1956. Now I know that Dr. Zetzel (1956) defined it and elaborated the concept. I just used it in the course of a sentence in 1954, again, as if it were taken for granted. But what you were getting at was something important about your view of this sort of phenomenon, the patient's vacation.

Langs: I was saying, and this I developed in my new book, *The Therapeutic Interaction* (Langs, 1976b), that the concept of the real relationship is used in several different ways. It's a concept that I don't entirely subscribe to, in that I prefer to think of the total relationship, and then we can isolate the realistic or nontransference components.

Stone: That's a legitimate reservation in the semantic sphere.

Langs: So, the main point that I wish to make is that once a deviation has been invoked, by patient, by analyst, or whatever, I take all of the material from the patient as a commentary on that deviation.

Stone: You're including in "deviation" the patient taking a vacation?

Langs: Yes, we're going to get into that specific one in a moment. And taking all of the material as commentary—something that I learned to do through my own experiences with the frame once I became sensitized to it—in essence, I attempted to sort out the valid comments on what we have just done in altering the frame, or on a proposal of that kind, from those that are essentially distortions and fantasies, though obviously they blend. And one has a rather difficult job in sorting these out. It requires a great deal of self-knowledge, and extensive use of what I have called the "validating process" (Langs, 1976b). The stress throughout is on *derivative* expression— indirectly expressed perceptions and fantasies.

Stone: Oh, it's not always easy, no disagreement about that.

Langs: Now, using this as my model, the conclusions which I have come to—and again, I know they sound extreme, but I have not seen exceptions to them—are that the therapeutic situation, the analytic work, the bipersonal field, the patient, and the therapeutic qualities within its province are not served by this kind of flexibility. Even when it is done in the name of humanity or in the name of so-called sensibility, the patient unconsciously does not perceive it as a positive act, he detects countertransference-based needs and defenses, and these are, in part, valid perceptions.

Stone: Which kind of flexibility? I don't know which you're talking about—the question of fees, or taking a vacation? As for what the patient "perceives": he sometimes perceives a loving woman as a devouring monster.

Langs: With the fees and with taking a vacation both.

Stone: You mean that, if there is an understanding, originally to the effect that the patient never takes a vacation, except when you are away. You see, it all depends on how you set up the "frame." To repeat: the patient goes away only when the analyst does, there should be no deviation from that

Langs: Well, this brings up the issue of whether there is, indeed, one valid set of grounds rules. It seems to me there is, although I would want to reserve the final judgment for now. Empirically, I am saying that when this is the arrangement, even though the justifications are quite human and seem on the surface to be quite sensible, there is always an element of acting out involved for both patient and analyst, there's always an element of disrupting the analysis, of rationalized flight, and more broadly, of transference gratification, and it will consistently disturb the therapeutic qualities of the bipersonal field and produce negative unconscious introjects.

Stone: If there has been such a field set up, assuming that the patient wasn't "acting out" a masochistic propensity in accepting such an arrangement at the outset. But suppose you never mentioned anything about whether vacations could occur?

Langs: If you do not establish such a ground rule, I think you do not establish the best therapeutic field and hold for the patient.

Stone: Well, that I would think would be "open to discussion," to understate my view.

Langs: Oh, right. I'm stating it in such a forthright manner because I want to show you the evidence I garner for that position from this clinical material.

Stone: I would be interested to hear it.

Langs: Because this material fits in with what I would predict. And, I also want to establish a definitive position for our dialogue.

Stone: Well, as you saw, the contrasting position depended on the original position, that it would have to have been a part of the ground rules that there are no vacations unless the analyst takes one. This, of course, is a special thing in itself, because it assumes that only the analyst really deserves a vacation as such, when he needs it. (This is separate from the question of equity in fees.) The other person is in effect a "function" of the analyst; for that reason this approach would not recommend itself to me a priori. This is a deviation from the principle of adult human rights—a consideration which must also impinge on the analysis. But let's say, for the sake of argument, that the ground rules are laid down. And if there is any deviation, you feel it's going to have an impact on the analytic process which will then have to be dealt with, regardless of justice, humane aspects, or anything else. No doubt that would be so.

Langs: Yes, you see, I can comfortably maintain this position with humanity and concern, and analyze the patient's responses because of my utter clinical conviction—and finding—that this is best for the patient. Without that, and confirmation from the patient, I could never do so.

Stone: I know that; I understand that. (A belief is a belief!) But you see, it implies that analyzing it, if there has been a deviation from the "ground rules," might not be just as effective, and in some instances more effective, than "prohibiting" or "penalizing" the deviation. Not that one really can control an adult's behavior. But an atmosphere of that sort can be established in the sphere of transference, which could be highly destructive. Especially if the person really needed the vacation desperately for very good reason. All right, then it will create some change in the material, and certain subtle impingements on the transference, but my belief would be that those can be analyzed. I mean the entire occasion has not been a matter of gross acting out that has been overlooked by the analyst. That's an entirely different thing. If the analyst overlooks acting out, he can't analyze it, in the patient or himself.

Langs: But then we come back to realities in the analytic situation: that there are certain realistic consequences to these interventions, and certain very real unconscious communications contained in them. Many analysts overlook such actualities. And as a result of them, the patient's reactions are not simply confined to fantasy, which is the erroneous view of many analysts. Actually, unconsciously, the patient is quite perceptive in this regard, and there are realistic consequences as well: the patient would gratify certain pathological unconscious fantasies and needs and would experience in reality the reinforcement of certain pathological defenses. You know, analysts have tended to back away from a full investigation of their errors in technique. The little work that has been done relates to errors in interpreting, and it is seldom recognized that mismanagement of the frame is another important sphere filled with potential for error. This brings up another point: under these conditions, when the analyst makes an error, he is experienced in certain ways that are in keeping with the patient's pathological, unconscious fantasies and introjects, and this thereby reinforces his neurotic adaptation. In other words, there are certain reality impingements that follow managements of the frame that then reinforce and gratify the neurotic components.

Stone: If they are overlooked analytically.

Langs: Well, you see, now the question comes up: if this realistic reinforcement occurs, can that be modified with words? That is, one can analyze and identify it, but the actual satisfaction has occurred. What then are the overlooked limitations of interpretive work?

Stone: I would say more easily modified "by words," as you say, if the patient has damn well really deeply needed a vacation, than if the analyst, by virtue of the authority vested in him by the transference, denies him that. Now, of course, it is true that the analysand lives as a free agent; he can get up and take a vacation if he wants to, and as a matter of fact, he is entitled to make that decision; that goes without saying. But if he goes away feeling that the analyst disapproves of it, that's also an impingement on the frame, as I mentioned before, possibly a very serious one.

Langs: Yes, oh yes. That's another way in which my viewpoint has been distorted. I never express approval or disapproval. I think that's a deviation in neutrality, to ever explicitly or implicitly tell a patient what to do.

Stone: Or what not to do.

Langs: Exactly. My position would be to analyze the unconscious meanings of the proposed vacation.

Stone: That goes without saying. But we are omitting again the contingency that the need for a vacation may be wholly or in large part determined by realities. Even when the vacations coincide, the truth is that to the patient it may still mean "the analyst is taking a vacation, so I'm taking a vacation too. But I'm taking it at his time!" And this assumes a different meaning, from the other kind of vacation.

Langs: Yes, it has all kinds of ramifications.

Stone: See, those are the neglected realities. The realities that are implicit in "good practice." There are certain things that nobody disagrees about, for example, that a patient should pay his fees, and if he goes along two or three months without paying—and without discussing it—it would be indeed strange if the analyst didn't say something about it. And that at a certain point, the saying something about it must go beyond just analyzing it. There must be some confrontation with the ordinary realities, perhaps the equities of the situation. Certainly that's going to impinge on the transference situation. But I think there would be more harm done if it were allowed to go on its own momentum for six or eight months. That sort of thing happened to me in my very early career, without anything being done, when I was a little too timid about handling certain things. Once or twice that happened, with a certain type of patient. You know—a mixture of complicated rationalizations; maybe some degree of actual financial stringency, but, more strikingly, a great deal of manipulation of the situation involved. Well, anyway, that gets back into times when I did or didn't do things, in a sense, because I just didn't know any better. Or rather, I did know better; but I was unable to handle the situation effectively, for an extended period. In two instances the patient's severe oral disturbances were importantly involved.

Langs: Yes, and you had found that the consequences are . . .

Stone: Of course, detrimental. Although, even then, not permanently irremediable—except in one instance where I really think it was due more largely to the patient's malignant oral pathology.

Langs: There's one other principle I would state before getting to the specifics. It relates to the question of the optimal ground rules, an important issue. One of the studies that I made—and it's led to a lot of controversy at this point—well, I did something that I thought was rather scientific. You know, I claim to be a scientist, and there's a certain innocence about being a scientist that can get one into difficulty.

Stone: That is true. I don't know about the difficulty, but there must be a certain innocence to be a genuine scientist.

Langs: I said, let's take today's ground rules as I have defined them (Langs, 1973, 1974, 1975b)—I'd been working in this area for three or four years, and as I said, I do feel that there is an optimal set of ground rules—and see if there is any way of confirming their validity. It occurred to me that we had Freud's case histories, which would be interesting to study in this respect. There they are, years ago, and these were not exactly his ground rules, and they were especially not how he explicated them. As you know Freud (1912b, 1913) wrote a set of papers on analytic technique and the ground rules, and when you read his case histories, you find that he did things which contradict his own principles.

Stone: Practically all of his published analyses.

Langs: So, as I mentioned before, I took the present ground rules as a template, as a scientific measure, however roughly drawn it would have to be; I know they weren't his tenets exactly, although they were to some extent, and, of course, he was experimenting. I grant you all of that. I proposed that we develop such a template and every time he stepped outside of that template, we should examine the material from the patient, wherever it is available. It seemed like a perfectly legitimate exercise, and many have accepted it very readily. Others keep saying that they weren't Freud's ground rules—but I'm not saying that they were.

What was fascinating to me is that when I found a deviation from my template, the material from his patients, in virtually every instance, was identical to the material we're about to study with your own patients, and to the material I've consistently observed with my patients and in supervision. That is, his patients unconsciously perceived implications of deviations, responded to them, communicated about them, and made unconscious efforts to help the analyst to correct the frame, along the lines I've discussed with you, and that I hope also to demonstrate from this material. But the most interesting part of Freud's material was his notes on the Rat Man. There we learn that not only did Freud, as was well known, feed his patient, but there was a prior deviation: there was a postcard from Freud to the Rat Man that preceded the feeding; most people have overlooked this. And the material from the Rat Man—both Beigler (1975) in Chicago and I (Langs, 1978a) have written about this—is identical to the kinds of material that we see from our patients today. I hope to demonstrate it from your papers too.

So, for me, all of this says something about the concept of a basic set of ground rules.

There was a fellow named Bleger (1967), who wrote a paper—I've mentioned it before—on the psychoanalysis of the psychoanalytic frame; he extended Winnicott's (1958, 1965) thinking, and considered the frame to be in some way analogous—and this is Greenacre's (1959) concept too—to the positive symbiotic tie between mother and child out of which growth occurs, out of which the ego develops.

Stone: In relation to which, I have an almost opposite view.

Langs: Right. You emphasize the other side.

Stone: I emphasize the experience of separation, latently implicit in the analytic situation.

Langs: But you still, when you talk about separation, talk about how it has growth potential.

Stone: I'm not speaking of the potential, but the view of the frame as it is. That we hope this will stimulate and give a "second chance" to developmental processes that didn't originally come off satisfactorily is certainly true. I refer, of course, to the unconscious meaning to the patient. It starts with the basic deprivation. But I don't want to intrude my ideas.

Langs: Well, we'll get back to that. I had never realized that there are two contrasting positions until we had talked. I (Langs, 1975b, 1976a,b) had followed the line of Winnicott (1958, 1965), Greenacre

(1954, 1959), and Bleger (1967), thinking of the frame as creating a fundamental matrix, out of which growth can occur, you see—that quality of securing, holding, of the frame's function as securing the medium for maturation through analysis and identification.

Stone: Oh yes, when the patient can grow up to the meaning of the frame as it is, then he is, to say it too aphoristically, he's analyzed.

Langs: Now, what I've realized, too, after we had last spoken, that I had emphasized, for whatever reasons—and I'm still exploring them—the holding qualities, and while I acknowledged the deprivational qualities of the frame, and even stated them in some detail, they were somewhat peripheral to my thinking.

My personal investigations of the frame produced, for me, a series of exciting discoveries and realizations. The last thing that I uncovered was a surprise to me, though it probably would not have surprised you at all, coming from a more explicit acknowledgment of the deprivational qualities of the hold. Let me review the sequence of my findings: first came the basic importance of the hold for the entire analytic experience, in terms of defining the therapeutic field and creating the maternal matrix and tie out of which growth can occur. I noticed, for example, that when the frame was secured, one would get positive introjections of the analyst, in addition to new material from the patient: transference material, analyzable material that could lead to interpretations, insight, and interchange. And this would have a very positive effect, as predicted.

But then something would happen: the patient would become frightened and anxious; there would be some regression. Now, initially I was at a loss to understand this. And the way in which I finally did comprehend what was happening was that I re-examined the analogy between the mother-child relationship and that of the patient and the analyst, and I realized that the analogy broke down at some point. There are important differences in that the hold that the analyst offers is one that has certain special deprivations as well, designed to foster suitable regression, to enable the patient to become analyzable, to generate the analytic material. This means communicating and experiencing on some level very primitive inner fantasies, anxieties, conflicts, and the like. Now, that's not a characteristic of the maternal hold at all. That's where the analogy, as every analogy does, breaks down: the maternal hold fosters security and growth, without regression; and that's where the other elements in the analytic situation come in as crucial to what makes analysis distictive and viable.

Stone: To me, it's the distinctive and central dynamics of analysis; the core of separation and the deprivation, in a primitive sense and reference. Obviously there's an important gratification at another level to whose ultimate full development the patients and we are aspiring.

Langs: So you see how my clinical observations led me to develop a clearer statement of both functions of the frame. The frame then is a unique construct; I think it defies metaphor. "Frame" is so rigid a term; there are important human qualities and we really need a three-dimensional metaphor. The frame is fascinating for its gratifying and for its frustrating, deprivational qualities. In fact, of late I have tried to stress the analyst's *management* of the frame, and the unconscious communications so conveyed, as a way of highlighting the human elements.

Stone: It's a unique human relationship; no doubt about it. It is a fact that Freud discovered more than he even knew!

Langs: Yes, it's a marvelous thing to study. Now, let's turn to your clinical material. We see that the patient then, as described in the introductory paragraph . . .

Stone: Took a vacation, about which he had had conflict.

Langs: What was the setting—as much as we can establish—in which the vacation occurred? You weren't studying the vacation, so you didn't offer much material.

Stone: Yes, I don't really remember. Whatever would be available for our consideration would be in the article. I remember this patient, as a person, as if it were yesterday, but not the circumstances for his taking the vacation other than as the paper gives them.

Langs: Well, okay. The little bit that you say, to go back a bit more (Stone, 1947), is that he was working over issues related to rivalry, to his need to carry out all functions himself. Rivalry had appeared in the relationship with the analyst, and it related to the need to rival all other objects, including children and women.

Stone: Yes, narcissistic, all-encompassing rivalry with everybody.

Langs: Right. And you wrote (Stone, 1947, p. 26): "It is likely that the nursing fantasy"—there had been a nursing fantasy—"underlay the obvious fellatio fantasy and the auto-fellatio fantasy, incorporated in his masturbation. A dream illustrating the ambivalent fellatio and auto-fellatio fantasy follows: the patient is in a sail-boat fishing with P.L. The patient tells P.L. to 'pull his line in and out.' Close to shore, P.L. draws his line in and catches a huge fish. He grabs the fish close to the head and removes the hook. The patient pulls his own line up and down, and catches a huge but strange fish. He is uncertain whether it is a dogfish or an 'eating' fish. The patient wakes with an erection, and a feeling of sexual excitement, not present in the dream. The man in the dream is a rich man's (and woman's) son, extremely selfish, apparently not likeable even to his own children, with an inexplicable aversion to sexual intercourse with his attractive wife. The patient spontaneously describes his companion's grip on the fish as similar to the manual grasp of an erect penis. The sail-boat suggests that he is giving up the sport for the summer, as a matter of economy. . . ." (This was all during the summer; there had been a reference to the daughter being away at camp.) To continue: ". . . a procedure unnecessary to P.L., whose two successive inheritances the patient frankly envied the night before, at a dinner at P.L.'s house. (The emphasis on the death of both parents should be noted.) Also, he ate excessively in an almost conscious effort to allay his anxiety about business. After several such associations, the patient thinks of the dream largely in terms of his 'sleeping symptom.' "

And then you go over to the business of his wanting to analyze himself, and his sense of rivalry. It would appear that some of this probably was occurring in anticipation of a vacation that you were going to take sometime during the summer. But that's very speculative. The circumstances aren't mentioned. That's one limitation of our data.

Stone: Well, you can be sure that I took a summer vacation, but just when—that year—I don't know.

Langs: So we don't know exactly what prompted him to go away, for what we have assumed was a brief spring vacation. Now the patient came back and something happened that led him to ask for sedatives. Let's take that sequence in terms of the thesis that I want to develop. But first, you might be able to recall the frame that you had created with this patient, at least as far as vacations were concerned?

Stone: That vacation would have been discussed like any other intercurrent reality. As to its realistic merits, or whether it was acting out, or not, presumably, if I didn't intervene, I thought the vacation was justified. That is the reasonable assumption. And we're not entirely clear as to all the details.

Langs: So, the patient takes the vacation and breaks the frame; roughly speaking, we could say that the next thing that happens is that he comes in and asks you for medication, after the vacation. Now, that comes out of a principle I mentioned before, one that Freud (1912b) stated and that Greenacre (1959) echoed—and, by the way, I (Langs, 1976a) have observed it again and again—that once the patient evokes a modification in the frame, he wants more. One deviation begets another. This is very characteristic, and we'll try to see what the implications are.

Stone: I don't disagree with that, in (reserved) principle, if the deviations are matters of indulgence. Let us take, for example, my going to visit the patient whom I mentioned, in his home. He was, let's face it, in a borderline type of depression, rather than a full-blown psychotic depression, in that he never lost contact with me, or with the realities of his situation, and so on. But the realities didn't govern his behavior, or the depth of depression.
He has not tried since then to get into a psychotic depression to have me come to his house. My action was just sheer necessity at the time. The choice was whether to let this patient regress, and as I say, go to hell. Or whether to continue to try to help him analytically. Now, if letting the old patient whom we have been discussing take a vacation was just pure indulgence, then I would say probably what

followed would be to get more, you see. I'm not sure of that, of course, in the sense of scientific certainty. But I would think it very unlikely.

Langs: The indulgence issue is a little bit different from what I am discussing, in that, even where . . .

Stone: That there may be transference gratification?

Langs: In other words—Greenacre (1959) says this too—there may be times when one has no choice but to make such a deviation, though often in retrospect one finds otherwise; but virtually always one will find that, of course, one pays a price for any deviation. What I'm saying is this: even after a valid deviation, the patient will, while not specifically seeking the same kind of gratification . . .

Stone: But he'll look for more?

Langs: He'll look for more. Take this patient: he came back from his vacation; then he may have asked for medication, or he may have asked for an extra hour, or a change in an hour; but in some form or another he's now going to see if he can maintain this kind of gratification, this kind of interaction. Yet, simultaneously, he may well be trying to see whether you will restore the frame, whether you will then begin to set limits.

Stone: In principle, I accept that. Again, with one reservation, which I shall state briefly, and even anterior to that, I would say that much of this has to do with the maturity of the patient's ego, and the degree to which, at this time or retrospectively, he can perceive the legitimacy of the deprivation. But anyway, it's similar to what I've said many times, that the "price that you pay" (as you put it) is that you have to analyze the sequels. "Paying a price" has acquired a pejorative sound. After all, we pay (we hope!) a reasonable price for food, shelter, clothing, and other necessities. There's nothing inherently wrong with that. Paying this "price" doesn't mean the destruction of the analysis, and the price of refusing a legitimate request may be far greater, because it will evoke rage, or indignation, based in good part on a sense of the reality. For exaggerated example: "this son of a bitch is willing to let me die to keep up his god-damn frame!"

Now, that is much harder to get around than: "All right, the frame was stretched and I like the indulgence; it's a temptation to ask him for more."

Langs: Well, for the moment I only want to state this as an observation—and one has to be prepared for it.

Stone: Correct.

Langs: Again, here's an area where we would agree. You have several indications for modifications of the frame: one group involves requests and things that you feel are relatively innocuous and minor, while the other group is emergency situations. And when it comes to emergency situations, I am much more in agreement with you. I have never ever felt that the frame is more important than a patient's life or . . .

Stone: Exigent clinical—that is, human—realities? That's the only point that I absolutely insist on.

Langs: It's a principle that should be explicitly stated, and one must then accept the consequences. But there is another point that is often misunderstood when I take this position: I agree that this can lead to viable analytic work, but I am suggesting that in addition it may leave certain unmodifiable destructive residuals. . .

Stone: No doubt.

Langs: . . . and they may never get resolved.

Stone: They never get resolved, usually, only if the analyst isn't aware of them, or for some reason can't handle them emotionally! Because otherwise they can be brought into the analysis by the analyst, even if the patient doesn't mention them. You see, I don't believe in the *absolute* rule of passivity. If a patient for several days doesn't mention an incident that occurred at the door, when she stopped and said something just as she walked out, *I* will mention it before too much time has elapsed.

Langs: Yes, but I carry that out a little differently. It's implicit in what you're saying. I feel that there is no conceivable way that the patient will not indirectly communicate material related to it on some level—most often indirectly, in derivative form, to that incident, and I will bring it in when this occurs. I try always to use the material from the patient, and not to introduce anything not present in the manifest or latent content. I play back such derivatives if the context has not been mentioned. I allow each session to be its own creation and the patient to lead the way.

Stone: Well, that may be true in, say, ninety-five percent of such incidents in a demonstrable sense. But free association is not the infallible instrument we like to think. One does not always get clearly interpretable material. Acting out is the most formidable resistance, and minor episodes at the door are simply minor forms of it. We can't let an idealization of free association transcend even small-but-hard realities.

Langs: But we agree that eventually it would come up; I really like to follow the patient, to allow him to unconsciously lead the way.

Again, to establish the first point: as I mentioned, Freud was on vacation and he sent a post card to the Rat Man. It's interesting that Freud mentioned the post card after he had related some material that had actually followed the receipt of the post card. Just as here, you mention the dream and then get around to what prompted it; Freud (1909) did the same kind of thing. It turned out that in response to the card, the Rat Man became furious with Freud; he felt that Freud was trying to be seductive and that he was disrespectful in sending this card. As you know, he had developed similar, apparently paranoid fantasies after the feeding by Freud, culminating in an accusation that Freud was trying to prolong the analysis through the feeding, which took time from the analysis. But, in any case, that was the basic sequence: a post card, then the request for a feeding. With your patient, there was the vacation, then a request for sedatives. Now you responded—and again we don't have all of the data—for whatever reason, by offering an alternative modification in the frame, namely, an extra session.

Stone: Well, this I don't regard as a great modification. Your approach is procrustean. Although I don't mind being compared to Freud!

Langs: I understand your position here.

Stone: Assuming again that there was a good reason for it, that it wasn't because I liked to see the patient, or needed the money for the extra hour, or was responding in some maternal way to something in the patient.

Langs: Well, I have found that the very things that you said are present as a rule; that it isn't only the fantasies that the patient would have about it, but the perceptions, often valid perceptions, of unconscious needs in the analyst. That is, the patient will come to believe that there is a special need within the analyst who offers this kind of deviation.

Stone: Well, I should let you make your point, then I'll respond.

Langs: But you did it for me. We'll see how it connects with what you said in terms of the data. Here, we should try to sort out what the patient perceives about the analyst's offer from his fantasies and distortions of it. So, again based on the data that we have, the analyst proposed a Saturday visit. Now, that proposal clearly was the day residue for the dream; I think we have clear evidence for that, so, let's go back over it.

Stone: The extra hour was suggested, instead of pills.

Langs: My own position would be not to offer an alternative deviation, but to analyze the meaning of the request for pills, and it probably would have been analyzed in terms of the implications of the vacation and other issues in the analytic interaction.

Stone: Yes, or maybe something more fundamental, in his orality. This man had bouts of very severe insomnia, and/or depression, in addition to his character disturbance and his ulcer. Are you sure you are not (inadvertently) trying to fit this material to your technical views? If your view of his fantasy and "perceptual" reaction to my offer is correct, his putative reaction would have to be based more on his profound pathology than on this offer. I would reject your referring to the hypothetical countertransference possibilities which I mentioned as being what the patient actually perceived. They were just not there! As I've said before, our analytical work is based largely on the patient's false perceptions. To separate what fraction is "veridical" is important. The only element that is clearly of that character here is that the patient was offered an extra hour instead of pills, to facilitate the analytic work. He wanted pills for his insomnia.

Langs: I will not pursue a further defense of my position for the moment. What I would stress is my proposal that the analytic route to the orality would have to be through the perceptions of what had transpired in the interaction with the analyst. Without that it would be avoiding the central issue and become isolated intellectualizing. The patient's intrapsychic dynamics and genetics can be used to avoid the unconscious implications of the analyst's interventions.

Stone: Well, that's because of your assumption that the interaction constituted the whole occasion for his asking for the pills. Certainly the patient's major pathology would appear in the transference. Indeed, the paper was written to elucidate the archaic elements in that transference. And certainly the everyday clinical transactions would impinge on them—as evidenced by the particular dream which you selected.

Langs: I wouldn't consider it the whole occasion—just an important part of what you call the proximal cause, and what I term the *adaptive context*.

Stone: Or rather, the day residue for it. But overall, I remain, shall I say, skeptical that the patient's vacation had any significant connection with the request for pills and the germane material that we are discussing.

Langs: The day residue has to be determined and then worked over in order to get at the unconscious factors. That material will also crowd out the unconscious factors, in my experience, if it is disregarded. There is both reality and fantasy, but one can only get to the unconscious and distorted aspects through working first with the actualities or at least being well aware of them.

Stone: Yes, that I agree with and have long practiced and taught, but I do feel that we may place different weight and even a different qualitative evaluation on these actualities. But I should let you finish your argument.

Langs: So, let's see: the patient had taken the vacation; he hadn't had the stomach trouble; the depression wasn't as bad. Now, we don't have the sequence clearly, but he had some old sedatives, and he had taken one, which, by my definition of the frame, is another modification. I believe analysis should occur without medication.

Stone: I am afraid that is an undue "prohibitive" extension of a frame. Besides it is a bit paradoxical in your own schema. One analyzes such questions, rather than involving oneself directly. Besides, how many patients do you have who have no access to medication? They take their wives' sedatives, or vice versa; their internists give them medication, and so forth. It is sometimes the case with my patients, who have often had multiple previous analyses, that they have medicine cabinets full of pills. So my only rule is that *I* don't prescribe their medications, except in a real emergency. I mean, for example, anti-depressants. I usually refer them to somebody else. I have some patients who are sick enough to require them at least for a time; but in that reference I'm rather strict. I feel that the analytic situation is less burdened if that sphere is taken care of by somebody else. It does avoid precisely the "materialization" of transference, which we are discussing. To impose that rule in my practice would be utterly unrealistic, and, in my view, a violation of an important principle. When they come in and say, "So I took a so and so," I try to analyze why they "took that" instead of dealing with it on some direct control or self-analytic basis, while waiting until the next session.

Langs: I never say to the patient, "No, you can't take medication." To me we are dealing with an implicit ground rule, so that when it's modified unilaterally by the patient, I will deal with it analytically, as you do. Incidentally, the use of another physician to prescribe medication modifies another basic tenet: the one-to-one relationship.

Stone: I don't regard this as an absolute rule. We call on other physicians for medical and surgical consultation. I prefer invoking the consultation to playing the dual role of psychological physician and oral medicator.

Langs: So he had taken this capsule; he had asked you for medication, you had not given it to him and you suggested a Saturday session.

Stone: It must have been that I thought he was pretty disturbed, if I suggested the Saturday session.

Langs: Right. And he had gone to bed Friday night; you hadn't given him a prescription; he had some medication in the apartment and he had taken a sedative. Okay. Then he had a dream.

Stone: Excuse me. Not that I *mean* to be a wise guy! But most of my patients have had multiple analyses in which ground rules were observed very strictly. To the point where it was sometimes experienced as harshness, rigidity, lack of compassion, and so on. You see, you mustn't forget that my orientation toward these things comes to some degree from my clinical experience. I refer to the question of which is the lesser evil. Also it has often seemed to me—since there are sometimes startling exceptions—that overstrict maintenance of ground rules is often a convenience, if not a countertransference gratification, for the analyst. Again, the shoe on the other foot.

Langs: This was the background of your book, *The Psychoanalytic Situation* (Stone, 1961). I appreciate that, and I appreciate very much the potential for countertransference abuses of my general viewpoint too.

Stone: Correct. There too, you see, countertransference abuses are usually seen in terms of "indulgence." Not to speak of seduction and unequivocal abuses of that sort. That they can occur in the form of

outright harshness or bouts of anger, all the way to just incon-
siderateness, and lack of compassion, is a neglected sphere. Do you
see what I mean? But let us go back to the dream!

Langs: All right. He had the dream: in it, he was looking at the
bottle from which he had just taken the sedative. There was one
capsule in it which seemed slightly chewed. To his dismay, the
chewed appearance was due to two small worms, with heads like
little rag dolls, in the bottle. He immediately became concerned lest
he had done himself harm by ingesting something contaminated by
worms. That, in essence, is the manifest content.

Now, the associations are selected in terms of the analytic material
you were developing: he felt that the taking of the sedative related to
the insomnia and that it had to do with a breast fantasy. The worms
he associated with biting into an apple; the two dolls' heads he
associated with the rag dolls his sister had kept on her bed as a
youngster. Then you pointed out to him that there was a fear of
disastrous consequences from the sedative, which you related to his
hostility toward the prototype of the worms, his sister and his
children, and toward the breast which fed them. He accepted that for
consideration. And that's the sequence. For me, your intervention is
interesting because it contains what I think is an implicit commentary on this interaction. Often, an analyst's manifest intervention
contains important latent contents. I would postulate the following,
which is not readily documented, but is in keeping with many other
observations: that, while the manifest content of the dream relates to
the pills, the latent content has a bearing on the offer of an extra
hour. In other words, since that offer was part of the day residue, the
adaptive context, I would view the dream as a commentary on that
proposal, some of which would be nontransference—valid unconscious perceptions and the like—and some of which would be
transference—pathological distortions and unconscious fantasies—
the dream communicates both.

In this context, then, the extra hour, I would postulate, is first of all
viewed by the patient as the offer of a breast, and as equivalent to the
offer of the pills. You can quickly sense here a mixture of reality and
fantasy—nontransference and transference. You have, in actuality,
offered some kind of special gratification; it doesn't take the form of
the capsule but of an additional hour. But the material related to the

breast fantasy is, I think, very pertinent, not only reflecting his experience of inappropriate gratification and not only experiencing it as fantasy, but also in that the offer constituted an actual gratification of unconscious wishes—of that wish for breast.

Stone: This issue has a most fundamental importance. First, let me concede something. You know this involves our common interest in the scientific aspect. If I did not comment in the article on the extra hour and its meaning to him, I omitted something important. Probably I did comment. Again, you see, this is four years of analysis in a few pages, and written in relation to a particular central topic. Again, as for the meaning to him: I would say that the dream is a reaction to the fact that I didn't give him the pills. That in giving him the hour—mind you, I would not defend not mentioning it, or not raising the question of what it meant to him—the response was intimately germane to what I regard as the very basis of the analytic situation. You may remember how I started out to develop it. The patient wanted a tit in his mouth; instead he got an analytic hour, words. Which, to me, is from the beginning a matter grudgingly accepted by the baby instead of a breast. Later it develops in its role as a gratification *faute de mieux*, and soon elaborates its own autonomy as a gratification and vehicle of relatedness of supreme importance. But the archaic substratum is, "I want momma and her titty; I don't want this blah, blah, blah, all this talk!" Thus the poisonous quality, the worms, the sibling rivalry to me would mean in the transference, "Look, the bastard probably gives his girl patients pills and he tells me, no, I'm a big boy; I've got to come in tomorrow and talk!" So, you see, we would differ as to the interpretation.

Langs: Okay. I think what you're saying has validity. But again we differ, in part, because you are picking up the deprivation, while I'm focusing on the gratification. Both are involved. This is what I term a *transversal communication*—it traverses several spheres simultaneously.

Stone: Yes, but I recognize the gratification. The gratification of what I call the "mature transference," the post-symbiotic type of urge which is part of the phenomenology of development. The fact that one can also relate to mamma and pappa in a different way, talking with them, learning, and so on.

Langs: I believe there is also a gratification of a primitive transference in giving the patient the extra hour.

Stone: There we would disagree. He might "try" to find such gratification in it, just as he dreamed about the pill. Just as he might "find" father or mother in the person of the analyst. But the reality and the fantasy were more sharply differentiated than usual, in this particular instance. Acutally, this patient traveled in from a considerable distance, and it was not easy to come in on a Saturday.

Langs: This would be an important point for us to try to sort out: it is because of your concept of the mature transference and the reasonableness of certain gratifications which I would view as inappropriate, that you work within the framework that you do. Now, I would say—let's call it an interpretation and it's based on the minimum amount of material; we both acknowledge that—but I believe that your interpretation of the dream and my interpretation of the dream are both correct. And that there are different levels. I'm thinking of the two worms, two contaminants, and I think that you are right by frustrating certain very direct wishes for gratification. You helped to prompt the dream and evoked certain transferences, because the dream suggests that he experienced that limitation. But I still feel that I'm right that on another level he experienced a kind of inappropriate gratification as well. What's interesting is that even in the manifest dream the capsule is there, but it's not available to him.

Stone: But after he took it, he was afraid he had hurt himself.

Langs: He sees the capsule as slightly chewed, and he sees the two worms.

Stone: He says, he's afraid he's done himself harm, after he takes it.

Langs: Yes—I was alluding to another aspect of the dream. He ingests a contaminated capsule, exactly. So he gets something, but he also cannot get more.

Stone: He had taken one the night before.

Langs: He takes something in, but it's contaminated, it's spoiled —an image that lends itself to the compromise that you had worked out. It also supports the point that I was developing. You created a certain amount of frustration that's reflected in this material in a perfectly valid way which you spelled out. And I should keep that in focus. Now, on a second level, you also afforded him a certain degree of gratification, and that was based on a modification of the frame, the extra hour; that is represented in his mind—in this dream and his associations—as a dangerous contaminated gratification.

Stone: That's your interpretation; I don't believe that's so. Nor, if I may be so presumptuous, do I believe that our interpretations are equally valid. You are omitting the fact that all the material must be seen in the light of the genesis and dynamics of a profound oral neurosis—you place all the emphasis on the fact that he was given an extra hour (for legitimate reasons). Suppose he had had the same dream after an unusually careful and profound interpretation! Ultimately, his transference sleep symptom came to revolve around the complexities of just that verbal interchange. Within his dream he carried out the gratification that he *didn't* get. Do you see what I mean? I don't mean to defend everything I did as perfect. But I really believe there is an issue of principle here, and it happens to touch on some of my strongest convictions about the dynamics of the psycho-analytic situation. If you put it in an oversimplified epitome, just as I said earlier, I believe that when the patient can wholeheartedly accept the analytic process (with its preponderant dependence on talking between two people) as the exclusively important relationship, he is practically analyzed. That is, when they are ready to give up the literal needs for physical proximity and its proximal derivatives which constitute the primordial transference urge.

Langs: It is at this point that I am reminded of the limitations of our data. I am not trying to prove a clinical thesis, but to show how your material fits in with a model that I have developed and validated from other sources. But I would like to clarify one point: I am not proposing a neglect of genetic and dynamic factors, nor of possible distortions by the patient. Ultimately, these would all be recognized and analyzed. I am stressing a possible unconscious meaning and communication relevant to your deviation which I believe must also be given due consideration—denial in this area would be as disruptive as any failure to work through contributions from the patient's pathology. I am trying to define a balanced view that considers all sides and stresses, for the moment, aspects that I feel are generally overlooked. And I am developing another issue: the difference in the dynamics of the situation when the analyst has inappropriately gratified the patient on some level—say, orally—and where he has not. I do not believe material exists qua material; it arises from the unconscious communicative interaction.

So, I take issue with you as to whether an extra session does or does not gratify the primordial urge, his inappropriate, transference-based needs. I believe it does. In other words, I would amend that part of your comment by suggesting that it is when the patient can accept both verbal communication and the frame—the agreed-upon frequency of visits as defined in the ground rules—that he is cured.

Stone: In overstrict and rather arbitrary principle, yes. I would agree that extra sessions, gratuitously given, or given just because the patient wants them, or is habituated to indulgences, would be an undue transference gratification, albeit not as serious as giving him a pill for the asking. However, I do not accept the assumption that there was improper gratification in this instance, or that my offer of an extra hour reflected my countertransference. But nevertheless, a questionable gratification can then become a basis for further demands or for habituation, if successful transference and countertransference analysis does not reinstate a more viable situation.

Langs: Or for reinforcing of the neurosis. You see, this is another point that I wanted to make; this is exactly where the issue that I tried to define earlier comes to life. Your view is that you behaved differently from earlier past pathogenic figures. My view is that you did and didn't do so. Your interpretation of this material at this point is based on the idea that what was primary was the frustration, which had generated a dream and a fantasy of the gratification that he was deprived of.

Stone: Yes, that's right.

Langs: My position is that what was primary was the extra session, a transference gratification, rather than a frustration. I agree that there was a frustration in regard to the pill, but that did not prevail because of the substitute gratification of the session. This influences, in a critical way, the nature of both our management of the frame and our subsequent interventions.

Stone: The gratification was on quite a different level, in actuality. Strange as it may seem, it's a bit like analyzing a patient in the first place, instead of treating him medically. That's where we would disagree. You see, I go so far as to say, that a patient of his type, as I remember him, with his intense envy and his sense of chronic deprivation in all spheres, possibly might not have brought that dream were it not for the fact that he did receive something, at a level that was more acceptable. Now, that's a hypothesis. You can say just the opposite: that he might have brought it eventually and gotten more out of it, if it weren't for the extra session. That would be a matter of judgment. You see, I am not even convinced, in the first place, that the frame need be such an absolute constant. I believe that the frame exists to give tenable and viable frames of reference and format to the process and content of psychoanalysis. In this sense, secondarily, especially insofar as it subserves the principles of abstinence, it achieves its own great dynamic power, on which you and I agree. But as you know, I have not been satisfied with the arbitrary, rigid frame of abstinence, which has evolved the way Topsy grew. There are times when the analytic process is propelled forward by reasonable modifications of the sort we are discussing. No disagreement about understanding and analyzing the "consequences" (which are not bogey-men when the modification was a rational one); but, as I said, you would no doubt think differently. I think that once in a while, anybody who deals with severe cases recognizes that an extra session might be necessary. For example Jacobson (1954) even speaks of prolonging sessions and so on, with certain depressed patients. That's hard to do with a regular analytic schedule, unless they come at the end of the day. But an extra session one can arrange, even if one's inconvenienced.

Langs: This is a position that I know to exist, and I agree, we have different interpretations. But I wanted to add to my comment that because my starting point is a focus on the extra session, this dream also tells me something about your not having given him medication, which he then provides for himself, nonetheless, so that on one level . . .

Stone: He gets the extra session—yes.

Langs: He also gratifies himself, and indirectly he then says that even his gratifying himself, his taking a pill, is a contamination of the analytic situation. On another level, where the dream also has to do with the extra session, it begins with his perception of the gratification in the extra session and then it extends into his fantasies. As a whole, it takes a very special, individual form. But what he's saying in this dream is that the extra session provided him with gratification that was contaminated, and my point is that this is a valid perception of one meaning of the extra session. It is not primarily fantasy. The fantasy part comes in the form in which it is experienced—as a breast—in its connections to the pills, in the images of the worms and the associations to the doll heads—associations that take him back into the past. You see, a present inappropriate gratification has its genetic antecedents. Not all genetics tie to transferences.

Stone: Of course. But again, I must reject your statement that his (presumed) reaction to the extra session as a contaminated gratification was a "valid perception, not primarily fantasy." The patient sees things in the light of his illness; again, that recognition and its interpretation is the core of analytic work. That patients sometimes see things correctly is true; we agree on that. I said so almost twenty-five years ago. But I think it is sort of a fantasy world in itself to believe that every manifest dream content is a correct appraisal of the analyst's behavior. An honest, reasonable, clinical maneuver is just that, and furthermore, I believe (in contradistinction to your own view) that the patient, if not too ill, usually knows it, and that fact renders his distorted, unconscious view of it analyzable.

Langs: Please understand that I am alluding to a veridical core which may then, of course, be subjected to considerable transference-based distortion. Nor did I suggest that manifest dreams may contain valid perceptions, though on a latent level this may be so—there are all sorts of mixtures of perceptions and distortions in all latent contents. Remember, I found derivative meaning in the dream by organizing it around a specific adaptive context; I did not allude to manifest contents alone. The patient has a perspective regarding unspoken realities realted to the analyst's good intentions on the one hand, but on the other he unconsciously understands the analyst's unconsciously misguided intentions as well. Without reiterating or elaborating further for now, let me just say again that the genetics are always there, but they have different implications in the two situations. If you've really gratified him—and I refer here to the extra hour—as he was inappropriately gratified in the past, it's different from what happens when you frustrate him and he then generates a fantasy of such gratification.

Stone: See, we disagree here. He was *not* gratified as he was in the past. For example, he didn't ask for an extra session. I suggested it. It's different if a patient is looking for extra time. I have one such patient who almost habitually will ask for extra sessions, or if something comes up and I have to miss a session, feels it must be immediately replaced by another session. The sensitive handling of such a situation is not as simple as rules of thumb would suggest. The patient we are discussing didn't ask for an extra hour; he asked for a pill. Furthermore, this is a fact; one of the few vivid facts that I recall. This man was not too eager to come regularly; still less to come for an extra session. You remember, he's the man in relation to whom I had to lay down a condition the last time he came back to me. And that was that he would persist in the analysis until by mutual agreement, we decided to stop. Because, I think, two or three times, as soon as he got some symptomatic improvement, he quit, in a burst of "independence." So, whether this was a gratification in the ordinary sense, or a gratification only at the level of the child who wants titty (with all its dread complications), but will accept momma's talking to him and the opportunity of babbling with her, I would have an open mind. I believe it was the latter. In any case, I don't accept your interpretation of the dream. In long-undocumented retrospect perhaps I could have done better at the time, but as later developments bore out, it was not a destructive maneuver in any "valid" sense. I would guess that it was probably productive. What I accept is, that without question the meaning of the extra session should have been discussed for whatever it was. I would assume it was, but I have no scientific certainty. The paper is now my only record. Certainly, such discussion would be taken for granted in my work of the last many years.

Langs: No, I understand that part, that's not an issue at all. Basically, I've tried to offer you an alternative view, which is why I want to continue in this way, because this will come up as we go through each vignette, and I'll attempt to show you how this alternative view can be utilized and supported in each of the vignettes we examine. Through this we can develop the differences in our opinions. Perhaps I'm being too repetitious, but we get around to breast fantasy, to his sister and her having these dolls in bed—another form of concrete gratification. My hypothesis would be that in part all of this reflects a valid perception of the situation. In fact, let me take it a little bit further. I introduce this with an apology, but we do have to look at the analyst in this kind of situation, since what I have found is that the patient perceives certain needs in the analyst who makes such an offer.

Stone: You feel that he may perceive certain needs correctly?

Langs: Yes. He may speculate about it, unconsciously communicate his ideas, and then the analyst will have to ask, "Is he right? Is there something valid in what the patient is conveying?"

Stone: Of course; but the patient, as I said before, may also perceive the analyst's need to be an honest doctor, to try to help, within the reasonable limits of an established framework. He may also perceive that the analyst who never extends himself in an emergency is unconsciously rationalizing his laziness, or stinginess, or robotlike adherence to rules, or overconcern for his convenience.

Langs: I would propose, for example, that the fact that the pills were slightly chewed, by someone else, reflects a question in his mind about your need for inappropriate gratification—viewing this dream as an introjection of your needs and inner state. He experiences your seeing him or for the extra session in this way. Despite your insistence that it was not based on some need to offer yourself to him as breast, nonetheless this was his unconscious perception of the situation.

Stone: There we would disagree, to understate it! Where I said "not" you have arbitrarily made it "yes," for my patient of more than thirty years ago!

Langs: As a model only. I agree with you regarding the limitations we face in interpreting this material. Let me just add that he saw it as a need to be an inappropriate breast—a "contaminated" offer.

Stone: No, you made that "point" clear— see Ella Sharpe's paper (1940)—but I don't accept it. In fact, I think it utterly wrong. You see, I would say that the interpretation was essentially valid (he had enormous rivalry with his younger sister). The chewing of the pills was a projection of his oral rage to the baby who was at the breast, which is not infrequent. You know, "the baby is gonna eat up momma," or something of the sort. Children may actually say this. So I can't accept your view of the patient's "valid" perception. The only thing that I accept, I repeat, is the question of the need to discuss the extra session. Also, that the genetic elements should have been clearly integrated with the current transference. From the great emphasis on the pill, it is reasonable to infer they were. But I cannot document the actual wording.

Langs: I suggest we let it stand as stated for now. At this point we've established some of the divergences in opinion that I wanted to get to.

Stone: Oh, very clear and very important.

Langs: There are alternative ways of conceptualizing the situation, and we don't have sufficient data to resolve these issues for the moment. I am stressing that the unconscious communicative interaction has primacy; you are adopting the prevailing position of the primacy of intrapsychic processes within the patient. When I work with supervisees, I offer my hypotheses, as you would offer yours, and we then have subsequent material from the patient with which to test them out and attempt to validate them. Here, in my discussions with you, we don't have that.

Stone: Well, we have subsequent material; we have the whole course of the analysis! Incidentally, in regard to my view, I don't believe in the unqualified primacy of the intrapsychic process. Certainly the patient reacts to the analyst and what he says, but he does so in the light of his preestablished psychic set.

Langs: In principle, I would quite agree with you there. By the way, the material that followed, concerning incestuous gratification with the sister, with the sister figure, with the daughter, which again, he did not consummate: this, to my way of thinking, is also a reflection of the compromise that you worked out. You didn't gratify him entirely through the pills, but did so in a more limited way, through the extra session. You would have an alternative interpretation.

Stone: I would say so. This would derive from his whole behavior in the analysis, his falling asleep, and so on. Also, his early ejaculatory interruption in masturbation. Naturally, the transference relationship would be the immediate reference.

Langs: He has the dream about the daughter, as you recall, where he just presses on her body, and he remembers jiggling her on his foot. Again, to me this would also convey his unconscious perception of the offer of the additional session: the inappropriate gratification, the child with the parent, making some degree of physical contact and being stimulated, but nonetheless achieving a compromise. The act is restricted, it's not blatant incest. And his remark that he would not wish to hurt his daughter brings up the theme of the harmful parent—a common theme in this context—and the hurtful qualities of this kind of deviation.

Stone: Yes, but that's unclear, you see; there is a disproportionate emphasis, even *if* you were right that it was a mistake to give him the extra hour. I believe you have things a bit muddled. Instead of seeing a lifetime severe neurosis as causing certain distorted reactions to the analyst, you see a benign clinical maneuver as possibly having caused even his early trouble with his sister! I think, you see, the "untoward" impact of such things is really minimal. And it can readily be undone. The affirmative effects, if the maneuver is well conceived, usually far outweigh them, so long as they are within the framework of the basic purpose of analysis, which is to translate into understanding those urgencies that derive from primitive sources.

But I don't believe your views, I don't accept any of those interpretations about the patient's valid perception. This becomes a sort of upsidedown world.

Langs: Well, I can only ask you to give some thought at some point; your caricature of my position leads me to wonder why it comes across so strangely to you. I'm simply trying to suggest that so long as these actual gratifications occur they modify the analytic work and outcome, and that these then have to be rectified and analyzed as a first-order task. I think that they have a major impact. I am in no way denying the role of the patient's own psychopathology. I am trying to simply give full cognizance as well to the much neglected role of the analyst's unconscious communications to the patient. I will not offer a further defense; perhaps our later discussion of clinical material will prove clarifying.

Stone: Attention to the possible un_onscious communications of the analyst is reasonable, but I believe this can be overdone in the sense of an a priori assumption of pathology in the analyst. The principle of adhering to a frame so long as there is no good reason to alter it is correct; but suppose, for discussion, I had given him the pills. Doctors often prescribe sedatives.

Langs: I feel that the consequences would have been the same at the core, with other, specific reactions related to the sedatives, and they would have been more dramatic than with the extra hour.

Stone: I think they would be, and I would be the first to criticize myself. First of all, it was asked for. He just wanted it. Secondly, it is on a level which is not analytic. I mean the gratification in the form of something to put in his mouth. Now, what was done was to reinstate analysis as the mode of contact. That he had an extra hour is what *you* are emphasizing, but this guy didn't look for extra hours.

Langs: No, I understand that. I do not place as much stress as you do on a direct request for a deviation. I see the pills and the extra hour on a very definite continuum, in terms of their consequences.

Stone: A continuum, but very far apart.

Langs: Well, you see them much more apart than I do, though I agree with you that the impact of the pill would even be greater because it has implications related to concrete gratification and is not verbal in its form, and also because it leads away from insight and analytic work. But to some extent, so does the extra hour.

Stone: There are doctors, analysts, who give pills when they think they are necessary. And that is not always terrible. I think that sometimes it is, if they're not aware of the consequences; if they give them with no justification. There is a difference when the patient says, "I'm having a little trouble sleeping, can you give me some pills," and you promptly write him a prescription, and, on the other hand, a situation where you've seen a patient through three weeks of stark sleeplessness and perhaps a state of physical exhaustion, and the analysis isn't quite getting to this. There you might decide that it is wise to provide the medication. I rarely do it. Maybe once in several years I have written a sedative for a patient. But there are others who do it a little more freely than I do. As I say, my patients usually have so damn many pills to start with, that that isn't the issue. The issue is to analyze why they take them so readily. Anyway, you feel that anything that happened thereafter in this analysis was governed by the fact that I saw him for an extra hour. I don't.

Langs: I would say that it has an influence; I don't say that everything that happens would bear on it, though it might. I would also say that in order to get to the patient's intrapsychic conflicts and fantasies, and to resolve the pathological aspects, the route has to be through that actuality.

But now, having established our contrasting positions, I would like to go on to additional vignettes so that we can elaborate on them.

Stone: Perhaps presenting some similar issues?

Langs: Yes, that is important to me, because that's where we would want to look further.

Stone: Yes, you see, as I reflect on this, I am convinced of its importance, from the sphere of practicality to the deepest reaches of theory. A current case, yours or mine, would be better, but there are obvious impediments. This was my case, but it was thirty years ago, and a published (extreme) condensation provides our only data. The publication, too, was offered to accent certain issues. The rest is my necessarily uncertain memory, as far as details are concerned. I'm sure that many things in my views would have changed or become more definitely crystallized since then—less often in essentials than in details or degrees.

You see, I can't remember just how strongly I felt the exigencies of the particular situation. I might still offer an extra hour to a patient if I felt that his clinical state was really bad and that the alternative, let's say, was to give him medication or to give him some reassurance ("support") or other placebo of an emotional nature; I have indeed done that occasionally in the last year, with no monsters returning to haunt the situation permanently! I know positively that this man could become very depressed. You remember, that was the alternative to his ulcer syndrome. It was one of the things that interested me especially in retrospect, because it is one of the not too frequent clear demonstrations of the oral gastric complex and its position in the psychopathology of depression. Also, his sleeplessness could be very severe. In general, he was a very sick man (this was the comment of an older colleague, very much interested in the "borderlines") with a mixture of characterological problems, depression, and the ulcer as a sort of pathoneurosis. In the light of developments nowadays I don't know whether the ulcer was entirely of psychological etiology, but certainly the psychological sphere was a demonstrably important participant in the ulcer. The final clinical response was good.

There were other symptomatic phenomena apart from the character sphere. I recall there were some fluctuating potency difficulties at one point, although that was not a presenting symptom. My guess would be that at that time, even assuming that my threshold was a little lower then, I might still be concerned about him, and think the offer of an extra hour the best thing to do. But as I say, my threshold might be a little higher now. I might be inclined to say, "Let's see how things go; I'll see you Monday." And then, maybe, deal with his rage. I don't recall if that request came up early in the hour. But apart from all the contingencies and unknowns, I do not think that an extra hour, unless determined by a neurotic countertransference on my side, would have consequences that couldn't *easily* be analyzed. He might say, "Look, as I look back on it, why did you indulge me with an extra hour?" He might say that, or something like that or equivalent to it—or "dream" it, in terms of his infantile conflicts. And I would say, "Because I thought that you were suffering a great deal and that an extra hour in which we could do some progressive work was much better than just giving you a pill." And, of course, analyze the distortions introduced by his psychopathology, probably with a productive outcome. But we have differences here; I think that while I give the frame, as such, tremendous importance, it's far more important to you.

Langs: Yes, and to our patients.

Stone: Granted that on both sides, we would agree on the importance of analyzing the impact, and—speaking for myself, although I think you would agree—that "modifications" always remain within certain strict limits (which I have tried to define).

Langs: That's what has come through. Some of it comes from your great sensitivity to the deprivational qualities of the situation, and some of it comes from my greater awareness of the gratifying qualities. But having established this, we'll continue to go through some vignettes and develop our ideas further.

Stone: Sure. That was a good case, because it's one of the few cases—I don't know, maybe the only one—that I wrote in detail and published. Even though the lapse of time introduces the problems which we have both mentioned.

Langs: We'll certainly have a lot to clarify at our next meeting.

Chapter 4
INTERACTIONAL MECHANISMS

Langs: You know, one of the moving spirits behind my book, *The Therapeutic Interaction* (Langs, 1976b), was a desire to attempt a history of our thinking on the analytic relationship, and to understand, as far as possible, the lives of some of the contributors to this literature. I was interested in what you had to say last time about the origins of the term "real relationship." I found that I have given you priority in my book, when I looked it up.

Stone: You didn't happen to look up the term "therapeutic alliance," did you? Because I am certain I used it in the "Widening Scope" paper (Stone, 1954).

Langs: No, but as I recall, Zetzel (1966), who was the first to define it in detail, credited Bibring (1937) with the phrase, in the Marienbad symposium on the effects of analysis.

Stone: Yes, I've often referred to that symposium. He used it there. Incidentally, since you mention that symposium, I noticed, in going over our previous conversations, that we spoke of Strachey's (1934) contribution, and I said something to the effect that I thought it was a

brilliant and very worthwhile paper, but perhaps a little too narrow.
As I remember, it was in that symposium—I think it was Fenichel
(1937) who stated a kind of blunt commonsense reaction to Strachey's
paper. He said, "I don't think"—mind you, this is not a verbatim
quote, but it is the idea—"I don't feel it's necessary to say that because
a person agrees with you, he has incorporated parts of you." He was
making, inadvertently, the tremendous distinction between cognitive understanding in terms of verbal communications and the more
primitive processes. Strachey was talking about the patient introjecting "parts of the good object" when a successful interpretation is
made in the transference; this is relevant to our earlier discussion
about the matter of giving pills versus offering an extra analytic
hour.

Langs: You know, your remarks bring up an interesting point. I
found in speaking to classical analysts—and some of this comes up
in my own writings now and in some of the informal reactions I'm
receiving—that classical analysts, by and large, were indeed critical
of Strachey's (1934) presentation; and they question or doubt the
specific effects of introjective processes in analysis. Many of them
conveyed feelings or opinions that are in keeping with what you said
about Fenichel (1937), that the identificatory element is to be set
somewhat to the side, and cognitive insight is to be given precedence.
And the reactions to my work, especially *The Bipersonal Field*
(Langs, 1976a), but also to *The Therapeutic Interaction* (Langs,
1976b), were in keeping with such attitudes. What I attempted to
draw together there—actually, it turned out this way; it was not a
conscious intention, although I did recognize the importance of
conceptualizing the two spheres—was to clarify the respective contributions of the cognitive sphere, of cognitive insight, and the interactional sphere—identificatory and introjective processes. Now,
whether you tend to think of it, as you said, as a more primitive
sphere—because I guess you're saying that actually, and certainly,
the introjective process is more primitive, more basic—there are
interactional mechanisms clearly present long before verbalization
or cognition.

Stone: Without question.

Langs: Though in a sense, there is some very primitive form of cognition from the beginning of life. But I made the statement, at the very end of the book (Langs, 1976b), that those analysts who have emphasized interaction tend to neglect cognitive insight. I think it is true that Strachey (1934) did not attempt to counterbalance his presentation with a discussion of the cognitive side. On the other hand, I believe that his paper was essentially an attempt to establish a second mode of structural change in addition to cognitive insight. This is how I think of it.

Stone: I have always had high regard for Strachey's (1934) paper. I think I made that clear. And you see, because of my own idiosyncratic view of this thing, the problem, to me, is not of difference but of increase in understanding, in the sense that I regard these things as on a continuum. That is, all the way from incorporation through somewhat more generalized abstract concepts, like introjection, all the way up to verbal communication in its most extreme, representational, cognitive sense. The analytic process to me consists in the gradual substitution of the one for the other. So I can agree with Strachey (1934), in the sense of his very acute but limited insight; but I believe that ultimately the patient becomes able to think about his most profound experiences, genuinely in terms of verbal representations.

Langs: The way I conceptualize this area is somewhat different, though once again we both acknowledge the importance of the two spheres—something many analysts have not accepted. So, while I agree that ultimately the patient develops cognitive tools, and the use of verbalization and specific insights . . .

Stone: And with that, memory as such can begin to replace the outmoded reaction patterns associated with old experience.

Langs: Right, but my point is that cognitive understanding is not an alternative to introjection, that it doesn't substitute for it or replace it; it goes hand in hand with it. There's development in both spheres. In other words, I think of them as two parallel tracks, with many interconnections, distinctive, yet influencing each other, and even, at times, one form carrying over into the other, for example, identifications that lead to specific insights.

Stone: Well, I don't see them as parallel, but as on a continuum, in which, I would agree, introjection never entirely disappears. If you and I have conferences, there'd be some kind of mutual introjective processes going on. But they will be of a very low grade in intensity and importance as compared with the exchange of ideas as such.

Langs: This is an area I've tried to investigate carefully, and, on the basis of my findings, I would say that they are, as a rule, not of low grade importance. My impression, clinically, is that they make a significant contribution to all adult interactions; they continue to supplement cognitive processes. This issue comes up in the literature when object relationships and narcissistic development are discussed. You know, Kohut (1971, 1977) believes that there is a series of transformations in the narcissistic realm that unfolds with maturation. And some have taken issue with him, though I don't see a solid basis for their criticism. Goldberg (1976) defended Kohut.

Stone: Well, with what did they take issue? With the fact that he regards this as a separate development, not continuous with object relations?

Langs: They criticized his notion of separate development. Goldberg had an interesting answer which I had not heard before, and I think it makes some sense. He said, "Look, aggression and sexuality interact all the time; yet, for theoretical purposes and for analytic study, you do separate them to some degree." This is the spirit of Kohut's writings. I had always been critical of the separate development notion too.

Stone: So have I. But I do think it's a very interesting contribution.

Langs: Right. When it's put that way—that they're isolating it more for study and they acknowledge interaction—I think one can hardly begin to split hairs. But they also took issue with the concept of a maturational sequence for narcissistic needs and expressions, and I can't see any basis for that. Goldberg (1976), of course, said that he felt that there is a maturational process in the narcissistic sphere.

Now, the same would occur, to get back to our main discussion, I think the same developmental unfolding occurs in the cognitive sphere, with its own characteristics, of course. In the course of a successful analysis, there is, in the patient, a growing, cognitive sophistication, the development of new and richer insights, growing conscious understanding and capacity for verbal communication. But accompanying this maturational sequence is a parallel and interrelated maturation in the realm of introjective processes, which initially are characteristically more primitive. In the course of an analysis they too mature, involve clearer self-object distinctions, fewer distortions, and more sophistication.

At the end of my book (Langs, 1976b), having written a good deal about interaction, I stated that analysts who write about interaction are criticized for overlooking the important role of interpretation and reconstruction in analysis, and that this was not my own intention. I believe you cannot have a successful interpretive-reconstructive experience without a positive, introjective interaction. Nor, in my opinion, can you have with the analyst—and this is an issue that comes up in our discussion—a successful, positive introjective experience without an analyst who is offering definitive interpretations and reconstruction. So I feel that one relies on the other, that they go hand in hand.

Stone: Yes. That they coexist, and that the one is never entirely abolished, and that it forms a part of the important adult relationships, I think, is true, and is even a part of folklore, just as the way husband and wife begin to be like one another in some respects in old folk observations. It doesn't always happen, but sometimes its very striking. A certain amount of mutual identification in its highest development occurs. And sometimes it occurs just as a mechanism of understanding; you know what the patient is experiencing by empathy, which requires a benign introjective process. But the thing that I would emphasize is this: that in the analytic process, there is a gradual replacement of the primitive mechanisms by the special functions of speech and cognitive understanding. As I see the continuum of coexistence and interaction of these processes, it would be very well epitomized in a specific sector by Money-Kyrle's paper (1956) which highlighted the introjective processes that occur in the analyst when the analyst's understanding fails. For example, in the ordinary sense: when he doesn't know what is happening in his patient, then he is liable to introject the patient. In other words, there will be an automatic regression to the more primitive process. And he describes the fairly complex series of possible, mutual, introjective and projective processes between patient and analyst, phenomena that may occur when the regular process of understanding and its communication fails. (Of course, one should consult the paper for details.) Now, that I would see as demonstrating very vividly the continued existence (if often latent) of the introjective process. Indeed, the analyst (thus, the analysis) may get stuck in such a process, unless or until communicable understanding is established.

Langs: Yes. What I feel he was describing there is a pathological form of introjection.

Stone: Yes, it's a regressive phenomenon.

Langs: A regressive form, which can be utilized to understand the patient, if one recognizes it.

Stone: Utilized, if the analyst can develop communicable, good insight into what is happening.

Langs: Becomes aware of it—which may be difficult, because it is an unconscious process. However, I think that here you're bringing up the other side of the analytic experience: what goes on within the analyst. I think, and this is based, of course, on the paper by Fleiss (1942), that certain introjective processes are inherent in the empathic functioning of the analyst, processes that he will, one should hope, repeatedly utilize in a nonpathological way throughout his analytic work.

Stone: That's what I had in mind in my earlier remark. And it's used through all adult life, in varying degrees.

Langs: And it remains there. You see, when I wrote *The Technique of Psychoanalytic Psychotherapy* (Langs, 1973, 1974), I included a chapter on forms of confirmation, because there was so little literature on what should be a crucial aspect of our work: defining what constitutes confirmation of an intervention. I identified various forms of validation, much of it on a cognitive level, in terms of the modification of repressive defenses and the emergence of new material. And I also found that at times confirmation could take the form of derivatives related to—or indications of—a kind of positive introjection or identification, as I called it then, with the therapist or analyst. But I discovered as I became more interested in interaction that it is really characteristic that if you make a correct interpretation, confirmation occurs in both spheres almost all of the time. That is, in the cognitive sphere you get new, really fresh, unexpected material, not just some bit of repetitition, but something that really permits a new integration of old stuff. In addition, somewhere along the line, the patient's response will include an indication of what I call a positive, introjective identification with the helpful therapist or analyst; characteristically, he will talk about some positive figure, some positive experience, even some asset of his own. In other words, you can really see the response in both realms—cognitive and interactional—in terms of derivative communication.

Stone: I have no doubt that that occurs. But that ultimately the process of understanding, as such, replaces certainly the pathological or primitive introjective phenomena. It utilizes the energies hitherto bound in these fixed and primitive mechanisms. In the course of this dynamic economic shift, the benign and useful multiple-function aspects of introjection—for example—are also freed of conflictual burdening. Instead of the inevitably frustrated, usually guilty wish to swallow the object (not to speak of devouring him), a viable, potential psychological process is established, compounded at first of primitive sensory impressions, later predominately the visual and auditory sphere, and ultimately the entire complex of human associative and integrative thought. This may lead to transitory empathic experience ("regression in the service of the ego"), or to the complex, relatively permanent phenomena of identification. Thus, I would agree that there is an important connection between successful interpretation in the transference and augmentation of the benign introjective capacity, pari passu, and in a dynamic economic relationship.

Langs: Yes, what you're saying is in keeping with something that I have also said in a way, that as far as I can tell—and this is an area that I'm still actively studying—there are definite limitations to the helpful effects of these positive introjects. Let me elaborate a bit. One clinical problem, one issue in technique that no one, as far as I know, has studied—and I have suggested that we have to look at it very carefully—is the relationship between the two realms, the interactional-introjective and interpretive-cognitive. What does each sphere contribute to structural change? My impression is the following, and perhaps you have some thought on it. Number one, that adaptive inner changes derived from one sphere can spread into the other; that cognitive understanding can merge into identificatory processes, and identificatory processes include a certain amount of understanding, so there isn't, as I said before, a total separation. And secondly—and this, I think, is crucial, particularly to nonanalytic therapies: that the positive identifications depend on the analyst's capacity to interpret and reconstruct. That's his central function, and on some level, the patient expects it. If he fails in that, in any kind of therapy, the patient's introjection will be incomplete, and even damaged.

Stone: Well, it will be based, on his side, on his original, as I would have it, primordial transferences. To the extent that the merger, or fusion, or incorporative tendencies remain in the ascendancy, both the translation into word-symbols and memories on the one hand, and the residual freeing of benign introjective processes of their conflictual burdening, on the other, will be impeded. That the analyst must provide most of the cognitive wherewithal for this exchange, in the light of an evolving transference relationship, goes without saying. I view speech, as you have noted, I'm sure, as one of the vehicles for replacement of and the (ultimately) willing renunciation of the need for merger, or fusion, or incorporation, or symbiosis (depending on the quality and degree) with the object. Speech is the alternative bridge. The analyst in effect extends the use of speech and the cognition that is intimately associated with it into the specific form and function of interpretation. Let us take the most simple paradigm of all: the oedipus complex, the classical incestuous complex. I would view it, and this of course involves my own as yet idiosyncratic view of these things.

Langs: Not entirely.

Stone: . . . that the incest complex is in itself an expression of the irredentist need to remain in close apposition to the original object, simply in terms of the particular phase-specific attitude of that time. That this is a way of getting back to mother in relation to certain biological pleasure capacities of the period and in the form provided by that phase. Then, ultimately, this can be translated into the terms of a wish that can be represented psychologically, in words, more and more genuinely, and the inappropriateness of the wish to the person's current needs and the ethical standards and other related matters which provide a context in which he lives can be demonstrated. The patient will gradually accept that and the available modes of relatedness with other objects that can be mediated by it, instead of the original wish. Also, the crystalization or precipitation of memory—whether by recollection or reconstruction—will permit the same adult processes to be brought to bear on the experience of early childhood. And he can then stand off and, in verbal terms, think of this as something he wanted as a little boy, that is no longer appropriate to the present; further, he can understand and relinquish the infantile modes of thought which alone made such ambition tenable at the time, in addition to their own exigent power.

Of course, the process by which he achieves that insight, or which renders him willing to accept it, will be very complicated, because obviously it will depend to some extent on the evolving relationship with the analyst. And that, I'm sure, includes introjective phenomena in itself. I mean, in the sense of Sterba's (1934) early paper, concerning the identification of the observing portion of the ego with the analyst. I don't question that these processes go on. But they go on, I think, in a different sense and general mode from, let's say, what happens in a boy who identifies himself with his mother because he can't have her as a sexual object and cannot relinquish his wish for her. He must submit to the tyrannical power of his father, as he sees it, but then instead of renouncing her he incorporates her, and *becomes* his mother. Once again, he may be confronted with the same tyrant, but in a different context! And all of this occurs, in a sense, willy-nilly in response to sheer inveterate drive requirements. So I think there are places here where one can state a sense of difference in terms of broad categories, and yet agree that the processes (granting differences in form) are never mutually, absolutely exclusive.

Langs: Yes, I think there's more agreement between us than it seemed at first. To restate it in a very condensed way, what you're describing then is a process of working through toward adaptive mastery, toward renunciation, toward the resolution of the unconscious fantasies and memories that are pathological—the pathological residue. What you've added to my own thinking is the idea that without interpretation and reconstruction, the indentificatory processes will remain largely in the realm of pathological processes.

Stone: Largely.

Langs: That is, first, they will not lead to the development of more adaptive or healthier identifications. Secondly, my empirical observations indicate that not only do these identificatory processes, in their most adaptive sense, rely on the analyst's capacity to interpret and reconstruct—this is what you're saying, too—but that there are limitations to what identifications, in themselves, can contribute to adaptive mastery.

Stone: Sure.

Langs: My impression, in general, is that positive introjective identifications afford the patient a kind of general ego strength, but not the definitive tools to master specific conflicts; these can come only from specific interpretive insights. I believe that is really another way to express what you're saying.

Stone: Yes, that is. You see, I had thought of it in an oversimplified paradigm: that the interpretation is an extended, elaborated, special version of the child learning to speak. That this is a mode of contact, let's say, originally, with his mother, which enables some distance and substitutes for the immediate bodily contact that at first is so essential. Now, of course, for some children, there is objection to this—objection to the physical removal, and objection to the substitute which is offered. That doesn't mean that some people who can attain extreme verbal fluency because of certain constitutional capacities may not still be among the people who have never attained the real and viable state of separation. In those instances, the capacity for speech (sometimes torrential) remains too largely a mode of oral-auditory contact (faute de mieux) at the expense of its other functions. Sometimes, as in "flight of ideas," there is a desperate reaction against a depressive trend to mutism. One has to deal with speech both as an autonomous, biologically given capacity and a special function that it may serve for a given individual. In general, I would be in essential agreement with your last remarks, although I must always enter the pithy reservation that no interpretation, however canny, will ever effect the revisions of which we speak if the basic affective relationship between analyst and patient is unsatisfactory.

Langs: This becomes your paradigm, then—cognitive matura-tion. Now, we have to introduce one other factor to round out this discussion: we've talked about the introjective mode, but we haven't said anything about the projective mode. And that's interesting in itself. It seems to me that it's much easier to conceptualize the role of introjective processes than projective processes. I think classical analysts would acknowledge that introjective processes are very crucial to both empathy and cognitive understanding, although they are very wary on the issue. Rangell (1968, 1969), for example, played down the role of any interactional factor except an identification with the analyst in terms of his analyzing function. And Annie Reich (1960), too, said something similar. But then, what of projective processes?

Stone: But the other occurs, of course, all the time.

Langs: Which, now?

Stone: Identifications with the analyst beyond his analyzing function.

Langs: Right—and I can't see how you can write them off. I think you have to take them into account and recognize the positive contribution they make, and the ways in which they may also contribute to resistances as well.

Stone: Certainly.

Langs: I would stress here that an analyst should not rely on introjective processes, because they can be based on a pathological idealization and on what I call a *misalliance* (Langs, 1975a, 1976a,b), a narcissistic kind of a collusion. Many a patient is willing to introject aspects of his analyst in order to avoid dealing with his conflicts, anxieties, and terrifying introjects and inner self. There can be very intense pathological uses of introjection. It is not solely a constructive mechanism.

But then there is the problem of projective processes, which I think is an interesting issue, because for the Kleinian analyst, as I understand it, projective processes, particularly in the form of projective identification—which I'll attempt to define somewhat—along with the counterpart, which I would call introjective identification, are considered to be the basic interactional mechanisms in the analytic relationship.

Stone: Introjection and projective identification?

Langs: Yes, they see projective identification as the basic interactional mechanism, as fundamental to the psychoanalytic process. Now, if we start off by getting rid of certain immediate, obvious problems—for example, if we don't assume that there are parallel processes in both subject and object. But let's start with a definition. As I understand it, projective identification—*interactional projection* as I prefer to call it—is a mechanism that is utilized from the very earliest months of life, even before self-object differentiation, and its basic action consists of taking some part of what's inside of you, and placing it, either in fantasy or in actuality, into the object, into a container, as Bion (1977) has written recently.

Stone: It can't be in actuality, it must be in fantasy, unless the object responds to it—a sort of folie à deux.

Langs: In my view, projective identification, to distinguish it from projection, always entails actual interactional pressures. Now, in addition, the object, the recipient, is open to his or her response; that is, the object may accept these contents or may repudiate them. Most of the time, most people, most patients, most analysts, are receptive to projective identifications. I've seldom seen it otherwise.

I've studied something the Kleinians have hardly considered: the analyst's and the therapist's pathological projective identifications into the patient. The Kleinians almost always see this process as being initiated by the patient. It turns out, of course, that it can begin with either party. I've seen only one or two occasions when the material from the patient indicated to me the patient was refusing to contain—was refractory to—the pathological projective identifications of the analyst. But most human beings are open to projective identifications. Now, this is a mechanism that apparently begins as an omnipotent fantasy, and then becomes a kind of interactional mode. That's how I would distinguish it from projection. That is, as I see it, projection is basically an intrapsychic process, in which you attribute something inside of yourself to someone else.

Stone: Yes, that's the basic conception.

Langs: Now, what is projective identification? Well, the term *identification* is used differently there from the way we normally use it. Usually identification is introjective in its mode: I identify with you; I take in something from you. Projective identification means, "I put something of myself into you, with which I remain identified." It also implies evoking an identification with me in you. It's unfortunate that they use that word. Melanie Klein, of course, did in her paper on schizoid mechanism (Klein, 1946). But, it means two things. It means I place a part of myself into you that I remain identified with, and that . . .

Stone: You then react to me as if I accepted that.

Langs: Yes, and I am attempting to invoke in you an identification with me. I'm going to put into you something that will enable you to identifiy with me, to experience on some level something that I'm experiencing. Martin Wangh's 1962 paper on the evocation of a proxy, which we discussed earlier, is, I think, really another description of projective identification. I have suggested calling it "interactional projection" instead, to emphasize that there is some actual effort to stir something up in the other person, to place certain moods, states, even fantasies, into the other individual. Hanna Segal (1967) emphasizes that aspect; much of it has to do with attempting, as Wangh points out, to evoke adaptive responses—trying to manage an inner problem outside of oneself, through someone else, where it can be handled in another way, not available to the subject. The concept, as originally stated by the Kleinians, stressed the notion of placing good parts into another person for safekeeping and placing bad parts into someone else in order to get rid of them. Wangh (1962) pointed out that there's an adaptive element too, that you often place these parts into another person to see if they can help you adapt to your own inner struggle.

Stone: Well, these are extensions of the original idea of projective identification. And I have no doubt that occasionally people respond and lend themselves to these roles. But the basic idea would be, that I'm going to react to you as if you were what I put into you or, as if you had those traits. It remains intrapsychic, in the individual. For example, in the analytic situation, some of the transference mechanisms occur that way. Some of the phenomena, for example, that would be regarded as parts of the narcissistic transference—what they call the "mirror transference"—would be phenomena of that general class. "I see, you have the same taste as I do, probably you like French movies, Impressionist paintings, classical music. I have that feeling that you're the same kind of person as I am," and so on. Perhaps Ferenczi's old emphases (1909) on the role of introjection in transference would be relevant: what is projected onto the analyst is an early introject. You know, it could range from relatively benign, unimportant specifications of that sort all the way up to very serious and important deficits or distortions of character and attitudes. But, with regard to something that's closer to the phenomenology you've been mentioning, not too long ago, I was reading some of Bowlby's material about loss, about childhood loss and mourning (1963). And there, one of the several mechanisms of solution, for example, is to find somebody who can be oneself, so to speak, as the grieving one, and then take care of the person and comfort him. So that would be an example of the utilization of "projective" identification for defense, of a relatively adaptive sort. I mean, only relatively. If a person evades his own, possibly very serious, mourning that way, in the long run it won't usually hold up. Mourning "has to be mourned," sooner or later. But he mentions that as one very important mechanism for warding off even the fact of loss. And that, I think, one sees in everyday life not too seldom.

Langs: I want to make two points about what you said. First of all, I'll just mention a paper that Sandler (1976) wrote. Classical analysts, I think, are moving toward interaction, and the next ten years will bring very significant contributions, without discarding the id and what is intrapsychic; now there are ego psychology, object relationships, and interaction. Sandler (1976) calls one aspect of this sphere "the evocation of roles." He insists that this is different, and I think that he's right, from projective identification.

Stone: You mean, the actual evocation of the role in the other person. In other words, the "other" must participate to provide the materialization?

Langs: Yes, that's where it gets interesting. Sandler (1976) was talking about the analytic relationship. Freud said, in "Remembering, Repeating, and Working Through" (1914) and elaborated in *Beyond the Pleasure Principle* (Freud, 1920), that the patient will try to have the analyst condemn him as his father had, and all of that. Sandler (1976) pointed out that this is translated into attempts to evoke responses in the analyst that actually gratify unconscious transference wishes and confirm the patient's unconscious introjects, the pathological introjects. He calls that the *evocation of roles.* There is a prior literature in that area (see Langs, 1976b). The Kleinians do imply something that is a bit different, though it is all related to actuality on some level. Again, it's this transition that I find classical analysts have some difficulty in making—distinguishing between having a fantasy which distorts your perception of another person so that you react to him in an inappropriate way, and actually doing something in order to place into him some inner content or state, which is more than simply evoking a role response. The way that works becomes very elusive—it begins to sound mysterious, almost as if it is magical thinking, though it is not.

Stone: But that is the phenomenon of acting out, in a way; it's certainly related to acting out. Furthermore, as you mention, a great deal of this was actually specified by Freud. So, like many other things, it's a matter of "old wine in new bottles." True, the mechanisms are probably more complicated than we have thought—at least as implied by our simplistic semantics about them. (This is true

of the whole field of transference, from the beginning.) Surely there is
a difference between transference-wish or fantasy and its materialization—to whatever degree? You recall Nunberg's (1951) distinction
between "transference readiness" and "transference" (when the materialization occurs in the form of the transference illusion). In this
reference, I demurred to the significance of his distinctions in my
own paper (Stone, 1967). Many of these distinctions of mechanisms
have to do with how the ego handles the exigencies of drives in
general, although, in fact, closer to the origins of these functional
interrelationships. Beyond transference illusion, of course, is the
actual "evocation" of the role in the other person, or something
supporting the subject's illusion. We saw that as an ephemeral
fragment in the case of the young woman, mentioned earlier, who
drove me to a display of irritation about an alternative appointment.
There are people who imagine what they need in others, those who
(especially in a masochistic sense) can evoke certain necessary reactions, and those who, by sheer interpersonal charisma, can force or
seduce certain suitable objects into the mold they require.

Langs: Leon Grinberg (1962) discussed the issue specifically. It's
hard to grasp without clinical data, but what he said, for example, is
that in situations where the patient projectively identifies into the
analyst on a massive scale, there is the danger of his being over-
whelmed and massively reprojecting back into the patient without
conscious understanding. He calls the process "projective counteridentification." In *The Bipersonal Field* (Langs, 1976a), I attempted
to provide documentary evidence, clinical material that reflects
projective identifications.

Stone: You mean, to document the materialization of it in the
sense that you were mentioning, not just the fantasy of materialization?

Langs: Materialization of it in the actual clinical interaction. After
I finished my technique books (1973, 1974) and while I was assem-
bling the material for *The Therapeutic Interaction* (1976b), I began,
under pressure of clinical findings, and through a study of the
therapeutic alliance and misalliance, as we earlier discussed, to look
into interaction. It's interesting to ask: "Where, for a classical

analyst, does interaction arise, as an issue?" It doesn't come up especially with transference, because he thinks of that as essentially intrapsychic. But it does come up in the very term "alliance," if not so much in the original concept. We know there's a transference component to the therapeutic alliance, but we tend to play it down. Well, coming to interaction through the alliance as I did, and seeing the alliance as that aspect of the analytic interaction that is geared toward insight for the patient, I found, clinically, that there are interactions that are constructed not toward the development of insight, but toward some kind of pathological reinforcement of defenses or gratification for the patient, and to some degree for the analyst. I called those *therapeutic misalliances* (Langs, 1974, 1975a, 1976a,b), and for reasons that are still unclear to me, I've been criticized by some classical analysts for that idea. Greenson told me that he thought the term was an excellent one.

Stone: I don't see anything wrong, a priori. It states succinctly what can happen, and sometimes does happen.

Langs: It happens more often than many analysts acknowledge. In any event, I was simultaneously wrestling with these ideas, collecting clinical data; in going through the literature I came across the papers from the first Pan-American Congress. Litman edited them in 1966—*Psychoanalysis in the Americas.* I found there a paper by the Barangers on the idea, new to me, of the bipersonal field. The Barangers are Kleinians, and their paper put projective identification into the center of the analytic interaction. I remember writing in my notes, why *projective identification?* Why not just *projection?* Why do we need something more? Why interactional mechanisms? In other words, I could not really comprehend it when I first began to read about it. I think that this experience typifies how the classical psychoanalyst reacts to this concept. I was very struck with the fact that you mention projective identification in *The Psychoanalytic Situation* (Stone, 1961), only briefly, but it was a concept that at least you had some idea about.

Stone: It's a concept that, even now, puzzles me a little bit, bothers me, because there is something in the term that's intrinsically confusing. A projection is a projection. An identification implies something that happens in the subject, and yet, it is meant to convey the idea that it happens, somehow, in the object. So it is confusing in its very nature, and yet it means something that probably is useful. Perhaps it has a somewhat more holistic significance than "projection" as we ordinarily conceive of it. We say, "See, I'm very hostile to you, and I'm unaware of that but I keep feeling that you're hostile, persecutory toward me." Or whatever earlier sexual vicissitudes may be involved in that. That's undoubtedly projection, but you see, if I'm a fellow who suffers an irreparable loss and persists in denying its importance and keeping up a cheerful front, and I picked you up somewhere because you momentarily had a sad look in your face, and decided that you need my care and supervision and consolation, that's different, in the sense that the identification has something more to do with a whole person, involved in a total and profound experience. But I don't know if that's what you have in mind.

Langs: Allow me to extend what you just said because you're very close. It concerns me greatly, I say it to you very directly, that many classical analysts have not been willing to struggle with this concept. They have rejected it out of hand, unfortunately, though some are now beginning to consider it.

Stone: Yes, because they know there is something potentially useful in it.

Langs: Secondly, I think you have to extend the idea further. You say, I come to you with my sad look; that could be a projection, but it also could be an actuality. In that case, your focus on my sad face carries little fragments of your depression, your sadness. You know, you just said something that is absolutely crucial. I described it in a very formal way in *The Bipersonal Field* (Langs, 1976a).

Stone: Something that excites the idea of a potentiality there.

Langs: Of a potentiality. The container concept (Bion, 1977; Langs, 1976a,b) comes in, because you're looking for somebody to contain your depression. That metaphor seems to make sense in the context of what you're saying. The "container" metaphor of Bion's was a telling stroke; it's one that can be used very well. In your example, you noticed my sad look and unconsciously you realized that I can be a container for your depression. I'm actually inviting that, by conveying to you something of my own underlying depressive constellation. This brings up a point about projective identification. We don't just projectively identify into the world; we really look for available people.

Stone: We look for a suitable object, of course.

Langs: People who are suitable, who invite contents and wish to contain. And this is part of every interaction; it goes on all the time. In marriages, with one's children, projective identification is a significant human interactional mechanism. It has levels of maturation; it ranges from omnipotent fantasies to much more mature forms that are quite adaptive.

Stone: That's a very important point, you see, because there may be people who are so ill, and who, in terms of the relative importance of drive and reality, allow the cognitive sphere and judgment relatively little place. That is, anybody will do. As an absurd extreme: you walk in and see a healthy, cheerful, bustling person, and say "God, you look sad today! Can I do something for you?" Or, "Talk to me, I'll be your friend." That would be a really sick example. But the other that you mention sometimes is, or can be, a *relatively* mature thing: to find someone who might potentially need this help and in whom this "need of the subject" can be "deposited," which will then serve as a defense against your awareness of your loss, your need for mourning, or your depression, as the case may be. It isn't satisfactory in the long run, as we agreed, in relation to the simple phenomenon of mourning. It won't do, because in the long run a person has to mourn and work through his grief and—as I recall Bowlby's view (1963)—his anger and his irredentist wish for the object's return. But, no doubt there are differences in how adaptively and appropriately it may be done. For some, it may provide a relatively viable character pattern for a long time. If you pick out some unfortunate kid who really needs help, it may work out excellently, at least for the kid.

Langs: Yes. One develops a symbiosis, which Bion described. What one finds is that, in general, more primitively fixated patients, who are more toward the nonneurotic end of the scale, tend to utilize more primitive forms of projective identification, and to use it more massively and more frequently.

Stone: More massively, and with an omnipotent disregard of reality.

Langs: Yes, Bion (1977) makes an interesting point: that what's really crucial about the development of the individual is whether he attempts to actualize his omnipotent fantasies of projective identification, or does not do so. He feels that those individuals who do not carry them into reality are the ones who eventually become psychotic.

Stone: The ones who do not?

Langs: Yes, who do not, who disregard reality, maintain the omnipotent fantasies, and don't tend to place them into the mother. They do not tolerate the frustration involved. It gets very complicated, and his books are really very difficult, I find. I mention this to you because he has worked over this concept in some very interesting ways.

But you see, this concept, clinically considered, places the analyst in a little different position regarding his subjective experiences, because he begins to realize that those experiences are not just a matter of empathy, that at times in the analytic interaction the patient is attempting to stir up and place into him a certain kind of state or mood or unconscious fantasy, and that helps him to clarify and understand his own—and the patient's—inner state. In the end, it all gets translated into an interpretation.

In any event, I continued to read the Kleinian literature, because I needed an interactional language, and that was where they were and are. And little by little I began to understand the concept of projective identification—at least I have a version of it that I think can be validated. The papers that helped most were Malin and Grotstein (1966), and Hanna Segal's (1967) paper on the Kleinian position.

Now Segal takes the example of a mother, who is, let's say, agitated, and depressed. Now, she has two children and they're in a playroom. They start to play with some toys, and she takes the toys away from them. She says, you can't play with those toys. She doesn't come at them directly, she doesn't communicate *verbally* something of her mood: she just takes these toys away. The communication is in her behavior. The children go to the blackboard, and they start writing on the blackboard. Don't mess up the room, she says, and she takes the blackboard away. They go to some other toys, or whatever; she takes those away. Well, by the end of that morning, these two children are in a state of agitation, depressed, hurt, and they're in a frenzy. Now she either spanks them, scolds them, or forgives them. She talks to them and soothes them or she punishes them.

In any case, I think this is a nice illustration of projective identification. The mother takes her inner agitation and finds interactional ways of placing it into her children. And it's important that we see that it was not done through projection, by intrapsychically attributing something within herself to her children. In *The Bipersonal Field* (Langs, 1976a), I offered examples where there is projection of inner contents, while the interactional projection takes an entirely different form.

Stone: No, that's quite apparent. From what you say, she actually produces a state in the children resembling her own by her specific impact on them, by her morbid maneuvers, whether or not planned or purposive. Now this may indeed represent her pathological need, and, in her experience, may represent a materialization of what is suggested by the term "projective identification." But in the children, in that specific situation, there is certainly no projective element, and not necessarily an identification. They may simply react directly to mother's neurotic behavior. Nor is the mother's behavior necessarily the need to put something in them, as opposed to some simpler conceptualization of her abuse of them for certain specific morbid reasons of her own. The "container" idea is of course engaging, like many other concepts derived from physical or mechanical metaphors, but by the same token arouses in me an a priori skepticism.

Langs: These matters are too abstract to be convincing in the absence of clinical data. To continue the line of thought, if I may, the mother actually tries to produce a state in her children—they are free to accept it or not, and to respond in keeping with their own needs and fantasies—but if they do take it in, she then manages it outside herself in a way in which she handles the children, feeling some degree of relief. Kleinians feel that there is also some degree of depletion when you get rid of a projective identification. I myself begin to wonder; when the image gets too concrete I have lots of questions.

Stone: Would Segal imply that that is projective identification, or a somewhat different phenomenon?

Langs: That it is projective identification.

Stone: I mean, if the mother came in and said to the children who were being relatively quiet, just behaving normally as children do when they're playing, and said, "Oh, what is disturbing you today, you can't seem to sit still and you look so unhappy? Is something bothering you? Can't you sit still and think some nice thoughts?" That I can see might be projective identification (with her own experience)—but the other?

Langs: Well, let's start with that for a moment. That's projection, as I define it. Initially, it's projection: attributing to the children her own inner state.

Stone: But, as I have suggested, in its more extensive sense of their suffering a phenomenon that she is suffering . . .

Langs: Yes, but you'd have to add something about the way in which she actually does it: she suddenly surprises her children with this communication

Stone: A form of drive distortion of cognition, you see.

Langs: I think that would be seen primarily as projection, though it could extend into a projective identification. If she keeps insisting to the kids that they are upset, even if they don't feel upset at first, pretty soon, they're going to be upset. Your example needs that added factor to make the transition from projection to projective identification.

Stone: I'll admit, though, that it still could be regarded as projection in its broadest sense. Yet "creating" the materialization could be a side effect of other motivations, conscious or unconscious. That it may, in the end, satisfy an urge for "projective identification," given a compliant object, is also true.

Langs: But if it is translated into an actual attempt to create the inner state in the children, then it becomes, in addition, projective identification. Now, in Segal's (1967) example, where the mother never says to the kids, "You look agitated," where she never attributes to them cognitively or verbally her own inner state—never feels they are depressed or sad, and yet creates that state in them through her behaviors —that would be placing into them a part of herself, a bad part of herself—we're using "bad" in a very wide sense—a disturbed part of herself, that she's still identified with, that she has evoked now in them, in the object, an identification with her.

Stone: That is the way "they" would use it. And it must materialize to fulfill the requirement. How would it apply to the analytic situation? Let's think of the analyst, in the ideal, originally abstract sense; he is continuously an analyst and "just analyzes." He shows no special mood manifestations. But the patient keeps talking about the analyst being in a very depressed mood. Yes, the patient thinks, he does handle it well, and it is quite remarkable how he keeps his appointments, hour to hour, and day to day, and seems to interpret quite intelligently and yet there's a strong feeling, which the patient can't shake, that the analyst is deeply depressed. There is, of course, material which indicates the patient's strong latent depression, against which he defends himself by this mechanism. And this I can understand is projective identification, rather than uncomplicated projection, because I think of projection as a primitive defense mechanism, having to do with certain specific drives, or at least drive-motivated elements, like a persecutory idea, or the less specific attribution of anger or hostility, occasionally even erotic attitudes. This is different from an identification which makes the person take on traits which characterize the subject, including his suffering. That I would think of as projective identification, to the extent that I can make conceptual sense of the term, and differentiate it from projection. I may be wrong. It is the untolerated portion of the "self" rather than a drive.

Langs: Let me extend your example again, because I think you are still essentially describing a projection, not of a persecutory element, but of a depressive element. Now, let's take it this way. This patient is saying that the analyst is depressed. It's an aside, but the analyst would have first to determine whether this is a valid, conscious perception.

Stone: We take it for granted that the analyst is just being himself, doing his work, and even feeling fine that day.

Langs: Okay. He's working with this patient, and the patient keeps telling him that he's depressed. And the analyst interprets one aspect of the depression and then another, from the patient's material, but the patient does not accept any of the interpretations. He keeps conveying his belief that the analyst is depressed. This goes on for one week, two weeks, three weeks. Pretty soon the analyst realizes he's getting nowhere at all with this patient; he can't do anything right; he can't reach this patient; he begins to feel depressed.

Stone: Well, that may be his introjection, in the sense of Money-Kyrle (1956) which we mentioned before. Although, of course, he may become depressed on the basis of any of several other mechanisms.

Langs: That's an introjection.

Stone: Of a patient with depressions?

Langs: Okay, and in this language, that is an introjection, an introjective identification with the projective identification of the patient. This is now inside the analyst. Now what the analyst does with it then becomes crucial, because he can do any of the following: he can experience that depression in a controlled way, and then interpret it to the patient, and there would be additional, clarifying associations to make it more specific, but he would point out that the patient has a wish to have him depressed in actuality.

Stone: Well, this may have started at the very beginning, long before he got depressed. The complementary mechanisms, which you condense quite elegantly, may of course be the fact. But there are many anterior, less complicated, more probable possibilities. There's a point. He might get depressed in Money-Kyrle's (1956) sense, as an introjective phenomenon, because he has failed to see and communicate his patient's transference wish—or indeed, before that, to analyze adequately the structure of his patient's depression. In our own hypothetical case, the patient's wish would be almost too blatant for an intelligent analyst to miss, i.e., that the patient wants or needs that he be depressed. Of course, he could become depressed because of a sense of failure in relation to an unusually exigent ego-ideal. But in any case I do not believe that the analyst's experience can be regarded as the patient's projective identification.

Langs: My view would be that the analyst's experience could be *in part based on* the patient's projective identification. The analyst may experience such a sense of depression initially in what I call, and Olinick (1969) and others have termed, a kind of signal function; that is, he may experience a modicum of the depression that he then utilizes to understand the patient.

Stone: Ordinary empathy, as that has been construed and employed for some time?

Langs: It would be related to empathy and the introjective, projective aspects of it. If the analyst fails to do that, it may become more massive. Grinberg (1962) makes the point that, in response to a massive projective identification—sometimes patients will come in and blatantly evoke a mood in you—that there's a danger, and it's a very common one, of responding by not being aware of what the patient is trying to put into you, but by reprojecting it out, back into the patient, responding in a countertransference way with what Grinberg (1962) calls, for better or worse, *projective counteridentification.* Now, with the inexperienced therapists that I worked with, I observed, and described in *The Bipersonal Field* (Langs, 1976a), what I think are very clear examples of an interchange of this kind, where the patient puts something into the therapist, and the therapist is unaware of it. The therapist's job is to contain it, understand it, metabolize it, as Fleiss (1942) put it—to ultize it to understand the patient, and to interpret. Failing that, where a countertransference problem interferes, sometimes the analyst will refuse to contain the mood or inner contents. He will immediately bounce it back into the patient, alter the frame, or intervene incorrectly to stir up the patient. Sometimes the analyst will take it in, suffer with it, and put it back into the patient. And I have sequences where you can see this kind of exchange, back and forth—the patient putting it into the therapist, the therapist putting that mood back into the patient, the patient putting it back—neither conscious of what is going on interactionally.

Stone: Well, there I would again have the same trouble with the conceptualizations involved, because I really still don't think that one person can put something into the other psychologically, simply because of his own powerful dynamic urge to do so. The other person must react in a complementary way for that to be a functional phenomenon. Furthermore, granting the archaic prototypes in the oral-anal sphere, I think that it is a mechanistic oversimplification to see these massive and complicated interactions as if there were a medicine ball being passed back and forth. Except in very regressed patients the interactions occur in a complex form, with many adult nuances involved.

The analyst can invest the patient with something in his psyche and react to it, as in projection, or in what I would regard as a still acceptable conception of projective identification, if one can genuinely separate it from ordinary projection. When he begins to react as if he were like the patient, then he is introjecting something. And that is his, you might say, active defensive process. He can't handle this patient, something is going on, he regresses and executes a primitive defensive phenomenon. And one would hope, of course, that those are minimal in the analyst who really knows himself and watches himself. But the next stage, in the sense of one person putting it into the other, and the other person putting it back—that I have trouble with.

Langs: That's because I have not completed the picture. What you've said is exactly to the point. To summarize: the object is not a passive victim of the projective identification.

Stone: No, he can't be, with rare folie à deux exceptions, involving complementary personalities (as I mentioned earlier).

Langs: An effort is made by the subject. The object then responds, in keeping with his own needs. His own introjective processes may or may not be mobilized, and they are influenced by his own pathological and nonpathological needs.

Stone: Yes, that's right.

Langs: So the analyst is open to respond to the patient. I am not suggesting a necessity for parallel states at all. Similarly, the patient, as I said earlier, can be open or refractory to the analyst's interactional projection, or he may just shut it out and want no part of it. Kids are much more helpless, but adults can sometimes refuse to introject or contain. Observationally, most often, people are open to this kind of interaction, but it is always stamped with the individuality of the container. And I think this is a valid criticism of the Kleinians: they say little about the recipient. I tried to correct that (Langs, 1976a,b) by pointing out that the total process always has the stamp of the recipient. He has choices, makes contributions, conscious and unconscious.

Stone: It's really only little kids, in that example that you quoted from Hanna Segal, who in a sense are victims of it, because they are so actually dependent on this person.

Langs: And even with them, it is relative, obviously. Certain children may refuse to contain projective identifications.

Stone: Oh yes, some children go off and say, "I don't like the way Mamma is behaving today!" and walk out of the room. But there, admittedly, it is a question of degree. For practical purposes, one would have to admit that children can sometimes be victims of this process. I should mention that by "this process" I mean any process deriving from an important object which seeks to engraft a role on the child. It doesn't have to be a "projective identification," although this as a defensive process may be more frequent than is thought. And yet even then, I'm not so sure that that is often a projective identification, in the strict sense of bringing about its own "materialization," so to speak. The subject's process, the object's process, and the interactional process have to be spearated for study.

To take an oversimplified paradigm: the patient may say, "You're acting like a tyrannical old moralistic son of a bitch in our relationship." And then, when you make some clarifying remark or interpretation, he may say, "Well, after all, on second thought you haven't done anything. I realize that, and this must be something coming from within me." Then you are able to interpret the father transference with good analytic response. This involves a different ego state from that of the patient who suddenly stamps out of the room saying "I won't stay in the room with such a tyrannical bastard. You're no analyst for me!" Or ruminates on his transference grievance all night, oblivious to interventions, to return the next day, seeking to pick a fight with the analyst, to get him to fulfil the ornery role his unconscious demands. There is a difference between the statement of a fantasy, with the willingness to look at it, and the compulsion to bring about in actuality the painful situation of the past. Thus, there may be a projective identification by the patient in analysis, where he says, "You have the same temperament as I have, I can tell it. You're compulsive as hell too, and fret about the tiniest detail." Or he may find in you something from his archaic superego or ego ideal. But he may then stop and think, if he's a nonpsychotic patient, and generally not too sick, and say, "Well, I don't know if there is any particular evidence for that." Of course he won't usually be so quick to do that, you see, but being able to do it is the important issue, with the realistic control of his behavior. Another patient, successful or not, may blindly continue an intensive effort to provoke the analyst to fill his bill. And failing that, create even greater difficulty in his life, and even more formidable resistance to finding the right object outside.

Langs: You mean in terms of the actualization? Some Kleinians, as I understand it, do distinguish between fantasies of projective identification, fantasies of having someone to contain, and their actualization. Again, I think it's just semantics—there are such fantasies, which I think of more as projection, and I think of the efforts at actualization as projective identification.

Stone: Well, I guess the effort must be there, if the term is to justify its separate meaning. Just as there often is such effort in the transference. It's latent, and it's a question of degree, you know, that the patient would want you to "fill the (transference) bill," somehow or other, and if it were possible, there would be that little germ of acting out within the situation, to do or say something that might provoke a response that could be interpreted as excessively rigid, or contemptuous, or something of that sort. The effort is implicit in the analytic situation. I guess that the latent urge toward evocative, if not provocative, action is implicit all the time, in patients' psychoanalytic attitudes. You may remember that Ferenczi and Rank, whom Alexander (1954) referred to in his later work, actually thought that the analyst conceding to some of these hostile-fearful fantasies, as I remember it, could enliven the analytic drama. This, in a sense, was opposite to the later "corrective emotional experience." I must admit that, just as I said at the very beginning, there is something a little puzzling to me in that concept of projective identification, yet I certainly believe that there is something useful in it, and that at times it can describe something that isn't very satisfactorily covered by other terms. But the semantic and conceptual confusions persist—in that a form of interaction between two persons, which may indeed occur, is as it were attributed to the psychic mechanism in one person. This is, of course, different from my own conceptualization. But I didn't coin the term. And I think it's nearer to what they mean, and to what you have been describing.

Langs: Yes. What we're doing opens up the opportunity, at least, to read the Kleinian literature about that issue, without closing one's mind to their use of that concept.

Stone: Oh, that I agree. One has to read, and try to understand. Do you know that in England I met an Indian analyst at the last Congress in London—a Kleinian? He sent me one of his papers (Amrith, 1975), a Kleinian paper, on projective identification. He was very much taken with the conception and its importance.

Langs: Really, all that I'm attempting to do is to open up a dialogue. You know that in general the direction is quite the opposite. The divergence between classical and Kleinian analysts seems to be growing greater, and there needs to be a rapprochement. You and I, certainly, would continue to feel that certain Kleinian concepts are not especially useful or valid, and I question certain

Kleinian techniques, but that needn't mean an outright rejection of all of their observations and formulations.

Stone: Well, I would emphatically agree that some of their concepts are definitely useful, at the very least, in one important sense. They should be thought about and explored, like these matters that we're talking about. They do deal with an archaic sphere, which we are prone to dismiss. They have created what seems to me a special "language" for it—which they, of course, regard as more than a language, rather, a description of facts and phenomena. Some of the concepts may, indeed, have more in them than meets the eye. They tend to elicit, in the non-believer, some a priori objection, like these internal good and bad objects, and the reciprocal behavior in relation to them, and the very complicated and varied processes of introjection and projection that they describe for them. Even there, there may be something more in these ideas or behind them than we are ready to acknowledge, although the a priori reaction to them is, "This is too strange, this is beyond verification, this is a system whereby the analysts' fantasies are being engrafted onto the patient," and so on. Those things I still view with a certain distance, and a certain (intellectual) suspicion that they may not be specific, in the long run. And certainly from what I've heard and read of some of their techniques, I feel a strong sense of rejection, as if these things were quite remote, quite strange to me, without intelligible rationale in any frame of reference. But that one should listen and read, and try to understand, is certainly an important responsibility.

Langs: And possibly learn. It turned out that in *The Bipersonal Field* (Langs, 1976a)—and this was not my particular intention, but I really attempted to document it—some of these concepts can be validated, clinically. The other mechanism that the Kleinians stress —and I have not really studied this especially, though Kernberg (1975) has to some extent—is splitting.

Stone: Oh, splitting. Well, Kernberg certainly uses that to the extreme degree in his work with borderlines.

Langs: I had an example yesterday, which I thought was really splitting par excellence. It came from a patient with a very serious physical illness, who was being reported to me in supervision. What this patient said was, "I have the illness, and I know it. But what you don't understand is that I also know that I don't have the illness." Just like that—and this is not repression—splitting really seemed an apt way of describing it. She had a whole set of thoughts about having this disastrous illness, but by and large those thoughts were set aside and covered over by another constellation, in which she was able to maintain a series of thoughts in which the notion of being seriously ill did not exist at all, like two separate states of mind. Clearly, there's denial involved.

Stone: Well, there's no question that splitting exists. Whether it is the pervasive and all-important phenomenon, let's say with certain borderlines, I don't know. But that it exists, and that it exists more often in borderlines, I would fully agree. I had a patient who varied on successive days, but could tell me with full, strong affect that I was utterly useless, that I had failed her completely, that her whole analysis was a flop. But she could also tell me after a very short interval, with no apparent sense of incongruity, that she thought I had worked wonderfully; that she had improved marvelously, and further that I was the *only* person who could have done it. Well, perhaps this isn't splitting, in the demonstrable sense that it occurs within a few minutes. But there's no doubt that there were (and are) two utterly different, coexisting conceptions (or images) of me. Oh no, I don't question the usefulness of the idea of splitting, and the importance of it in psychopathology, and of its recognition in the therapeutic process.

Langs: On that note, perhaps we can shift the mood and get back to a little bit of clinical material. I think that through it we can develop in a specific context some of the interactional issues we have been discussing in general terms.

Stone: I still haven't read that case over—my own old published case! I'll have to deal with it as you present it.

Langs: Well, I'm going to offer another segment from the patient with transference sleep neurosis with duodenal ulcer (Stone, 1947). We had discussed one issue related to the frame, and a relevant dream.

Now I want to take a second vignette. I selected this segment because
it too relates to the analytic situation, to the basic ground rules. As I
may have told you, I read everything you wrote, and as I did I selected
some clinical material related to the frame. At a point in your
presentation here regarding this patient's second period of analysis,
you make this statement (Stone, 1947, p. 29): "Of special importance
was the patient's disclosure, after long concealment, with great guilt,
that his earnings had been very large, out of all proportion to the
small fee he was paying, on a partial credit basis."

Now, the "partial credit" comment, as we discussed earlier, caught
my eye, because here was a modification of the frame. I responded as I
had in working with Freud's material (Langs, 1976c, 1978a,b): each
time his presentation indicated a modification of the frame—today's
frame as I define it—I then went to the antecedent material and went
through the subsequent material with the altered frame as the
adaptive context, the context for organizing the material. So, what
I'd like to do with you is go back over the clinical material that
precedes this particular revelation to see what it illuminates.

Stone: Freud, in his earlier work, didn't have a well-defined concept of the frame. The frame evolved and crystallized out of his work.

Langs: I agree. In this instance, let me give you the material that
precedes this allusion to the fee. Your paper really was not written
with the frame in mind, just as Freud did not write his case histories
to illuminate issues of the ground rules, but let's see what the
antecedent material brings out. I'll begin in the middle of your
discussion of this particular phase of the analysis, the interval after
his first return.

Stone: I think he was there on three separate occasions.

Langs: Here, in a single interval visit—he returned after a few
months—depression was the major symptom. I'll summarize. There
were suicidal ruminations; nocturnal wakefulness and "stewing"
were conspicuous, but the stomach pains were relatively in
conspicuous. And then, his depression was quite highly developed.
The sense of defeat and failure in business and analysis was strong.
There were a lot of escape fantasies, especially in the occupational

sphere. There was an element of feminine identification. There was a sense of grievance, reproach, and disappointment about the analysis, but now usually not acknowledged as active anger, except in an occasional sense, in response to persistent interpretations of deep hostilities that were autoplastically implied in the depression, and directed toward the analyst and the patient's siblings. Throughout this period, the struggle was with the symptomatic passivity. There was nocturnal awareness of the inclination to stay home in the morning and just not go to work, and obsessive rumination. He had an unusually frank wish that his parents would die and that he have his full inheritance—that wish came up.

Now, I'll pause here: we see a very strong depressive constellation, intense passive wishes, some reference to anger, and a rather strikingly frank wish that the parents die.

Stone: Striking in this sense, that this man was one of the few examples I have seen of depression, psychosomatic illness, and oral character tendencies, all highly developed in a relatively viable adult. To some extent they were interchangeable, but very often operating simultaneously. It shows how profound in the patient was what people would call the orality.

Langs: This syndrome is one of the reasons that you wrote the paper. You state that the advantages of acquisition by full inheritance over gifts from the living were seriously discussed by the patient. So, here we hear of an inheritance and we hear about gifts.

Stone: I can see your drift.

Langs: To continue: "A urinary urge was frequent with the nocturnal ruminations; there was an occasional impulse to go to the bathroom to drink water; there were occasional headaches or dizziness." And you mention that this dizziness had occurred before. "In general, the stomach-ache soon became the predominant nocturnal problem, with the biphasic obsessive rumination."

"In this period there was more frank expression of diffuse death-wishing envy, hostility, and grasping impulses, the corresponding inhibition and passivity, the objects ranging from wife and parents, through analyst and business associates; there was deeper analytic working through of these attitudes."

"A long period of extreme sexual apathy inevitably evoked more detailed attention to sexual problems. The early (second) operation [that he had had] was recalled more vividly" (Stone, 1947, p. 28).

Stone: I asked if he had a hypospadias, a partial opening at the bottom of the penis. He had a partial hypospadias—although he referred to the operation as his "second circumcision."

Langs: This "was recalled more vividly, with memories of sitting on the pot with a 'big bandage' on his penis. The patient recalled intense pain for two or three days, during which he'd *much rather have suppressed urination.* This came into association with a dream in which he was able to watch his penis through his wife's transparent abdominal wall, as though to reassure himself of its presence. The pain in urination was further associated (by the analyst) with the tears which the patient recalled in his early voluntary mechanical suppression of bladder impulse. Frank sexual comparison and rivalry (genital structure, size and noise of urinary stream) with the father appeared in dream material and childhood memories, as well as their rivalry with his mother in other dreams. The father's attack on the brother also reappeared, and the stated recollection that the patient concealed his interest in his mother from his father thereafter."

It is interesting that a reference to concealing appears in this antecedent material, in the particular context of the fee issue. So whatever we're picking up may well be derivatives related to what you and he were doing at the time, and the material may contain implications related to their influence on his interaction with you, all of which has specific genetic meanings for him, specific genetic antecedents. I stress that point because often students are confused; they say, "Well, if there is a genetic factor, then it must be transference." And they don't recognize that nontransference components, things that are actually happening in the interaction and which are filled with unconscious implications, also have their genetic counterparts.

Stone: Well, also they can be a part of the person's character, you see. He would behave the same way with anybody else. For example, he might very well conceal something in order to get something, whether in the state of active transference or not. Because, in a way, a character structure is an expression in structuralized form of latent, old transferences that have become integrated as part of the ego.

Langs: Right. I'm adding a different dimension: the distinction between a pathological fantasy—a distortion within the analytic relationship, transference—and some level of the actual interaction—a nondistorted aspect. I've already revealed my point by describing what came up later. But we know that he was involved secretly in gratifying certain unconscious transference fantasies in the relationship with you, and you were an inadvertent participant. That actuality also has its unconscious implications and genetic antecedents. That is, genetics do not determine the distinction between current reality and fantasy.

Stone: You mean concealing his interest in his mother from his father? But this is implicit in the psychoanalytic process, all the time. I mean, the gradual revelation of unconscious trends through derivatives.

Langs: I am trying to organize the material around a specific (hidden) adaptive context, to give it immediate dynamic meaning. The patient's intrapsychic propensities are evoked by the actualities of the analytic interaction, and take on unconscious meaning and function accordingly. What I am saying is that he had actualized an aspect of his genetic past in his relationship with you.

Stone: Yes, by concealing something. No doubt about it.

Langs: And the genetic component doesn't determine whether this falls primarily into the realm of transference or nontransference fantasy or actuality—unconscious perceptiveness—or both intermixed. That is, both have a genetic counterpart.

Stone: Right, but that would be a question of, as they say, the person's ego structure, and the corresponding character. Actually, I believe it was not even mentioned in the paper because it might have been too revealing, but a similar deception was going on in his everyday life when he began with me, and had antedated the analysis for a considerable period: getting a striking concession on a "poor-mouth" basis.

Langs: Yes. It would also be a reflection of the nature of the actual interaction between the patient and analyst, on both sides.

Stone: Yes. That would enter of course, but I am not clear about my side of it. Naturally, one deals with the patient's character.

Langs: Okay, so we see how this particular behavior has very highly personalized genetic meanings. And there is the stated recollection that the patient concealed his interest in his mother from his father thereafter. To continue (Stone, 1947, p. 28): "Of childhood or infantile masturbation, only the school-room episode was recalled." In other words, there were some masturbatory components as well. But then we begin to see a whole constellation emerge; we can see the unconscious derivatives, fantasies of punishment, of exciting him.

You go on: "However the memory of his brother's punishment was revived in an hour in which adolescent masturbation was reviewed in some detail. The unconscious offer to reconcile the opposing psychic tendencies was vividly expressed in the dream material in which, for instance, a threatened jibe in a sailboat becomes a normal tack without a change of direction, or even more pointedly and naively in a dream of coitus in which both the patient and his wife are both flat on their backs."

Now, again, I'm narrowing the field of consideration, leaving out a lot of things about the relevant intrapsychic dynamics, transference implications, and the like. I'm attempting to relate this material to a subsequent revelation about the frame.

So he had two dreams. They occur at a point where he's beginning to approach this subject, at least in his own mind. In one, there is a threatened jibe in a sailboat that becomes a normal tack without changing direction.

Stone: You are a sailor, are you?

Langs: No, so I'm asking you what that would mean.

Stone: When you change your tack, or you want to come about, you turn into the wind. He, incidentally, was quite an avid sailor, although not on a large scale, not what you'd call a yachtsman, but he liked to sail a small boat and apparently was fairly expert at it. A tack, coming about, normally is done into the wind. You turn into the wind with the use of your rudder, so that you come about slowly, and the sail gradually fills when you have turned sufficiently. Normally, you change direction by this method. This makes it a gradual thing and the sail fills gradually. A jibe is one in which you turn *with* the wind, instead of into it. Say the wind is coming from this side, and you want to turn around, if you turn that way, you get the full and sudden force of the wind into the sail, and this could be dangerous. It might jerk out all of a sudden and even capsize a small boat. A jibe is sometimes correctly done by highly skilled people for racing purposes, on occasion. Otherwise a jibe is to be avoided as an accident or mishap.

Langs: He said, a threatened jibe in a sailboat becomes a normal tack without change of direction.

Stone: You see, a threatened jibe means that your position is such that the wind may catch you unaware, and turn you in the other direction, swinging the boom, with sudden impact. In the dream, this becomes a normal tack, without changing direction. It's as if the two things have cancelled one another and you're going straight ahead—an effort to handle two conflicting impulses.

Langs: I see. I'm reminded of one thing, which may or may not be pertinent. I remember in *The Psychoanalytic Situation* (Stone, 1961) you used, as an example of what you considered to be a relatively innocuous revelation, acknowledging a knowledge of sailing. Does that imply that this particular patient may have known of your interest?

Stone: No; actually I saw him in the period before I got much involved in the sport. The reference in the book is to a couple of later patients. In this case, the patient alone was the sailor.

Langs: So this didn't carry a personal meaning.

Stone: No, no.

Langs: The second dream was of coitus, in which both the patient and his wife were lying flat on their backs. You go on: "In a pithy dream expressing the essential non-specificity of his passive wishes, the patient is receiving a packet of bonds with which to 'make his fortune.' The donor is his mother, then his father, then alternating; then he is uncertain about the identity."

Now, could you say anything related to what that is about? Now we're getting closer of course to the revelation.

Stone: No doubt the transference was involved, as in any important dream, and the deception was from the beginning a part of the transference context. But it is a fact that he wanted something from everybody. And he wanted a great deal from both parents. And there is in it, perhaps, the idea of his mother as a phallic person, or conversely some reference to the penis as breast. It's so far back, I'd have to read the details in sequence. But it continues the general theme of broadly conflicting, powerful impulses, in a series of representations. Now the "getting closer to the revelation" was the result of the analytic work. The deception was, so to speak, a symptomatic phenomenon begun long before. The "righting" of the situation as in the sailboat dream was an expression of the disavowal of the predominance of the very impulses expressed in the dream. You must also recall the material you recently read concerning the advantages of inheritance.

Langs: On a more superficial level, anticipating the revelation that's to follow, it seems to me that if we look at these three dreams, the first one is related to danger. The second is related to him and his wife in a sexual position; this begins to raise the issue of alliance and misalliance—fantasies or unconscious perceptions on his part that there is some kind of shared gratification going on. Now he gets to the third dream, where he's receiving a packet of bonds, which is more clearly a reference to the credit that he is receiving—a derivative.

Stone: Well, I don't know how "clearly" it is, because there were always actual things of this nature going on, which may be mentioned somewhere. I know that he was promised money if he didn't smoke, for example; somewhere that's mentioned. As I say, I've not reread this material, and it's almost thirty years ago. There were many actualities which also participated. But what is certain, along the lines you mention, was that his financial deception of me, and the attendant, secret, guilty gratification, was an integral element in the transference evolution. I wouldn't question that. What one doesn't know, however, can't readily be analyzed! But the analytic spade-work around his general problem did permit this to emerge. Perhaps, had I been smarter then, I would have perceived his deceit in the analytic material earlier. This would have been a feather in my cap, no doubt. Whether such hotshot perception would have improved on what was really, ultimately, a quite good analysis, I am at a loss to say.

Langs: The facts are, one, that he was receiving credit, two, that he was receiving it based on a deception of you. Again, this reminds us that, clinically, things are never really simple. One of the things that I've observed, very often, around modifications in the ground rules, is that frequently the patient consciously or unconsciously exploits the modification and that there is an element of corruption inherent in many of these situations. It is a common theme in this context, so this is not exceptional material in my clinical experience; it's rather more the rule. I'm not saying that it's always the case, but very often it turns out that there has been some corrupt element in a modification of the frame.

Stone: Well, no, there is no a priori reason to assume there is usually a corrupt element in the modification of the frame, unless one attributes some sacrosanct quality to the frame as such, so that, a priori, it's corrupt to modify it. Such assumption I do not accept. And certainly I do not accept it on an empirical basis. That the modification may cater to a particular latent transference attitude of the patient is true, and that would ultimately have to be analyzed.

Langs: This is what I'm saying.

Stone: But it isn't necessarily a corruption. In some instances the "modification" may have been something necessary, or necessitated by an urgent reality, or genuinely thought to be, and as such it remains entirely analyzable. In fact, the refusal to do it might make

certain attitudes unanalyzable, and—if irrational or unempathic in
the refusal—could also be a real corruption. If, for example, I said
that you had to pay me so much and that it must be paid within three
days after you get the bill, then, if in the face of very real financial
troubles, this frame were not modified, your response would take the
form of chronic anger and resentment, which even if you suppressed
it, or "came to terms" with it, would remain as a permanent
distortion in the analysis, largely unanalyzable. I say "largely"
instead of "entirely" because if a rationally decent and considerate
adult relationship is understood as a necessary (even if tacit) part of
the compact (or frame), it is not impossible that circumscribed errors
in this sphere (if not too frequent) can also be corrected—at their own
level, not by a "transference" interpretation!

So, I would say, one can take a much more benign view of
"modification" depending on its rationality, the degree to which it
takes cognizance of reality, and the degree to which it's free of
countertransference contaminations. In that period (really quite
early in my analytic career), I was perhaps unusually easy with
people, financially; it may have been to some degree a transitional
characterological thing, or, you might say, a diffuse countertransference manifestation (in the sense of Ferenczi's "stages"), or
to some degree just a matter of learning; I became more realistic in
this sphere as time went on. I may have been a little too easy in
judging this patient, although, even in restrospect, I think it more
likely that it was a part of his character to carry out this particular
type of deception, and I accepted his presentation of himself. He was
an interesting patient, and I thought he had a family to support; he
could pay only so much; and he could owe a little more. That
probably seemed entirely reasonable to me. Parenthetically: we were
still in a different phase of American economic history at that time;
and patients were often seen privately for fees that now would be
regarded as at the very lowest clinic level. Now that that introduced
something complex into the transference is clear and obvious. And
that it played a role in the evolution of the transference, there is no
doubt. But, you see, the point that I make about the relative benignness of it, insofar as there wasn't something "crazy" in the arrangement on my side, is the fact that he did ultimately tell the whole story;
further, that he paid up; and still further, accepted a reasonable
increase in fee.

As I said before, I am not so sure that my being a more successful detective earlier in the game would have brought about a better result. So that the point of the preeminent importance of the rigid frame, I don't accept. True, it must have certain basic, unalterable qualities and boundaries, which cannot be transgressed, but within those limits, there must be room for variation, because, after all, it's like the frame of a picture: it should be appropriate to what it frames. It's very important, and it does influence the content, but it's not as important as the basic transactions within the frame. As you say, the dream about his father and mother giving him bonds is undoubtedly related to the transference: I don't argue that point. He wanted everything from me—up to and including incorporative sleep and the nullification of speech. These things later came up, not least in his sleeping phenomenon—you know, the intense, primitive, oral acquisitive and aggressive fantasies. I don't think the successful analysis of a hidden psychopathic fragment is to be sneezed at.

Langs: Unfortunately, I cannot for the moment present my own data. I can only assure you that my base is entirely empirical. One of the points I would make, and you may well disagree, is that the nature of the frame and, of course, the way in which it is maintained determine the nature of the interaction within it, and the properties of the field within which it occurs.

Stone: Contributes to it or determines it?

Langs: It is one determinant.

Stone: One determinant, yes, operating in relation to all of the profound realities of human nature and its general context, as expressed in a relationship between two people, with their own specific variants, one a trained analyst, the other a patient with his specific illness. For example, to say that to accept a patient on partial credit was an "alteration of the frame" could also be questioned. Again, it would depend on your conception of the frame. I don't know how it is nowadays, but in the old days it was not an infrequent thing, especially during the period when money was very tight and people often couldn't pay a reasonable fee, but may have had some prospects for the future. It was not unusual, at least among people whom I knew. If one were to stickle on that, one could say that patients treated privately would also have to pay a fee within a certain range, because unusually high or low fees cause people to feel "exceptionally" treated, especially if they compare notes with acquaintances. Of course, this impinges on the (psycho-)economic aspects of the transferences, as does an important real element inside the relationship. Certainly, a credit arrangement has similar dynamic potentialities. But, again, how do the special transference reactions balance out against the exigencies of the reality? We cannot sidestep reality for an abstract, streamlining conception without, in my view, courting more severe, even if sometimes less obvious, troubles. Incidentally, not that it disestablishes our general problem in principle, as I think over this whole interlude years later, two related questions come to mind: (1) Did the patient deceive me from the outset? Or did he withhold communication of his increasing prosperity? Either could have been true, but the latter more probably so; (2) Did he or did he not complain of ineffectuality in business, as part of his original trouble? I believe he did.

Langs: Yes, many new questions arise inevitably. Now, insofar as the ground rule for fees is concerned, I would define it in terms of a basic, agreed-upon fee which is within the analyst's usual range of fees, and which is paid in full within a reasonable period of time. I've learned, and it was somewhat surprising to me, that there are analysts who do ask for payment within three days, or who do other things of this sort. I would question these practices too.

Stone: Of course. They suggest that a person has no adult reaction to the analyst as another human being. Could a patient not think, "Is this guy an analyst, or is he primarily a Shylock?" The latter inference doesn't help the analytic situation.

Langs: It could reflect a countertransference greed, and things of that sort.

Stone: That's right. There is indeed a countertransference danger in the other direction. I, in that period, to the best of my recollection, was rather, I would say, too easy about those things. And this situation may have been a reflection of it, to some degree. Maybe somebody else would have been more exacting about an explanation of his exact financial situation. But this, in principle, I object to.

Langs: I do too.

Stone: Yes, because I feel that a person tells you about his capacity to meet financial obligations, and I'm not going to be an accountant, auditing his books. Is that not already an alteration of the relationship at the outset? But that was the situation. That it entered into the transference I don't doubt. By assiduous analytic spade work around—and touching on—his hidden false element, it came to rectify itself.

Langs: The question which I think is really unanswered is the extent to which anything like this, where credit is afforded, carries with it a large potential for what I call a misalliance (Langs, 1975), in which there can be a transference-countertransference gratification, and where an aspect of the relationship gets split off and is not discussed, but denied or repressed in the way the Barangers (1966) described. They call it a bastion, a situation where a piece of the analytic relationship, an unconscious piece, gets split off by both participants.

Stone: It can be, if one is not aware of it and doesn't deal with it. Of course, a deception in reality (as in this instance) is something one can't as readily cut through as one might wish. Incidentally, apart from the financial sphere, it's probably more frequent in analysis than usually is recognized—for example, isolated items of guilt or humiliation, minor perverse practices, etc. The saving element here was its connection with the massive and pervasive oral complex which was under constant analysis; also its close relationship to the constant manifest "poormouthing," greed, and envy. I understand that his is a case in point. But why is it emphasized (or at least implied) that only a "modification" tends to get segregated as a pathologic "bastion"? "Modifications" are conspicuous; by their nature, they can alert both participants. Naturally, if counter-transference gratification plays a part, this type of sequestration can occur. This can occur with anything. Whole segments of the transference-countertransference system can have been ignored or unobserved in the most orderly, "unmodified" authoritarian-coded analyses. The most blatant example in my recent experience was from such an analysis.

Langs: There are, of course, many ways bastions can be created; for the moment we are discussing the influence of alterations in the frame. Such arrangements create the potential for a bastion, for a kind of misalliance in which the terms are accepted and the derivatives are not examined in relation to this special arrangement.

Stone: No doubt about it. That it should be part of the analytic work, that's without question. But the same should be true of the patient's perhaps massive, although not necessarily expressed, reactions to the analyst's sometimes overwrought and stereotyped "correctnesses."

Langs: Nonetheless, we come back to actualities. The patient clearly exploited this actual arrangement in terms of his own neurotic needs, but in addition, it really has seductive qualities, in and of itself—and there is his sexual dream. It also had aggressive qualities, in his exploitation of you, and it had certain corrupting qualities. The extent to which this even included your inadvertent participation leaves some residual as an actuality within the patient. This I think remains unresolved. That a great deal can be analyzed profitably, I'm in entire agreement. What residual remains unanalyzable, unalterable with words because of the actuality, I think is an interesting area for research. The arrangement is an actuality filled with unconscious communications and implications.

Stone: Well, I don't believe that the residuals will be important if the analyst is aware of them, and looks for the evidences. I think you read more into this than was there. It isn't quite the original sin to have been a bit lenient with a patient financially. Patients recover from such things better than from their opposite counterparts. Whether I was as sharp then as I might be now, or even ten years ago, in picking up such relationships and sequelae I couldn't say. I would hope that I'm more experienced and smart now than I was then. Although on the whole, this was a very satisfactory analytic experience, considering the patient's rather severe troubles. But I think I would do better now, without question.

The point is, though, that there are very few analyses—and this we're inclined to forget—where realities of one sort or another don't impinge on the situation, because analysis occurs in a real world; and furthermore, the analytic undertaking in itself has certain inevitable agreements and certain conventions, and so forth. They are all operative in it. They're part of it. The relative silence of the analyst, for example; or his noncommunicativeness about himself. To be sure, these have important affirmative functions. But they can also have a dysfunction in certain instances, and be exploited by the patient neurotically. They can lead to something like the "misalliance" which you emphasize. Nothing is free of this potentiality, in the light of a given patient's neurosis. I believe that in *The Psychoanalytic Situation* (Stone, 1961) I mentioned a paper by a German analyst (Scheunert, I think), devoted to the rule of abstinence. He mentions a patient, as I recall it, to whom the couch was such a gratification that the principle of abstinence would have required renouncing it. Some time ago, I saw for the third time a sophisticated person who had been treated by an analyst of great distinction. No specification, so it's all right to mention that. An analyst who operates according to certain very well-defined principles, validated intellectually in a very rational and thoroughly competent way.

This person had seen me a couple of times, with the intention of leaving this analyst; in fact, had stopped a few months before, and did not wish to go back; although paradoxically, and that's what made the consultation the more complicated and interesting, felt he had been helped. He could not stand this person's detachment; this person's insistence on—as the old classical aphorism used to have it—"just analyzing it." But "just analyzing" to the point of only interpreting. Disregarding, for example, the person's pleas that his reality situation be given some cognizance in estimating something that had happened—not *only* the interpretation of the patient's unconscious role in it. I sent him back with the suggestion that he request an interview with his original analyst, to talk things over with him, state his complaint, and see if some sense of rapport could be reestablished by the exchange. There was an interval of a few weeks; he didn't do it; he called me again, wanted to see me again and came back and said, he just couldn't go back. The were a few further telephone contacts. Finally he carried out my suggestion. He could not, however, go on with his original analyst. This is not as simple as it sounds. Obviously, there may be things in this person that made intolerable to him what another person or many persons might find entirely tolerable. But I introduce it only to indicate that even in very skilled hands something that could be regarded as an integral part of the process and a very correct attitude can be found to reproduce something in a given person's early life in an uncanny way, and therefore proves intolerably painful. That sort of thing is operating all the time, in terms of the realities of technique, of the real situation, the financial relationship, and everything. This is not meant to be defensive, you understand. It isn't to deny the imperfections of my own work, or to say that all virtue resides in "modifications."

Langs: No, I understand your point.

Stone: Maybe I didn't pick up early enough some clues that this patient was reacting in a specific way to his financial relationship with me.

Langs: Yes, the derivatives were there.

Stone: No doubt, although one could say that his way of handling it was a sort of built-in secret acting out of all the lively core material in the analysis—a sort of reverse, but related view? As it was, whatever the most specific instrumentality was, it somehow or another enabled him to "make his confession." As I said before, I believe it was the fact that all the other transference material analyzed was ultimately related to this financial element.

Langs: What's interesting, too, is that it shows you something about derivatives. Here is a series of communications. Knowing what's to follow and using it as the adaptive context, one can see derivative expressions in response to the fee situation, disguised allusions to it. So again, as you say, if one is really alert to this as an issue that the patient will be responding to, and recognizes that the frame is important to the patient and that one should be sensitive to any sort of modification, even slight, one would be ready earlier rather than later to think of this as a communication related to the frame.

Stone: No question about the relationship. But it's not just that the "frame" was modified, but that something was established that may have "acted out" for him important elements in his transference, for a time. The communications were not about the "frame" being tampered with, but about his having pulled the wool over my eyes, and the impingement of that maneuver on the transference. His deception was his act, not mine.

Langs: There's another point that I want to make apropos of our earlier discussion. If we think of the two spheres that we were discussing before, the cognitive and the identificatory, it's interesting that cognitively, I think, there's little question that one would expect that once this secret has been revealed, a great deal of insight and working through can be achieved. Whether the patient would maintain residual secrets or not, we wouldn't know; that question would come up. In the identificatory sphere, there's another set of experiences. During the period in which the patient has in some way duped the analyst, there is an identificatory process with the analyst who has not detected the derivatives, and who is inadvertently participating. There's some kind of negative introjective identification. Once it's revealed and worked over with the analyst and, I would stress, *rectified*, there are positive introjects. But then the question comes up, what is the fate of the earlier negative introjects?

So you see, important and unsettled issues come up when one is thinking in these spheres. Does one ever entirely modify those initial negative introjects? I don't really know the answer. My hunch is that there are probably some residuals, but that a great deal is accomplished with an analyst who is able to recognize the true situation, analyze it, and rectify it. I think, though, that the rectification of the frame becomes essential to establishing the communication that's needed for the cognitive material and for establishing the proper identificatory processes.

Stone: There is a "residual" from every human experience. But why the aura of almost religious gloom hangs about a modification of the frame I don't understand, especially if its undertaken—and often successfully—for rational and benevolent reasons! It may be a derivative of the Kleinian view that the patient's perception of reality is given no importance. The rectification of the frame is certainly desirable; but in some instances, it may be less important than the analysis of the impingement of the frame or its modification on the transference relationship. I mean, for example, we don't make financial concessions as much nowadays as in the past. It's part of the sociology of analysis. Some people still do it. Previously one might treat people who couldn't approximate what one regarded as an adequate fee, adequate for one's livelihood. And one might make great concessions because this person was thought to be worthwhile or interesting. Now that would already constitute a modification of which the person could be—or become—aware.

Langs: It certainly is.

Stone: One can speculate on the historical reasons, perhaps with some cynicism. But whatever the reason, analysts have accepted more thoroughly their position as persons who treat patients who can pay adequate fees. Except, of course, in clinics. In early days one might make considerable concessions as to fees, mode of payment, and so on. True, one might speculate here, too, on the elements of economic determinism. In any case, this might be something that would remain necessary through a considerable portion of an analysis. Then maybe later the person would get a much better job and there would be some corresponding increase in fee, perhaps still not approximating what one might want, but which would be quite adequate for the patient. Sometimes quite helpful analyses were done that way. I would agree with you, certainly, that the person's feeling, even about paying a lower fee than others, and what it would mean, in reality, would impinge on the transference. The idea the analyst is a benefactor, and so forth. These are complicated things and they would have to be dealt with to the best of one's ability, yet it still might be a very worthwhile undertaking to analyze such individuals, and try to do good analytic work within those limitations, provided you were aware of them and tried to make even the special transference responses useful to the patient.

Langs: One could undoubtedly accomplish sectors of valid analytic work; and I would prefer that to not treating the patient. But certain bastions or sectors of misalliance would continue to exist in actuality and to some extent would preclude a certain degree of analytic work in important areas, because the realistic gratification involved inevitably has its neurotic components.

Stone: No doubt about that. But realistically speaking are there not areas or sectors of that sort actually or potentially present in all analyses? Does a streamlined, rigidly outlined setup exclude the myriad (often subtle and hidden) things that can go wrong between two people—often much less accessible and more damaging than matters like fees, or visiting the hospital, and similar matters?

Langs: Of course, and their proper analysis and rectification can prove quite helpful for all concerned. As long as one recognizes there is a limitation, a sector of misalliance, and one attempts to deal with it to the best extent. But we really don't know as yet the extent to which an arrangement of that kind alters the entire bipersonal field, and both the identificatory and communicative processes involved. In those situations where one can rectify the frame, one will have a better outcome than in those situations where it can't be done.

Stone: Oh, sure. One can rectify the frame. But you see, for example, if one rectifies the frame, and I don't mean to be acid about this, although I've sometimes been a little sarcastic, if it is rectified as some analysts have occasionally done—now I do not say the majority, for the great majority of analysts are very decent people—but occasional analysts have rectified the frame—or kept it inviolable in the first place—by having a person who works for an ordinary salary, a working person, a secretary, a clerk or what not, beg, borrow, or steal money to pay what they regard as an adequate fee, and even see them for a considerably reduced number of hours to get this fee, all right, in some respects, one aspect of the frame is being maintained, and they pay an adequate analytic fee on time, no credit, but they're paying an unjust fee. Of course, the other side appears. And what I meant by the acid attitude is that it sometimes has seemed to me that this kind of thing is better tolerated than the "unanalytic" behavior of a less demanding analyst who charges a low fee. That's seriously "wrong," like saying to the patient, "Sorry you've had all that trouble," when a child has been sick or even died, for example, as compared with being tough about the payment of a fee being delayed. The latter is often regarded as "good" analysis; the first is a "serious mistake." Now, I'm saying it in caricature. But the general principle of trying to maintain or restore a sensible working frame, I don't question. The principle you stated is correct. I would only wish that we saw it in reference to more profoundly important issues. You see, I don't conceive of the frame as having its importance in a sort of ritualistic sphere, nor as an end in itself. I see it as deriving broadly from: (1) the need for a consistent frame of reference and context; (2) the rule of abstinence, judiciously and reasonably applied; (3) the general proprieties and limitations of a professional—specifically medical—relationship; (4) the specific technical procedures and ancillary requirements of the psychoanalytic process. That it is a major participant in the dynamics of analysis I have long thought and taught. But I do not think that it—or the patient in it—is so mortally and potentially irremediably vulnerable to its rational and considered modification as you may feel.

Langs: I believe you have quite overstated my position. But rather than trying to reiterate and clarify, it seems best to finish up the vignette and discuss it. After the dream about the bonds and making his fortune, the patient spoke often of the killer instinct in true males. This he illustrated by a dream of wheeling two criminals—you see two criminals—strapped to a carriage; they were trying to get at him with murderous intent, with their mouths. This dream was associated with the analytic situation. So, now he begins to bring the derivatives toward the analytic situation, and the reference to two criminals manifesting what I consider again the duality, the misalliance.

Stone: Well, you have your own interpretation. I would interpret that as his father and mother, as in the other (alternating) dream about the bonds. I am both in the transference (alternatively).

Langs: I would agree that they are the genetic counterparts of what he is experiencing in actuality.

Stone: And I am both. It's a clear projection of his oral destructiveness, the fundament of his neurosis. I see no connection with "what he is experiencing in reality."

Langs: I am trying to say that on another level this is an unconscious perception of the something he is experiencing in the actuality of this arrangement, another level of viewing the situation.

Stone: Yes, I understand your direction of thought. Except that I am certain that he regarded himself as the criminal, and the projection was to his parents and thus to me.

Langs: To quote a bit more (Stone, 1947, p. 28): "This was associated with the analytic situation. He spoke of probable impulses to assault women sexually, in line with the previous dream material."

Incidentally, just to express my view, I want to also mention the business about the murderous intentions. Now here, there's a deception involved.

Stone: A deception which is not available to me.

Langs: Not yet. In general, patients see these modifications as ultimately destructive to themselves.

Stone: Yes, I know, you've said that. I do not accept your generalization, for reasons which I have tried to explain before. Certainly, I don't think that was true of him. He was the destroyer, the criminal, and felt enormously guilty. And this was continuous with his lifelong neurosis.

Langs: Yet he's working over something on that level; both are operating: the intrapsychic and the interactional, projective and introjective processes. To quote a bit more, "He mentions his father's annoying requests for confidences about women, and his injunctions about controlling natural sexual 'brutality' toward them. The manifest violent wish to tyrannize over his wife and daughters frequently emerged."

Now here we're seeing, once again, his image of himself as tyrannical, but there's also a frame reference: the allusion to a father who wishes to modify usual boundaries of confidentiality. "Toward the close of the second period, a few developments in the patient's actual life were of special importance. His wife resumed remunerative work. His own business showed remarkable improvement, partly because of changes in him, partly from purely external accidental factors. His sister moved to his near vicinity, mobilizing many attacks of pain and much material about her which was worked through."

"Of special importance was the patient's disclosure after long concealment, with great guilt, that his earnings had been very large, out of all proportions to the small fee he was paying on a partial credit basis. The patient had been practicing the same characteristic concealment in relation to his father, lest he 'lose out' to his two siblings. The patient liquidated his debt and gladly arranged a moderate increase in fee. He showed marked symptomatic improvement in all spheres. However, he again forced the termination of the analysis in an uncontrollable burst of 'independence,' although in a much better condition than on the previous similar occasion."

I'll just go over the last paragraph.

Stone: Then we'll have to quit; and we can resume right there.

Langs: Okay; I'll summarize: When the patient returned for the last analytic period of a few months, the complaint was that of severe gastric upset, precipitated by a fight with his wife, over the question of whether he loved her. The patient was X-rayed, and his physician stated in a telephone conversation that he had a duodenal ulcer, and so forth.

So, in all, this is what led up to this particular revelation. There was improvement then, apparently due to the rectification of the frame and whatever analytic work you did around that issue.

Stone: It is undoubtedly true that material like this "killer instinct" involving the mouth, and so on, was under fairly continuous interpretation. To the extent that that was a transference dream, myself as both parents, you might say that, even though it was not, in the current manner, "interpreted upward," in relation to the actual situation, because I didn't know that he was withholding, concealing something from me, it is quite likely that it contributed to his becoming able to tell me that he was doing something "bad" to me, in the real sphere. (In those days, incidentally, while I understood many things pretty well, I was impelled to be much more stilted in my interventions, permitting imaginative reconstruction very little play.) So, what I'm saying is that the work wasn't lost. Of course, what you don't know, you can't interpret. "You are concealing your true financial situation from me." Later, I don't know whether it's mentioned there, one would think that—even retrospectively—the meaning of the concealment would have been brought into the analysis. But your idea that just the fact of a modification of the frame was the essential "crime"—I don't think you mean that, nor that that is why he continued to conceal it. At least, *I* don't see things that way. I think such a view absurd.

Langs: Oh, no. I didn't imply that. I did not introduce notions of sin or crime, though many who hear my views bring up such ideas— regardless of my founding them on extensive clinical data.

Stone: But that I should have been more actively participant in the interpretative work of the analysis? Well, probably so; but again it's the paradox that I didn't know it.

Langs: There's no question about it. In fact, what's missing here, and it would have been fascinating, is the sequence of the sessions, the specific material, and the analytic interpretive work that facilitated the revelation. As it unfolds in your description, some of it seems to stem from the fact that in reality he became extremely comfortable; it heightened his guilt, and he finally revealed it. But I would seriously doubt that that was the only factor. I'll postulate something which I have observed quite often in supervision: that at times, even though the therapist or analyst is not aware of this specific problem, he picks it up unconsciously, and he may then shape interventions that convey this unconscious realization. The message begins to get across to the patient, and that helps to allow him to make his secret explicit. No, I was only attempting to say that this material raises issues related to the influence of actualities of that kind on the analytic relationship and work, and on the patient's communications.

Stone: There is no doubt it played a part in it. It must have played a role, as does every other important reality. It's the more evident, if it's a reality that deviates in any striking way from the convention. But the only thing I would stick on is that such "deviations" should be made, certainly can be made, and ought to be made, if they are consonant with, actually justified by the reality. To withhold a reasonable concession, like being overdemanding or greedy, would be even more seriously damaging and yet would conventionally be overlooked. See, you've picked up something in this case, even though I reject the extreme implications you find in these matters. But if somebody had charged this patient a stiff fee, and he was really in financial trouble, it would probably not be emphasized that the patient was overpaying. That might be ignored. And the resulting damage might be really deep-going.

Langs: No, I understand fully. You're talking about choices of this kind.

Stone: Of the dynamic part that it played, there is no question. The question of benignness vs. depth and severity is another matter.

Langs: Well, we'll stop at this point. Next time, I'll also have the third vignette, and I have some others that aren't yours, because I would like to try to establish some of the recurrent themes that occur in this kind of a context.

Chapter 5
FURTHER DEBATE
ON CLINICAL MATERIAL

Langs: Today, I thought we could discuss one more vignette from your material, which I did want to use as our focal point. I thought, though, that we could add another clinical exerpt from someone else's material!

Stone: It would be a relief to talk about somebody else's material!

Langs: But it's interesting to have your own because you have experienced it. Well, we'll go over the two vignettes. I also hope to ask you some general questions, in terms of the clinical experiences you have had over this span of years. Perhaps you could extend some of the ideas in your paper on problems and potentialities in analysis (Stone, 1975); it would be useful, I think, to follow the extension of clinical issues into the broader concerns that exist within analysis today. But I suspect we may have to reserve that discussion for a later meeting.

Now the paper from which I selected the vignette is entitled "Psychoanalysis and Brief Psychotherapy" (Stone, 1951), delivered in Montreal in 1949. I chose it because I thought it relevant to an issue related to the framework that came up. I'd like to read it to you and then we can discuss it, perhaps more briefly than some of the others. It has been mentioned before.

In the paper you're talking about some of the distinctions between analysis and psychotherapy, and brief therapy. And you give a closing example, from a clinic case, of "a young man who had reacted well to a short period of treatment for hypochondriacal fears. He had always been excessively jealous. He returned after an absence of ten months, acutely disturbed by jealousy. At an office party, a pleasant man named Bill (also the patient's name), with whom he had been drinking, had put his arm around the patient's wife in an innocuous way. The patient suggested that the therapist see his wife so that she might become more cooperative about his treatment. This was an actual problem to him, as she had a mildly derisive attitude about it. A reserved willingness to see his wife was expressed, with the expressed preference that he settle the problem himself. No interpretation of the implication in the transference was made, an important decision, made at the moment, obviously susceptible to discussion. Considerations stated earlier in the paper would be relevant." This refers to some of your comments, made earlier in the paper, about dealing with transference in psychotherapy. That is another topic we want to talk about a bit.

To continue: "The patient returned without his wife, feeling much better and bringing up a dream: a man called him from the office, addressing him as Bill, and said, 'We couldn't help it, standing there, and I just kissed your wife.' The patient started for the place, found himself with a blonde in an apartment, and had a seminal emission. He recalled he had proposed a foursome date with Bill and his wife. The man in the dream had the name of a girl whose picture in a bathing suit he had seen in the paper and who was to marry a senator. In addition to the projection of his own extramarital wishes and jealousy, as a reaction to something which he himself wished, the interpretation was given that he wished to share his wife with a man whom he obviously liked; that it could express his affection for this man; moreover, it could be an avoidance of conflict and complications about the exclusive possession of a woman. Had he not previously recalled playing with his sister in bed on two occasions while his brother was in the next bed? Might it not be possible that (then and now) there was an impulse to share sexual guilt and avoid rivalry at the same time? The patient had been fond of his brother; also he had had a dream in which his wife and sister had been manifestly interchanged. During the following interview he related several instances from adolescence of making, with a friend, joint sexual overtures toward the same girl. A few weeks later he reported that he had eaten some good dinners at his brother's house, had enjoyed a party at which his friend Bill had been present, and had shown a naive competitiveness with his brother's wife, in tobogganing with his brother."

Stone: Competitiveness with his brother's wife?

Langs: Right. "These responses suggest that the interpretation was to some degree effective; however, it must be noted that his wife had quit working in this period, a change for which he had devoutly wished. The normality of this wish had previously been confirmed by the therapist, while interpreting his envy of certain features of the woman's role in life. The immediately relevant question is whether there is a special advantage in brief psy:hotherapeutic contacts in trying to integrate a single interpretation, in a concept available to the personality from multiple points of view, in acceptable language, elements of defense, aggression, and libido, including a clearly available genetic parallel."

"Brief interpretive psychotherapy, based on psychoanalytic principles, is a field for empirical research by psychoanalysts to determine its therapeutic effectiveness, scope of applicability, and techniques" (Stone, 1951, pp. 233-234). That's how the paper ends.

Once, again, there's very little material, but I bring it in because it raises an issue related to the ground rules and frame.

Stone: Of course, I think some of the patients referred to in this paper, as I remember them, were not seen so much that there would be a lot of material about them. They were usually rather brief contacts, and infrequent. Does it say how often?

Langs: It doesn't say.

Stone: Maybe once a week, at the most, I would say. There was another, a young woman who was seen for a while, somewhat more than once a week, but only about fifteen sessions in all, as I recall it.

Again, I have not looked at this paper for many years, although obviously everything in it is very familiar to me—or should be.

Langs: Yes, I didn't develop the background. To reconstruct a bit, one of the problems that you're taking up is the issue of how one deals with the transference in brief psychotherapy, and even more broadly, the therapeutic relationship. So we don't assume it's only transference, but consider nontransference elements as well. We can extend this to the question of how one deals with this area in basic psychoanalytic psychotherapy, as compared to analysis.

Stone: Some of these questions I have kept on thinking about even currently and perhaps formulated a little bit in the later paper, "The Widening Scope" (Stone, 1954). The interest continues. But I did have some definite ideas even then.

Langs: This vignette, which I selected for its allusion to the frame, actually raises several questions. One is the issue of psychotherapy versus psychoanalysis, especially how one deals with the relationship. The second is a related question, in that this then determines how one interprets or does not interpret in this area. Third is the question of the frame in psychotherapy, and the particular aspect of the ground rules that involves seeing a spouse. We have talked about third parties to treatment before, and I'd like to try to clarify that issue in the context of this vignette. And then, fourthly, this is a clinic patient, which raises an important question today: the influence of the clinic on the therapeutic relationship.

Let me begin by asking you the broader questions; we'll get to the more specific ones in a moment. What do you recall of your position about psychotherapy versus analysis at the time you gave this paper? And has it changed in your thinking, with particular reference to dealing with the therapeutic relationship as compared to the analytic relationship?

Stone: Well, I don't believe that there are basic changes, in principle. The skeletal, linear clarity of distinction between the two has perhaps diminished somewhat. I mean that perhaps, as time has gone on, I can recognize a grey area which is much broader than I would have said at that time. And the very clear-cut distinctions are perhaps somewhat less clear-cut. Although one might say that, conceptually, the general patterns of distinction would still obtain, and that matters of degree would in my mind now become matters of qualitative distinction when the degrees become very great. (Something like the quantitative considerations involved in color, or musical pitch.)

For example, if you see a person once a week, sitting up and facing you, and have a fairly active exchange with him, ask more questions than one ordinarily would in analytic work, feel freer to comment on things (as one might in everyday consultative conversation) than in the regular analytic context, but always within the scope of the therapeutic atmosphere and purpose, I don't think there's much difficulty in distinguishing psychotherapeutic from analytic work, even if you are always an analyst, always aware of the transference and the meanings of things in an analytic sense. If, on the other hand, you see a person three times a week, and he speaks largely in free association, and you are, relatively speaking, quite passive as to response, perhaps increasingly so as he becomes more involved in the material, there the fact that he sits up or that it's three times a week, instead of four, not to speak of five or six times a week, becomes, to me, a less important distinguishing feature, in relation to psychoanalysis. The distinguishing feature would then begin to reside in the question of whether your purpose, manifest or latent, takes a certain direction—to allow him to develop a "full-blown" (now almost a cliché) transference neurosis, with the ultimate purpose being to reduce that interpretatively—or whether you have maintained some more limited goals in mind, and would be more inclined to settle matters on the basis of certain confronting sectors of the person's unconscious life as they may present themselves—some particular conflict, or some particular relationships?

The maintenance of these limited or specified goals or sector interests would then provide, broadly, the "definition" of psychotherapy, because analysis does have that implied quality of a spontaneous, unlimited, or unmodified deepening of the whole latent transference neurosis. And of course, in that sphere are its greatest and most highly specific potentialities for thereapeutic effect of a unique sort, and also certain of the elements that constitute unique problems with certain patients, especially when time is limited, and the person's potentialities are limited, or regressive potentialities are

very great, and so forth. I would say that, broadly speaking, many of
the things, in fact, most of the things that I stated in that paper, I
would still think are true in principle. The paper might now be a
little stuffily certain and "correct" about some things. I'm not so sure
about every technical detail. For that, I would have to reread it, and
discuss it in great detail. I'm not sure, for example, whether I would
now *always* wait with regard to transference interpretations, as
clearly as I think I stated in that paper about the patients there, where
it would only be the confronting emergence of transference material
that would lead to a transference interpretation. But I still think it's
true, in a general way (and I follow that general plan with patients),
that the focus should be more on the patient's life and its external
relations than might be the case in analysis. Even transference
material, unless confronting and very grossly and obviously stimulated by the situation itself, as opposed to outside-integrated transferences, I would in most instances still think should be kept in or
allowed to be worked out as far as possible in the patient's actual life,
even interpretatively. The "unless" involves certain germane conditions: for example, that the failure to interpret the therapeutic
transference would fortify resistance to further progress, as in the
traditional analytic view. Or, more pointedly, that a new or exacer-
bated symptom formation might occur. Or, still more in point, in
relation to my later views, that such development might present the
crucial opportunity for the specific therapeutic effect that one seeks.

Of course, as I remarked in the later reference to this, in the paper
on the "Widening Scope" (Stone, 1954), it did seem to me that there
was a certain pattern that could be thought of in relation to "psychotherapy," in this sense: in view of the analyst's greater activity and
involvement, and lack of reticence, in the sense of every-day (physicianly) responses, little comments, little bits of advice in areas where
the analyst's competence as a physician, or even as an analyst, might
make him authoritatively competent to mention such things—
responses of approval or calling attention to matters that were
thought to be manifestations of poor judgment in the patient's
activities—I assumed that this give and take (and I still have found
this to be the case, even in relatively recent experiences with one or
two once-a-week therapies) tends to militate against the deepening,
regressive aspects of the transference neurosis. It maintains the
relationship affectively closer to the level of the professional inter-

personal reality. And then when certain specific elements, which are clearly irrational, nonadaptive, and very often ego-dystonic, begin to manifest themselves as evidences of a sector of regressed relationship to the therapist, I would think that the full resources of the therapist's analytic understanding, especially in terms of his understanding and interpretation of the transference element, should be mobilized and utilized in this focal application. This can become the decisive element in the treatment. And there is a distinction even in that type of intervention, because in analysis, at least as I see it nowadays—and I think many others see it that way now, although for a long time there was a certain almost stereotyped traditional reaction against it—one anticipates transference elements, sees them in their integrated appearance in the patient's everyday life or in the material, long before this becomes an issue in the patient's consciousness, and that seeing these, anticipating them, and interpreting them, is not only salutary per se, but, if anything, facilitates acceptance of the subjective aspects of the transference neurosis in the patient. This, I think, I would still tend to keep out of what I would call an actual, a "real" psychotherapy, where limited frequency and a more generally reality-oriented relationship obtains. Those broad differentiations I would still hold with. And for scientific-didactic reasons, I still hope that further, more specific, categories can be evolved. However, as I said, I think that the blurring and the merging of the two modalities of treatment is perhaps more frequently evident to me nowadays, especially in the sphere of modified psychoanalysis as applied to more difficult patients. It's a long speech, I know.

Langs: No, it defines your thinking very nicely, and it raises a number of issues. Initially, I would just like to clarify one point, in terms of your experience and your clinical opinion. As you undoubtedly know, many therapists, analytically trained both in the classical sense and otherwise, will place patients on the couch, even though they're being seen with a frequency of only once a week, let alone twice. Certainly, many, many will do it with patients coming three times a week. Have you had any experience with that?

Stone: Well, I have opinions about it, and of course the opinions are based on some experience. I may have mentioned it in that paper. It was also quite a number of years ago, so I'm not certain. But there was one experience that I never forgot (indeed, I mentioned it to you once before in an earlier conversation), and that was where a rather good analyst, who was one of the senior people in an early Institute clinic of mixed composition which I headed up, used to see a patient once a week, which at that time was the usual frequency there. Sometimes visits were even less frequent, but not more. The analyst employed the couch for this once-a-week therapy, and took an analytic position, that is, affectively, and in terms of frequency of intervention, and so on. The therapist was soon confronted with a very severe, very disturbing regression in this patient.

Now that to me was a kind of demonstration—I understand that many other patients may *not* have experienced that type of regression—of the general technical inadvisability of an analytic-like context for infrequent treatment contacts. Perhaps it was a premature, insufficiently supported inference, a partly intuitive, a priori view, already in existence. But this was a frightening experience and there were reasons, all the more since this was a very competent analyst, for assuming that the structure of the situation had something to do with the regression. That, of course, interacting with the patient's intrinsic pathology. As I remember, the analyst and I agreed on that. He turned to me for consultation, and we talked it over, and I do not think that he disagreed about that consideration. At any rate, we had to deal with the situation, and it righted itself.

That became kind of a paradigmatic experience for me, and thus part of my general feeling about these things. That the lying down, the not seeing the analyst, the analyst's infrequent interventions, and the general affective cast of the relationship are things that are not dealt with in infrequent interviews. That the stop against regression, or too rapid regression in the analytic situation, includes, along with elements in the timing and the judgment of the analyst about interventions, the sheer frequency of contact. The frequency of contact is something of a protection in more than one way. You know, there is just a gratification in that sheer frequency of contact that is very potent. You've spoken of these considerations as the "holding element." There is also the opportunity of the analyst to intervene more frequently and effectively. In general, I do not utilize the couch in infrequent contacts. Once I had a patient (this was post-analytically), somebody whom I could, literally, not persuade to sit up when he would come back to see me, short of an ultimatum. It was a matter of almost an obsessively entrenched habit. But in general, with patients where I create the setting, unless I'm going to see the patient quite frequently, approximating traditional analytic frequency, I don't use the couch. This coincides not only with my empirical experience, but my general theoretical view of these matters.

Langs: Yes, in my technique books (Langs, 1973, 1974), I adopted such a position, based too on a rather dramatic vignette that had been presented to me. More recently, as I have heard presentations from nonanalysts who have patients on the couch, and as I try to draw upon that experience, I've developed a less firm and more questioning attitude. I don't know the answer. I'm convinced that the couch itself, in addition to other factors, fosters a regressive experience, and the regressive aspects of the therapeutic relationship.

However, I also think that patients and competent therapists do have the resources to deal with them, and that it may therefore enhance the therapeutic experience and outcome. So, there is the question whether the couch itself has a salutary effect for the treatment; in other words, whether there can be some justification for using the couch with a once-a-week or twice-a-week patient.

Stone: Whether it has a salutary effect?

Langs: Yes. Why use it unless you feel that there's an advantage over the face to face mode?

Stone: The advantage it offers seems to me to lie in the context of analysis, and its purposes. (Even there, as with any technical modality, it may occasionally backfire.) That is, it facilitates, by the lack of the perceptual impingement of the immediate reality, the evolution of fantasy, not to speak of the earlier traditional idea or the early introduced idea that it was easier—as many patients say—easier to talk more freely to somebody when you're not looking at them, and so on. I do not know how many colleagues experience Freud's discomfort in being looked at all day, at the other end. But in my conception of psychotherapy, which includes the tight anchoring— or tight as possible anchoring—to immediate realities, this is not an advantage.

Langs: I have no question in my mind about it being an advantage in analysis. But, is it an advantage in insight-oriented therapy? And what you're saying leads me right to another point. I have been interested in how these ideas about the use of the couch are really interrelated with one's conception of psychotherapy—which inter-digitates with how one conceives of the frame and of the goals of any kind of treatment. And it's difficult, in spelling out one's thinking in one area, to do justice to it without really stating one's total position.

So, since part of the answer would depend on one's conception of psychotherapy, I would like to address that point, in terms of my own thinking. When I wrote the technique books (Langs, 1973, 1974), my position on psychotherapy as compared to analysis was very much in keeping with yours. One of the reviewers of that work commented, critically, on the position he saw there, that the focus in psycho-therapy should be on the patient's life situation, and that interpreta-tions of transference, of aspects of the relationship, should be made primarily when this area relates to a resistance or an urgent problem, or happens to be the vehicle for a core fantasy or memory. This reviewer felt that such an approach tended to underestimate the importance of the relationship in psychotherapy, as reflected in my own extensive case material.

Stone: In what sense?

Langs: Well, first of all, in the sense of its inherent therapeutic potential and its basic importance. I don't think he spelled it out, but I would add, also, in terms of the extent to which the patient, despite any efforts of the therapist to the contrary, is unconsciously preoc-cupied with and reacting adaptively to the relationship.

Stone: That there is that unconscious preoccupation is, I think, true. But it is more readily—what is the word that I've sometimes used?—deployed in the patient's everyday life.

Langs: That's one of the basic issues. Is it most therapeutic to deploy and displace the work with these unconscious fantasies and perceptions to outside relationships? Or must they be dealt with in terms of the therapeutic relationship itself? You know, when I received this review, I recognized that, even though I had made this position statement—really, again, very similar to yours; it was the one that I had been taught—my own clinical material absolutely belied it. That is, if I looked at the clinical material that I had presented in the two volumes (Langs, 1973, 1974), if I looked at the vignettes that I had chosen for various other purposes throughout the book, to illustrate interpretations and confrontations, resistances and all, the material related preponderantly to the therapist and to the need to intervene in that area. It seemed almost overwhelming. In other words, my response to his criticism was, "It's true; I said this. But if you look at the book and what the work entailed, the therapeutic relationship comes up again and again." That experience was one of many that began to lead me to reconsider my views, and eventually to alter them. But I think there are some important consequences for understanding the patient and for technique. We know in analysis that very subtle differences can be extremely crucial.

One of the concepts that I now maintain—we've discussed it before, and you're implying some agreement with it—is that in the latent content of the material from the patient both in psychotherapy and psychoanalysis there is a great deal that has to do with the therapist, in terms of both transference and nontransference; what I call unconscious fantasy and memory, and unconscious perception. When we begin to realize that, and I think you're acknowledging my point, one then has the question of how one best deals with it. Through deployment or through direct interpretation?

Stone: By deployment I didn't mean something you do actively. That you "send it back" into the outer world. Rather that you do not facilitate—still less encourage—its deintegration from it's appearances in the daily life of the patient. You try to understand and interpret it there, in situ, unless or until the economics and reality-dystonic aspects point clearly to the therapeutic situation. Then (1) the interpretation is obligatory; and (2) it often provides maximal opportunity for therapeutic effect.

Langs: I undertstand that, although sometimes therapists actually do that—interpreting it in that outer sphere, rather than in the inner sphere.

Stone: That's right. And often they are right. Sometimes—unfortunately, because of lack of analytic acuteness—they are very wrong.

Langs: Well, as my observations have expanded, I have found more and more that interpretations outside the therapeutic relationship, even in psychotherapy, function dynamically as a defensive avoidance by the therapist of unconscious perceptions and fantasies related to himself—not always, but remarkably often.

Perhaps this is not a logical sequence. Let me introduce another position: I feel now, on the basis of accumulated experience, personally and in supervision, that the best psychotherapy is based on interpreting the derivatives where they apply—within the therapeutic interaction. I have found too that adherence to the frame of psychotherapy is also essential for sound therapeutic work.

Stone: Of psychotherapy, as differentiated from analysis?

Langs: As differentiated from analysis. But the same principle applies to analysis. I often say that the patient in therapy doesn't know that he's not supposed to think about his therapist, consciously or unconsciously, or that he should accept modifications in the frame.

Stone: But you're speaking of the frame as if they were identical. I conceive of a different frame for psychotherapy. But granted that your aphorism is intrinsically sound, I wouldn't know to what conception it applies. I know no one who thinks that psychotherapy patients are not supposed to think about their therapists. Some of us may believe that such thinking is not to be interpretatively stimulated, that the patients are not to be led into an overwrought preoccupation with him, if it doesn't occur spontaneously. By the same token, I would not favor the anticipatory interpretive precipitation (separation) of transference elements integrated in important extratherapeutic relationships, so long as that may be advantageously interpreted in situ. As long as the patient thinks of his doctor preponderantly as an understanding and helpfully clarifying doctor, well and good. When he changes, clearly and emphatically, interpretative skill must be ready.

Langs: No, I don't consider the frames identical. But the only modifications in technique that I envision as necessary, by and large, in turning from analysis to psychotherapy, are based on the differences in the frame of the two situations: basically, the frequency of the sessions and, for the moment, until we decide otherwise, the mode or positions of the participants. I'm open about that, but the frequency then, instead of being four or five or six times a week, as in analysis, is once or twice in therapy. That difference in frequency . . .

Stone: With a "grey area" in between.

Langs: But with a fundamentally interpretive and frame-securing approach in psychotherapy too. I have validated the patient's unconscious need for such a stance through extensive clinical observation.

Stone: Well, analysis can sometimes be conducted at three times a week. I'm rather skeptical at any attempt to do it with fewer sessions. And that would only be with certain cases under certain conditions.

Langs: Could you say anything about those certain cases, certain conditions since you mention it—patients whom you might see three times a week?

Stone: Well, I mean, there are probably still cases of the type Freud mentioned—for whom three times a week would suffice—"light" or "mild" cases, I forget what his exact words were. Also, I have frequently tapered off intensive schedules at this rate; occasionally, at the end, even less. Sometimes I have applied it to patients who have previously had long analyses. And there are cases where the difficulties of commuting from great distance or other reality factors may necessitate curtailed schedules.

Langs: Such as financial.

Stone: Yes, but that I would not take quite as seriously as other obstacles because that can be dealt with in other ways. Commutation, work, getting to the analysis and so on, could necessitate a curtailed schedule, and it might work out satisfactorily where the non-severity of symptoms would permit the lighter schedule to be a reasonable thing—or, at a later period in analyses that have been conducted intensively, for long periods, where I have sometimes felt that diminishing the schedule brings out certain material, provides an anticipation of ultimate termination, which some people, I find, cannot tolerate if it comes abruptly. Then it may have a much more complicated affirmative effect than just the ordinary sense of tapering, of gradualism. It brings out material about the intervals, and creates in the patient the anticipation of termination. It is true that some patients fight this. But my observation is that such patients have especially severe problems of separation, and recoil with fear even from the implicit testing. So there are situations where I think the diminished schedule is useful. And it does permit some of the essential continuities of analysis, of free association, and the reasonably effective context for the remembering of dreams, which, you know, can be difficult on a once a week basis, and so on.

Langs: To clarify one point: you are saying that you would consider or prefer a reduction in fees, under certain conditions, in order to establish a four times a week analytic situation?

Stone: Yes, if you're going to analyze this patient, instead of referring him to someone else who is glad to accept the lower fee. I don't think it's very often necessary; still less is it desirable, to conduct an analysis with a curtailed schedule, just because of the fee. I don't want to be too sanctimonious about that, but there may be instances where for some reason it's necessary. I don't think that's often the case.

Langs: Well, in any case then, you see major distinctions in the situations and techniques with the once or twice a week patient as compared to the four or five times a week patient?

Stone: Yes, that's more of a potential conceptual differentiation.

Langs: The frequency of visits will certainly influence the intensities of the relationship, and perhaps, to some extent, the nature of the communications. Let's assume for the moment that the once or twice a week patient is in the face-to-face mode rather than lying on the couch. That, too, will influence communications and the nature of available derivatives. But I do not inherently assume a modification in the therapist's attitude in psychotherapy compared to analysis; that is, I don't know whether we disagree there. You were saying something about a different stance?

Stone: Oh, a difference in the whole mode. That's where I differ from you.

Langs: And you would consider that part of the frame of psychotherapy?

Stone: Oh, most definitely.

Langs: So you use a distinctive approach, because I do not consider any basic modification in the therapist's approach to intervening as part of the frame of psychotherapy.

Stone: I do.

Langs: Certainly this is something that is considerably debated. Incidentally, I am not implying that, empirically, interventions do not differ in the two forms of treatment—indeed they do—I am simply suggesting that these differences do not stem from, or need not arise from, the a priori adoption of a unique stance in psychotherapy—they come from the differences in frequency and mode instead. Much of this is based on my observations of many patients in which these alterations were attempted, where various modifications in attitude and limited advice-giving were utilized. Granted, much of this was in the hands of inexperienced therapists, but the literature on such work from experienced analysts shows the same negative outcome, expressed mostly through responsive indirect derivatives. You know, one of the things that I have learned through our discussions and through talks I had with Dr. Phyllis Greenacre is that once I get away from specific clinical material there is something about my position in these areas that sounds either unreasonable, harsh, inappropriate, or not sensible. I am aware of that; so much of it comes from latent content, unconscious communication, and so much of it requires renunciations by the analyst. It's hard to offer abstract justifications. For example, one might conclude from the foregoing discussion that I am suggesting that one should attempt to analyze every patient in some deep sense. Obviously, this could lead to a lot of difficulty, trying to get to primitive material, in inappropriate situations. And that's not at all what my position implies. Instead, it suggests that patients unconsciously expect unique, interpretive interventions from a therapist—and they can be properly developed—and such interventions offer the greatest opportunity for cure, because, empirically, therapy patients are unconsciously angered and disappointed when this does not happen, and they resent so-called supportive interventions. Then others say that my position seems very rigid and inappropriately harsh. But this too is not the case. My position came out of extensive clinical observations; it relates to the patient's overriding unconscious needs, though again, just as with the couch issue, there are always many variables. Just as in the situation with the analyst you observed, he may have had a specific countertransference problem that made the situation such that he didn't manage the material that he was getting properly.

Stone: Oh, there's always innumerable possibilities for something going wrong. But in that case, as I mentioned, I think we (the therapist and I) both rather came to the conclusion—and after all, I was uninvolved—that the primary mistake lay in the way the treatment mode was set up from the beginning. It may not have been true, naturally! But all my experience over many years tends to confirm the fact that it was true. Again, I should say a word about your passing remark, "Much of this is in the hands of inexperienced therapists." I do not think that such material provides a basis for adequate comparison, at least direct comparison. It is difficult for a person to utilize rationally something that he does not yet really understand, i.e., analysis. Both his countertransferences and his lack of knowledge of both theory and technique get in his way.

Langs: I am not making comparisons; I am attempting to derive general principles. We have discussed the issue of my main sources of published data before, and I can add little to my previous comments. I can only assure you that the principles that I am proposing have been validated in my own clinical work and by other experienced analysts. I only wish I could review such data with you, but part of my own adherence to the basic frame includes the maintenance of total confidentiality—which precludes the presentation of vignettes from my own practice.

These are very difficult questions to resolve. You see, I no longer draw conclusions without hearing specific sessions. If you look at our literature, unfortunately, this approach is by far the exception, still. All I can say, because I always feel the need to justify this, partly because my position tends to isolate me from my colleagues and to draw criticisms without a confrontation through clinical material, is that my position is basically and entirely empirical. It is based on listening for derivative material with each deviation as the organizing adaptive context—and attending to both valid unconscious perceptions and distorted fantasies. That's why I have welcomed the chance to go over some specific vignettes with you. But I also wanted to get into some of these general issues.

Stone: May I say a few words about what you were just saying, because there are some implications that you may not have quite grasped my point of view. In the first place, I don't think there's anything strange or harsh about your view. Indeed, contrary to what you think, I think it is the dominant view. Most residents in hospitals, as I see them, or hear about them from the people who supervise them, practice what they think is "like analysis" in the more limited setting—the sitting up, facing the therapist, with infrequent interviews. And to me, to show how polar our experience and attitudes may be, this is one of the causes of the trouble. That they believe, first, that there is only one way to help the patient, and that is by just listening for extended periods, and making progressively "deeper" interpretations, and second, that they must maintain a certain distance and aloofness, and not think in rather holistic terms, of the limitations of the patient's personality and and illness, in relation to those imposed by time, economic circumstances, and so on. In relation to the latter, one can reformulate, from psychoanalytic concepts and knowledge, a more appropriate technical approach.

Now to me, psychotherapy can range all the way from simply listening to a patient and responding in terms of support and advice, although always alert and sensitive to his specific psychopathology. Only when confronted with reactions of a quite specific and different nature does the therapist call on analytic knowledge in an attempt to get an interpretation of this across to the patient, and largely (or very often) in the terms that I tried to set forth as a kind of special technical modality, which I called an "integrative interpretation." This kind of interpretation gives the person something about a large area in his psychic life that would include several mechanisms at once, and which would not require the establishment of more progressive cleavages within his personality. The assumption is that he can better handle such interventions in a limited situation, than the type we traditionally associate with analysis. I think it is not only the sitting up and the infrequency, but another question: a determination as to whether progressively deepening interpretations and the development, then resolution, of the transference neurosis are the goals, or whether the limitation of technique and (one hopes) response to some sector of this person's life and functioning is more appropriate.

In any case, on the affirmative side, I don't think that your point of view can be thought of as rigid or harsh. It's a legitimate (in the sense of "arguable") point of view. It's just that I have found that it does not work psychotherapeutically and that one can use all of one's resources as an analyst at the particular point that specifically indicates their application, while at other times they operate latently in terms of understanding what is "behind the scenes"—and dealing with special understanding with the "scene" itself

You did touch on some other things, which I don't want to go by entirely without some comment. You see, you said for example that the psychotherapy patient "doesn't know he's not supposed to have thoughts about the analyst." This is obviously true. And that the patient develops, or finds stimulated by the situation, certain unconscious fantasies about the analyst or therapist is a fact, a truism. However, as I said before, there are nuances of difference, sometimes gross difference, as to how one responds to these thoughts in analysis and psychotherapy respectively. All this has something to do with one's theory of the transference. From my view, all human relationships develop out of a single original relationship, which gave rise to the primordial transference, and then later, by way of language and certain cognitive developments, into what I spoke of, in a poorly selected term, as the "mature transference" (Stone, 1961, 1967). So in a way, a person is living with his transference all the time, therapy or no therapy. With every relationship, there is an element of transference, of varying degree, although it may be in no way manifest as separate or different from the other elements in the relationship. They are integrated, fused, so to speak, in the sphere of conscious awareness and behavior. Not to speak of the transmutations that urges that might have been transferences have undergone in the process of maturation, different functional forms that they have assumed, i.e., real needs towards appropriate objects.

So in a sense you are interpreting, and can interpret, transferences or transference derivatives in the everyday relationship in a special and limited way. The question is whether these urges have to be, or it is desirable that they should be, brought into relationship with oneself in every instance. This is partly an economic (-psychological) problem. I made a point, I think in *The Psychoanalytic Situation* (Stone, 1961), that the very intensiveness of the analytic relationship makes it more of an actual and confronting reality; that is, the relationship with this one individual whom you see every day, or nearly every day, for a long period, as opposed to the relationship with a therapist who sees a patient once a week, while he has a boss whom he sees every day, or a wife with whom he lives all the time. True, the "abstinences" involved in even the most active (if professionally delimited) therapies, plus the "resemblances" of the therapist's role to certain aspects of parental figures, do tend to mobilize ego-dystonic as well as ego-syntonic transferences. This is true of other figures in most patients' lives: conspicuously teachers, physicians, clergymen. But the economic element must be taken into consideration, as well as the advantages or disadvantages of a broadly regressive transference neurosis under limited conditions. But somewhere in most therapies, even so-called supportive therapies, the relationship to the therapist will have a focal character, will become a confronting issue; that I do not doubt. And that that's where the real, critical juncture in the therapy may crystallize. There are exceptions into which I do not enter at the moment. But the great likelihood that such issues will arise is the reason that even supportive therapy, if extended in character, requires alert analytic perceptiveness.

Langs: I follow what you are saying. I think it is true. I meant something in a little different sense: I realize that there are many naive resident therapists who attempt to do something that in their minds is related to or is a form of analysis with all patients, that borders on wild analysis. This is not my proposal, though I can see how my approach could be misunderstood in that way. Within the position that I'm developing, one responds to the patient's needs within the session. It is a matter of following the patient's unconscious leads and being prepared to intervene wherever his neurosis is expressed—and in therapy, as in analysis, this occurs in response to the therapist's interventions. They prove empirically to be the critical adaptive contexts for the patient's material.

For example, one may intervene more frequently, without other kinds of modifications. One may intervene in ways that are in tune with the patient's needs as they are reflected in a once-a-week therapy, even with a basically interpretive approach. It doesn't imply in any sense a sort of blind, interpretive pushing ahead. It includes a great deal of sensitivity and even a decision not to interpret in certain areas, or to interpret upward.

Stone: I think we would agree on that. But I also believe that the whole pattern of the relationship should usually be significantly different from that which obtains in analysis, within the professional pattern that I mentioned earlier.

Langs: I observed (Langs, 1973)—and this is why I take exception to a modified and so-called supportive or noninterpretive stand in psychotherapy—many presentations of the supportive approach. Listening to the material in the adaptive context of the interventions that were intended to be supportive—and that is what most therapists fail to do; they accept surface responses and do not recognize the indirect, latent communications—I found again and again that the patient unconsciously reacted very negatively to such interventions.

Stone: What kind of actively supportive interventions?

Langs: Advice, suggestions, leading questions, reassurances, praise, and the like. First of all, it really surprised me because I did not expect it. I had been taught to accept certain supportive measures in therapy; I was forced by the data to change my view. Now this has to be qualified, because one might say, "Well, in more skillful hands this would not occur." I don't believe that's true. Many observations, of my own work and that of others, have convinced me that if we study the patient's unconscious communications and introjective identifications, we will discover that he experiences a negative introject in response to seemingly supportive interventions; while patients will accept them, as a rule—though not always—on the surface, there is a split, and the unconscious response is characteristically adverse and negative. The patient experiences the intervention as an intrusion, as a seduction, as a loss of autonomy, and as a reflection of countertransference problems in the therapist. And the material from the patient will reflect various kinds of detected unconscious meanings. I don't mean now just fantasies, as perceived validly from the therapist. I mean that these measures convey these kinds of actual implications to the patient. See again, that's where one needs the data.

Stone: The data, yes. Well, just to respond to that. I would not find it hard to agree with you, if by active support (you see all of these things have to be defined) you mean gratuitous reassurances and the taking a sort of Jewish mother attitude toward the patient, automatically absolving him from all responsibilities and so forth. If by support you mean the support that comes from listening with a sympathetic, interested attitude, not being unwilling to answer a simple question that might be quite natural for the patient in the setting, and treating him with the respect that is due him as an adult, well then I don't think that support per se produces these untoward responses, without some additional, unspecific adventitious factor.

Langs: No, I would agree. Though I do mean to imply that virtually all noninterpretive interventions will have such unconscious effects. I'm talking about active, supportive interventions of which there is a continuum ranging from those of a gratuitous, Jewish mother type, totally inappropriate, to those that the analyst feels are necessary modifications in neutrality, undertaken in the interests of the patient and based on his analytic insight and skills. I'm talking about any such active intervention, as contrasted especially with the inherently supportive aspect of the therapist's basic hold and interpretive position, which, as I have said, I believe to be greatly underestimated. I think the regular once-a-week frequency, and the set time, and his concern, and his ability to interpret—all have very important and inherent supportive qualities. In psychotherapy, too, there is a basically supportive holding component which does not entail any sort of modification in, let's call it an essentially analytic stance or attitude. This provides the patient the best opportunity, however limited, for adaptive inner change. There's a distinction, and many analysts, interestingly enough, don't make this distinction, between active efforts of support and implicit attitudes of this kind.

Stone: I don't think that most analysts ignore the inherently supportive aspects of the regular and dependable hours, the patient listening, etc. Nor do patients. In fact, intuitively, some people just seek "someone to talk to." What may be ignored sometimes is the fact that a transference breakthrough may occur even when this setting, with minimal or no interpretation, is the prevailing modality of treatment. Indeed, this is largely what is meant by supportive therapy, in a skeletal sense. What may be added, according to judgment, in relation to the particular exigencies of the situation, might be occasional interventions of a didactic, explanatory, or counselling nature, clarifications, occasionally even broad, simple, interpretive remarks, closely bound to immediate realities, of the general type mentioned earlier. And yes, when really indicated, even an expression of sympathy or reassurance! The effort is not (to borrow your term) to seduce the patient into an increasing (usually futile) preoccupation with his unconscious (or the terminology connected with it), but to help him to deal better with the painful psychological or material realities of his life. In truth, over many years of work, I have not seen the calamitous effects of which you speak. Again, I feel a paradox at work—with a sort of Calvinistic aura. Whatever is usually good and useful in "human relationships seems doomed to turn out badly!"

Langs: No, the results often are not calamitous, but quietly unhelpful or what I term (Langs, 1975a) "misalliance cures." I am describing an empirically derived position. It bears out Freud's (1912b) warning: matters are different in psychoanalysis—and psychotherapy—from the social sphere, including the nature of truly helpful responses. For me, the most supportive and kind intervention available to the therapist is a well-timed, meaningful interpretation.

In supervision—and then in my own work when I still responded in such ways—I found that patients experience active and direct so-called support far differently from inherent or implicit support. The latter is essential; we agree on that. It's the question of the more sophisticated, active interventions to which I have found patients reacting negatively—sometimes directly so, but most often on an unconscious level.

Stone: Again, the only thing I would disagree with strongly is the fact that active—leaving aside for the moment the definition of "active"—support is per se necessarily bad. There may be times when it is necessary and where its lack will produce the same negative effects which you describe. Incidentally, we have not discussed the indications for supportive therapy as such. Have you tried supportive therapy with a patient with advanced heart disease or carcinomatous metastases to bone? You see, I think the question of appropriateness and of meeting the real needs of the patient and the context in which it occurs has to be considered in every instance. And I think the maintenance of the frame as such, which you emphasize so strongly, is a fallacy, as this then assumes almost a greater importance than the interaction between the two people on an adult level.

Langs: Let me clarify, because you are right: my position can be destructive in its extreme—but so can yours. Essentially I am discussing a basic choice. This is crucial, because this is not just frame for frame's sake. There is a critical alternative here between a supportive intervention and an interpretation. Interpretation leads to insight and adaptive inner change, while so-called support is suffused within latent but real negative effects—empirically.

Stone: Oh, of course, there's a difference. Persons who are susceptible to the deep revisions of interpretive psychotherapy are not usually treated with essentially supportive therapy.

Langs: Here, again, our thinking differs, since I feel that all patients will benefit from an interpretive approach that is in keeping with their pathology and needs. For me, the issue is whether one makes the interpretation, or offers support. I believe on the basis of what I have observed, that the interpretive intervention is in all cases preferable to the supportive one, and I would go even further. Often the supportive intervention arises out of a failure to understand the material and from an inability to interpret.

Stone: Oh yes. We're not speaking of things that are done because somebody doesn't know how to do better. Also, our tracks may have diverged a bit. An occasional judicious broad interpretation may have an ancillary position in supportive therapy, just as occasionally strongly indicated support may have a minor, but very important, position in interpretive psychotherapy. There are things that require support and there are things that require interpretation. And obviously, support will not accomplish what interpretation would accomplish, when interpretation is the thing that is required. I believe they're just two different modalities. And also there are many kinds of support. So I would not be able to go along with the generalization about interpretation *always* being the advantageous modality. It is sometimes wasted, confusing, misunderstood, irrelevant or even exacerbating to existing illness.

Langs: That's really where we disagree. But again, the best we can do is establish contrasting positions and at least we can define it as an empirical question. Unfortunately, so much of my position derives from a form of listening to the patient that is unique in the field. It is difficult for me to allude to clinical data and formulations that you could readily comprehend. Let me say simply, that my observations indicate that a supportive intervention, offered by an experienced analyst who feels that this is indicated as a positive and helpful maneuver, may well be revealed, by analysis of the specific material and interaction, to contain countertransference problems. I exclude here emergencies, such as suicidal or homicidal crises, where a lot of questions would come up about the therapeutic interaction anyhow.

Stone: I have no doubt that that occurs, at least now and then. The only thing that I would stick on, and this has appeared in some of our previous discussions . . .

Langs: Oh yes, we get back to the same issues.

Stone: . . . is that the opposite may also be true. That a countertransference may enter into the analyst's stiffness, his refusal or inability to respond in a reasonable and appropriately supportive way at times. And that this can be equally destructive, and sometimes more destructive, if it occurs in a critical situation. I do *not* mean just to keep telling the patient that he's all right, or that what he did was fine and not to worry about it, or nonsensical businesses of that sort. But just occasionally a word, a phrase, or an attitude, or a tone of voice that may indicate to the patient, "Look, we're still working on this, and you know that you have me with you" may be critical at times. Another thing I must mention again—rather, two things: (1) The concept that the interpretation is not only the only valid psychoanalytic (and thus psychotherapeutic) tool—and further, the only inherently nondestructive one I do not accept; and (2) I do not usually conceive of supportive psychotherapy (as a general modality) as applicable to people who can utilize interpretive work genuinely and constructively.

Langs: Here again it is my in-depth observations that have led to my position—the patient's indirect rather than direct responses. I find that it's quite feasible to convey support implicitly, in many ways. I think it is true that many analysts, apparently mistakenly, have elaborated upon your position by very actively reassuring the patient at times when they're being not only gratuitous but really reflecting their ignorance, anxiety, and countertransferences. In terms of a wider area, when one develops a position in which one constantly monitors the material from the patient for unconscious communications and processes—not only unconscious fantasies about the analyst, but the unconscious perceptions and introjects as well—one learns from both a subjective reassessment and the material from the patient that an incorrectly supportive intervention communicates to the patient a failure to have understood the material. The nature of the intervention then expresses the analyst's need to be supportive when he should be interpretive. It also communicates a whole constellation of pathological unconscious meanings from within the analyst; these the patient then, of course, generally introjects, and then has to work over. Erroneous interventions convey critical unconscious, pathological projective identifications from the therapist into the patient.

Stone: It can communicate it, if it's so. No doubt about it, and that it may often be so. Just as Money-Kyrle (1956) pointed out, these introjective-projective phenomena can occur instead of understanding and good interpretation. But the opposite can be so. You see, I must insist on that because I have too often dealt with the results of the opposite, so I know of its existence. There is no aura of sanctity about interpretation as such. It may be incorrect, ill-timed, or influenced just as much by countertransferences or a sense of helplessness in the analyst as any other form of intervention, which is more readily made a whipping boy (even when indicated). I've said before, "correctness" is often the most secure hiding place.

Langs: I understand that. They too constitute pathological projective identifications when erroneous, though not when correct and indirectly validated by the patient. I think that the condition that you've seen so often is part of a constellation in which there are interpretative failures, human failures.

Stone: Without question. Still, the offer of an interpretation instead of a supportive maneuver can in some instances be a "failure."

Langs: I think that without a sound stance of concern and the like therapy becomes what you are describing. Once it becomes barren of an inherent sense of support, then it can be a terrible phenomenon.

Stone: Well, I don't disagree with that. That's why I was at pains earlier to correct the idea that I believe that all people who follow strict rules are necessarily harming their patients. That would be an absurdity. I certainly have greater respect for that attitude than I have for a sloppy "Jewish mama" interpretation of psychoanalytic work or even psychotherapeutic work for that matter. I conduct psychotherapy in quite conservative fashion, when I do have such cases. And I have always had one or two, in which the affective contact is not strikingly dissimilar to that which obtains in analytic work, with due regard for the differences that I've mentioned in activity, relative openness, and the interpretive format. I have in mind somewhat different goals; I have in mind the fact that the patient requires or needs something different from me, when he is seeing me once a week (and that's all he has), than he does when he's coming every day, or four times a week; and that this different arrangement has been set up for reasons of different indications. And certainly I think it's appropriate that there be differences. But I do not get involved in any overtly parental attitude toward the patient. As you know, I regard the realities of a therapeutic situation as very important. If one is a doctor one should remain one. One can always offer that to the patient genuinely. If one imitates a parent, one can stimulate expectations that in the long run must meet with disappointment that may be catastrophic. I believe that in the long run that is where Gertrud Schwing's (1954) brilliant efforts went awry.

Langs: I agree that there are different needs. Much of this is dealt with in my approach by more frequent interventions, again ultimately interpretive. One develops a different rhythm, uses a different sense of timing, works at a different level—there's no question about it. One makes interventions that one might have waited to offer with an analytic patient, for two or three sessions of build-up; but in general, when one has a once-a-week patient, one attempts to do the best with the material at the time. As to whether one then makes the interpretation within the framework of the therapeutic relationship or outside of it—I feel that, just as in analysis, one makes the former type of intervention in both because that is where the important neurotic (and nonneurotic) material lies.

Stone: I would say the preponderance, to me, is importantly different.

Langs: Yes, I understand that, but I have found empirically that the issues related to the therapeutic relationship will predominate in therapy too. You see, given that the area in which the therapist intervenes is determined by where the patient is at the moment . . .

Stone: Naturally.

Langs: What I've observed in psychotherapy is that the patient is, as a rule, dealing with issues related to the therapist and the therapeutic situation. What surprised me, when I finally became willing to follow the patient, was the frequency with which issues related to the therapy, the therapist—what he said, what he didn't say, when he's going on vacation: issues of that kind—would come up in a once-a-week therapy.

Stone: Well, of course they do. I have not meant to contradict that. You said you must follow where the patient is at the moment. But you see, even there, there are complications in the way one conceptualizes it. Because in a sense the patient is always at this earliest relationship with his mother, to some degree. And one doesn't interpret it that way.

Langs: Right. But I am referring here to the immediate critical adaptive stimuli for his behaviors and associations; the rest is traced out from there.

Stone: It is also a fact that this has evolved into an elaborate system of relationships with the whole world, with different components and ingredients, cognitive, aggressive, libidinal, and the Lord knows what. If a person is fighting with his boss, we'll say, or fighting with his wife, it's extremely important, I think, not to depart immediately from the realities of those situations, but rather to make sure that, to the maximum degree possible, the person first becomes aware of the realities there, and then the irrational aspects, and then of certain ego-dystonic elements that are finding indirect expression in those areas. And then, you see, they can be interpreted, sometimes in fairly direct relation to genetic aspects. That there will be, sooner or later, a residue that perhaps can be experienced only in the transference situation, I'm convinced is true in psychotherapy too. But that should be allowed to precipitate out, while being monitored. Not squeezed out, or pulled out, much less plastered onto the patient's thinking about the realities of life, and that I've explicitly stated. My own emphasis would be on trying to exploit to a maximum what is out there, and can be seen out there, and leave for the transference those elements that are of such a nature and such an origin that they really can be seen only "there."

Langs: I must stress, because it does not seem to be coming across, the extent to which I allow the patient to create the session and my interpretations. I follow him and introduce virtually nothing beyond the reshaping of his communications—I do not force things onto him. I can't help but feel again that much of our disagreement stems from differences in the level at which we listen to material and in how we formulate transference-based expressions. I am stressing a focus in derivative communication because of the finding that this is how neurotic responses are conveyed. I also am emphasizing the continuous unconscious communicative interaction far more than you seem to. I approach all of this within the concept of the *adaptive context.* And I think that it's crucial continually to assess the central adaptive stimulus for the patient's material. And obviously, in a situation where, let's say, there is a quarrel with the wife, for me, the first responsibility is to determine whether the central intrapsychic conflict and adaptive context for the moment is displaced from the therapeutic relationship, or whether an aspect of the communicative interaction is being expressed in derivative form in that way.

Stone: Indeed, it may be a reaction to the therapeutic relationship. But why is that the *first* responsibility?

Langs: Because empirically it is the overriding source of the patient's unconscious responses; it is the realm that generates indirectly validated interpretations. If it is primarily a reaction to the therapeutic relationship, one must then deal with the question of how much is transference and distortion, and how much of it is not. That is, how much has been evoked by some error of the moment, how much involves unconscious perceptions and introjections of the analyst's pathology. There are lots of questions. I have no hesitation to interpret the material as related to the therapist, nor do I refrain, if the main adaptive context is actually in the relationship with the wife, from interpreting in that sphere. But even in psychotherapy, you see, I am concerned, just as I am in analysis, when I make interpretations that do not include a reference to me, at least ultimately. I mean this as related to interpretations of unconscious fantasies and memories and the rest. I always feel that something is missing at such a point. In essence, I may begin an intervention with a comment about an outside relationship, but I always link it up to some aspect of the interaction between patient and therapist or analyst.

Stone: Sooner or later, though, the transference will show itself at a time when the patient has been prepared on the basis of the progress of other clarifications and interpretations of what's going on, and the fact that it is so clearly in relation to the analyst, that he will accept the interpretation, both the cognitive and affective references. He's at a point where he can understand that this relationship is an active and important thing in his life, in ways that he had not hitherto thought likely. You see, in the usual psychotherapy, you haven't had much chance to prepare him for that interpretatively. And you have not occupied, quantitatively, the position in his life that you do when he comes to see you every day. So, while I agree that sooner or later, it will appear, in fact, I'm quite certain of that, and that then it has to be dealt with, and probably is the critical thing in most interpretative psychotherapies, I don't regard it as the active medium of exchange, until it signals its activity in an economic sense. I don't speak of those cases where you may see a person for a long time in, say, some largely reactive problem, for example physical illness, where it may play a relatively minor role, compared with the integrated real relationship. But in most psychotherapies it will ultimately prove itself to be the critical thing, in the focal sense that I have mentioned. Then, of course, one has to interpret it as such.

Langs: There are other differences in our views. When there is no reference to the therapeutic relationship, I think that something is missing right at the moment, rather than just later on. While the frequency of visits is only once or twice a week, the therapist does take on a very special meaning for the patient, and you seem to agree with this. I think that a psychoanalytically trained psychotherapist has a very special function that nobody else can fulfill for the patient, namely, to offer interpretations and insight, and special introjects based on that capacity. There's nobody else who can do this with any consistency. In other words, it's a special opportunity to handle conflicts with a certain kind of adaptive, inner resolution that is not available in any other relationship. Other relationships may be curative in other ways, but not through verbalized, cognitive interpretations, and the unconscious incorporation of the therapist on such a basis.

Stone: You say that he has a special meaning to the patient. Now, there is no question about that. And I would further agree that sooner or later, if this is a suitable patient, one who is capable of using an interpretative psychotherapy in a genuine sense, interpretation is explicitly indicated. Not just to learn a different way of saying what bothers him, as many patients do utilize interpretation. Sooner or later the unconscious aspects of this relationship, with its genetic background, will become a focus of that therapy, and that will be a moment of critical importance, where the analytically trained therapist has something unique to offer. But he also has the unique capacity, from his knowledge, his reconstructive or tentative knowledge of the patient, to use other modalities, to know when "support" is helpful and when it might flood the patient with guilt or produce angry or disturbed responses or diminshed self-esteem, and also, to fashion other useful elements of intervention, other elements of interchange and communication.

Now, the other thing is this: while it is certainly true that the therapist is important from the beginning, there are different levels and aspects of his importance, and the only special thing that is implicit in what I've been saying is that, for example, your importance to the patient as a doctor is very great. That integrates in itself many things, from my theoretical point of view—for example, the mother who cared for him, and is close to him, and is uniquely important to him. In psychotherapy, I believe, that can remain as an integrated phenomemon for a long time, as opposed to being prematurely precipitated out—or (not unlikely) being driven under a permanent cloak of resistance—by early interpretations. This can remain an aspect of the relationship, while the physician is engaged in helping him to understand what's going on in his life.

At some point, disturbances in certain of the fundamental elements in that phenomenon will appear, in various forms: for example, in the case of certain women patients who go frequently to male doctors and are always falling in love with them; this appears most often as a simple female "oedipal" phenomenon in the sense of the evolution mentioned earlier, a "father" transference because the doctor so readily becomes the "caring parent" and the fixated person's sexual feelings are harnessed to that anaclitic need. Well, when that sort of thing begins to show itself, obviously there is a unique opportunity. There are other things that are less simple and "classical" than that. So, while I agree with you about the unique importance of the therapist from the beginning, I see it in a somewhat different way, which to me remains fundamentally important: that your uniqueness includes the fact that you are the patient's doctor, and I say "doctor" in the broadest sense. I made some brief remarks about the word in *The Psychoanalytic Situation* (Stone, 1961). You might, in the situation described above, be a lay therapist and still be a very good doctor to the patient. And that meaning of the therapist should not be lost sight of.

Langs: I think we have covered this topic from several different viewpoints. Perhaps to just round this out, we can say something about the specific vignette I presented. We've said all we can about psychotherapy for the moment.

Stone: I'm sure we're both still interested in studying that. I mean, I'm not fully satisfied with my own contribution to date.

Langs: Yes, I agree with you fully. Let me just say this: The vignette was a situation in which the patient, who was in some form of brief psychotherapy, had brought in an incident at an office party with Bill, who put his arms around the patient's wife. He then in the session suggested a modification in the frame: that you see his wife. Now, I think we would agree that in psychotherapy the one-to-one relationship should prevail, without third parties; that would be basic to the frame.

Stone: Yes, but in the nature of the situation, somewhat more readily subject to exception and variation than in analysis. Although, of course, it does occur even in analysis, that one might have to see a marital partner.

Langs: You would be more prepared to modify it in psychotherapy?

Stone: More ready, in general, because of the more limited interpretative armamentarium, and the more frequent exigencies of this kind.

Langs: And I would be, of course, not so inclined.

Stone: I don't mean that the tendency to keep it "one to one," if something is not seriously lost thereby, would not be there. Remember, I said to this fellow, a rather naive patient, that I would prefer that he solve it himself. But I would be more ready, given the limited treatment possibilities, to utilize all possible methods of promoting the treatment.

Langs: My data produce a different attitude. In this context, which is not an emergency in any way, the patient suggests to the therapist that he see his wife. Now I would essentially, of course, see this as a request for a modification in the frame, and I would not tentatively agree to see the wife while stating a preference to do otherwise. I wouldn't even say anything initially; I would wait for associations, especially for him to change the subject and offer indirect material, which will contain the crucial unconscious meanings of the request—not just fantasies, but actual implications, functions, and consequences. But technically, if the patient pressed me, I would say, Let's explore it, let's see what comes to mind.

Stone: Yes, here you do the same thing as the psychoanalyst. Incidentally, the patient's request, while it no doubt also has unconscious meanings, is not a request for a "modification of the frame." That is a matter of your conceptualization. He is asking that one see his wife (for more than one reason). Now, if you treated it in a standard analytic fashion, instead of my conditional response, with a disturbed young man, you might have gotten the material you anticipate, or you might not! You might have gotten an angry, perplexed response and a suppression of the same material, which actually did present itself vividly and availably in this case. This choice, like the later choice as to interpretive direction, would, of course, be a matter of judgment. In the latter reference, it was, of course, following a tentative principle of psychotherapeutic interpretation as well.

Langs: Here you allude to manifest reactions. If the therapist does not inherently agree to participate, the material from the patient, in addition to revealing his fantasies about what such a modification would mean, will dictate the actual answer. The patient unconsciously communicates the answer, which, characteristically, is that the frame should be maintained in the best interests of the treatment. He will also then reveal the *unconscious* meanings and functions of the proposal. Once you even tentatively agree to alter the frame— how did you put it: a "reserved willingness"—once you've expressed a reserved willingness to see the wife, even with the preference that the patient deal with it himself, you've already indicated to the patient that you are prepared to modify the frame.

Stone: Yes. But as I said, with all respect for the meaning of the frame, I believe the patient remains more concerned with the inner transactions—and reacts to the frame only as he recognizes its validity. By the way, my alternative hypotheses about the patient's reaction included his possible anger as an adult, which would, of course, have much to do with his further state of cooperativeness in the treatment.

Langs: That fact, though, will have certain meanings for him, of the kind that I think are revealed in this material. These involve not only fantasied implications, but also realistic meanings and consequences. There are very subtle differences in my position compared to the usual understanding; it's been very hard to get them across to analysts. Students accept these ideas much more readily because, as analysts, we're so trained in thinking of the material from the patient in terms of transference and fantasy that we've neglected the actual implications it contains, its perceptive aspects and the introjections of ourselves based on consciously and unconsciously communicated realities. In any case you handled it by the "reserved willingness," the preference for the other approach, without an interpretation of the transference and nontransference implications. Now, here you didn't state what you might have interpreted to the patient. Would you want to suggest what relationship meaning you felt the request contained?

Stone: In addition to the reality basis for the request? That he might have wanted me to enter into some closer, sharing relationship with him, by way of seeing his wife.

Langs: I agree. One of the meanings of this request—and requests to modify the frame always have these kinds of actual meanings—involves special and inappropriate gratifications, for both patient and therapist.

Stone: Oh, this is a frequent thing. Although I should first register my objection to your last statement. Very few things are "always." One must remember Hamlet's famous remark to Horatio. This is too sharp a departure from empiricism. For example, apart from sometimes overwhelming realities, such requests sometimes originate with the marital partner, and sometimes from his or her own specific psychopathology. There was one once-a-week patient a few years ago who wanted me to take over his wife's treatment from another doctor. But the situation there was such that it could be handled in a fairly direct, if tactful, interpretative way, because this person also had a mild, pathological jealousy as one of his problems, was securely in treatment for some time, and, despite this request, was a psychologically intuitive person. None of this was true of the patient you are discussing. And it was useful as something that could be integrated with his understanding of his jealousy, as it had been previously gradually developed, in relation to "outside" material. That's what I mean by something "coming to a focus" in the transference.

Langs: Well, here's a brief psychotherapy where it does come to focus in the relationship, in a very intense way.

Stone: I am not so sure that this had "come to a focus" in a sense that would have been assimilable to the patient. The reality was in the foreground. Also I elected not to interpret it there because I was influenced by my feeling that there was sufficient material about the name, "Bill," and his brother, and so on, that could and should come first. Ordinarily, a young male has to be introduced to his homosexuality gradually and circumspectly, under the best of conditions (apart from the special technical and economic principle elaborated earlier). Thus the special principle of interpretation. Incidentally, if a pragmatic view means anything, the patient did not do too badly for a sick young man on rather sparse treatment hours.

Langs: In many respects, our views diverge again, though I fully agree on the need for tact.

Stone: Well, I wouldn't want you to think that I would necessarily do exactly the same thing now, or always even then. I might have elected now to call his attention to the fact that this had something to do with his feelings toward me, even in psychotherapy. But would that be better? Or would it be in part the result of a longer ingrained psychoanalytic habit and long years with a different kind of patient, under different conditions. I think that at that time I felt that the situation was so intense an experience for him in its own setting; and the fact that the question of my seeing his wife had such a clear purpose in his mind might still be preponderant. That's another thing. She was deriding his psychotherapy and creating trouble for him, and if he had felt that it was necessary, I might have considered it, and then have the interpretation follow it. Because, for example, he could very well have brought a dream thereafter which involved an obvious substitute figure and his wife, and made the issue a matter of indisputable clarity. Let me explain the difference: If it was interpreted, as soon as he brought it up, it would have been interpreting a matter which to him made perfect sense. Interpreting something in that state is not optimum. Especially when the reality factors are not "real." Don't forget that to him I was not some hocus-pocus figure who doesn't see people. I was a doctor; and doctors see wives or husbands at times, explain things. That was probably what swung the balance for me then, plus what was at that time a much more heavily weighted principle of trying to interpret the thing in its own setting where it was active, and where it had quantities of demonstrable affect involved in it. Also the interpretative emphases on ego-dystonic, unconscious aspects of the transference (if it worked) would be launching the patient on a long and stormy voyage for which his treatment vessel might not be adequate. I don't know with any certainty how I would do it now. I would have to be confronted by the entire situation de novo. But apart from a certain element of obstinacy, I must say that I still adhere in general to some of the principles that guided me then, albeit in a less doctrinaire, more pragmatic way.

Langs: I see the therapist's and analyst's functioning as different from the usual physician—because of therapeutic necessity. Unfortunately, we don't have sufficient clinical material. Let me tell you what my experience is; it helps to explain why the accent would be different. Patients, I have noted, will often bring up modifications in the frame when they're involved in some difficulty in the therapeutic relationship. Sometimes these are based largely on transference distortions, sometimes on countertransference distortions—often, on both. But the request can be taken as a signal that there may well be an unrecognized problem in the therapeutic relationship that has to be resolved; that has been an extremely frequent observation in my material. One of the most significant factors in the wife's derision of your patient's therapy might well be his use of her to split off and disown his own criticisms of you as a therapist. And seeing the wife, then, would of course bypass the unconscious uses that he is making of this particular division—his resistances. In other words, participation in an interview with the wife, for me, would have the hallmarks of what I call a *therapeutic misalliance* (Langs, 1975, 1976a,b), in which certain unconscious fantasies and defenses are not only bypassed, but are directly gratified.

My conception would lead to a difference in my understanding of the dream that would follow such an interview, a difference that would stem from the fact that you had actually gratified, let's say, his wishes for you to share his wife with him. The unconscious gratification would relate, on one level, to his unconscious fantasies, which are related, of course, to some of his pathology—there's some kind of unconscious homosexual conflict involved here. If the therapist were actually to accept the modification in the frame, the patient then directly gratifies in a disguised way the homosexual fantasies and directly defends against them, and their genetic counterparts then take a different shape than seen in essentially transference situations. In transference, the homosexual wish is in a fantasied form, the analyst does not gratify it or directly avoid it, and he is thereby different from, say, the father who did on some level gratify or flee from these homosexual wishes. The current situation would be different from the patient's past situation, and the analyst different from the patient's intojects. Reality within the therapy would not correspond to his pathological intrapsychic or inner situation. On the basis of that differentiating grade—if I can use that term a bit differently than it has been used by others, although somewhat in the fashion of Loewald (1960)—the material then is analyzed. The patient has an opportunity for a new resolution of the fantasies and conflicts involved. In contrast, in the situation where the analyst complies, he now has behaved in a way comparable to the traumatizing, pathogenic father. He now in a way confirms the pathological introject, and the patient's pathology is reaffirmed.

Stone: Some of the things you say are quite acute insights into what might be. I myself could speculate endlessly about the depth or psychopathology of the person and process. The use of the marital partner to voice the patient's warded-off criticisms can indeed occur, and spectacularly. But these are only "mights." And even as hypothetical, they are only parts of any attitudes or wishes which emerge as ego syntonic in a nonpsychotic patient. The pathologic aspect must separate out, and preferably, gradually. Tact and timing are also necessary in psychotherapy—only more so! Ignoring the patient's reality a priori is not helpful. I think some of your speculative reconstructions (and again I object to their universalization) are a little too far removed from the realities.

There's another thing, you view these things a little—not a little— much more than I do in terms of unconscious psychic reality, which ignores other psychic realities. You know, there are ego perceptions of reality, integrated relations between patient and doctor, as I said before. And when you say that by seeing his wife I "necessarily" gratify his homosexual fantasy, there is an important basic mistake. I don't gratify it. I'm not having sexual intercourse with his wife, nor putting my arms around her, still less with him. And in my attitude toward him, including the (general) "countertransference," latent in being a doctor, whether it be *the* best judgment or short of the best judgment, I'm doing it as a doctor trying to help, seeing his wife to explain why his treatment is necessary, and why it might be helpful to him. Now, these realities are extremely important. On them depend the structure and integrity of the therapeutic situation at the very bottom.

So if there is an unconscious gratification, it is still in his fantasy, and thereafter, he might come and bring a dream, let's say that I put my arm around his wife—something of that sort. It could be interpreted, and the fact is, sometimes with very striking impact. True— the entire sequence might be different now, because I might be a little more ready to include an ("anticipatory") transference interpretation with a psychotherapy patient than I was then. As I said, or implied, earlier, the grey area is larger for me nowadays than it was then with certain patients, under certain conditions. With this patient, under the conditions of treatment, I just can't say. But sometimes these things are better interpreted after the fact, assuming that you didn't do any monkey business with his wife or show any phony attitude toward him, or want to see his wife because you heard she was a strikingly pretty girl, or something like that. Surely such matters would destroy the treatment. If you see her honestly, for an honest reason, it might stimulate certain fantasies. It would be very unlikely that they would be stimulated to a destructive degree. Incidentally, that has never happened in my personal clinical experience.

Let me present the following as an example. Two or more years ago I saw the wife of a younger analytic patient, for the simple reason that there was a real threat to that marriage and the young woman was jangling my phone, creating emergencies, and saying that he was crazy, when he wasn't. She turned to his doctor, you see, because there was a lot of trouble between them. I saw them together; I would not see the wife separately. (This occurred on very rare occasions, but not under those circumstances.) Even the joint interview was followed by dreams that involved the homosexual aspects of the triangle, dreams in which the wife exposed herself to me and matters of that sort. But these matters could be interpreted to advantage, no psychoanalytic harm was done, some clinical perspective was established. Of course, it is true that the patient's neurosis will usually incorporate such incidents into his reactions in the psychoanalytic process, invest them with this neurosis and his transference, and evidence this in his material. But where the occasion is "clean" I have yet to see a malignant reaction to such episodes. Indeed, some are even productive. What to do about the *spouse's* transferences (positive or negative) is sometimes a more knotty matter.

Langs: Here too I am alluding to derivative but *real* pathological gratification, not overt sexuality. On a derivative level, the patient's dream of the wife who exposed herself to you could represent an introjection of the exposure on your part of unconscious sexual needs and fantasies. Without attempting to respond in further detail to your comments, allow me to continue delineating my position. I would stress one other factor. Not only is there the homosexual gratification, there is also the defense against the homosexual transference and perhaps countertransference enacted by bringing the woman in. That part is even more apparent and actual. But, to return to your point . . .

Stone: Your reference to the introjection of my needs could be so, like any of a million other things. But there was no evidence in that direction in the subsequent analysis. The patient's own impulse to homosexual sharing determined his dream and thus invested that incident with his sexual fantasy.

We start all this with the reservation that I am not defending the technical perfections of the way I approached it. I was aware, obviously, from what I said, that there was another way to do things. I left it to the patient, with my statement of preference. He took the option, did not bring his wife in, and—I think—instead brought the dream. Possibly the option and the waiver were in themselves important.

Langs: Yes, we're going to get to that in a minute.

Stone: Well, now, you see, if one refused, that's another thing. We wouldn't have the same affective context—granted its diagrammatically firm position in the principle of abstinence. We don't know if the patient felt desperately hurt by his wife, and in real trouble because she humiliated him about going to treatment. If I had refused, then he would have had to deal with the other side of this two-layered situation (to oversimplify it). "What kind of a doctor is this who won't talk to my wife, when she's giving me a hell of a lot of trouble?" That might be as difficult, or, as I said, sometimes more difficult to deal with. The average, nonpsychotic person is not going to react with an uncontrollable intensity, homosexual or otherwise, to one's seeing his wife. He may have fantasies, but they will certainly emerge as such.

Langs: Your point is well taken, though I do not fully agree. But I do think you have crystallized something very critical. First of all, as a therapist or analyst I never refuse or direct, or tell a patient what to do.

Stone: You just interpret the request, right?

Langs: The patient generates his own answer; it's in his indirect associations. The patient really becomes the key determinant of this decision, and given this approach it's almost never a problem, although it seems like it would be. But the material has the answers; the patient unconsciously answers his question so readily, just as this patient consciously did so in this case by not bringing the wife.

But you said that you and I address realities and psychic realities somewhat differently, and that you pay greater attention to certain realities that I tend to put more aside. That's the critical statement. I do treat all of this in terms of analyzable material, and I do indeed set the realities to the periphery. I do not ignore or deny them, but as a therapist and analyst I constantly seek out the unconscious meanings and functions so contained. My responsibility as a doctor who helps by interpreting remains the central one, and I would indeed take all of this material and focus almost entirely on its unconscious meanings and implications—fantasies and perceptions—and I would not simply consider the reality involved in a sense divorced from my central role—for example, in terms of my being a doctor who could explain things to his wife. Tarachow (1962) made the statement that as soon as the analyst—and I would say the therapist as well—accepts as reality, as a realistic need, some aspect of the patient's communications and wishes, one no longer has the transference illusion, or the as-if transference relationship. In a sense, it is no longer analyzable.

Stone: I don't agree with that. I feel that transference or other fantasy material never emerges genuinely as such, if the patient's reality is ignored. It may emerge in a placating "good pupil'—or even in a masochistic-submissive sense.

Langs: All transference material emerges in interaction with various aspects of reality, centrally those which exist in therapy. There are matters of definition here, but still, there can be no question that your position is different.

Stone: Very different.

Langs: I agree. It's much easier to formulate this in terms of a homosexual transference—and hypothetically, often I find that the therapist has contributed to such a request by unnecessarily modifying the frame, or by failing to intervene, by misintervening, though this need not have been a factor here—but we can assume that the patient is looking for the presence of his wife to protect him from his homosexual fantasies, and possibly perceptions, and from their gratification in some derivative form. Very often, less experienced therapists will alter the frame to protect themselves against an unresolved homosexual countertransference. This leads to a situation where the homosexual material is not adequately interpreted. It is indirectly gratified and defended against. The patient at such a juncture—and I'm not suggesting that this was true here, I'm using this as a model—will attempt to deal with homosexual anxieties by bringing the wife in, for one reason or another. Therefore, the presence of the wife has real meaning, even though it will prompt the patient, certainly, to dream and work over his reaction to your seeing her, or offering to do so. But I believe that the actuality is a significant one. The fact that the therapist participates in this defense or its disguised gratification creates a misalliance, designed, not for insight, but for something else, here I think, for avoidance, protection, and gratification of latent homosexual fantasies and wishes in the patient, and often in the therapist. That this creates a situation that has provided the patient with a moment of shared, inappropriate defensiveness and gratification doesn't imply that subsequently this cannot be worked through. It certainly can, though probably with some residual effect, but if the therapist is aware of the implications of seeing the wife in terms of the defense against the homosexuality, the offering of a sexual object and all . . .

Stone: That goes without saying. In a given instance, any or all of these things may be true. Quite frequently the patient may offer his wife instead of himself, and so on ad infinitum. But they may not be true—or they may be, economically, of secondary importance. And in any case, the analyst may not be in any way a real participant in these fantasies any more than his existence as a transference object for the patient, by treating him, means that he is thereby creating a misalliance. How can the reality be ignored? That's what starts the whole thing, and that's where we hope to end up.

Langs: It is odd to hear you imply that I ignore reality when I am actually stressing it—realities of which the analyst may be unaware. You are addressing manifest reality; I acknowledge its presence and add latent reality, if I may use that phrase, as well.

Under the circumstances I described, the patient's responses could be worked over. Here, the therapist can't rectify his deviation, but he could implicitly acknowledge its implications if he recognized them, and interpret the patients subsequent distortions. All of this would be available in derivative form in the patient's material. But you and I would differ. I would argue that the patient has actually perceived, unconsciously, kernels of truth regarding unconscious motives within yourself for deviating. These would be communicated indirectly, as a rule, in what he's saying, and his response would not be totally distorted. Granted that the therapist is not consciously involved in homosexual fantasies about the patient, granted that he does not have conscious, sexual wishes for his wife, nonetheless, I think the patient would be entitled to feel that there are some unresolved, unconscious, homosexual and seductive problems within the therapist and that they were expressed through the acceptance of the modification in the frame.

Stone: I think you're absolutely wrong there, due to the fact that unconscious fantasy is given a preeminence and predominance in life that is utterly unrealistic. For example, as I have said, every doctor to the patient at some level is a primordial mother, but that doesn't guide either his or the doctor's behavior. And when you say that the patient must perceive correctly that there is a homosexual countertransference, and that gives him a sense of justification in thinking, for example, that there is something seductive or something self-gratifying in the doctor's behavior, the idea is just wrong. For example, if a doctor, a general practitioner, comes to the house and feels the patient's abdomen, or let's say, if the patient happens to be a rather pretty young woman, lifts her breasts and applies his stethoscope, one could say he's acting out something from his unconscious incestuous fantasies toward his patient. But this is ridiculous. He is doing his job, just what he's supposed to do. Or, in the same sense you could say, "Why didn't he see her in his office? It's a break in the frame that he saw her at home." Maybe he is one of the few remaining doctors who makes house calls when the patient is too sick to go to the office. Now, if there is some overflow, if there is something that breaks out of his integrated function as a doctor, so that he gives a little extra caress to that breast, which the patient senses, and she sees something in his eyes that's different, well then, something has happened.

Now, that's just what I have tried to convey to you in this instance. If I saw this fellow's wife, it would have been solely and exclusively to try to promote a difficult, limited therapy by taking away misconceptions. She might come and say (these were working-class people, as I remember it), "What kind of sissy is my husband, coming to see a man all the time to talk, and what the hell's the matter with him? He worries about being sick all the time, and there's no sense in it."

I may exaggerate; it might not have been so coarse or untutored, but it could very well have been in that direction. I would have explained to her that this is an illness, like any other illness, but that it's susceptible to a different kind of treatment and that if she would be understanding, and not always make him feel that every time he came for his hour he was a sissy in his wife's eyes, it might facilitate his treatment.

Now, from your point of view those things would be relatively unimportant. All that would count was the fact that I saw this man's wife and that he would interpret this as an interest in her or as vicariously gratifying him through her. It's clear that there would be some such reaction to it, but that it would be ego-dystonic, far from the surface, and that if it were mobilized by this episode, it could be interpreted. This is all with the reservation that I do believe the fewer, in general, there are of such contacts, the better. Now, I say "in general" advisedly, because as I get older, there is an exception to every exception in my mind. There may be instances where it actually does promote and facilitate the therapy, and where it removes blocks, and where, as I say, to ignore such potentiality would be a mistake. So, I just don't go along with these gloomy generalized forebodings. With rare exceptions, I think they don't hold up.

Langs: Your comments border on proposing that the analyst's interventions reflect entirely his conscious intentions, and lack unconscious communicative implications of which he may be quite unaware. This is an attitude reflected in the analytic literature as well. Using your own model, I would regard the seeing of the wife as, unconsciously, the extra caress.

Stone: Why is it the extra caress? Are you "wild analyzing" me? Of course, I realize that an analyst's conscious motivations may not always be the exclusive phenomenon—whether in interpretations or other interventions. But we assume that the analyst knows himself reasonably well and is willing to examine his ongoing work, as well as the responses of his patient. The type of reaction that you attribute to me and apparently to all other analysts who do not maintain a rigid frame has not been validated by my experience.

Langs: Forgive me; I am simply trying to derive all possible implications in this material by organizing it around the prevailing adaptive context—honestly seeking out all possible meanings. I know that this sometimes seems like "wild analysis," but it is meant to be a reading of available inference from the unconscious communicative interaction. Seeing the wife could on a derivative level be experienced as the extra caress because, as I—and patients, unconsciously—define the framework of therapy and the function of the therapist, it is to see that patient and to see the patient alone, and because therapists too can have unresolved unconscious wishes. But mainly because the analysis of such behaviors has consistently revealed such unconscious meanings. Here, once again, I wish I could share such data with you.

Stone: Well, then I would say your frame is too rigid, based more on a mathematical model than an inclusive view of the complexities of human problems. It's absolutely rigid, because the frame, like a frame to the picture, as I think I said before, is there to facilitate the best presentation of the material. It's a poor analogy, because a picture is largely an aesthetic object. The frame in psychotherapy or analysis is there to facilitate the processes between the two individuals and their special functions. And I include the rationally interpreted rule of abstinence as an important part of the frame. It is not, however, there to make the process into a bed of Procrustes.

Langs: You are saying that at the point at which you modify the frame, you modify the nature of the relationship between yourself and the patient, and communicative properties of what I call the bipersonal field.

Stone: Of course you modify them, but not necessarily disadvantageously. Furthermore, I would hitch the cart and horse differently. Something arises in the requirements of the therapeutic relationship between the patient and yourself that necessitates a change in the frame.

Langs: Obviously, I do mean disadvantageously. It does really change the nature of the bipersonal field, and takes away from the uniqueness of that field, and brings into the situation unconscious contaminations.

Stone: Well, I think too great a sequestration from the ordinary processes of life is disadvantageous. Incidentally, since you say that these matters are only to be interpreted, I am reminded that I used that phrase (or something close to it) in *The Psychoanalytic Situation* (Stone, 1961)—I quoted it, because I was in contact with many of the analysts of a generation definitely older than my own. Some were colleagues of the greatest distinction; and one especially was very fond of the phrase—yes—"only to analyze." He was also known to depart from this dictum more widely than most. Although, in fact, of the people I knew, very few adhered to this principle as strictly in practice as the words might have sounded. You know, there were many, many "deviations"; I think by this time that is a matter of history. Beginning with Freud himself, of course.

And again I must enter the reservation that I do not mean to be critical. It was such contacts that contributed to my puzzlement about the teaching and practice of the later generations. Was psychoanalysis suffering a reverse arteriosclerosis? Was it a disease of the younger generation? We must base our work ultimately on empirical experience; there's no other view that really stands the acid test, other than the pragmatic one, except in the realm of abstract thought. You will recall I mentioned the person who was seen by one of the outstanding men in the profession, and (paradoxically) had been helped. I say "paradoxically," in view of the fact that the patient had left him, and I had been unable to persuade him to go back. Whenever this patient would bring up something painful, whatever the sphere, the analyst would only interpret his reaction to it. And this made him frantic, as time went on. As if these occurrences had no connection with reality; that his environment had no part in how he felt. If something untoward had happened, it was almost as if he alone had created it. Now, this is intolerable to some human beings, and if one doesn't take cognizance of that simple fact of human nature, I would say one is placing too great an emphasis on one's conception of the frame, and the frame which is supposed to help one do something for the patient can be something that militates against the effectiveness of your effort.

Langs: What you're describing is not in any way inherent in my attitude. In fact, through the adaptive context, every intervention I make begins with reality and from there extends into unconscious contents and processes. I think what was involved there would be part of a much more elaborate countertransference problem. My position doesn't imply making the patient responsible for everything that happens. Nor does it imply being insensitive to the realities of his life or his human needs. For example, that the wife is realistically picking away at her husband's treatment, this would be taken in, be understood. But I would interpret, within the context of the material, how the patient responds, how he's presenting it, how he's using it unconsciously, in addition to the reality, and it all would depend on the context of the material.

Stone: Exactly. All right, then, we agree. With one important exception: that, if the reality is not recognized, sometimes explicitly, the patient cannot give genuine attention to the other factors.

Langs: Not entirely. We've both said, so many times, that both your position and mine could be caricatured, abused, and misapplied, terribly. There's no basic disregard of the realities. My quest, and my job, is to get to the unconscious meanings of the material, as it's presented in a particular context.

Stone: Well, in that, you and I would have the same principle. Except that we might disagree as to what forms the best background for such access to the unconscious.

Langs: Oh, there's no question about that. Now, if we can just conclude the clinical discussion—the dream is not superfluous. You had not seen the wife, she did not come in, and then he had a dream about a man calling him from the office threatening his girl; he couldn't help but say, "I just kissed your wife." So he now tells you that unconsciously he was offering his wife to you for seductive purposes.

Stone: Right.

Langs: For me that unconscious meaning is extremely important. Sure there's the reality—the wife's complaining and all that. I feel that if he gets his homosexual fantasies worked through, and works through his own criticisms of the therapy, he'll handle the wife. But, what he's stating here is that not only would it be his fantasy that you permitted him to offer his wife to you seductively, but he would have some substantiation for his belief.

Stone: My attitude toward his request was just what I expressed; and I have mentioned some factors that entered into my choice of option. My countertransference was definitely not involved and I do not accept your theoretical conviction that the patient must react as if it were involved. Had the patient reacted thus, he would have had a symptomatic flare-up, or then flight, instead of bringing a readily interpretable dream and reacting well to the interpretation which was offered. This is not "caricature," but it is Procrustean. Again whether or not my way was the best way, "under the aspect of eternity" . . .

Langs: No, no, I'm again using the model—if it had occurred. Or, let's say, the model of a reserved willingness to see her. For him, the dream element, "I just kissed your wife," would be a representation not only of his fantasy, but again of how he unconsciously experienced the reserved willingness, and, if you had actually seen her, how he would have experienced the interview.

Stone: Or what he would have wished for, in my seeing her.

Langs: Wished for and gratified—in actuality. In other words, this alludes to what he unconsciously attempted to gratify.

Stone: Right, what he wanted to bring about. But his "unconscious" perception of my reserved willingness was *not* a correct perception, and the patient in the ego sphere knew that. It was an anticipated fantasy gratification, not a true perception.

Langs: He wanted the therapist to see his wife, and that unconsciously meant, "I want you to kiss my wife," which, we know, unconsciously means I want you to seduce her, to go to bed with her; I want you to allow me to offer her to you. Had you seen her, some gratification of these wishes would be involved—that would create a different climate.

Stone: The question of the analyst's real and unconscious motivations has much to do with determining the climate of understanding versus hidden gratification. You put the emphasis on the gratification of the wishes, which could only be in the fantasy sphere. I would have accepted the fact that in a good therapeutic climate, the contact with the marital partner that was being considered, and the latent fantasies which it stimulated, would likely stimulate still further the expression of the fairly direct unconscious wish (in the characteristic dream form of consummation). The gratification of which you speak isn't an actual gratification. It's symbolic gratification, or a very remote, derivative gratification which is sufficiently in the direction of his wish to enable him to state more concretely what the wish is.

Langs: We seem unable to resolve a key issue: the basis for, and the influence of, seeing a patient's wife. In sum, for me this conveys a failure to analyze an unconscious interactional issue—for example, a homosexually tinged misalliance—and involves a bilateral action (acting out) instead. And while the pathological gratification is symbolic (i.e., not directly sexual), it is real (i.e., latently sexual). You stress the derivative quality and suggest his response to the deviation would be essentially fantasied. I stress that in addition to the fantasied level, justifiable and valid unconscious perceptions would be generated and have a negative effect. The actualization of unconscious countertransferences and the reality of the implications of the analyst's active interventions have been quite neglected by classical analysts. Your offer of a possible session with the wife conjured up both realistic perceptions and distorted fantasies in my view, though only the latter in yours. Incidentally, you mention how this can then promote the therapeutic process. I agree that it may then be processed in that way. In fact, most erroneous interventions have a therapeutic wish contained within them.

Stone: I wouldn't say that it would be a matter of principle to do it, merely because it would promote the therapeutic process. It would be a matter of principle to do it, if the *reality* reasons were sufficiently preponderant. Some affirmative response might then indeed occur. But if it were done as a therapeutic trick, I would expect the response to be negative. No, I don't think "tricks" are desirable.

As for your remarks about the transactions in the sphere of unconscious realities, I must regard these as entirely in the realm of assumption. The "reserved willingness" to see the patient's wife was offered exclusively for the purpose of gaining her understanding so that the patient could continue his treatment without extreme domestic unhappiness and loss of his wife's esteem. In other words, whatever gratification he would actually gain would be in this sphere, which might then enable the understanding of the unconscious fantasies involved.

Langs: In the dream, the patient says, "He started for the place, found himself with a blonde in an apartment and had a seminal emission" (Stone, 1951, p. 233). Given the context of "reserved willingness," which for me is a lesser version of seeing the wife, this dream element would represent an introjective identification with the therapist, who has said he might see the wife, and who, in the patient's unconscious view, has gratified himself sexually with her. Here, I think, is an imbalance; where we say that the patient behaves in certain ways on the surface and that these behaviors gratify unconscious fantasies, I think we also have to apply that to the analyst. The analyst can behave in certain ways on the surface, and this, too, is often symbolic, and it can gratify certain unconscious fantasies.

Stone: They may or may not; if the patient's system of wish and fantasy is active, it will very likely utilize the analyst's behavior for its purposes. But again, this would be fantasy gratification and, if the therapist's behavior was soundly motivated and the patient not psychotic, the observing portion of the patient's ego—identified with the therapist in a manner different from the one you specified— would realize that and respond accordingly.

Langs: Perhaps I can further summarize the differences in our positions, and identify something of their basis. It seems to me that, with each of these vignettes, you are stressing your conscious good intentions, the surface reality of the incidents that call forth the deviations, the surface realities of the nature of the deviations themselves, and the direct and apparent salutary effects that their invocation elicits. You emphasize too, the patient's capacity to perceive these realities, and you view impressions and reactions beyond that level in terms of distortions based on transference and neurosis. On the other hand, I would, in general, accept the relevance of all of that, but I would insist on listening to all of the subsequent material from the patient as a commentary—realistic and fantasied—on a given deviation. I am suggesting that this more indirect material reveals first, additional distortions, but secondly, a series of valid unconscious perceptions and introjections of the unconscious meanings of the deviation. It is this realm that analysts have very much neglected. It contains expressions of unconscious countertransference fantasies and influences the patient's transference and nontransference responses, his reality testing, and his symptoms.

I cannot document the validity of your patient's unconscious perceptions of the hidden meanings of your proposed deviation here. I can only say that they are reflected in this material, may well be valid, and that they should direct you to search for possible countertransferences. In my clinical experience, there is as much truth to these perceptions as fantasy. And, by the way, I do not see the patient as the therapist's victim here—nor the reverse. These are circular interactions with continual inputs from both participants. I must stress again the empirical derivation of these concepts and their basic acceptance of the patient's unconscious sensitivities—not as an alternative to his neurotic functioning, but in addition to it. I am trying to add an important dimension; I have not discarded any basic aspect of the usual analytic conceptions in these areas. And this addendum is reflected in my interpretive work: I do not treat everything from the patient as fantasy and distortion, but instead sort out the patient's communications for fantasy and reality, conscious and unconscious, and respond accordingly.

I hope that clarifies aspects of our disagreement. This is why I am suggesting that your patient experienced, on one level, the proposed deviation as an unconscious, shared defense and gratification. And if I am correct, two points follow: one, that this aspect must be both rectified and analyzed before anything else; and two, that my position regarding the frame is not rigid or inhuman, but a sensitive, empirically validated response to the patient's therapeutic needs—an avoidance of undue traumatization by the therapist, carried out not because of fear, not through a belief that it is sacrilegious to break the frame, but out of a wish to offer the best possible therapeutic setting and relationship. On that basis, unplanned deviations can be rectified and analyzed quite comfortably and effectively—with gains for both patient and therapist.

This is the statement of a position—validation with this material is really not feasible. In your description of the session, the patient went on to mention the name of a girl. That brings up the issue of the other person's sexual identity—this was a girl marrying a senator—and then you offer an interpretation—and consciously decided to leave out the therapeutic relationship, interpreting in a more general way.

Stone: No. A very specific way. His friend, and his brother, with a specific historical background.

Langs: I meant that you intervened in terms of other relationships without linking it up to the therapeutic relationship. I don't mean to imply total nonspecificity, because you do offer definitive comments regarding these other people.

Stone: The omission of the transference there, if it was so, would have been determined by my specific point of view of that time about the methodology of interpretation in once-a-week therapy. Does it say anything more about it? As I have said, while I would still follow the same general principle I might be less rigid nowadays; if the patient continued for a longer period, and the relationship to me (other than as a physician) was clearly presenting itself, I would interpret the transference element.

Langs: I don't think that you specifically get to the relationship with yourself. I think perhaps that we have here finally crystallized from some of our discussion: the definitive issue that emerges is whether the therapist, who for good reasons seemingly related to reality, modifies the frame, for instance, by seeing a third party, by such action inherently gratifies some neurotic components for both the patient and himself. I believe on the basis of my observations that these modifications offer inappropriate gratifications or inappropriate defenses to both participants and that the patient will have a grasp, usually unconscious, of that residual of reality. I don't mean to imply that it becomes a hopeless situation, but basically, it requires rectification and a great deal of analytic work.

Stone: Well, I know it isn't a hopeless situation, from sheer empirical observation. And as I have said repeatedly, I think it is a serious and to me inexplicable error to minimize reality, to think that for a neurotic patient (I don't speak of psychotics) reality is nothing more than a crystallization of fantasy. All of our work depends on the maintenance of contact with the continuing reality of our roles and the therapeutic situation.

Langs: My conception of reality is not that it is nothing more than a crystallization of fantasy; it seems difficult to get my concept across to you. Reality is given full consideration, but its unconscious implications are given their full and necessary emphasis. A deviation is a reality that will leave a residual image, but if one is sensitive to the meanings for the patient, and for himself, one can do some self-analysis to modify whatever was inappropriate within the therapist. This can be and almost always is an extremely important therapeutic experience, for both participants. It does mobilize a great deal of material that when properly analyzed can have very significant therapeutic benefits for the patient. But the whole issue of the extent to which this does constitute some unconscious gratification is one that maybe we'll have to discuss further.

Stone: May I say a few words about it now, because it's in line. It's repetitive. But it requires repetition. There is, I think, an overestimation of the frame, important as it is. I don't see it the same way. The frame is important; the frame of a bed is important; the frame of a picture is important; the box in which one carries one's tools is important. It's not more important than the contents. It's there to serve the contents, to keep them usefully available. Now in your thinking, if I get it right, it attains a certain over-growth. You know, it's like the tail of the dog. The tail begins to be more important than all the rest of the animal. And the idea that there is always some neurotic purpose being served for the therapist if he finds it necessary or desirable to modify a rather overrigidly conceived frame is pure, unjustified assumption. Just to take the examples at hand: "Perhaps I will see your wife and try to discuss this with her if necessary. It would be better if you could work it out yourself." As a matter of fact, such necessities also involve the analyst in similar situations, although much less frequently, because of the different situation. Or, with the published analytic case, you found something similarly ominous in the fact that I would suggest an extra hour, instead of the medication. This I think is a pure (and not well-grounded) hypothesis. It is as if the person's conception of his functions and his commitment, if it is thought necessary to vary an abstractly conceived structure for good reasons, has only a neurotic basis. It could imply then that he analyzes people for neurotic reasons. He is a "young Jewish doctor who is afraid of blood, that's why he just sits and talks with people. One can reduce this to an absurdity very readily. There are good reasons for doing certain things and there are bad reasons. Or there are inadequate reasons relative to other consequences, and I think one has to preserve important differentiations there. If a patient whose unacknowledged, rigidly warded-off homosexuality frantically demands that the analyst see his wife, because she is neglecting her graduate courses for her bridge lessons, it would be folly that the analyst comply. You see, a person for example can raise a fee (1) because he's greedy; (2) because he needs the money; (3) because he thinks that the fee is inequitable and also that the patient will benefit from a more equitable fee. Now any of those may operate, or any of many other more complicated reasons. He may raise the fee, because he's afraid to be thought a sissy by his psychoanalytic group, or by his supervisor, or because he is reacting too strongly against his countertransferences being too mushy and wanting to give too much to the patient, or to be thought a good guy. Any number of reasons may operate, and the same is true of these things that involve modifications of the frame.

Langs: I understand what you're saying. I have already tried to clarify or disclaim some of your characterization of my position. I won't restate all of that again. I will say just two things though. One is that the contents remain one central concern, but the management of the ground rules and impingements on them also have analytic importance; but the argument is, of course, that with the modification in the frame comes modifications in the contents. The second is that these deviations empirically (not because I make it up, but because patients have consistently demonstrated it through derivatives) are detrimental to the therapeutic work. So my position isn't a disregard for the main body of analytic or therapeutic work.

Stone: But the results may be highly informative, and "no harm done," when rational variations, within certain limits of course, are introduced for *good* reason.

Langs: I understand that. But I think we can say for the moment that my thesis is offered as a hypothesis for further empirical testing.

Stone: I think it valid to test any such hypothesis, although I've been testing it throughout my career!

Langs: I think it points to an area whose implications and consequences could be now perhaps more profitably studied. I think we've established our positions and we can't do any more for now. We've both drawn upon our experiences as analysts, and we should let it rest at that—and leave it as a hypothesis for clarification.

Stone: For further clarification and study.

Langs: Perhaps in our final discussion we can look over more data. But one can always say, "Well, there are other situations in which this or that is a valid approach." That kind of objection won't resolve anything. What I wanted to do—and this is why I came to you in the first place—was present some of the differences in our positions.

Stone: I understand that, and I value it. Actually, I think that most truth lies in some dialectical sphere rather than at one pole or the other; that I certainly accept, in principle, about most things. It's just that one takes one's position according to one's observations and experience as to what is in general best. The fact is that I too, for many reasons, believe in the maintenance of structure. There are deviations which I regard as never acceptable. But it's a much broader, more flexible frame than yours—I think less based on a priori conceptions and much more on what I regard as demonstrable psychological realities. I am sure there are patients who are better treated in a rather strictly delineated fashion; whether they are the majority of patients, I don't know, even among neurotic patients, where the sense of adult human reactivity in relation to the analyst is not readily subordinated to the analyst's system of basic assumptions, when the latter are not clearly demonstrable as rational and realistic.

Langs: I am unable to get across to you that I have adopted not an a priori position but one based on a seemingly unique level of listening, derivatives in context being the key. This is where my position sounds very harsh and extreme, and I'm aware of it. I can only say that I have developed my approach empirically, and that I carry it out with tact and humanity, and that I have validated it over and over again. Inherently, I prefer a more flexible approach, but I have discovered serious pitfalls in such an approach and have to respond to the data. I think for our last meeting I'll pick out some non-Stone vignettes.

Stone: You'll have more time to change than I. I have had a few decades in which to become convinced of my view. Unfortunately, I'm nearer the end of my career (to state it euphemistically). But the dialectic, the mutual critique, is always useful. Nothing is airtight. And things do change somewhat with the perspective of time. As with my own old material.

Langs: I'm still working it over. But the fact that you are open to thinking about this is really what matters. Because many analysts really are not open to any important degree. Yet one has to remain open-minded as long as one is working in this field.

Stone: Of course. You can't get *anywhere* that's worthwhile if you don't remain open. Things become absolutely static and frozen. I have said I don't think your position is harsh or rigid. It's just that I don't agree that it is the best way. Nor do I agree with some of the theoretical substrata on which it is founded. The question isn't about being human or harsh.

Langs: We can stop by agreeing on that—until next time.

Chapter 6
CONCLUDING STATEMENTS OF CONTRASTING POSITIONS

Langs: Today I wanted to do two things. One is that I would like to take another vignette or two, not drawn from your material, for discussion. And I thought we could possibly discuss some of the issues brought up in your paper on problems and potentialities of psychoanalysis (Stone, 1975). I'm sure you have some kind of a perspective on your work, and on psychoanalysis, that would be of interest, to round things out.

Let me turn first to some vignettes. The first I am taking because the author referred to you. We both know the risks involved in writing, the problems of misinterpretation by others. So I thought that it would be interesting to read you some sections of a paper that was published in 1974, as part of a panel in Boston on regression, by a psychiatrist—I believe he may be an analyst—John Gudeman. The title of his paper is "Uncontrolled Regression in Therapy and Analysis." The paper centers upon a case report of a patient in analysis; I'll summarize excerpts. There are a number of modifications in the frame—deviations in technique. The patient, a twenty-eight-year-old married woman, two children, was referred by her gynecologist because of a nagging problem of frigidity; she herself felt the need to develop more in her role as mother and wife, and felt that she had marital problems. Her difficulties had begun two years before the consultation, when her husband told her of another woman he wanted to marry. She reappraised her marriage; she was unhappy sexually; did not have orgasms. Her husband remained with the marriage, she felt, because of the children. She had some counseling over the next two years. Her husband refused help, and then she herself came for analysis, because she felt she held back feelings, especially sexually. Sex had seldom been fulfilling for her; she felt inhibited, and they were having relations only once a month. She was aware of long-standing wishes to be cuddled and taken care of, wishes for passive love, dependency, an idealization of a beautiful world, and indecisiveness.

She began analysis with what Gudeman describes as a flood of material, immediately presenting a dream in which she was a nurse and she was not married. She worked at a hospital. She saw a baby born; it was ugly, because it had a big head. It was a casual place, not like any hospital she had seen. She sent the girl home with the baby, sent her out with a fellow. There were no direct associations. The analyst didn't comment on it, but went on to speculate about the dream: the "casual place" referred to where he worked. He thought of the baby possibly as the patient. The large head was seen as a need for intelligence, time to take the analysis, desire to be different, and some sense of ugliness of the self. The patient was the baby, who would grow up either deformed or intelligent. The analytic setting is represented by the hospital.

Stone: These are all the analyst's responses to the dream?

Langs: Yes, and he felt there was a charged sense as she related it, seductiveness and openness. He was concerned with whether this dream was predictive of regression.

To continue: During the initial sessions the patient described her early development and confessed many indiscretions; there had been a grandmother who had been in a state hospital, the death of a grandfather when the patient was nine, and then she became klep-tomaniac. She confessed to masturbation, and related it to the stealing. There was a seduction in her early adolescence by an older man, but not sexual intimacy, and other early seductions. She acknowledged being more than just passive.

Then, early in the course of treatment, following a moving description of the death of her grandfather, she came early to a session, walking up the corridor to the analyst's office, carrying a bouquet of fall flowers. The analyst stated that it was evident she was living out the wish for a wedding.

Stone: She brought *him* the flowers?

Langs: Yes. He said, "I accepted the flowers but not without some degree of discomfort, saying nothing immediately but undoubtedly conveying this discomfort. Knowing that acceptance of a gift might well enhance erotic components of the transference, it seemed at that moment that the rejection of the gift would mobilize, early in the treatment, separation anxiety and anger beyond the patient's ability and capacity to understand and analyze. Indeed, the presentation of a gift could well be the harbinger of fragile ego boundaries and a significant regressive potential. There can be little question—I feared severe regression and loss of boundaries for the patient" (Gudeman, 1974, p. 327).

Stone: This is early. Just in the first few weeks?

Langs: Early in the course of treatment. What do you think about such a gift offer from an analytic patient?

Stone: Well, you see, that would sound almost as if it were over the borderline already. Early in the analysis, for no special reason a patient brings a bouquet of flowers to the analyst. It seems to me a little bit bizarre. Of course, I don't know the context, the duration, and so on. In general, I approve of the rule about not accepting gifts. But I do feel that like any other rule, there are times when exceptions should be permitted. As I've often explained, it is different if things occur in the context of the patient's whole scheme of life and background, as with somebody who has grown up with the idea that at Christmas you give something to somebody whom you like, or respect; if such people bring some homemade cookies, or something of that sort, ordinarily it would not be necessary to reject them. "Reject," of course, is a term in itself that is pejorative. I mean, decline to accept them, with explanation. If the person is sufficiently sophisticated and well integrated, you might decide that the better thing to do is to get started right there and now, so to speak, and explain that it's much better if you analyze the impulse. If the patient is fragile, and of course I know there's a variation in use of those terms, then it becomes a matter of judgment.

Langs: Yes, he's concerned about that.

Stone: Or quite ill, and then if the gift is something that has not represented a sacrifice for the patient. Obviously, if somebody walks in with an expensive gift, there is something wrong there, a priori, that certainly should be treated immediately. But, as I say, if it's a token gift, a little thing, then it might be better to accept it, and then to say that ordinarily these things are not done, as part of the general analytic contract, and it would be better hereafter, if such an impulse arises, to try to understand it, rather than to act on it. I've found that sometimes that it's better accepted than the primary rejection, and I don't feel that harm has resulted from it. This incident, you see, strikes me in two ways: first, there's something to me that sounds bizarre about a bouquet of flowers to a male analyst early in the treatment, not because it's Easter, and it would be something fitting into the person's habits and customs, or some other (possibly) explicable occasion. This was out of the clear blue sky, and I would have the feeling that I would be concerned about what it means. And he apparently was concerned about the fragility of the patient's ego boundaries, or the vagueness of them, and he thought it best to accept it.

Langs: Yes.

Stone: Well, in the light of his reaction to the patient and his hypotheses, I would say that it might quite possibly be all right, and could be followed by an actual explanation, in relation to the usual customs and procedures.

I don't think those things are disastrous. They can be disastrous if they are dealt with as a matter of course, accepted as such, and if there is anything that makes the patient feel that the analyst likes or wants this kind of treatment, and omits all discussion of what the usual provisions are.

Langs: I understand what you're saying. Again, of course, this is where we have quite contrasting positions. I have tried to think this out again and again. When I first read this, I reacted somewhat along the lines of your response, only in a more definitive fashion. Obviously, I now know what follows. However, I really was able actually to predict in a general way what did follow. My position is often misunderstood as implying that I would simply say, "No, no, thank you." It's not what I do at all.

Stone: Well, I don't think you would say that. That would be just a bald rejection—No, thank you, without further explanations.

Langs: I do it differently, even in regard to explanations. I would simply not accept the gift, and indicate to the patient in an open-ended way that we will explore this as we explore anything else. Now, that is a certain level of rejection, in that it isn't the direct acceptance of the gift. But it is also turning to the analytic situation and to basic analytic work, in essence implying to the patient that we will analyze her offer, and from her associations, we will make a decision, and also understand how the gift offer came to be actualized on the basis of unconscious needs and behaviors in both herself and the analyst, who often has unconsciously set the stage for this to happen, by failing to maintain the frame or missing important interventions, whatever the additional contributions from the patient's pathology. I have had experience with various approaches— accepting, not accepting, or simply saying "Let's analyze it and see." This last attitude makes a significant difference, in that the analyst does not immediately participate. If one accepts the gift, then there is participation, unconscious gratification, and the patient reacts accordingly. Even direct refusal without suggesting a need for exploration is a kind of participation. In other words, it's back to the point I've made many times before. For me, these ground rules took on meaning in terms of the image of the analytic relationship as occurring within a bipersonal field, a setting, a space with properties and serving as a medium of communication. The concept of space is being used a great deal by Kleinian analysts.

Stone: A figure of speech, that matter of "space." One can begin to confuse figures of speech with the realities on which they are based.

Anyway, not accepting the gift is not accepting it, however gracefully done; it does not mean that one is not involved. It may be right, mind you. But it is not an avoidance of participation. It's just "no" instead of "yes."

Langs: Actually, I used the word *participation* in a different sense. As I said, when a patient asks the analyst to participate in a deviation, he has no choice but to respond. However, invoking the basic tenets of analytic practice is the most neutral response possible under such conditions. If one thinks of the analytic situation as having a three-dimensional quality, and recognizes that any of the ground rules can influence the nature and the properties of the therapeutic space, or if one realizes that the frame is essential to the properties and qualities of what goes on within its confines, then one takes these ground rules, and even the slightest modification of them, with a different degree of seriousness. In principle, the analyst's refusal to participate—that is, to join in and accept the gift—means that the patient is free to go on to associate in an uncontaminated space or field. Now I always listen to the material with the gift as the adaptive context, the situation that's evoking the patient's responses, and as the therapeutic context too—an indication for an interpretive intervention. But there is another special provision related to this: that I don't immediately think of the material as simply the patient's fantasies about the gift. I do think of it partly in terms of fantasy, but also in terms of the realistic implications of the offer and possible acceptance of the gift. The patient—and this happens rather characteristically—will generally go on to say something about the matter at first directly and then indirectly. To offer a hypothetical illustration, in this case the patient's association might be to when she first got her engagement ring. This would indicate that accepting the flowers would gratify her wish to be engaged to, involved with the analyst, and on that basis, one could then offer such an interpretation and the patient could examine her wish to have you accept the gift in the light of its unconscious meaning. Acceptance would entail derivative and direct gratification of these fantasies.

Stone. Right. But you see, this gift would seem to be purely in the realm of fantasy, just by its nature and timing. And it would be quite different from the sort of thing that I mentioned, somebody bringing a little package of cookies at Christmas time.

Langs: Let's take that as a model. What do you feel the difference is?

Stone: In giving the cookies the person is doing what—let us say "she," because it is most often women, and especially young and naive women, who have done this in my experience, and perhaps more often people who come from places away from New York—what she had done all her life with people who are important to her, and she regards it as a token of respect, gratitude, affection, or whatever it may be. Or sometimes just as "something you do." Now you see, it has quite a different meaning from the sudden bringing of a spring bouquet to a male analyst, without specification of any convention involved. Mind you, I'm not saying—don't misunderstand me—that every time one of this other kind of gift occurs—the ones I refere to, with which I am more familiar—it must be accepted. One, for instance, was a girl from another part of the country where this was just a part of the Christmas season to her, and she was a *relatively* healthy person, psychologically, but most often they are shy, schizoid girls to whom this means some kind of gesture of warmth, affection, and closeness, such as they might do with a teacher, or an uncle or an aunt who has been nice to them.

You see, the point is—and this you do not believe—that this does not have to have a very important fantasy significance, any more than the fact that some of these people will say "Hello" a certain way, or leave the room a certain way that's in keeping with their general breeding and background, which may be different from that of a New York sophisticate. You know, one can analyze that too. But that one might analyze quite late; it might take on some additional significance. If this token gift is not accepted from a shy person, who doesn't automatically know the ground rules—you don't start out by telling them to everybody in detail, and usually this is something that occurs (or doesn't occur) as time goes on—there may be a "hurt" which is also integrated into the analysis. This is the part in your thinking, which to me represents something of an omission—although I agree with you, in general, about the soundness of this type of ground rule. "What is this? You didn't take my gift—just a little package of cookies that showed my respect and affection for you—something that I do with anybody of importance in my life." It isn't seen that this too may occasion a warping or a deflection in the analysis, a

shifting of the whole picture of the analyst. Just as there are unconscious fantasies that are involved in these things, there are reactions
to the whole person and to the whole situation, as a reality. In
general, the question of accepting it or not accepting it could often be
a rather trivial thing in either direction. But I submit that very often
the acceptance can then be followed by a somewhat better understanding by the patient that, in the future, such gifts are not a part of
the analytic situation, and that it is much better, if such an impulse
arises subsequently, to discuss it. I've seen this happen repeatedly.
(Now, again we are talking of analysis and "psychotherapy" as if
their ground rules were identical. In my view, of course, they are not.)

Langs: One of the reasons that I think there is so much uncertainty
about my observations is that there is a split in the patient in response
to such incidents of implicit or explicit nonacceptance of an offered
gift (see Langs, 1975, 1976a,b), usually in the form of conscious
resentment and objection, and unconscious acceptance, confirmatory material, and understanding. You see, the point that there is a hurt
involved—a necessary and therapeutic frustration—and that this
then makes the analyst different from these other family figures and
the rest, is essential to what I'm attempting to create, in any case. It is
essential to creating a therapeutic, analyzable relationship and field.

Stone: Well, different in a different way. Different in the sense of
the person's accessibility as a human being. Not that you want him to
be like an uncle or a father, or whatever it is. But he does occupy a
position in reality like that, for example, of a respected teacher, at
least in part. The split in which you are interested is the split in
unconscious fantasy. Also the analyst, as you say, does have a
distinctive functional role. But it is important, at least to many
patients, that he not thereby lose all of the traits and characteristics
which are valued in important figures on whom they rely in reality.

Langs: The split I alluded to involves both unconscious fantasy
and unconscious perception. This stance does not imply insen-
sitivity or inaccessibility. It involves the development of a specifically therapeutic attitude. The nonparticipation marks the ways in
which the analyst is indeed different, as related to pathogenic factors.

Stone: Oh yes, of course. But right at that moment, the distinction may be too sharply impressed on the patient, instead of being gradually developed. With certain individuals, in certain contexts (as mentioned before), this may possibly yield more difficulty than the immediate advantage gained.

Langs: I understand what you're saying, but I do feel that this situation seems ambiguous, partly because the analyst dealing with it, at times because of his own countertransference-based needs, will hear only the conscious response, which is, characteristically, "I want to offer the gift, I want it accepted, and I want to just express simple appreciation." The indirect material, the derivatives in the subsequent indirect associations, the things they then go on to talk about that are supposedly not related to the deviation, characteristically communicate the negative valence, the perception of it as a seduction, as an inappropriate form of interaction and the like. This aspect is not conveyed directly by ninety-nine percent of patients. I think there's been a failure really to maintain the gift as the framework for listening to indirect derivatives, and to recognize that this can very strikingly diverge from the conscious material. For example, recently I supervised a situation where a patient consciously wanted the therapist to sign an insurance form.

Stone: Well, they often want it now, but do you mean to sign it incorrectly, to their illicit advantage?

Langs: No, just to bring the insurance company in, as a third party, and as an alteration in total confidentiality.

Stone: Well, they often have to do that.

Langs: Yes, this is what's being done. But if you don't participate initially, if you allow the patient to go on to associate, and this is again characteristic, the patient will consciously continue to express his wish just to have the money. But the indirect associations—and I have never seen an exception to this—have to do with inappropriate gratifications.

Stone: Even in the case of legitimate insurance?

Langs: Oh, yes.

Stone: You mean that the signing will be experienced by the patient as an inappropriate gratification?

Langs: As an inappropriate gratification of the exposure to the third party, bringing in an outside observer. You get all sorts of material related to the inappropriate exposure of one's secrets to another person. This has a certain truth to it, because the patient's secrets are going to be exposed.

Stone: Of course, for his own need.

Langs: Right. I have found (Langs, 1976a,b) that this modifies the therapeutic field, the image of the therapist, the communicative properties of the field, and compromises certain aspects of the outcome. There's certain material that you will never have an opportunity to analyze and resolve. The way in which I discovered this is that if you at some point—let's say, when the form is to be renewed—don't sign it—you've done it in the past, but now you don't sign it—at the point at which you don't participate, you get material that you never heard before. So signing such a form is a compromise. It's a very difficult situation in reality. I'm well aware of it. But I think it's quite possible—and I have had such personal experiences, of course—to adopt a position that this request, too, will be handled analytically and explored.

Stone: The wish to get insurance forms signed?

Langs: Patients, when they recognize the many implications, can decide to forego this contamination of the therapy or analysis.

Stone: You mean to forgo the insurance? This, I think, in ordinary circumstances, would be too formidable a reality for most patients. I have seen two patients who sacrificed their insurance to stay with me, rather than expect me to manipulate the "date first seen." I have no doubt the other may also occur, but I would think it would be rare. One cannot analyze a formidable reality forever. If the patient has paid premiums and is entitled to insurance payments, there are few who would waive this, for the reasons you mention.

Langs: Yes, in the interests of the treatment and the therapeutic outcome—based on their own unconscious appreciation of the situation.

Stone: Well, there are some things where there are theoretical divergences between us, even though there are areas of agreement. Basically, I think that the matter of gifts is an important "ground rule" (I adopt your term there). Because, you see, if it isn't maintained (at least in principle) there is an opening of the way to ultimate exploitation, in a very distorted way. Now, we assume analysts are aware of their countertransference needs as well as their own ordinary, conscious greeds and so on.

Langs: I don't assume that—I really don't. I've had too many experiences to the contrary.

Stone: Well, I feel that you are postulating analysis out of existence if you feel that. If we can't have a body of practitioners, who are committed to their patients and to the dignity and importance of their task and its science, I'd say it's too damn bad. For example, there are patients—and I've had this at least twice in my life—people of considerable wealth, who have proposed really large or expensive gifts as a matter of course, and even pretended to be somewhat hurt and miffed with me, because other people have accepted them, and so on. Obviously, that would be catastrophic. You see, that's why even the quantitative aspect of the expense of the gift has some importance. Because a token gift is like a symbol. If it is going to produce something in the transference it can be treated as if it were a symbol, a symbolic gratification or the offering of a symbolic gratification to the analyst (not that this means it should always be accepted!). If it is expensive and large, the entire significance is, a priori, different. Incidentally, do you trust yourself in these matters? Or do you feel that the "frame" obviates the need to make such a decision?

Langs: I adopt as neutral a stance as possible, initially saying neither yes nor no. I allow the patient's subsequent derivative communications, organized around the adaptive context of the proffered gift, to provide the answer. In working this way I have seen not a single exception to my finding that the patient communicates a prediction of clearly detrimental consequences for the treatment and the relationship were the gift to be accepted. You treat the token gift as symbolic, but there is an actual gratification.

Stone: Yes, very small.

Langs: Please understand: I am not impugning the dedication of most analysts. I am questioning their sensitivity to more subtle expressions of countertransference. The literature reflects many failures to recognize or search for countertransference—and unconscious communications—in many of their interventions. They do not monitor every intervention for that factor, and they fail to study their subjective responses and the material from the patient for valid indications of expressions of countertransference elements, however large or small. It is a fundamentally different attitude: constantly searching versus assuming it is largely known. As for even a small gift, once accepted it takes it out of the realm of symbol into actuality.

Stone: Well, it's a relative thing. You see, this, as I've mentioned before, has to do with almost every step in the analysis. You know, there are some people to whom making more interpretations in an hour is a gift, a symbolic gift, a feeding; in a sense, it's actual—you talked more in that hour. This can readily be brought to the state of a reductio ad absurdum. Years ago, believe it or not, a patient shyly confided that she regarded the presentation of my bill as a gift! It was a tangible piece of paper and, in those years, usually in my own handwriting. However, I'll admit that a real gift is far more tangible. A package of homemade cookies is still a package of homemade cookies; it is a feeding gift to you. But it is not, economically, so important that it can't be lifted from the position of an important contamination, if the acceptance was carried out in good faith, because you thought it was better to accept it, not because you were hungry for cookies at that time. My wife makes excellent cookies; I don't need those brought me by patients; and as it does anybody, it always bothers me a little when those things happen. It doesn't happen often, but once in a while there is a patient who has this tendency, or makes a point of it. Recently, this has occurred with one of my few psychotherapy patients, seen once a week. Certainly in analysis it would not be allowed to continue after the first instance.

Well, I don't think that it need be very important; it can be blown up and exaggerated, on a doctrinaire basis. Just as I said in *The Psychoanalytic Situation* (Stone, 1961), that if a person knows or learns that I have been interested in sailing, this is not likely to become an important contamination of his transference neurosis. What may happen is that, whether he's a sailor or a nonsailor, this will fit in somewhere into his dreams and associations and will simply be part of the grist for the mill of everyday life. The fact that he's heard that you gave a paper somewhere (or perhaps has read your books!) is among those inevitabilities that we can't avoid; and I think they rarely disqualify analyses. We can't all hide behind screens. I still believe it to be essentially true, that if the image presented is too bare and too stark, it has an adverse influence on the evolution of transference. I didn't mean that you ought to sit there and keep telling things to the patient, to stimulate the transference neurosis. That would be an absurdity. But one doesn't fuss too much and too actively about commonplace material that may emerge in the natural course of things and that doesn't impinge directly on instinctual forces and their attendant conflicts, or similar matters germane to the transference neurosis and its evolution. For example, if you were to tell a person about your sexual habits or preferences, this could have a catastrophic effect. But the ordinary, remote, derivative phenomena that fill daily life I think are not too damn important, unless they become "contaminants" through their sheer quantitative conspicuousness or intrusion, their impedance to free association, their upsetting the general balance of communication, or their obvious idiosyncratic tendentiousness or other pathologic countertransference significance.

Langs: Again, you give credence to the reality along a quantitative scale. You put it in terms of "relatively minor" realities.

Stone: Quantitative and qualitative.

Langs: Agreed—there are certain qualities to any situation, of course, and you feel that when the reality is such that these are relatively minor, the rest is really quite workable.

Stone: And that sometimes the fussy withholding has an inimical effect on the progress of associations and development of fantasy.

Langs: I, in contrast, have become very sensitive to the unconscious gratifications, the actual unconscious gratifications involved in these relatively minor deviations. And while I also acknowledge a quantitative factor, I have found such deviations are in general more disruptive than a frustrating approach.

Stone: That that is your position, I understand.

Langs: So my comments are addressed to your acceptance of certain modifications that you define as "minor."

Stone: In accordance with judgment applied to the exigencies of the individual case.

Langs: And my emphasis, as we clarified last time, is on the unconscious gratification.

Stone: We were going back to the insurance. I know that some of this is circumlocution; that's in the nature of these things. Insurance, as a matter of fact, bothers me, as an historically developing intrusion into the analytic framework. Because I believe that to have an expensive procedure, which originally was regarded as a personal sacrifice, taken care of by a third party at the very outset vitiates, in many ways, some of the personal expenditure of funds and energy and interest and so on that one accepts as an important, if not literally integral, part of an analytic commitment. On the other hand, in reality, since insurance exists, and since people pay well for it and are entitled to its benefits, it would be utterly unrealistic, I think, to expect them not to accept the advantages, under legitimate conditions. You see, there would be another distortion: "This analyst wants me to work my balls off and not take advantage of something to which I'm legitimately entitled!"

I have a relatively short experience with this, because it's really only in the last few years that people have begun to bring me these forms. Before that, for some reason, I had very few patients who had insurance. The idea that a patient may at first expect you to predate or postdate, for example, the time of the first contact, which is usually asked for, is of course something that just can't be done, that I have never done for anybody. If they bring me the form, and it has to be filled out, it will be filled out exactly as I think is correct. What I will not do is answer certain questions which, I think, are not fair, because in a way they ask you sometimes to place yourself, knowingly or inadvertently, in a position of possibly contradicting your patient about a history for which he is usually your sole source, and which he can furnish to the company as well as you can. So usually I just don't answer things like: past illnesses, or when did symptoms begin, etc. I leave them blank, and as a matter of fact most insurance companies have respected that. But if they ask when I first saw the patient, which is a practically unvarying question, that will be answered correctly. In one instance, the patient actually could not benefit by the insurance because of my insistence on that. Another person did get certain benefits anyway. The fact was accepted, and it did appear later that there might have been some undesirable unconscious consequences of entering into something that would have been a kind of conspiracy against a third party, apart from the fact that it could never have been a tenable conscious position for me. Now, as to omitting direct response altogether, or refusing to cooperate, refusing to fill out the form, as you say—that is an entirely different sphere.

Langs: No, I do not take such a stand.

Stone: You see, it's again a place where the emphasis on the element of abstinence and deprivation overrides what I would regard as realistic common sense. One could not expect the patient to have a reasonably workable attitude toward one thereafter.

Langs: First of all, I don't refuse to fill it out. I simply say that this, too, is something that we will explore.

Stone: Well, it will be explored anyway. The patient will talk about the insurance as a matter of course, and one can't defer a reality indefinitely, for a doctrinaire principle of analyzing in abstinence.

Langs: Yes, but it comes down to two propositions, which my experience substantiates. The first proposition is that there is a significant difference in the material that you get if you fill it out and then explore it, or if you don't fill it out, leave it open as to whether it will be done or not, and then let the patient go on to associate.

Stone: A significant difference in the timing maybe, and shaping, not in the ultimate outcome. Unless, of course, a sense of justified indignation and anger introduces a permanent distortion.

Langs: Well, I feel that there is a marked difference in what will be both communicated and introjected. The second proposition is that the presence of an insurance company through the completion of such a form significantly modifies the bipersonal field and with it the flow of the analysis, the material available for analysis, the image of the analyst, the unconscious introjections of the analyst, and the ultimate outcome of the analysis. These are hard realities, but attention to derivative communication leads to unmistakable conclusions of the kind I am discussing.

Now, what I cannot state, because I don't know how one could ever measure it, is how significant these modifications are. To what extent do they render significant pathological problems unmodifiable in analysis? I happen to feel that all of my data point to this being of great significance, and that basic properties of the field as well as therapeutic outcome are affected.

For example, the patient I mentioned has a significant homosexual problem. It's a male therapist, and a male patient. The material indicates that his homosexuality was gratified and reinforced—and also covered over and defended against—by the completion of the insurance forms, to the point where the analytic resolution of that problem will not be feasible. It did not appear in his associations in an analyzable form. That doesn't mean that he might not ever give up the homosexuality, because he might, on the basis of what I call a "misalliance cure" (Langs, 1975, 1976a,b), that is, because he's gratified and frightened of the gratification, or because he's going to prove to the therapist, whom he now unconsciously sees as homosexual, that he can repudiate his homosexuality. There are lots of possible dynamisms to symptom change, but the analytic work related to that symptom will not be feasible under those conditions. And that is a hell of a conclusion; it's one that many therapists immediately object to, but I'm talking about clinical observations and validated inferences, or even conclusions, based on a sensitivity to this area, to the implications of this kind of modification in the frame.

Stone: Well, I would not come to quite as pessimistic a conclusion as you do. Furthermore, to me it sounds rather magical—that the filling out of an insurance form gratifies homosexuality to an unanalyzable degree. Either the patient is psychotic or the analytic effort is inadequate. Suppose the same patient found that handing him a bill—or, let us say, a statement for his income tax—gratified his homosexuality. I do believe that the third-party involvement is an intrusion which may alter the cast of analytic work. It's here, obviously, to stay, and if anything, is going to increase, and so we have to adapt ourselves to it. I think that if people could get along without it, it would be better. I do see that if people are getting away with a great deal, paying very little for important services, and the larger part paid by an outside agency, obviously that has important effects on the whole cast of the relationship and will alter the evolution of the transference. If the relationship has been an entirely honest thing, I believe the matter can be analyzed.

Langs: What about the modification in confidentiality, the release of information about the patient?

Stone: The modification in confidentiality is very little, because the diagnoses that are given are very rarely searching diagnoses, nor do they have to be. Further, they are released entirely in the patient's interest, and only at his request. They have to be diagnoses that fit the situation sufficiently and are adequately classificatory. They don't have to tell anything significant about the patient's personal life or development. It is true that somewhere it's written down that this person has a psychoneurosis, or depressive illness, or whatever. Well, I have rarely seen the patient to whom that meant a great deal, so long as it remained relatively impersonal. It means something to him if it's going to affect his future jobs, or future insurance applications, or matters of that sort. Again, it's largely in the sphere of reality. These matters don't involve the analyst particularly, because the thing is specifically done at the patient's request and to meet his needs. So that I don't give it quite the formidable unconscious significance that you do. Yet I do regard it as an intrusion and in some ways, even under the best circumstances, a vitiation of certain elements in the actual "compact" that we took for granted before.

Analysis, at least, was exclusively a contract between two people.

As always, of course, there are a couple of exceptions that immediately come to mind. For example, I never specialized in the
treatment of children, nor of adolescents. But earlier in my work I did
have some younger people, apart from occasional consultations.
Maybe the youngest was seventeen or so when she began; another
was, say, twenty, somewhere in that range. These patients were
entirely dependent on their parents for the analytic fee. You see, you
have a similar problem there. If we're going to take it too seriously
and literally, no children can be treated at all, and rather few
adolescents. It is occasionally true of young adults, also many wives,
who are strictly housewives, and thus financially dependent on their
husbands. All of those things enter into analysis, not only in reality
but, occasionally, in the sense of powerful unconscious dynamics. In
the case of wives, it can sometimes be quite a formidable element: for
example, continuing to make the husband spend money for reasons
other than just the immediate clinical needs, to take a simple
concrete thing; or the relatively manifest overwrought guilt connected to the same thing. I don't mean that that necessarily occurs
often, but it's a simple example of where the reality can become
harnessed to and put in the service of certain unconscious propensities. Naturally, the transference neurosis tends to "assimilate" this
phenomenon to its intrinsic dynamics. Children, too. I remember
vividly cases—actually I refer to a couple of young adults, dependent
on parents—where there was no question that a revenge motive
emerged in this sphere.

I'm taking the simplest, most easily stated thing. There may have
been more subtle complications. You see, this is where I stick, and
where I think we perhaps don't quite get together, and maybe we
never will on a theoretical basis. I believe that those things can
usually be analyzed in patients in the neurotic range; maybe in
extreme instances where they can't be, it's because there is something
irrational in the arrangement, not adequately justified by the realities, something essentially overindulgent, or whatever. But assuming it is a reasonable thing, these complications can be analyzed. If it
is an arrangement that is really determined by the reality, especially
by necessity, and will persist no longer than that necessity, that
reality is exigent, and requires it. It will, of course, not be analyzable
or analyzable only with great difficulty if it involves the participant
neurosis of the third person; you know, the sort of concealed folie à

deux, where, for whatever reason, a third party is involved, and wants to be involved, on a necessarily irrational basis. (I omit possible "Machiavellian" motives—"keeping" a child or marital partner in analysis for ulterior motives.) I think it's something like the insurance, only much more so. If it's on the level, and it's a firm obligatory reality, it's okay. Or take a clinic treatment, where patients pay a very low fee and know it, and often react to that, very sensitively, with a variety of feelings. They often picture the analyst as a student or a candidate, as he often is, and develop secondary transferences to the unknown supervisor. What are you going to do? It's there. People can't be treated at that level otherwise. And yet I believe some of the student clinic analyses come out quite well. I don't believe that the situation permanently invalidates the analysis. I think the unconscious impact of the adventitious can be analyzed, for practical purposes. The realities, of course, remain. But I think we underestimate the degree to which such realities, gross or subtle, cultural or individual, may be entering into most if not all analyses.

Langs: I think that in some situations it does invalidate the analyses. In all situations it limits the therapeutic and analytic work. It definitely creates what the Barangers (1966), whom we discussed before, called a "bastion," a sector of material that is set aside and will not be openly communicated, or open to analysis.

Stone: You might be surprised at how well these things can be communicated. Well, you've had experience with it, but surprisingly, it sometimes is a very open matter.

Langs: I'm not referring to a direct discussion. The identification of the bastion is very complicated. It doesn't suggest that just the fee arrangement would be split off, but refers to a situation where the modified qualities of the fee arrangement correspond to an aspect of the patient's neurosis, and to a neurotic aspect of the analytic interaction, in which the patient and analyst share inappropriate or pathological unconscious fantasies. It is this area that will be split off.

Also I believe, and my observations appear to confirm this, that in those situations where, let's say, an adolescent is in treatment and the parents are paying for it entirely, there are modifications in the therapeutic field and in therapeutic outcome. I don't feel that this means therapy is invalidated, though it may be. I, of course, have also treated adolescents, with a certain degree of success, but there are residuals that remain quite unresolved. But there is a very great difference between the insurance arrangement and this kind of fee arrangement, in that the analyst or therapist need not modify confidentiality. There are analysts and therapists who see the parents of adolescents, and who communicate with them from time to time. But this need not be the case. So with parents and spouses there is a likely contamination, but the analyst does not actively participate in it. I believe we have much to learn in this area.

Stone: Yes, not all see the parents of adolescents, but many do, and regard it as integral to the treatment.

Langs: Right. I think that further modifies the field. But where the therapist does not do so, he at least does not participate in these arrangements, and I think that has its positive effects. At least confidentiality is maintained, though he's participating in a different alteration of the field by treating the patient under these circumstances. Look, I am not up in some idealized cloud. I know these are very hard realities and hard decisions to make. That if one does not work under these conditions with certain patients, then there is nothing available to them in the way of therapy. I just think we must look very, very carefully at how detrimental such arrangements actually are: what are the negatives, what is feasible. Beyond that, there are very important social issues involved, of course. They are basic with patients where these modifications might be deemed necessary, where for various reasons we accept this modification because we see no other alternative. But social need cannot alter scientific observations.

Stone: May I say one word about that? You see, it isn't that there is any disagreement that any or all of these things introduce certain modifications in the analytic process or field. But one disagreement is over how formidably and irretrievably they distort the situation. My feeling is that to some degree it is contingent on the rational necessity of the modification, because that is something to which the patient's ego can respond, and which can make it analyzable.

The second thing is that there is an overlooking of the universality of this kind of—I don't know whether the word used is a good one—"faulting" in the ideal analytic process. So that while you are right in these individual matters, including the special character of the unconscious responses, you are right in such universal reference that it all but stands on its head. To misquote—"To err is human, to be without error is divine!" Unfortunately none of us, nor any humanly contrived actual situation, is divine. For example, in everyday analysis, people are frequently referred by one analyst to another, sometimes to a peer, but quite frequently to a much younger analyst. There is immediately a special factor in the analysis. "Why couldn't I go to that older, more experienced person? I'm with somebody to whom he sent me, who had a lot of time." Or "Why does he have a lot of time? The other person doesn't have any time! He's much busier, so he must be much better." Those things are occurring every day, and they have to be dealt with. The things that you mention are glaring, it's true. They stand out in a special, qualitative way. But they are in a sense magnifications of what is happening all the time. It's happening all the time, for instance, that wives are being analyzed, while their husbands pay. True, many wives nowadays work and have their own income, but still there are many who don't. We take that as a matter of course, and we analyze the impact of it. In the case of insurance, you seem to put great emphasis on the fact that the third party must receive a diagnosis. Well, until a few years ago, in most instances, there were semiannual reports on the progress of the analytic candidate that often involved more than clinical diagnoses.

Langs: And it was a clearly destructive practice. And just because flaws are inevitable, that fact of our human limitations should not become license for knowing participation in disruptive practices. Are we not committed to offer the best possible therapeutic setting to the patient? You implied as much in your own comments, including those on training analyses. So I know something of your attitude toward that.

Stone: I know my attitude well, and there were two others before me who expressed similar attitudes—Kairys (1964) and F. McLaughlin (1967). I have felt especially strong about this (1) because

I feel that it can be eliminated without significant loss; (2) it involves much more than the breach of confidentiality; it involves the actual power of the analyst over the development of the candidate's career. As for your more general remarks, I am against sin too.

Langs: I think a lot of these things are unnecessary. Sometimes we do have realities that impose limitations, and one has to make a distinction between those situations and the others where no such reality impinges. Such unnecessary power is actually expressed in many deviations, including the signing of insurance forms. I would agree with you that the testing of the analytic frame is universal with patients, and I think it's an essential part of analysis.

Stone: Yes, I feel very strongly that that is so.

Langs: I think that there are certain differences between those situations where the analyst does participate in a modification in the frame and where he does not. You, on the other hand, it seems clear, would stand by what I would call your "principle of minor realities," and by another principle which you didn't specifically mention. I'll state it: you would, would you not, accept the principle that analysts who immediately refuse to, shall we say, bow to these minor realities may by this refusal do more damage to the field than they would by accepting them?

Stone: With certain patients and certain minor realities. There is an area where we can't abdicate judgment, and to follow the rule rigidly can be a serious mistake. I don't mean that the rule is always to be tossed out; but that a judgment must be involved as to the nature of the reality, and whether it is better to leave it with the refusal, or a conditional acceptance, or direct compliance.

Langs: Again, we're coming to the term "rigidity." Adopting the neutral attitude of allowing the material to provide an answer is not, I believe, rigidity. I know of no other area of analysis where the same findings virtually always appear; as a rule, there is almost nothing that is one hundred percent consistent in analysis. Yet when it comes to a test of the frame, the material from the patient will always, without exception in my experience, dictate the preference for its maintenance in the service of the treatment, rather than its modification. That's my observation.

Stone: But you have said so throughout. That is not my observation. I didn't say you were rigid. I'm talking about rigidity as a principle. What I would say is that the material will always exhibit the response to what occurred; that it does not necessarily always show that something that has happened is bad. Indeed, the response may have been favorable. It will show what it means to the patient, which is then a part of the analysis.

Langs: Let me go on now with a little more data from the vignette we are discussing. I'll move on to the session to which the patient had brought the flowers. The analyst has accepted them, uncomfortably. Perhaps it is unfair to the man who wrote this paper to zero in on one incident like this, but to me it isn't this specific example that's important. It's the general principles we are trying to derive, and I'm not concerned about this particular clinical interaction, except as a source of data. I have more material in *The Bipersonal Field* (Langs, 1976a) and plan to publish a series of cases with more experienced therapists in private practice, where issues like this come up.

Now, to return to the case at hand: you and the analyst both expressed concern—and I'm only using this as a kind of characteristic approach—with a certain inappropriateness in the patient. You focused first and foremost on the possibility of a certain kind of pathology in her.

Stone: I know nothing about it, except the bringing of the flowers and that little preliminary history.

Langs: This is true, but I would approach such incidents in terms of the interaction, and look to both patient and analyst for contributions. The stress on the patient has to be counterbalanced with something on the other side, which is generally put aside, and this author certainly tended to do so, though he later briefly acknowledged the possibility of these other factors. In my experience, in many, many instances when flowers have shown up unexpectedly, there has already been an unconscious countertransference problem in the analyst that has helped to create the conditions under which this occurs.

Stone: Why flowers more than chicken soup, or a painting? Unless you refer to the connection of flowers with intensely emotional situations of one sort or another? A priori, I doubt it always occurs.

Langs: I'm not saying this is always the situation. I'm saying that it may well be the case in this instance. That we don't know, but that very often such a contribution exists. For example, in my empirical studies of the erotized transference, I found that in a large number of cases, there's an erotized countertransference or a hostile coun-tertransference—something that has promoted this type of response in a patient who is, of course, herself prone to react in that way. Often the analyst's problem is expressed in failures properly to manage the frame, to intervene, thereby allowing the pathology to flourish. I would take the offer of the flowers as a very important signal to explore countertransferences, though I should not neglect the need to understand what this reflects of the patient's pathology. I assume that most analysts are quite dedicated to analytic principles—but to think of them as not having countertransference problems is a different level of assumption.

Stone: No. Altogether different. No one is absolutely free of at least potential countertransferences.

Langs: We all have certain sectors of countertransference. Our responsibility is to be aware of them and to keep their influence minimal. I do believe, though, that many analysts manifest sectors of countertransference that are expressed not only through failures of intervention, but through mismanagement of the frame, and that there is a tendency to ignore the extent of their influence. Now, the patient began the session to which she had brought the gift with the comment, "I want to come with snowflakes in my hair. I want you to love me and be my father. I want to know your first name. I am very surprised that this kind of thing happens so fast in analysis, at how much I'm involved" (Gudeman, 1974, p. 327).

You see the analyst is already getting material that tells us the meaning of the flowers. But had he not accepted them, there would have been different characteristics. To try briefly to define this: by accepting the flowers and accepting then this gift of love, he directly gratifies the pathological unconscious fantasies, and she must now respond to him as a participant, rather than as a nonparticipant. And these fantasies are not entirely oedipal; there are very strong preoedipal elements involved. In my opinion, his taking the flowers puts him in a compromised position, and the unconscious sexual gratification renders the patient vulnerable to further regression. We can postulate that she has within herself the residuals derived from experiences with seductive figures in her early relationships—her father—or there may have been a certain seductiveness in her mother and inappropriate interactions that helped to create her pathology. Now the analyst has behaved in a way that's in keeping with those earlier pathogenic figures, with the same loss of control and inappropriate seductiveness, and it's going to be very difficult for her to distinguish him from those earlier pathogenic figures.

Stone: I understand the principle quite well. That's why we have the rule. But nothing is quite so automatic. I don't know whether it was a big expensive bouquet, or just some spring flowers. Whether there was an immediate proviso that this would have to be discussed at length, and her associations listened to. And further, that in general, in the long run, we find it better for the analytic process that such gifts be withheld, and the impulse discussed. We would give her the privilege—as has, at times, been accepted—to say, "Perhaps I'm making a mistake, then," and to withdraw the thing. Or to ask that you keep the bouquet—and to begin her "learning" with that. The interchange is then deprived of that arbitrary, "cold turkey" significance. She decides, and with that the analysis is under way. Please understand that, given my slight knowledge of this case, I do not presume to recommend something clinically. We are dealing with hypothetical alternatives.

Langs: It is very important that one does something immediately to counterbalance to whatever extent one can the elements I am stressing. You can see that, despite the author's contention, accepting the gift only promotes fluidity, instead of enhancing the therapeutic alliance. This is where one of his ideas seems in error to me: that one has to do these things in order to promote the alliance. Such a position especially fails to recognize that securing the frame and offering valid interpretations, even with a patient with regressive potential, are the soundest, and probably the only, means of promoting the therapeutic alliance.

Stone: The principal means, in the right affective context, yes. Not the only means. People don't stop being human, because they are in treatment. Did you ever read Brunswick's paper of many years ago (1928) about her rather brief treatment of a paranoid young woman? It's full of "errors in the frame." But one can learn a lot from it about how very sick people react. Incidentally, this point is as good as any for mention of the "quantitative" element, which seems to puzzle you in my thinking. Or perhaps I'm wrong about that. I have mentioned already that I don't feel as you do about the exclusive value of interpretations, nor, of course, about the critical significance of the ground rules as such, within certain limits that I have tried to define. Both are extremely important, but so are other things, for example, the constant undercurrent of affective exchange. Cognitive or affective—there are certain kinds and degrees of gratifications which would certainly create serious difficulties. There are others which, I feel, are in a different class, like the "token gift" under certain circumstances, or the occasional transmission of relatively neutral minor information. We know that quantities can determine actual qualitative distinctions in the physical world. So—a priori— why does this distinction seem so strange? In her classic paper on the "as-if" personality, Helene Deutsch (1942) mentioned the empty early childhood of one of the principal patients, almost devoid of the normal stimulations of close contact with parents. Somewhere—I'm relying on my memory—she comments that the normal oedipus complex is unlikely to develop without such stimulations. Now these matters are, of course, not identical or exactly parallel. But there is a certain analogy between this concept and what I've said about the development of the transference neurosis, where the relationship is too artificial, too diagrammatic, too "unreal," in short.

Langs: Appropriate and therapeutically necessary deprivation is not the creation of a void or vacuum. Securing the frame is not the only means of establishing the therapeutic alliance—I'm not considering here such matters as the analyst's basic attitude and the stance he takes.

Next, the patient talked about wanting to please the analyst. He says, "I pointed out it would be of most use for us to talk about these feelings, and not always useful in our work to give a present although she might want to. The patient wanted a pat on the head from me and was angry when I did not give this" (Gudeman, 1974, p. 327).

Stone: She mentioned the pat on the head literally?

Langs: Yes. Which brings up the principle I have raised so often: if you modify one aspect of the frame, the patient will want other deviations.

Stone: If you don't absolutely exclude direct gratifications of that sort. Also, I have no reason in my experience to assume that she wanted a pat on the head only because of the flowers! Freud had a lot of experience with providing direct gratifications, although not in this sphere, as far as I know. And he was very explicit about the prohibitions. I refer to the Wolf Man, the Rat Man, and so on.

Langs: So the analyst attempted to indicate the limitations of his response, but she then sought further direct gratification. This was in the first month of analysis—really very early.

Stone: He did refuse the pat on the head?

Langs: Yes.

Stone: That wish he refused, unconditionally. Even with a psychotic patient, I feel that these demonstrations are to be excluded.

Langs: Physical contact, certainly. Yet, there are those who advocate hand holding, or things of that kind, with borderline and psychotic patients.

Stone: No, no, I do not concede to such wishes under any circumstances. Somebody who is sufficiently able to come to your office should be able to accept the fact that you won't hold his (or her) hand. Now, you will remember that Ferenczi, as part of his long cycle of experimentation, included such things in his period of conviction that neuroses in large part arose from insufficient parental love in infancy, which he then thought the analyst should supply.

Langs: So there shouldn't be any physical contact?

Stone: Well, conceivably in some acute panic. I remember a patient whom I visited in the hospital in a psychotic episode, who suddenly got down on his knees, grabbed my hand and kissed it. I mean, I wasn't going to yank it away abruptly. He released it in response to a gradual, firm, withdrawal movement. But aside from an absolute emergency situation in which the patient is psychotic and makes a sudden grab, I don't believe even such reserved compliance is indicated. I do not mean to be "holier than thou." I speak of the range of patients I've been treating. I know that people treating very disturbed psychotics are dealing with a different order of problem.

Langs: There are, indeed, modifications in the frame that the patient imposes upon the analyst and that he can't prevent, though one must always be certain he has not created the conditions under which it occurs: where the patient picks up the telephone and calls your office, where there's inadvertent contact outside the office. Under those circumstances, though, I always feel one has a major responsibility to examine any countertransference contribution. . .

Stone: Of course, without question.

Langs: . . . to analyze it subsequently, and to limit it to what the patient has imposed. Many modifications of the frame, of course, are not invoked under those conditions or are even analyst-evoked.
To continue with a little more material.

Stone: He tried to indicate that it was better to talk about these things. She asked for the pat on the head, which he didn't give, and she was angry, you say?

Langs: Yes, she became angry, and they continued to clarify. "In the first months of analysis, there were episodes of acting out of her feelings." I'm not sure what that means. "At one point, when her husband was away, she brought her children to the waiting room, as if for protection." This, to me, illustrates things that I've observed repeatedly, though I shall not attempt to validate it here: I believe that had he not accepted the flowers, had he analyzed it instead, she would not have felt the need for actual protection to the extent that she did.

Stone: Well, that's your bias. I have seen many minor instances of the kind—true, not in such obviously sick people—where no requests whatsoever followed.

Langs: Right, it is a bias—but, please, an observational one.

Stone: There's transference and there's countertransference. We assume that a well-prepared analyst, except when somebody gets to some particularly vulnerable, hidden spot, is aware of his countertransference. So, you see, to attribute too much to countertransference in general, I think, can be fallacious. There are still things that originate in the patient. People often become psychotic, without benefit of an analyst; and the same applies to many other impulsive behavioral reactions. People who are psychotic or borderline are going to make undue demands and develop regressive transferences, even if the analyst is "perfect" in his attitude (sometimes because he is too perfect. I include myself, in my early "sans reproche" period.)

Langs: No question about it. I know again that the first characterization of my position is in terms of its seeming rigidity. I must say that accumulation of experience has led me to take a very skeptical position about analysts. It sounds terrible to speak this way about my peers, colleagues, teachers, and otherwise, but I believe that there are many blind spots, and many sectors of unrecognized countertransference, and that there are even shared countertransferences that are widely denied. I think that much that has been written about the frame, for example, reflects shared countertransference difficulties. From what I can determine, from what has been written, and from those situations that I have heard presented and discussed, there are important areas of countertransference of which analysts are not generally aware. To identify their role in no way disregards factors within the patient; it stresses the interaction rather than overstating the patient's contributions and understating or denying those from the analyst.

Stone: Oh, I don't doubt for a second the importance of the general theme, but as I have said, most conscientious analysts are looking at their countertransferences, or should, as a part of their work. Most that I know do that. Of course, people don't know themselves completely in all instances. As far as the frame is concerned, I fear that my view of the "shared countertransferences" might be quite different—if not opposite—to yours!

Langs: In principle, such a search is always acknowledged, while in practice . . .

Stone: You don't think they do?

Langs: I don't find it reflected in the literature. I think that that's an ideal that is simply given lip service.

Stone: They don't write about them too often in the literature, that's true.

Langs: Not that they don't write about them. I can understand someone not writing about and revealing his countertransferences. But again and again, when they write about what happens with the patient, they exclude themselves. When things go wrong, they don't even look for countertransference contributions—again, with rare exceptions. That's why my position sounds so exaggerated in the direction of the responsibilities of the analyst, even though I'm quite aware of what the patient can bring to the situation. I take the literature as my barometer here, and there is no sign of consistent self-exploration. Here's a narrative which is typical, in which a whole series of things are done by the analyst in the name of what he sincerely felt to be an effort to create a therapeutic alliance.

Stone: What was sincerely done to support it, not to vitiate it.

Langs: And to do what he had been taught to do, and all the rest. But I believe that these decisions are significantly influenced by countertransferences that are not reflected upon, that are sanctioned by the group, through his own analysis and his learning at an institute. Please recognize this as speculation, but it is well founded, and there is almost no indication that he examined his decision as a possible vehicle for countertransference expression, though I can assure you the patient will experience it as such.

Stone: You argue from a point of view that I can understand. I shared it in the early years of my analytic practice to a degree where I once would not write a crucially necessary note to an employer about a patient's genuinely incapacitating height phobia. Contrary to your view, I think most analytic teaching is rather in the direction you espouse. Again, I think it's bias, exaggerated in one direction. I don't doubt the profound importance of a countertransference and that an unanalyzed countertransference may influence things. But you see, keeping the frame absolutely intact and unswerving is in itself an artificial protection against countertransferences, sometimes obviating the confronting need to understand them and work them through.

If the person has an answer for everything, there's no problem. I do not know this paper, this case. What I say depends on the few fragments you have given. Now, you see this analyst, I would first assume (maybe he shows a lot of things as he goes on), made an honest decision about the flowers. I would think that in that case the patient should have immediately learned that this was exceptional and that in the future it would be better that the impulse be controlled, and that it be expressed verbally in the analysis, and that thus it would, if anything, enhance the analytic procedure, right? But that all the other material follows necessarily because he took the flowers evokes my profound skepticism. She may have been a very disturbed patient, and maybe if he hadn't taken the flowers she might have had a psychotic storm in the same hour. Who knows?

Langs: Again, I must emphasize that this is something I discover anew in every such situation. It's really that basic attitude that I want to stress: that there is a need consistently to search for countertransferences, especially when deviating, through both self-analysis and detection of valid introjections and perceptions of the patient. I'm not saying that it's solely because of the first deviation that she now brings the children. It may have contributed significantly toward it, and in terms of my experience, it did. It's not the sole determinant, but it is an important one. That is, what with the husband away and her having erotic wishes and fantasies toward this analyst, and with his having accepted the flowers, she doesn't feel that she can be certain that he would not accept more serious advances. Even though he had said in words, "This isn't how we're going to work," his action is contradictory. I can also document from other material that she is still confused about the ground rules, the properties of the field, the rule of nongratification along with analyzing. It stands to reason that she doesn't know where the boundary line will be drawn.

Stone: Well, the boundaries should have been explained. Besides, it doesn't stand to reason. Of some four women whom I recall offhand, over many years, who brought children to my office waiting room, for one reason or another, not one had ever given me a gift prior to the event. One of them, definitely psychotic, brought me a gift from travel, in a secondary return to treatment, a very small gift, because she knew I would not accept any other kind. Yes, I accepted it.

Langs: There is much implied when you say, "Well, I'll do it this time, but we mustn't do it again." And there are many unconscious reasons why patients may feel unsafe in a given analytic situation.

Let me go on with some more of the material. This really helps crystallize the issues. Now, at another time, "she brought me tobacco as a present, having the previous day had her yearly gynecological exam and having become frightened of cancer." So now comes another gift.

Stone: Where's the connection? She brought him tobacco, having had her gynecological exam, as if there were some tie between the two?

Langs: It's clear that he must have taken the gift, because he writes: "Much later in the work, she would say she hoped I would smoke myself to death, but at this time, tobacco was only a gift. Simultaneously, she became frightened with the monthly bill. She wanted me to feel sorry for her and recognize her husband was a 'bear' with money, although he had agreed to support the analysis." So all this brings that issue in too. To continue: "It was months later when the patient acknowledged she had lied about her husband's salary, having been afraid to confront the issue of paying a higher fee" (Gudeman, 1974, pp. 327-328). She showed anxiety about the initial bills, a capacity to project internal conflicts onto her husband, the wish to be taken care of by the analyst, an almost clinging reaction, some annoyance with him, and a later confession that she withheld information.

All of this is described in terms of the patient. There is no sense of interaction, and the analyst is excluded. To continue: "As the patient proceeded with dreams and sexual material, she set up complicated triangular situations. I was fantasized as a loving, good person who could provide her gratifications" (which she has already confirmed in reality) "while her husband was seen as ungratifying, withholding, and hostile. The transference" (now, I would never use the term "transference" here; I would say the analytic relationship, or the patient's relationship to the analyst, and then I would want to distinguish what is transference and what is nontransference) "appeared to be a highly eroticized and idealized one." In retrospect, he then said there were a number of elements that prognosticated her severe regressive state.

Now, I don't take issue with this point, in that each patient, of course, reacts individually based on her own needs and propensities. He cited as prognostic the psychotic relative, the kleptomania, frigidity, a rapid, erotized reaction to the analyst, the projection of internal conflicts to the outside, manipulation of the analytic setting, a tendency toward splitting, and the withholding—all suggesting significant defensive functioning and an underlying fragile ego.

I don't even want to discuss that particular area: that's common parlance and I have nothing to add. To summarize now: he adds that nonetheless she had begun to work, and to recognize her rather controlling and aggressive ways. She acknowledged deprivation; she'd been able to observe herself at times and note sources of strain, and specific fears were identified. The patient then took a one-week vacation after the first nine months—you should notice—of treatment. This sounds like a unilateral vacation, but we don't know. Preceding her vacation, she dreamed of being stuffed with hot dog rolls and as a result missing a party—a reference to the analysis, to date, as not giving her enough, according to the author.

So, there was her vacation; then four weeks after the analyst's summer vacation, the patient brought in a request from her husband, with no prior reference in the analysis. We're now back to the fall, which sounds like about a year of analysis, because those were fall flowers that she originally brought. The husband had spoken with his physician and decided to obtain a vasectomy. He wanted to know if the analyst would write a letter stating that because of his wife's illness, his vasectomy would be medically indicated and medical insurance would then pay for this procedure. Here the analyst says: "I asked her for her thoughts." She goes on to say, "Maybe it would be better if he were sterilized. It would eliminate the problem of my being a woman. It would eliminate the problem of my having my tubes tied. I always feel that it would help to take a part of me and cut it out. I just don't want any more children. How would I feel if you wrote a letter? I don't think I would feel bothered not having any more children. Perhaps I couldn't predict. Over the next few days the patient talked about this, but then wanted a specific answer" (Gudeman, 1974, pp. 328-329).

The analyst responded that he could not write the letter, as he believed there were no specific psychiatric problems in her that would indicate her husband should have the vasectomy; but that they could talk about her thoughts.

Stone: Seems a reasonable and correct response.

Langs: Okay. So she goes on and says, "You mean you won't write a letter, then I could have another child who I can cut into little pieces. Why should I feel initially pleased and now disappointed? You took something away from me. Maybe I thought I could get you to write the letter. He'll be cross with me. Oh well, he'll survive."

A few days later she dreamed she was in the toilet. "There were toilets for deaf people and blind people. I felt exposed. Then there was a younger man being seduced by an older woman. I came to your office, and you said to me, that's it—I [the patient] sat up and we ended up talking" (Gudeman, 1974, p. 329).

That's where the dream ended. The analyst pointed out that she was indicating that he was not hearing or seeing something. The patient responded in general terms, indicating she was not getting away with the vasectomy request, but further clarification was not possible.

A day later she said that she must have done something terribly wrong as a child and that was why she always wanted to please the analyst. Then she anxiously stated that she hoped he wouldn't abandon her. He asked her about this, and she talked about feeling abandoned by her father, but there was nothing specific. Two days later, over a week-end, the analyst received a phone call from the patient's husband—the first contact with him—stating the wife was upset, thinking strange things about her father and grandfather. The husband seemed calm. The analyst talked with the husband and then with the patient. She described some of her feelings about some past involvement with the father and grandfather. He reassured her and said that he would see her the following Monday. And on Monday she came in rather upset and was talking, apparently in a rather dissociated way: "Any minute I know what it is that I did was bad—taking a knife to cut myself—my father beat me—my grandfather taught me to masturbate—Did I bleed—maybe that was the lost baby—It's as if I did it all again—did I lie—did I lie? People are telling me to make up—they say your mother is too weak" (Gudeman, 1974, p. 329). She's looking for someone to tell, "My father says you'll find someone to understand—if you didn't seduce me then I couldn't tell you—I keep hearing them say they are playing the game—it doesn't matter—as if I were never a virgin—masturbating—I hear people saying your hand's busy—the magic number is three—I keep blaming you—was it that I had my tonsils out—did my mother threaten to be unfaithful—yesterday I had to find the secret—my grandfather had three clocks—I am sure there is a secret in one of them." She was agitated. "I see dead babies. It's like a play. My father raping me." She goes on and on like that.

And the analyst says the patient was psychotic at this point. Attempts to define himself as separate were met with merging and incorporation of his ideas into her regressive state. He called the patient by telephone requesting her return that day, and he had her sit up. He stated he did not know exactly what was causing her acute distress, and asked if she felt like hurting herself; she said she wanted to die. She returned to the theme of her father raping her.

Stone: Her theme? I thought that was a fantasy. Had she not also said her grandfather had taught her to masturbate?

Langs: The analyst asked specifically whether any of this had happened and she said, "No." He decided then to put her on medication. Eventually there was some reconstitution.

Stone: But she remained an outpatient?

Langs: I believe so. In his discussion he wondered whether the acceptance of the gifts had set the stage for the expectations about the vasectomy. He noted that in the dream of deafness and blindness, and in the psychotic material, the patient both blamed and felt seduced by the analyst, as well as hurt and depressed. The acceptance of the gift, he wrote, had evident transference gratifications and may have contributed to the patient's idealization. He referred to Greenacre's work (1966) in this context, and discussed working with the psychotic and regressive episode. He does consider techniques. For example, should one have been supportive, should one have stuck to the analytic session differently, with earlier confrontations? The issue of fees, for example, could have been more structured, or the analyst could have refused to take the present of flowers early in the analysis. These are obviously matters of judgment, he states, and he cites you: "Stone (1961, 1967) has pointed out that there is a danger in the analyst becoming a distant, remote, artificial and cold person, rather than conveying in some manner that he is a real human being." He goes on: "There is no question that the usual working or therapeutic alliance broke down at the point of the psychotic episode. Whether the real aspects and the therapeutic alliance were not adequately nurtured in the first nine months of analysis is always open to question. If the analyst had been more of a real person and modified techniques earlier it might have made a difference. However, it does seem doubtful that these intense needs would not have surfaced, although it can be argued that they would have been more workable" (Gudeman, 1974, p. 337). He referred to Winnicott's concept of the good-enough mother—the analyst being such for the patient.

Stone: The patient was always on the couch free associating?

Langs: Yes, until the psychotic episode; apparently he then sat her up.

Stone: So how did this come out? What happened? Did the patient recover from the episode?

Langs: He continued to work with her and she reconstituted.

Stone: And resumed regular analytic work?

Langs: I believe so. He talked mostly about the work during the psychotic turmoil. There's a lot more material.

Stone: No, no, I don't mean the details. There's no doubt that she had a psychotic regression. I was just interested in what happened to her.

Langs: The analyst talked about whether the patient could return to analysis after the psychotic episode.

Stone: And wondered whether he could continue to analyze her thereafter?

Langs: Right.

Stone: What was his point; what was he trying to illustrate?

Langs: He was trying to illustrate the factors that contribute to regression, and how they should be managed in the course of an analysis. The main question that he asked is, "How does the therapist or analyst deal with regression?" And he demonstrated how he handled the regressive episode.

Stone: He handled it by sitting her up?

Langs: Yes, and by giving her medication, and reality testing.

Stone: Something more active.

Langs: He asks: How does uncontrolled regression come about? And he attempts to determine some of the factors. Also: Is such psychotic regression a contraindication of further insight-oriented work? How can it be a productive experience for the patient? How significant are the countertransference reactions of the therapist or analyst—he raises that as a side question, particularly in response to the actual regressive episode. He points out the danger of blaming oneself, the possible contributions to it, and some of the difficulties in working with borderline patients.

I presented this case because it has a sequence of modifications of

the frame which culminated with a psychotic episode which, interestingly enough, followed the analyst's efforts to then adhere to the
frame. Of course, we don't know how he handled it, we don't know
more of her associations, and we don't know whether he used the
material from the patient to come to this decision, though that seems
unlikely.

Stone: One doesn't know much about the patient, in general—her
actual emotional relationship to her parents, or even to the doctor,
except in dramatic highlights. Or even about the general traits and
qualities of the patient's ego, or her object relationships. It's conceivable that if an analyst, having established this atmosphere of
extreme permissiveness with a very sick person, whose reality testing
is deficient relative to the drives, reestablishes ordinary "demands" in
the situation, she might crack up because of a frustration that might
otherwise be normally accepted. It seems to me that it could be
explained to such a patient, for example, that to fulfill her request is
really cooperating in something dishonest or shady. Obviously you
would have to be careful, in talking to this patient, to be tactful, but
somehow, to let her know that such a letter could not even be a
statement of fact; that is, as he did say, it really had nothing to do with
her psychiatric condition. I don't know how he worded his answer,
how patient his explanation was, how it was related to everything
that went before. I don't believe in making authoritative statements
about a patient whom one doesn't even half know—and at that, third
hand.

Patients do not have to crack up because of rational non-
compliance with one of their requests, any more than with compliance, or even the succession of one and the other, when both are
justified. I have had abundant experience with all combinations in
this technical complex. I once had to refuse a schizophrenic girl a
letter of reference for rental of an apartment. The reality, the crucial
external relationships, the state of the transference, and the unconscious ramifications of the request must all be considered in full and
subtle detail. The countertransference I take for granted! One has to
do whatever one thinks is right, in any case, but this circumspection
makes for better handling and presentation of the decision, better
interpretation, and much better preparation for the consequences.
How do we know, for example, that this woman was not trying to

castrate her husband, with the analyst's cooperation? And what would his sterility as such really mean to her? And so, ad infinitum!

Langs: The dream conveys what are probably valid unconscious perceptions; she had been seduced and that destroyed the therapeutic alliance and hold. An erratic management of the frame creates strong regressive pressures on the patient, and someone as vulnerable as this woman, who needs the implicit ego support of a secure frame, would suffer terribly as a rule. I have nothing more to add for the moment regarding this case.

It occurred to me that I should also present some material from one of my own papers. There are a couple of vignettes in a paper on the "Therapeutic Relationship and Deviations in Technique" (Langs, 1975b), which are drawn from supervisory experiences. Perhaps I can demonstrate some of the kinds of data that I've made use of. I'll summarize (Langs, 1975b, pp. 119-129):

Mr. A: Severe character disorder; twice-weekly psychotherapy for severe depression that followed the suicide of an older sister whose own therapy had terminated just before her death. He was confused about his life goals, concerned about becoming a homosexual, unable to find a marriage partner. His parents were divorced. In all, a rather stormy situation. The treatment, which I supervised from time to time, had not gone well. The therapist had had some difficulty in understanding the patient and his interventions tended to be naive and incorrect. The patient had been openly resentful; questioned the efficacy of therapy and occasionally would miss sessions. There were indications of a kind of misalliance with bilateral obsessive , sadomasochistic, and some latent homosexual qualities. Now, in the session prior to those we're going to study, the patient was worried that he would not get any help in his treatment. He had an argument with the male cousin who had referred him to treatment and described fantasies of leaving treatment. He had been depressed. Without material from the patient, the therapist attempted to relate this material to the death of his sister. Unconsciously, then, the therapist had really set aside the patient's sense of hopelessness and rage vis-à-vis his therapy.

The patient's response was to describe how his mother never accepted responsibility for failures in their family. And this again, I think, is primarily an unconscious perception of the therapist's failure to see his role in the deterioration of the therapy, with a genetic tie to his mother.

Stone: Yes, albeit in a circular way, insofar as this includes a mother transference to the therapist.

Langs: What I would call a primarily countertransference response. Now in the next session, the patient described feeling exceptionally well, even though the previous day had been his sister's birthday and he had been quite depressed. He had thought of calling the therapist. He ruminated about fears of becoming dependent on the therapist, and about the guilt that the therapist had suggested that he had experienced about the death of his sister. When the therapist commented that Mr. A. seemed to have difficulties in discussing certain feelings with him, the patient complained that the therapist was cold, and likened him to a fellow with whom he, the patient, had lived.

Stone: A homosexual?

Langs: Yes, apparently—and with whom he had frequently quarreled. He thought of changing therapists; he felt they were getting nowhere, but he was afraid of offending the therapist.

Stone: Is this a clinic case?

Langs: Yes. He recalled that when he got mad at his father he was beaten, and when he got angry with his mother, she would just cry, but he always controlled his anger with other people.

Now, he arrived for the next session early in the morning in the midst of a terrible snowstorm. The therapist began the hour by asking the patient how the driving had been, and the patient said that it had been pretty bad for him; he then asked the therapist if he had had difficulty driving to the office. The therapist said that he lived nearby, within walking distance, and the patient fell silent.

So here's the modification in the frame. Do you feel that's relatively innocuous?

Stone: I would have to wait and see, though I would say it is superfluous, because it's a statement about his immediate personal life. It seems to me rather gratuitous; he could have made some more general answer. But that this is necessarily going to be important, I wouldn't say. That would remain sub judice. A priori, I rather doubt it.

Langs: The patient went on to say that he felt quite shy. He'd seen his father and had discussed his sister's suicide, and he had decided he wouldn't visit the father again. He didn't hate the father; he just felt sorry for him. Then he thought of the snow falling on his sister's grave. The therapist commented that he seemed to be preoccupied with his sister, and the patient said he felt guilty and didn't even want to see his mother again. With his mother, he gave the peace sign, but inside he was full of hate. His mother had gone away to the West Coast because his brother had been ill, but the situation wasn't serious and it was really an unnecessary trip.

Stone: It's an older brother or younger?

Langs: Older.

Stone: Both the sister who suicided and the brother are older.

Langs: It would have been better if his mother had stayed with her own sister, who was quite ill, and if she had given better care to the daughter that she had lost. The parents had a way of tearing their children into pieces. He then thought of how the sister had died. He was afraid that if he told his mother that he didn't want to see her, she'd go crazy; but if he didn't say something about it to his mother, he'd go crazy. At this point, the therapist offered the patient some information about the mother taken from the assessment interview carried out by another therapist in the clinic; the information related to an apparent psychotic depression and hospitalization which the patient's mother had undergone after his birth.

Stone: It was old material, based on a time when the mother had been a patient?

Langs: Right. The patient said that he really ought to find out more about what had happened; he hadn't heard from his mother for several days. She would disappear on purpose, so that everybody would feel that she had killed herself. Sometimes he said things that led people to be afraid that he might kill himself, but he had no recollection, afterward, of making such remarks. He had some fear that his mother would commit suicide and somehow he would be blamed.

So now the therapist has introduced material about the mother.

Stone: That, I would say, is entirely gratuitous, as well as an unethical revelation. It should be confidential material. You get the impression that the therapist has a way, in general, of abruptly just doing things, or bringing things in, that have nothing to do with the patient's production of material, so it's a kind of inept therapy all the way through, one in which it's practically impossible to judge "fine points."

Langs: Yes. In the paper, I went on to suggest that the modifications in the frame would be seen as homosexual gifts by this homosexual patient, and I thought the deviations were, in part, an effort by the therapist to undo his inadequacies in interpreting to the patient. And I also expected that it would intensify some of the patient's suicidal fantasies, his feelings of hopelessness, and that he'd look for further deviations.

Stone: I'd see this, in a sense, in a larger way; the fellow wasn't trying to make contact with what his patient was experiencing, enabling him to elaborate upon that, and then reacting. He is introducing all kinds of irrelevant and sometimes inappropriate or unjustified material on a hit-or-miss basis, such as bringing in the question of his mother's clinical depression.

Langs: In terms of the bipersonal field . . .

Stone: You mean you would interpret it immediately in terms of the therapist's countertransference?

Langs: I would see this as reflecting all of the things you noted.

Stone: A reflection of his inadequacies. Perhaps so. But there is first his apparent lack of understanding of the basic techniques of psychotherapy. It is hard for me to turn to interpersonal nuances in a framework of treatment which is so clumsily ataxic. Frankly, I'm not accustomed to cases where interventions are made without a considerable accumulation of anamnestic data, and a legitimate reconstruction in the doctor's mind of what is going on, and to what complications he is addressing himself. I don't doubt the probable countertransference complications, but does one get at them, usefully, in such a chaotic therapeutic context?

Langs: I would suggest that the specific interventions are a reflection of countertransference problems which prompt the therapist, in a sense, to put his pathology into the patient. Many would simply see this as a failure in empathy; I see it as that and considerably more. Using some of the patient's life events and communications, the therapist selects the erroneous intervention according to his own unresolved inner needs, and puts this into the patient.

Stone: Yes, it would sound that way, to a considerable degree. But does one know much about the therapist? It seems to me the work must proceed with reasonable technical adequacy, before one can call attention to countertransference problems in the treatment. These should then be left to self-analysis or to the therapist's analyst. As you know, I am skeptical about the very concept of a therapist (or anybody else) "putting things into" a patient. One would have to know infinitely more about these two people to arrive at such an idea, even as a speculation.

Langs: The patient, as I see it, is put under inner pressure from these introjects to work over the therapist's pathology. What I call the *interface* of the bipersonal field (Langs, 1976a,b) will shift now from the patient more toward the therapist, in terms of the major pathological inputs.

Stone: That's quite likely right. Whether I would see it immediately, as you do, in terms of depth-psychological processes between them, I very much doubt. I would first see the problem, as clinical, technical.

Langs: Yes. There are some who say that the errors we have discussed (and there were others in this therapy that I have not

thought it necessary to describe to you) are too blatant, not representative. But for me, the blatancy highlights what occurs more subtly,
with lesser errors. It's this kind of sequence that brings me back again
and again to issues of the frame in analysis and psychotherapy, and
you can see the kinds of data that have guided me there, why I focus so
much on the interaction, and why I believe that an incorrect intervention is a self-revelation of the therapist. The patient is in tune
with your unconscious communications in therapy, as well as in
analysis.

Stone: Of course.

Langs: And when an intervention is incorrect or the frame is
inappropriately managed, it unconsciously communicates to, and
places into—projectively identifies into—the patient a variety of the
pathological unconscious fantasies—the countertransferences of the
therapist. It involves specific contents which are inappropriately put
into the patient, who generally takes these contents as introjects that
he then works over. Patients exploit these errors; they respond to
them in terms of the genetics that such errors stir up, not as the
genetics related to transference, but initially at least, to nontransference, though they are always elaborated subsequently in
terms of transference distortions. Initially, however, there are reality-
based introjects filled with unconscious meanings, and then it
extends in one direction—I won't go into detail here—into efforts to
cure this pathological introject, to make even what I call *unconscious interpretations* (Langs, 1976a).

Stone: To treat the therapist.

Langs: Yes, to treat the therapist unconsciously as a rule.

Stone: Well, the only difference, and of course it is an important
difference, is that you make a more profound (it seems to me—a
priori) interpretation of the exchange than I would. And for that I
would need a very special context and a lot of data. As you read the
material, I see inept handling of the psychotherapeutic situation and
material all the way through. With all the intensities going on, one
really knows very little about this patient, his personality develop-

ment, the etiologic elements in his homosexuality—even the mysterious role of his sister's suicide death, his mother's illness, how they were related to his homosexuality, etc., etc. And, of course, we know even less about the therapist. So a great deal of depth psychology is being invoked about two people about whom we know very little. The therapist's approach seems out of contact with the patient's material, given the sudden brusque interjections of irrelevancies, gratuitous introduction of material, instead of efforts to follow or facilitate the flow of what's really bothering this man. So I wouldn't be able to evaluate what's happening in the therapist's unconscious and in the unconscious exchange. The man seemed to have come there at least in part because he was depressed because of his sister's suicide death, and the one time the patient began to talk about it, the doctor suddenly said something that had nothing to do with it.

Langs: As you can see, I have found that I can make many formulations regarding both the patient and the analyst from material like this; and they are validated in the derivatives from the patient—and even by the therapist's subsequent interventions. By the way, here, a particular image drawn from the metaphor of the therapist's containing functions (Bion, 1977; Langs, 1976a,b) comes up: his capacity to take in from the patient, contain, and work over an area of pathology such as the sister's suicide. Clearly, one level of communication from this therapist is that he cannot contain such pathology and introjects. He cannot handle it. My approach uses the patient as the mirror of the therapist, and obviously I do this in a very extensive way.

Stone: I know that. But while I acknowledge the seed of some merit in it, it strikes me as greatly overblown. It leads to the neglect of the urgent need to understand the patient.

Langs: Well, here again we differ, since I see this as one aspect of understanding the patient. As Bion's metaphor expresses it, the patient perceives the therapist's fear that he will take this material in and it will do terrible damage to him on some level; drive him crazy, according to the patient. And I have found that the patient is a rather sensitive mirror to the therapist, though "mirror" is a poor metaphor, because we are dealing with interactions and introjections.

"Container" is a more appropriate image. Sorting out how much of this comes from the patient's pathology and is distorting, and how much comes from what he's validly taking in and processing from the therapist, is a crucial problem. But recognizing this task creates a certain basic attitude. And that's really all I want to emphasize for the moment—that in listening to the material from the patient, certain accents come in. I would agree the first level of listening to the material remains the patient's pathology, detecting his unconscious fantasies and memories, and the distortions they contain. But there is another critical second level of listening, in which the material is taken to refer to the therapist or to the analyst, not in terms of distortions, but as valid perceptions and valid introjections. Once we've sorted that out, then we look secondarily for the distortions.

I think of interfaces. The first is the *me/not-me interface* (Langs, 1976b): the patient's communications, I feel, are always a reflection of himself and the therapist or analyst—of both; that's one pairing or interface. There is a second interface or pairing, which I think is also always present: the patient's associations have a certain degree of validity and distortion. We can call it the *transference-nontransference interface*. What I've objected to is the extent to which analysts have seen these communications primarily as reflections of the patient's inner state and object relations, and that of the patient alone, and as primarily involving transference and distortion, and distortion alone. Only begrudgingly do they acknowledge that on certain rare or special occasions it may be that the patient's communications are saying something about the analyst, and even more begrudgingly do they acknowledge that they may have said something valid about, and experienced something correctly from, the analyst. I find that if you place yourself more equidistant from, or if you more equally consider what is valid and what is distorted, what is the patient and what is yourself in the latent content, you perceive a remarkable degree of perceptiveness within patients.

Then I am accused of thinking that the patient is omniscient. I don't think so. A point that Searles (1975) explicitly developed—however difficult it will be to validate it—is that we're almost virtually born with sensitivities and therapeutic intentions: they appear in the infant. And there's an unconscious sensitivity, and unconscious perceptiveness and effort at cure in this kind of intimate therapeutic relationship that I find astonishing.

Stone: Are you thinking of the therapist or the patient?

Langs: Of both. If I had the therapist's associations, I could demonstrate these qualities within him. I have only the patient's free associations. But what they tell me is that really we come as natural-born therapists, that our training has to help us to actualize what we already have. You see, there is a difference: the patient can be an unconscious therapist, but the therapist and analyst have to be able to do this consciously.

Stone: Right.

Langs: Bridging that gap from these unconscious resources to what is conscious becomes very critical, but that's really the goal of our training—to enable our unconscious gifts to become conscious.

Furthermore, our training has to prepare us for a constant struggle to overcome inner resistances to working not only with our own subjective reactions, but with the patient's material as validly mirroring us, in order to detect unconscious, well-defended countertransferences. As I said, Margaret Little, in 1951, wrote a beautiful paper on countertransference in which she made these exact points and even wrote of unconscious interpretations and therapeutic efforts on the part of the patient toward the therapist, and Searles (1965, 1975) independently defined and clarified these therapeutic endeavors. As I've become sensitive to this entire area, I've been able to identify countertransference problems from the patient's material and to recognize when the patient is indeed attempting unconsciously to be helpful. You know, all the patient wants is not some banal response, "Oh thank you for that interpretation," but that your responses to him then change in a way that reflects the resolution of the countertransference difficulties.

Stone: I understand your drift, and I believe a great deal of it in certain remote areas is extremely important. I do think, however, that excessive enthusiasm for it can turn things upside down, and lead to profound neglects. And as I said, I cannot accept the wholesale substitution of archaic processes of "putting into" and "containers" for the later understanding and interpretations with which we live as adults. All these things began long ago in different terms, as I mentioned to you once before in our conversation. I was surprised to find that as correct a personality, quite an English (or Scottish?) personality, I think (I had correspondence with him, although I never met him), as Glover, back in the thirties, said that somewhere the patient is reacting to what we are in the very depths of our personalities, and that this can't be excluded. He said it without these more extensive, detailed invocations of archaic mechanisms. I have referred to what Glover said in that second technical paper of mine (Stone, 1954), and elaborated it somewhat in the Postscript to *The Psychoanalytic Situation* (Stone, 1961). I believe it is true. However, where one gets to that, and when one gets to that, would be a matter about which I would be much more conservative.

I mean, for example, in the case of the young doctor whom you cite, I would start with what seems to me his quite blatant technical clumsiness and lack of understanding of the general nature of the therapeutic relationship, and the fact that the patient first and foremost wants his problems and his material to be listened to with understanding, and without brusque interjections of things that have nothing to do with the case (at least in any sense of immediacy), and that reflect the failure to facilitate, at very least by passivity, the emergence of the things that really bother the patient. Then, next, if I had access to them, I would raise the question of whether some specific countertransferences, which incidentally would not be uncommon for a young doctor dealing with a manifestly homosexual patient, especially if the doctor had not come to terms with his own latent homosexuality, had distorted his work with this patient maybe further on; if one had a lot of work with him, one might perhaps begin to wonder about these more complicated mechanisms. If it got that far, it would be better that he be discussing things with his analyst. I do not approve of a dual role for the supervisors. So it isn't that I disagree for a second that these things may exist. I do disagree, or would have a reservation, about the emphasis (and I've said that elsewhere) on the pervasive, controlling aspect of the doctor's countertransference, as an a priori consideration. It may be true with people who don't know themselves at all, and are doing a therapy in which perhaps one of the first requirements is to know oneself.

Langs: I was going to ask you that specifically. But first let me respond quickly to your point. My emphasis on these mechanisms, and for the moment on the therapist, is often questioned in the case of *The Bipersonal Field* (Langs, 1976a), where I took tapes at random to try to illustrate some basic interactional mechanisms and functions of the frame, and I am asked, Why do you spend all your time talking about the therapist's pathology? What about the patient? I have a rather simple answer to that which is related to what you had said: because that's what the patient is working over at the time, and patients do that more often than generally acknowledged. As a matter of fact, my observations indicate that when the therapist's pathology is presented into the patient and into the field, the patient's pathology becomes camouflaged and hidden within it, and doesn't get worked over until the resolution of the therapist's problems. I do not see this as a dual role; it is all subsumed under one's functions as a supervisor—no therapeutic functions are implied. It is a matter of working where the problem exists.

Stone: Well, if the doctor's pathology is very strong and intrusive, and without insight. Most, if not all, doctors have some troubles of their own. You know what has always been said from way back, that there are analysts who may be quite ill, but who know themselves very well and whose *Arbeits Ich* or "working ego" (I believe it has been called that) may nonetheless function very well. Such colleagues can separate their own depressions or marital troubles, or whatever, from their work with patients. But if the doctor is quite ill and is not aware of it, and is operating in the light of his urgent pathology, then I would say that what you describe is probably so. Now how often that happens in people who have had good training, I don't know. I have not seen many examples in the range which you describe. It seems to me that it will happen in occasional cases, and then the candidates usually become aware of it, or the supervisor calls attention to a trend which is intruding. Then it is taken up elsewhere.

Langs: You stated it in terms of the extreme, as an occasional, intermittent occurrence. I see it as more often a kind of continuing process or pressure that is . . .

Stone: Always present to some degree?

Langs: Yes. There are certainly exceptions; there are analysts where this need not be a factor. But it's there more often than we've acknowledged and it's potentially there all the time. Even with a good analyst who has had a relatively good analysis, and knows himself, there will be periods in which he introduces some of this. And yes, with sophisticated analysts this can be brought to a minimum, though we should all be constantly on the alert for it. But there are many good analysts where this remains as a factor, even in a subtle form, and it can influence the analysis.

Stone: The last thing you said is important. I would unequivocally agree that the analyst's personality is always participant, and this, of course, includes his specific pathology. At times, this may be stimulated only by certain patients. But what can we do but be aware of this constantly, and to correct it by whatever means are available, whenever it appears? If you will be indulgent with the levity: we can't solve it by turning to our patients for therapy!—which may be an impulse in certain unhappy people. But I agree that we can listen more attentively to what they say about us—without writing it off *immediately* to transference. I think that this factor determines the unequivocal fact of variations in the effectivenss of analysts with certain patients.

You see, analysts may not be sick in the ordinary sense, and may be, as the cliché goes, pretty well-analyzed people who know themselves and are very conscientious (although of course there are residues of conflicts in all of us); and yet this variation in sub-clinical residues probably accounts for the fact that a patient can do well with one person, or do poorly with one person, make a transference in a later effort and do very well with a second analyst, and so on. Surely that isn't always just a technical matter; it has to do with these elements that you speak of, these things where the personal problems of the analyst, however slight, low-grade, or nonclinical they may be, do exhibit themselves in the work with the patient. I don't doubt the importance of the analyst's ability to accept certain things about the patient—slight or subtle feelings of rivalry or competitiveness—or an inability to accept certain erotic things. One has to include in this too a host of things not necessarily pathological: likes, dislikes, aversions, prejudices, preferences—which can also be "warded off" (but sometimes unsuccessfully) in committment to a professional stance. But in any case I doubt whether it means that, in every analysis, this is to be the predominant and first consideration, so that when the patient begins to produce transference reactions, the first question is, "What did I do to elicit them?" Such questions should appear after a considerable number of prior considerations. Patient's transference reactions will sometimes appear in absolute oppositeness to the latent state of the analyst, or of the analyst's countertransference, if he knows it and is handling it well. This can be seen in very simple things, where the patient will tell you what a rejecting, disliking feeling you have for him or her, in instances where if anything you're a little concerned because you rather like the person especially. It is true that the person might sense your feeling, and this might be a defensive response. But it also occurs as an outright—pure—genetically conditioned transference fantasy.

Langs: Again, you are focusing more on a manifest level while I am stressing latent, unconscious communications.

Stone: There are many combinations and permutations. But we cannot disestablish or ignore the sheer power of the patient's transference.

Langs: But I do think it is important for the analyst consistently to monitor the material for valid perceptions and images as well.

Stone: Of himself? No disagreement!

Langs: Yes; I don't think this need predominate, or that it implies that the analyst's own rectification of his countertransference difficulties need dominate analytic work, but I do think that in virtually any analytic experience, there will be such moments. The more untrained and unanalyzed the therapist, and the more the patient sets off particular unresolved residuals, the more this will predominate. We each have to face the limitations of our own analysis—our own inner resolutions and unstable areas—and we should maintain a kind of comfortable monitoring of the material in this way.

Stone: I think this should go on all the time, not only with our feelings but, of course, watching the material.

Langs: Yes, and there is such a narcissistic tendency in analysts immediately to think of it as the patient's pathology. This is really what I'm reacting to; just as you reacted to a certain rigidity in the application of the frame, I am reacting to a certain over-idealization of the analyst. An analyst told me that a very sophisticated analyst colleague, because of my teaching of therapists, was being attacked and being told that he was seductive with his patients—he was presenting his own cases to them. And this analyst said to me, "It can't be true. Look what you've done." I said, "But how can you say to me it can't be true? Neither you nor I have observed the material. Why should we assume that this analyst can't possibly be seductive?" But that is the assumption, that an analyst can't have blatant countertransference problems.

Stone: That, of course, is an absurdity. I have over the years seen four consultations with patients who were outrightly seduced by their analysts, and one consultation with an analyst who had carried out such a seduction, and, as a matter of fact, went back to analysis thereafter. So, there's no doubt that these things exist, and that one occasionally gets the backwash of literally extravagant things that have been said or done with patients whom one may reanalyze, reflecting all kinds of human failings, not to speak of one's own subtle mistakes of which one becomes aware. And of course, we may postulate that there are some which escape awareness, and that a conscientious analyst will be concerned about these things in himself.

Langs: Margaret Little (1951) said that analysts tend to be phobic about their countertransferences, and my reading of the literature confirmed this. That's all that I'm talking about. We tend, both classical and Kleinian analysts, to overidealize ourselves and to relegate countertransference to the background. I'm simply trying to say that there can be a kind of continuous monitoring. It doesn't have to be intrusive.

Stone: No, I think that that is correct. I don't like to see it the sole concentration of therapy, because it then is going to undermine the perception of the patient's transference as a major function of the analyst. The patient comes with pathology. The latent transferences were there in the nature of his illness. Obviously one expects them to appear. That these other things in ourselves may interfere with our perceptions, or may unduly gratify the transferences, may often be true.

Langs: I am only seeking a balanced approach, by considering areas that have been neglected. In no way do I advocate neglecting the ultimate focus on the patient's pathology. It's just that we must remember that there is another level of the interaction between patient and therapist, and I object to being blind to the analyst's contribution. Sometimes we begin an interpretation by alluding to an outside relationship.

Stone: Of course, because certain processes occur there that can't occur in the analytic or therapeutic relationship.

Langs: But there's always an echo in the analytic relationship and in the interaction, and we shouldn't be blind to it.

Stone: That I agree with.

Langs: In general, do you think that nonanalyzed therapists can do valid psychotherapy?

Stone: I have thought about it somewhat. You would have to know the therapist. There are some healthy people. I think Freud himself said—I may be inaccurate as to the words, but the general idea was conveyed by him in one of his major writings—that after all, the best that analysis can do is to enable the person to do what the healthy person is able to do anyway, without being analyzed. He doesn't need it. I mean that he makes certain adaptations, resolutions of conflicts without symptom formations, and so forth; he doesn't have a tyrannical superego, and the strength of his instincts isn't such that they're constantly pressing him. There are people who I think are healthy (in an inevitably relative sense) without analysis. And I think that such persons can be taught the technique. They may not have, perhaps, the profound perceptiveness that comes with becoming acquainted with certain things in oneself. But I'm not sure, because there have been some very perceptive analysts who were never analyzed. I don't know that they were any worse than some people who had years and years of analysis, if they had an intuitive gift which probably included some degree of self-analytic power. I think by and large, while I would hold with the sensible requirement that a person should have personal analysis as part of his preparation for doing the work, I would be inclined to think that there are some people who can do it without having had the benefit of what we call thorough analysis. Again, we are talking inclusively, about the entire field. The Institutes, of course, require analysis, and I have no quarrel with this requirement. I do have a quarrel, as you know, with the "reporting."

Langs: In your practical experience, in this real world, how often do you think someone like that turns up?

Stone: I would have to plead a certain degree of ignorance there, because since the days when I was chief of a clinic at Mt. Sinai and worked in a clinic at New York Hospital at another time (at Mt. Sinai, I was chief of the Monday, Wednesday, Friday clinic for a few years), I have had little contact with this sector of the profession. Even there, most of the people, if they weren't analysts, had had some analysis. There were few who hadn't. The people whom I've had contact with, even people who are nonanalysts who may come to me for consultation, have almost invariably had several years of analysis, so I don't have a good basis for specific judgment. What I was talking about before was sort of "in principle" and was also, to some degree, based on occasional contacts with nonprofessional people who, I feel, might be "naturals." I also have some knowledge of a few unanalyzed but nonetheless able analysts in the past. What is your feeling about that, because you continue to see residents?

Langs: Well, it's like Diogenes with the lantern. I find such people to be extremely rare. It is an ideal that is seldom accomplished in terms of the people who chose psychiatry or psychotherapy as their life work.

Stone: Even as a matter of a priori, I would not find it hard to agree with that. You remember, in that paper of mine which you've mentioned, "Problems and Potentialities" (Stone, 1975), that was one thing that persisted for me, as one of the indubitable values of lege artis analysis, which was a preparation for psychotherapy of any kind, whether the person was going to be an analyst, or just an intelligent, sensitive psychiatrist, or a psychotherapist. I do believe that it is truly helpful, and probably in most instances necessary.

Langs: Since you have mentioned that paper—and to enable us to round out this discussion: Where do you see the problems in analysis today? We've really been touching upon some of them in our dialogue, but what, specifically, are the areas that concern you?

Stone: You see, as a matter of fact, it's implicit in our whole dialogue. I mean, I don't have a claim to the ultimate truth, nor do I assign that to you. I feel, as was one of the burdens of that paper, and has been one of the burdens of my thinking for some time, that we still do not understand thoroughly enough the psychoanalytic process, its dynamics, ab initio, so to speak; what makes it go in the first place, what makes it feasible that a verbal exchange between two people can alter profound things in the patient's personality, or his symptoms. I think we have certain clichés, which we take for granted, about the nature of insight and what it does. I think the idea of working through was in itself an important step, and yet even that isn't understood sufficiently. As to the structure of the situation, I'm not satisfied about our understanding of the balances between gratification—whether cognitive or emotional—and abstinence, although I fully accept the fact that abstinence in certain important areas, especially in the instinctual life, is absolutely necessary to the structure of the analytic situation. I am not satisfied that we know, for example, the relative importances of emotional or cognitive exchange. What does it mean to a very sick, borderline patient, that the analyst patiently continues to work with him and wait, over a period, let's say, of many years, when the patient or possibly another analyst might have thrown up his or her hands? What is the impact of this on the dynamics of the person's illness, as compared with very clever interpretations as the exclusive therapeutic medium offered? All these other, more specific matters that you mention, like alterations in the frame, would, I think, if we had a better understanding of the fundamental dynamics of the situation, come into better and clearer light and evaluation. Now, for the rest of it, you say, what do I foresee? What are the problems?

Langs: What do you see as the problems among analysts, the problems for analysis? Are you concerned about basic attitudes?

Stone: This was one of the central themes in that paper, too. I'm, concerned about the fact that because analysis in its very nature has implicit in it large areas of uncertainty, it takes on, in reaction to that fact, certain aspects of a religion. This disturbs me a great deal. Analysis is full of rituals, of dogmas, of beliefs held as sacred, which are somehow or other conceived of as scientifically established, when they're not at all of that character. We may find that some of our fundamental conceptions are literally wrong. We haven't yet; the basic things have seemed to stand up very well. And they may, for a long time to come. But all kinds of intermediate things, and maybe even some of the basic assumptions which I, like others, regard as axiomatic, may eventually have to be radically reversed. The a priori resistance to such a concept in feeling and attitude, if not in words, is to me the chief obstacle to the progress of analysis.

The second thing is the position that analysis has in the reality of the community and the body politic in general: its extremely long duration, the very great expense in time and money, the necessary fact of restriction to a relatively few people who can afford it and benefit by it. Now, I don't say that that can be altered by fiat. So long as it's so, it's so. But then the result is a sort of "trickle down" aspect. And this "trickle down" aspect, even though I have borrowed the rather demeaning phrase from economics, I believe, has some real potential validity in it, in the sense that the "tricklings" may provide very valuable fluids. This aspect should be examined much more closely; psychotherapy should be given a much more important position than it's been given, among analysts. It should be taken very seriously. I know you do, because you're engaged in teaching it. The differences that are created by differences in frequency or spatial position, or visual stimulation, and all that sort of thing, should be examined very closely, and the effort to create rational, well-grounded psychotherapies should be a growing interest of analysts, instead of something that's tossed off to the side. You know, "They can only afford some psychotherapy, so we'll send them to some novice that we know, who is not yet privileged to do analysis."

Langs: The alternative, too, is that many analysts do psychotherapy as a kind of indulgence. They surrender their principles.

Stone: Well, that's right. And in fact, sometimes toss them over. You apparently follow the same technical principles that obtain within analysis. I would say that there should be modifications, carefully thought out, in standard formats, and/or in individual applications. The crux of the problem is the alteration in the dynamic psychological economy of the situations.

Langs: I accept the need for investigation, though I do feel that on one level the principles are indeed comparable.

Stone: Just one more thing. I now feel, by this time, and I've been very slow to come to it, as an older conservative analyst, that the question of psychopharmacology is here to stay. We have to concern ourselves not only about immediate, demonstrable psychopharmacological effects, but about where these drugs may fit into fundamental psychology and psychopathology. For example, what effects do some of them have on oral mechanisms, when they affect depression, and so on. I think that analysis must come to better terms with this field, understand it, gradually perhaps to begin to utilize it, and somewhere fit it into the schema of psychoanalytic work with more sick patients. Because I have no doubt that it is going to augment greatly the possibility of psychoanalytic treatment of psychotics or sick, borderline patients.

Langs: I would, if I may, only wish to add that we must include in such a study an investigation of the way in which the use of medication could influence the frame and the therapeutic field.

Stone: Of course, both, both. The way it influences the "frame" in the immediate manifest sense is that the analyst or his colleague consultant gives the patient medicine, and this I've already dealt with in a few patients. It's not an easy or simple matter, beginning with the question of who prescribes and monitors the drug. So far it has been my preference that this be separated from the analyst's commitment. But also there is the primary fact that a pharmacological agent alters the patient's feeling. How does this "competitive" agent affect his interest in purely psychological work? The unconscious symbolism may be profoundly important. And more deeply—how may the drug be altering certain instinctual mechanisms, apart from the obvious symptomatic effect? And I don't know what else. We keep on working and trying to understand things better in every sphere. Even the nature of transference; I'm not satisfied with our knowledge of it. Contributions have accumulated, there have been increments through the years, but there's still a lot to be learned.

Langs: Yes, I agree. You know Sandler, in his 1969 paper with a group of associates, made the statement that every analyst knows what transference is clinically, so there's no need to discuss that subject. I took great exception to that statement, which, to me, can only lead to a false sense of certainty, to a neglect of the distinction between transference and nontransference, and of the need continuously to monitor the patient's material for that aspect in the clinical situation. This relates, of course, to the work I've been doing regarding the nondistorted components of the analytic relationship, which I don't like to call the "real relationship."

Stone: That was a term I used years ago. I can see that it's susceptible to a great deal of improvement. I have never been sufficiently fussy about terminology. However, I think the idea was useful and clear.

Langs: Yes, because it tends to dichotomize and lead to many unnecessary modifications in technique. There are two points I'd like to make here: one is that a questioning and skeptical attitude leads to reevaluation of the nature of the patient's relationships to the analyst, and the second is that we have a lot to learn about interactional mechanisms in the analytic realtionship.

Stone: Well, I would accept that as another field that does require a great deal more exploration.

Langs: You know, it's quite refreshing to see this attitude at this point in your career: it shows that there is a vitality to analysis and that there are many avenues of important research that still remain open. There are others who are also moving in that direction. It's one of the reasons I appreciate Bion (1977). Despite his extreme difficulty, he comes up with ideas that are provocative of different lines of thought. For example, Hanna Segal (1977) has a paper on dreams that clinically illustrates an idea of Bion's—that certain dreams and certain communications are not designed for the possible understanding of unconscious fantasies, or even for verbal communication, but primarily to get rid of the contents involved, to evacuate them. Well, you know, classical American analysts would have a lot of difficulty with that concept, but at least it could open their minds to thinking of the different kinds of functions of communication, and different kinds of interactional spaces. This would lend an entirely different meaning to the concept of transference—that the analyst is being used as an object into whom one evacuates things.

Stone: Well, this is not really a departure from certain classical analytic concepts of transference. It's perhaps using it in a different context, and giving it a different symbolic language.

Langs: Yes, we could think of it in terms of acting out and acting in, or, as I prefer, "living out." But you see, that's another point. There are many Kleinian concepts that can be readily integrated into classical analytic thinking, and can extend and clarify it. I object to dichotomizing the Kleinians and Freudians, and to the extreme divergence that prevails, though in Europe that may be changing; but there's knowledge to be shared that could really be illuminating.

Stone: Well, I'm afraid that both sides may contribute to the lack of communication. You see, there are areas that can be shared, and I haven't the slightest question that there are things that we can learn even from their most extravagantly stated systems of fantasy and so on, but I think sometimes that their practice, as one hears about it, seems so far out, so divorced from reality, that that constitutes their contribution to the dichotomization.

Langs: There's no question about it. It's all very frustrating. I think Hanna Segal is somebody who has tried to write intelligently.

Stone: Well, she is one of the most intelligent. That little book of hers (Segal, 1967), I always value very much.

Langs: As an editor, I'm getting Kleinian papers and I've added Kleinian editors to the *International Journal of Psychoanalytic*

Psychotherapy. It's an attempt to open avenues of communication, but there are certain Kleinian papers that are completely out of all realm of actuality, completely flooded with the analyst's fantasies, without any kind of methodology, and with no effort even to establish the sources of their material. It's very disconcerting. But, for their own part, I find that the classical Freudian is a little too wedded to Freud's basic concepts, a bit too rigid and unimaginative, and a little too closed to expanding.

Stone: Well, the closed mind is certainly one of the difficult general attributes of classical psychoanalysis, not necessarily among the most distinguished minds, but among most who tend to "follow a line" and think that that is right and nothing else is right, in perpetuity. Even very distinguished minds, if very strongly committed to certain ideas, will look at the other view, but with a certain primary attitude of adverse judgment.

Langs: One last point and then we'll stop. Some fascinating issues came up in the 1975 London Congress, where I understand the classical Freudians and the Kleinians did not get along well at all. Rangell (1975) and Green (1975) offered rather different statements.

Stone: I was there, but I didn't go to the meetings in which these matters were thrashed out further. I just heard the exchange between Rangell and Green.

Langs: Now, the point, for instance, developed by Green and the Kleinians, based on the notion of the paranoid-schizoid position that the core of every neurosis is a psychosis, rather than a perversion, as they take Freud to have said, raises certain very interesting issues, very interesting considerations.

Stone: I thought that Rangell "talked down" in his dealings with the disagreement. He's a very smart and able man, but I thought he was a bit condescending.

Langs: Yes, he seemed to adhere rather rigidly to the basic classical position, and to be relatively closed to new ideas. That's why I think Bion should be read.

Stone: I'll have to read some of Bion. I know a little of it only by indirection and reference. I've never gone into his ideas thoroughly. I admit to a certain bias of my own: I tend to stick close to intelligible patterns of human thought and feeling.

Langs: Well, I found his *Experience in Groups* (Bion, 1959) relatively easy. He has a series of other little books (Bion, 1977) that are very difficult. One has to read them in sequence. Well, let me close out our dialogue. I think, at least for me, and I hope that the people who read this eventually will share it, it's been an extremely important and stimulating experience to have had this opportunity so frankly and openly to share our ideas, disagree, and agree, and discuss these basic issues.

Stone: Well, I've enjoyed it very much too.

Langs: And I'm really going to miss it. It's almost a year since I first called you. Do you want to say anything in concluding?

Stone: No, no, I've appreciated it and enjoyed it myself and we'll no doubt have some further contact.

Langs: Yes, I really hope so; and we'll eventually have reactions to what we've done that will be important for both of us—and I hope for our field as well.

REFERENCES

Alexander, F. (1954). Some quantitative aspects of psychoanalytic technique. *Journal of the American Psychoanalytic Association* 2:685-701.

——— (1956). *Psychoanalysis and Psychotherapy: Developments in Theory, Technique and Training.* New York: Norton.

Amrith, M. (1975). Introjective and projective identification. *Samiksa* 29:1-12.

Arlow J. (1969). Unconscious fantasy and disturbances of conscious experience. *Psychoanalytic Quarterly* 38:1-27.

Arlow, J., and Brenner, C. (1966). The psychoanalytic situation. In *Psychoanalysis in the Americas,* ed. R. Litman, pp. 23-43. New York: International Universities Press.

Bak, R. (1970). Recent developments in psychoanalysis: a critical summary of the main theme of the 26th International Psycho-Analytic Congress in Rome. *International Journal of Psycho-Analysis* 51:255-264.

Balint, M. (1968). *The Basic Fault: Therapeutic Aspects of Regression.* London: Tavistock.

Baranger, M., and Baranger, W. (1966). Insight in the analytic situation. In *Psychoanalysis in the Americas,* ed. R. Litman, pp. 56-72. New York: International Universities Press.

Beigler, J. (1975). A commentary on Freud's treatment of the Rat Man. *The Annual of Psychoanalysis* 3:271-286.

Benedek, T. (1962). Book review of *The Psychoanalytic Situation* by L. Stone. *Psychoanalytic Quarterly* 31:549-555.

Berman, L. (1949). Countertransference and attitudes of the analyst in the therapeutic process. *Psychiatry* 12:159-166.

Bibring, E. (1937). Contribution to the symposium on the theory of therapeutic results of psycho-analysis. *International Journal of Psycho-Analysis* 18:170-189.

Bion, W. (1959). *Experiences in Groups.* London: Tavistock.

——— (1977). *Seven Servants.* New York: Jason Aronson.

Bleger, J. (1967). Psycho-analysis of the psychoanalytic frame. *International Journal of Psycho-Analysis* 48:511-519.

Bowlby, J. (1963). Pathological mourning and childhood mourning. *Journal of the American Psychoanalytic Association* 11:500-541.

Brunswick, R. (1928). A supplement to Freud's "History of an infantile neurosis." *International Journal of Psycho-Analysis* 9:439-476.

——— (1929). The analysis of a case of paranoia (delusions of jealousy). *Journal of Nervous and Mental Disease* 70:1-22, 155-178.

Calef, V. (1971). Panel: Concluding remarks (to the panel on the transference neurosis). *Journal of the American Psychoanalytic Association* 19:89-97.

Calogeras, R. (1967). Silence as a technical parameter in psycho-analysis. *International Journal of Psycho-Analysis* 48:536-558.

Deutsch, H. (1942). Some forms of emotional disturbance and their relationship to schizophrenia. *Psychoanalytic Quarterly* 11:301-321.

Eissler, K. (1953). The effect of the structure of the ego on psychoanalytic technique. *Journal of the American Psychoanalytic Association* 1:104-143.

——— (1958). Remarks on some variations in psycho-analytic technique. *International Journal of Psycho-Analysis* 39:222-229.

——— (1974). On some theoretical and technical problems regarding the payment of fees for psychoanalytic treatment. *International Review of Psycho-Analysis* 1:73-101.

Fenichel, O. (1937). Contributions to the symposium on theory of therapeutic results of psycho-analysis. *International Journal of Psycho-Analysis* 18:133-138.

——— (1941). *Problems of Psychoanalytic Technique.* Trans. D. Brunswick. New York: Psychoanalytic Quarterly.

Ferenczi, S. (1909). Introjection and transference. In S. Ferenczi, *Sex in Psychoanalysis.* New York: Brunner, 1950.

——— (1919). On the technique of psycho-analysis. In S. Ferenczi, *Further Contributions to the Theory and Technique of Psycho-Analysis.* London: Hogarth Press, 1950.

——— (1921). The further development of an active therapy in psycho-analysis. In S. Ferenczi, *Further Contributions to the Theory and Technique of Psycho-Analysis,* pp. 198-217. New York: Basic Books, 1955.

——— (1925). Contra-indications to the "active" psychoanalytic technique. In S. Ferenczi, *Further Contributions to the Theory and Technique of Psycho-Analysis.* New York: Basic Books, 1955.

——— (1926). *Further Contributions to the Theory and Technique of Psycho-Analysis.* Chapter XIV. London: Hogarth Press.

Ferenczi, S., and Rank, O. (1925). *The Development of Psychoanalysis.* New York: Nervous and Mental Disease Publishing.

Fliess, R. (1942). The metapsychology of the analyst. *Psychoanalytic Quarterly* 11:211-227.

Freud, A. (1954a). Problems of technique in adult analysis. *Bulletin of the Philadelphia Association for Psychoanalysis* 4:44-70.

——— (1954b). Discussion: the widening scope of indications for psychoanalysis. *Journal of the American Psychoanalytic Association* 2:607-620.

Freud, S. (1900). The interpretation of dreams. *Standard Edition* 4/5.

——— (1905). Fragment of an analysis of a case of hysteria. *Standard Edition* 7:3-122.

——— (1909). Notes upon a case of obsessional neurosis. *Standard Edition* 10:153-320.

——— (1912a). The dynamics of transference. *Standard Edition* 12:97-108.

——— (1912b). Recommendations to physicians practising psychoanalysis. *Standard Edition* 12:111-120.

——— (1913). On beginning the treatment (further recommendations on the technique of psycho-analysis, I). *Standard Edition* 12:121-144.

——— (1914). Remembering, repeating and working-through (further recommendations on the technique of psycho-analysis, II). *Standard Edition* 12:145-156.

——— (1915). Observations on transference-love (further recommendations on the technique of psycho-analysis, III). *Standard Edition* 12:157-171.

——— (1918). From the history of an infantile neurosis. *Standard Edition* 17:3-122.

——— (1920). Beyond the pleasure principle. *Standard Edition* 18:3-64.

——— (1925). An autobiographical study. *Standard Edition* 20:3-74.

——— (1926). Inhibitions, symptoms and anxieties. *Standard Edition* 20:77-175.

——— (1937). Analysis terminable and interminable. *Standard Edition* 23:209-253.

——— (1940). An outline of psychoanalysis. *Standard Edition* 23:172-182.

Friedman, L. (1969). The therapeutic alliance. *International Journal of Psycho-Analysis* 50:139-153.

Gitelson, M. (1952). The emotional position of the analyst in the psychoanalytic situation. *International Journal of Psycho-Analysis* 33:1-10.

Glatzer, H., and Evans, W. (1977). On Guntrip's analysis with Fairbairn and Winnicott. *International Journal of Psychoanalytic Psychotherapy* 6:81-98.

Glover, E. (1937). Contribution to the symposium on the theory of therapeutic results of psycho-analysis. *International Journal of Psycho-Analysis* 18:125-132.

——— (1955). *The Technique of Psycho-Analysis.* New York: International Universities Press.

Goldberg, A. (1976). A discussion of the paper, "A critical examination of the new narcissism," by C. Hanly and J. Masson. *International Journal of Psycho-Analysis* 57:67-70.

Green, A. (1975). The analyst, symbolization and absence in the analytic setting (on changes in analytic practice and analytic experience). *International Journal of Psycho-Analysis* 56:1-22.

Greenacre, P. (1954). The role of the transference. *Journal of the American Psychoanalytic Association* 2:671-684.

——— (1959). Certain technical problems in the transference relationship. *Journal of the American Psychoanalytic Association* 7:484-502.

Greenson, R. (1965). The working alliance and the transference neurosis. *Psychoanalytic Quarterly* 34:155-181.

——— (1967). *The Technique and Practice of Psychoanalysis,* vol. I. New York: International Universities Press.

——— (1971). The "real" relationship between the patient and the psychoanalyst. In *The Unconscious Today,* ed. M. Kanzer, pp. 213-232. New York: International Universities Press.

——— (1972). Beyond transference and interpretation. *International Journal of Psycho-Analysis* 53:213-217.

——— (1974). Loving, hating, and indifference toward the patient. *International Review of Psycho-Analysis* 1:259-266.

Grinberg, L. (1962). On a specific aspect of counter-transference due to the patient's projective identification. *International Journal of Psycho-Analysis* 43:436-440.

Gudeman, J. (1974). Uncontrolled regression in therapy and analysis. *International Journal of Psychoanalytic Psychotherapy* 3:325-338.

Guntrip, H. (1975). My experience of analysis with Fairbairn and Winnicott. *International Review of Psycho-Analysis* 2:145-156.

Hartmann, H. (1939). *Ego Psychology and the Problem of Adaption.* New York: International Universities Press, 1958.

Heimann, P. (1950). On countertransference. *International Journal of Psycho-Analysis* 31:81-84.

Jacobson, E. (1954). Transference problems in the psychoanalytic treatment of severely depressive patients. *Journal of the American Psychoanalytic Association* 2:595-606.

Kairys, D. (1964). The training analysis; a critical review of the literature and a controversial proposal. *Psychoanalytic Quarterly* 33:485-512.

Kanzer, M. (1958). Image formation during free association. *Psychoanalytic Quarterly* 27:465-484.

——— (1961). Verbal and nonverbal aspects of free association. *Psychoanalytic Quarterly* 30:327-350.

——— (1963). Book review of *The Psychoanalytic Situation* by L. Stone. *International Journal of Psycho-Analysis* 44:108-110.

——— (1972). Superego aspects of free association and the fundamental rule. *Journal of the American Psychoanalytic Association* 20:246-266.

——— (1975). The therapeutic and working alliances: an assessment. *International Journal of Psychoanalytic Psychotherapy* 4:48-68.

Kernberg, O. (1975). *Borderline Conditions and Pathological Narcissism.* New York: Jason Aronson.

Khan, M. (1960). Regression and integration in the analytic setting. *International Journal of Psycho-Analysis* 41:130-156.

——— (1969). Vicissitudes of being, knowing, and experiencing in the therapeutic situation. *British Journal of Medical Psychology* 42:383-393.

Klein, M. (1946). Notes on some schizoid mechanisms. *International Journal of Psycho-Analysis* 27:99-110.

——— (1952). The origins of transference. *International Journal of Psycho-Analysis* 33:433-438.

Kohut, H. (1971). *The analysis of the self: A systematic approach to the psychoanalytic treatment of narcissistic personality disorders.* Psychoanalytic Study of the Child Monograph 4. New York: International Universities Press.

——— (1977). *The Restoration of the Self.* New York: International Universities Press.

Langs, R. (1971). Day residues, recall residues, and dreams: reality and the psyche. *Journal of the American Psychoanalytic Association* 19:499-523.

——— (1973). *The Technique of Psychoanalytic Psychotherapy*, vol. I. New York: Jason Aronson.

——— (1974). *The Technique of Psychoanalytic Psychotherapy*, vol. II. New York: Jason Aronson.

——— (1975a). Therapeutic misalliances. *International Journal of Psychoanalytic Psychotherapy* 4:77-105.

——— (1975b). The therapeutic relationship and deviations in technique. *International Journal of Psychoanalytic Psychotherapy* 4:106-141.

——— (1975c). The patient's unconscious perception of the therapist's errors. In *Tactics and Techniques in Psychoanalytic Therapy: Volume II. Countertransference*, ed. P. Giovacchini. New York: Jason Aronson.

——— (1976a). *The Bipersonal Field.* New York: Jason Aronson.

——— (1976b). *The Therapeutic Interaction*. 2 vols. New York: Jason Aronson.

——— (1976c). The misalliance dimension in Freud's case histories: I. The case of Dora. *International Journal of Psychoanalytic Psychotherapy* 5:301-318.

——— (1978a). Misalliance and framework in the case of the Rat Man. In R. Langs, *Technique in Transition*. New York: Jason Aronson

——— (1978b). Misalliance and framework in the case of the Wolf Man. In R. Langs, *Technique in Transition*. New York: Jason Aronson.

Litman, R. (1966). *Psychoanalysis in the Americas*. New York: International Universities Press.

Little, M. (1951). Counter-transference and the patient's response to it. *International Journal of Psycho-Analysis* 32:32-40.

Loewald, H. (1960). The therapeutic action of psycho-analysis. *International Journal of Psycho-Analysis* 41:16-33.

Loewenstein, R. (1951). The problem of interpretation. *Psychoanalytic Quarterly* 20:1-14.

Macalpine, I. (1950). The development of the transference. *Psychoanalytic Quarterly* 19:501-539.

McLaughlin, F. (1967). Addendum to a controversial proposal: some observations on the training analysis. *Psychoanalytic Quarterly* 36:230-247.

Malin, A., and Grotstein, J. (1966). Projective identification in the therapeutic process. *International Journal of Psycho-Analysis* 47:26-31.

Menaker, E. (1942). The masochistic factor in the psychoanalytic situation. *Psychoanalytic Quarterly* 9:171-186.

Milner, M. (1952). Aspects of symbolism in the comprehension of the non-self. *International Journal of Psycho-Analysis* 33:181-195.

——— (1969). *The Hands of the Living God*. New York: International Universities Press.

Money-Kyrle, R. (1956). Normal counter-transference and some of its deviations. *International Journal of Psycho-Analysis* 37:360-366.

Nacht, S. (1957). Technical remarks on the handling of the transference neurosis. *International Journal of Psycho-Analysis* 38:196-203.

——— (1958). Variations in technique. *International Journal of Psycho-Analysis* 39:235-237.

——— (1963). The non-verbal relationship in psycho-analytic treatment. *International Journal of Psycho-Analysis* 44:328-333.

Nacht, S., and Viderman, S. (1960). The pre-object universe and the transference situation. *International Journal of Psycho-Analysis* 41:385-388.

Nunberg, H. (1926). The will to recovery. *International Journal of Psycho-Analysis* 7:64-78.

Olinick, S. (1969). On empathy and regression in the service of the other. *British Journal of Medical Psychology* 42:41-49.

Racker, H. (1959). Notes on the theory of transference. *Psychoanalytic Quarterly* 28:78-86.

—— (1968). *Transference and Countertransference*. London: Hogarth Press.

Rangell, L. (1968) The psychoanalytic process. *International Journal of Psycho-Analysis* 49:19-26.

—— (1969). The intrapsychic process and its analysis: a recent line of thought and its current implications. *International Journal of Psycho-Analysis* 50:65-77.

—— (1975). Psychoanalysis and the process of change: an essay on the past, present and future. *International Journal of Psycho-Analysis* 56:87-98.

Rappaport, E. (1959). The first dream in an erotized transference. *International Journal of Psycho-Analysis* 40:240-245.

Reich, A. (1960). Further remarks on counter-transference. *International Journal of Psycho-Analysis* 41:389-395.

—— (1966). Empathy and countertransference. In A. Reich, *Psychoanalytic Contributions*, pp. 344-360. New York: International Universities Press, 1973.

Rosenfeld, H. (1972). A critical appreciation of James Strachey's paper on the nature of the therapeutic action of psycho-analysis. *International Journal of Psycho-Analysis* 53:455-461.

Roskin, G., and Rabiner, C. (1976). Psychotherapists' passivity: a major training problem. *International Journal of Psychoanalytic Psychotherapy* 5:319-332.

Sandler, J. (1976). Counter-transference and role-responsiveness. *International Review of Psycho-Analysis* 3:43-47.

Sandler, J., Holder, A., Kawenoka, M., Kennedy, H., and Neurath, L (1969). Notes on some theoretical and clinical aspects of transference. *International Journal of Psycho-Analysis* 50:633-645.

Scheunert, G. (1961). Die Abstinenzregel in der Psychoanalyse. *Psyche* 15:102-123.

Schwing, G. (1954). *A Way to the Soul of the Mentally Ill*. Trans. R. Ekstein and B. Hall. New York: International Universities Press.

Searles, H. (1965). *Collected Papers on Schizophrenia and Related Subjects*. New York: International Universities Press.

—— (1972). The functions of the patient's realistic perception of the analyst's delusional transference. *British Journal of Medical Psychology* 45:1-18.

—— (1975). The patient as therapist to his analyst. In *Tactics and Techniques of Psychoanalytic Therapy: Volume II. Countertransference*, ed. P. Giovacchini, New York: Jason Aronson.

Segal, H. (1964). *Introduction to the Work of Melanie Klein.* New York: Basic Books.

——— (1967). Melanie Klein's technique. *Psychoanalytic Forum* 2:197-211.

——— (in press). *The Work of Hanna Segal.* New York: Jason Aronson.

Sharpe. E. (1940). Psycho-physical problems revealed in language: an examination of metaphor. *International Journal of Psycho-Analysis* 21:201-213.

Silber, A. (1969). A patient's gift: its meaning and function. *International Journal of Psycho-Analysis* 50:335-341.

Spitz, R. (1965). Transference: the analytic setting and its prototype. *International Journal of Psycho-Analysis* 37:380-385.

Sterba, R. (1934). The fate of the ego in analytic therapy. *International Journal of Psycho-Analysis* 15:117-126.

Stern, A. (1948). Transference and borderline neurosis. *Psychoanalytic Quarterly* 17:527-528.

Stone, L. (1947). Transference sleep in a neurosis with duodenal ulcer. *International Journal of Psycho-Analysis* 28:18-32.

——— (1951). Psychoanalysis and brief psychotherapy. *Psychoanalytic Quarterly* 20:215-236.

——— (1954). The widening scope of indications for psychoanalysis. *Journal of the American Psychoanalytic Association* 2:567-594.

——— (1955). Two avenues of approach to the schizophrenic patient (review of *Direct Analysis: Selected Papers* by J. Rosen, and *A Way to the Soul of the Mentally Ill* by G. Schwing). *Journal of the American Psychoanalytic Association* 3:126-148.

——— (1957). Book review of F. Alexander, *Psychoanalysis and Psychotherapy: Developments in Theory, Technique and Training. Psychoanalytic Quarterly* 26:397-405.

——— (1961). *The Psychoanalytic Situation.* New York: International Universities Press.

——— (1967). The psychoanalytic situation and transference: postscript to an earlier communication. *Journal of the American Psychoanalytic Association* 15:3-58.

——— (1973). On resistance to the psychoanalytic process: some thoughts on its nature and motivation. In *Psychoanalysis And Contemporary Science,* vol 2, ed. B. Rubinstein, pp. 42-74. New York: Macmillan.

——— (1974). The assessment of students' progress. *The Annual of Psychoanalysis* 2:308-322.

——— (1975). Some problems and potentialities of present-day psychoanalysis. *Psychoanalytic Quarterly* 44:331-370.

Strachey, J. (1934). The nature of the therapeutic action of psycho-analysis. *International Journal of Psycho-Analysis* 15:127-159.

Szasz, T. (1963). The concept of transference. *International Journal of Psycho-Analysis* 44:432-443.

Tarachow, S. (1962). Interpretation and reality in psycho-therapy. *International Journal of Psycho-Analysis* 43:377-387.

Viderman, S. (1974). Interpretation in the analytic space. *International Review of Psycho-Analysis* 1:467-480.

Wangh, M. (1962). The "evocation of a proxy": a psychological maneuver, its use as a defense, its purposes and genesis. *Psychoanalytic Study of the Child* 17:451-469.

Winnicott, D. (1949). Hate in the countertransference. *International Journal of Psycho-Analysis* 30:69-74.

——— (1956). On transference. *International Journal of Psycho-Analysis* 37:386-388.

——— (1958). *Collected Papers*. London: Tavistock Publications.

——— (1965). *Maturational Processes and the Facilitating Environment*. New York: International Universities Press.

Zetzel, E. (1956). Current concepts of transference. *International Journal of Psycho-Analysis* 37:369-376.

——— (1958). Therapeutic alliance in the analysis of hysteria. In E. Zetzel, *Capacity for Emotional Growth*, pp. 182-196. New York: International Universities Press, 1970.

INDEX